THE
END OF
EVERYTHING

THE
END OF
EVERYTHING

HOW WARS DESCEND
INTO ANNIHILATION

NEW YORK TIMES–BESTSELLING AUTHOR OF *THE DYING CITIZEN*

VICTOR DAVIS HANSON

BASIC BOOKS

New York

Basic Books
Hachette Book Group
1290 Avenue of the Americas, New York, NY 10104
www.basicbooks.com

Printed in the United States of America

First Edition: May 2024

Published by Basic Books, an imprint of Hachette Book Group, Inc.
The Basic Books name and logo is a registered trademark of the Hachette Book Group.

The Hachette Speakers Bureau provides a wide range of authors for speaking events. To find out
more, go to www.hachettespeakersbureau.com or email HachetteSpeakers@hbgusa.com.

Basic books may be purchased in bulk for business, educational, or promotional use.
For more information, please contact your local bookseller or the Hachette Book Group
Special Markets Department at special.markets@hbgusa.com.

The publisher is not responsible for websites (or their content) that are not owned by the publisher.

Editorial production by Christine Marra, Marrathon Production Services,
www.marrathoneditorial.org.
Print book interior design by Jane Raese

Library of Congress Cataloging-in-Publication Data has been applied for.
ISBNs: 9781541673526 (hardcover), 9781541673502 (ebook)

LSC-C

Printing 1, 2024

CONTENTS

MAPS

PREFACE

I thank my editor at Basic Books, Lara Heimert, for encouragement and support during the publication of four books under her direction. Roger Labrie was once again of great help in carefully editing the manuscript. My agents of more than thirty years, Glen Hartley and Lynn Chu, offered their accustomed support, expertise, and encouragement. David Berkey, Megan Ring, Morgan Hunter, Christian Martin, and Andre Brilliant of the Hoover Institution were instrumental in proofing and editing the manuscript, providing me with research materials and advice, as well as preparing the illustrations and maps. I thank my wife, Jennifer, for her constant help that allowed me the time and provided the environment to write the book, as well as the encouragement of my daughter, Pauline Hanson Steinback, and son, William Hanson.

Unless where specified, I have translated all the classical Greek and Latin texts from primary sources. All dates in chapters 2 and 3 are BC, and AD in chapters 3 and 4.

For the last twenty-one years, I have been fortunate to have enjoyed residence at the Hoover Institution of Stanford University, along with the current and continual support of its director, Condoleezza Rice, and our former director, the late John Raisian, who first invited me to Hoover. My Hoover colleague Bruce Thornton read the entire manuscript and offered invaluable suggestions about both content and organization. I thank Bill Nelson for drafting the maps.

I owe a special debt of thanks for the direct help of Hoover overseers Martin Anderson, Lew Davies, Jim Jameson, Robert, Rebekah and Jennifer Mercer, Roger and Martha Mertz, Jeremiah Milbank, and Victor Trione.

Victor Davis Hanson
Martin and Illie Anderson Senior Fellow, Classics/Military History
Hoover Institution, Stanford University
Selma, California, August 31, 2023

FOR ROGER AND SUSAN HERTOG

*Quid dulcius quam habere quicum
omnia audeas sic loqui ut tecum?*

(What is sweeter than to have someone with whom
you dare to speak on every topic as with yourself?)

—**Cicero, *De Amicitia***

HOW CIVILIZATIONS DISAPPEAR

And on the pedestal, these words appear:
"My name is Ozymandias, King of Kings:
Look at my works, ye mighty, and despair!"
Nothing beside remains. Round the decay
Of that colossal wreck, boundless and bare
The lone and level sands stretch far away.
—Percy Bysshe Shelley, "Ozymandias"

THERE ARE LOTS of ways that states and their peoples can vanish from history, and all sorts of causes explain their disappearance. Both nature—earthquakes, tsunamis, volcanic eruptions, plagues, and climate change—and humans sometimes wipe out vulnerable populations. Indeed, entire cultures have often been obliterated, sometimes quickly, sometimes over decades. Yet this book focuses on the rarer abrupt *wartime* destruction of a civilization, a state, or a culture through force of arms, and uses as case studies classical Thebes, Punic Carthage, Byzantine Constantinople, and the Aztecs of Tenochtitlán. Its conclusions warn that the modern world, America included, is hardly immune from repeating these tragedies of the past.

The wartime end of everything has usually followed from a final siege or invasion. The coup de grâce predictably targeted a capital or the cultural, political, religious, or social center of a state. And the final blow resulted in the erasure of an entire people's way of life—and often much of the population itself. Strangely, the transition from normality to the end of days could occur rather quickly. A rendezvous with finality was often completely unexpected. Yet absolute defeat too late revealed long-unaddressed vulnerabilities, as economic, political, and social fissures widened only under wartime pressures. Waning empires rarely wished to accept, much less address, the fact that their once sprawling domains had been reduced to what the defenders could see from their walls.

Naïveté, hubris, flawed assessments of relative strengths and weaknesses, the loss of deterrence, new military technologies and tactics, totalitarian ideologies, and a retreat to fantasy can all explain why these usually rare catastrophic events nevertheless keep recurring—from the destruction of the Inca Empire to the end of the Cherokee nation to the genocide of a populous, vibrant, and Yiddish-speaking prewar Jewish people in Central and Eastern Europe. The continual disappearance of prior cultures across time and space should warn us that even familiar twenty-first-century states can become as fragile as their ancient counterparts, given that the arts of destruction march in tandem with improvements in defense. The gullibility, and indeed ignorance, of contemporary governments and leaders about the intent, hatred, ruthlessness, and capability of their enemies are not surprising. The retreat to comfortable nonchalance and credulousness, often the cargo of affluence and leisure, is predictable given unchanging human nature, despite the pretensions of a postmodern technologically advanced global village.

Even in our age of transnational wealth, an interconnected global economy, Davos, the United Nations, thousands of nongovernmental organizations, a rules-based international order, and major-power nuclear deterrence, the fates of Thebes, Carthage, Constantinople, and Tenochtitlán are not mere memories from a distant benighted past and thus irrelevant in the present. Of course, no modern state enslaves the entire surviving population of the defeated—one of the most effective ways in the past of erasing a civilization—in the fashion of Alexander the Great with Thebes, or Scipio Aemilianus with Carthage. And the United States at least is protected by two oceans, a formidable nuclear deterrent of nearly sixty-five hundred warheads, and the most powerful economy and military in history. How then could it be reduced to nothingness by any enemy on the world stage?

Unfortunately, the more things change technologically, the more human nature stays the same—a law that applies even to the United States, which often believes it is exempt from the misfortunes of other nations, past and present. This book makes clear, however, that there is no certainty that as scientific progress accelerates and leisure increases, and as the world shrinks on our computer and television screens, there is any corresponding advance in wisdom or morality, much less radical improvement in innate human nature.

The besieger of Tenochtitlán, Hernán Cortés, operated on the same principles as did Alexander the Great, some 1,788 years earlier, in assuming that almost all of the Aztecs he stormed would end up as serfs, slaves—or dead. If the world is now intolerant for the most part of slavery, cannibalism, and human sacrifice, nonetheless the tools of genocide—nuclear, chemical, and biological—are far more advanced than ever before. And they are at our fingertips. The years 1939 to 1945, with their seventy million dead, a mere two decades after twenty million perished in "the war to end all wars" of 1914–1918, taught us once again that with material and technological progress often comes moral retrogression, a lesson dating back to the seventh-century BC warnings of the Greek poet Hesiod.

The twenty-first century has already experienced bloody wars in places as diverse as Afghanistan, Chechnya, Crimea, Darfur, Ethiopia, Iraq, Lebanon, Libya, Niger, Nigeria, Ossetia, Pakistan, Sudan, Syria, the West Bank, and Yemen—all of which followed the end of the millennium genocides in Cambodia and Rwanda. Yet these gruesome conflicts are not even the most likely current flash points that threaten to draw in major powers possessing weapons of mass destruction, including most notably the United States. In the last few years alone, Russia has threatened to use nuclear weapons against Ukraine, China against Taiwan, Iran against Israel, Pakistan against India, and North Korea against South Korea, Japan, and the United States. Turkey has talked of sending missiles into Athens and Israel, or solving the Armenian "problem" in the manner of its forebears. These are just the threats of bombs and missiles, as we head into the age of gain-of-function pathogens and artificial-intelligence-guided munitions.

3

Note that the four ancient man-made Armageddons we discuss are different from the mysterious disappearances, or the monumental abrupt system collapses, of "lost civilizations" such as the Mycenaeans (ca. 1200 BC) or Mayans (ca. AD 900). They are clearly not the same as smaller extinctions like the mysterious ends of those on Easter, Pitcairn, or Roanoke Islands.[1]

Nor does the book focus on the gradual, internal decay that incessantly wastes away a nation or empire, such as the dissolution and partial absorption of fifth-century AD imperial Rome by the proverbial barbarians, and its slow metamorphosis into Europe of the so-called Dark and Middle Ages. These chapters are not studies of the political disappearances of state governments or the changing names of peoples, such as the formal end of the nomenclature and political existence of Prussia and Prussians, or Yugoslavia and Yugoslavians. Even the actual destruction of an enemy state—with borders, a government, and a unique history and culture—does not always equate to the genocide of an entire people, although at times a victorious siege certainly can result in mass death driven by racial, ethnic, or religious hatred.

But if states and cultures can be completely obliterated by wartime enemies, then when exactly is a people defined as vanquished or ended? When its nation is formally conquered, occupied, and its citizenry made permanently subservient? Or, as this book argues, when a state's government disappears, its infrastructure is leveled, most of its people killed, enslaved, or scattered, its culture fragmented and soon forgotten, and its space abandoned or given over to another and quite different people.

Of course, nothing ever quite ends, at least in its entirety. Political institutions implode. Culture wanes. Language lingers. And people scatter. Nonetheless, a few survivors can run for a time on the fumes of past glory. So, as we shall see, there can be gradations of "obliteration." We must examine carefully whether a Thebes or Carthage was really destroyed as recorded—and indeed exactly what is meant in our sources by verbs like "destroyed," "razed," and "leveled."

From the fall of Troy to the atomization of much of Hiroshima, the destruction of cities and occasionally their entire civilizations, as mentioned, is unusual but also not yet a thing of our savage past. A small number of these catastrophes still reverberate through the centuries. Sometimes these obliterations changed the lives of quite different peoples, well beyond the dead and enslaved. Millions far from ground zero grasped almost immediately that the ripples of destruction would ultimately alter their lives as well. Subsequent generations in retrospect realized these annihilations had marked the abrupt end of an age and a transition to something quite different. Whether the significance of an entire political system lost, a culture vanished, or a distinct people erased became obvious in real time or only later, there nonetheless remain certain similarities—and thus lessons—in these historic wartime disappearances of whole societies.[2]

The size and wealth of the targeted population made a difference. The ancient world rued the Athenian extinction of the tiny island of Melos and its culture in 415 BC. But the classical Greeks did not equate a world without the Melians with the loss of Hellenism, at least in the manner of the later razing of a much larger and more influential Thebes or Corinth. The language, literature, art, and science of the vanished, and their ability to transcend their own borders also mattered. The world of Asia Minor and the Mediterranean changed after the end of Byzantine Constantinople far more than following the obliteration of the barbarian Vandals in North Africa, Sicily, and Italy.

The case studies here—the leveling of Thebes by Alexander the Great, the erasure of Carthage by Scipio Aemilianus, Sultan Mehmet II's conquest and transformation of Constantinople, and the obliteration of Tenochtitlán by Hernán Cortés—all marked the end of cultures and civilizations. They were seen so by contemporaries and later generations alike. Alexander brought a close to the Classical Greece of hundreds of independent city-states with the extinction of Thebes and its inhabitants. The implosion of the independent city-state inaugurated a very different subsequent Hellenistic era of imperial kingdoms and values.

The destruction of Carthage and Punic civilization in Africa saw the disappearance of the last major obstacle to a Roman Western Mediterranean. Its obliteration brought North Africa into the West, and accelerated Rome's transformation from a republic to an imperial power. The fall of Constantinople confirmed the decline of the Mediterranean world as the nexus of European commerce. The loss of the city ended the formal European presence in Asia, even as it helped to inaugurate in the opposite direction a new Atlantic world dominated by Portugal, Spain, France, and later Holland and England. Cortés's annihilation of the Aztec Empire and its capital Tenochtitlán normalized the crushing of independent native states in the Americas while birthing a new Spanish-speaking civilization there, one neither altogether indigenous nor Spanish.

Often a great city—usually a capital, defined by its prior political centrality and influence or size and wealth—becomes a synecdoche, a shorthand to later generations for the collapse of its entire civilization. Of course, the players involved did not always realize the transformational roles they were playing. It is doubtful that Alexander ever thought about razing Thebes as anything much other than the erasure of a rebellious annoyance, a roadblock holding up his long-planned invasion and looting of the Persian Empire.

Similarly, Scipio Aemilianus, for all his supposed subsequent remorse and his philosophical pretensions, was likely more concerned with not damaging his own political career by failing to demolish Carthage after his two immediate and inept predecessors had faltered. Mehmet II appeared to have some idea of the historical and cultural significance of the fall of Constantinople, as he announced that he was now the only and rightful heir to the Roman Empire. But even the sultan did not foresee that his own choices would spur Western Europe to conquer the world by sea to avoid Ottoman Kostantiniyye's increasing control and disruption of East-West Mediterranean trade. Cortés envisioned his conquests in terms of career and financial interests, along with magnifying the power and name of his church, his king, and himself.

Chapter 1 reviews the fate of the city of Thebes, renowned in both history and myth. In 335 BC, the Thebans not only revolted against the Macedonian occupation of Greece, but defiantly dared Alexander the Great to take the legendary city.

He did just that, after a brief but savage one-day battle. He then quite unexpectedly enlisted other conquered Greek city-states to ratify his decision to raze the city, kill off most of the adult males, sell the surviving captives into slavery, and allow neighbors to appropriate Theban territory. Thereby Alexander ended for good the ancient citadel of Cadmus, mythical founder of the hallowed city.

More than just Thebes itself was destroyed. The annihilation of the Thebans marked the iconic finale of the entire era of independent city-states that the rebellious Thebans had sought to save. After the obliteration of Thebes, one empire or kingdom succeeded another on Greek soil—first Alexander and his Hellenistic *Diadochoi* ("Successors"), then Rome and Byzantium, then the Ottomans, and finally the independent Greek monarchy. Yet the creative polis civilization of the golden age, not just of Thebes but of Athens and the rest of Greece as well, vanished after Alexander.

Chapter 2 explores the lethal rivalry between Rome and Carthage that culminated in 146 BC, some 189 years after the end of Thebes, when the Carthaginians likewise disappeared *as a people,* thus marking the end of the Third Punic War. Punic civilization itself vanished with its capital city. Like the Thebans, they perished by siege, after their once distant frontiers had collapsed to just the city's suburbs. The once Mediterranean-wide Carthaginian language, literature, and people receded to only distant memories in the Greco-Roman centuries that followed.

Carthage in its three Punic Wars had fought Rome too long and become too vulnerable. Its existence became perceived as not so much an existential danger as a constant irritant to Rome. Its fate was mostly irrelevant to others. And Rome sought an opening to extinguish an economic rival and appropriate its wealth. The fall of Carthage, and the almost contemporary destruction of Corinth and creation of Roman provinces in Greece, traditionally were seen by historians as both the emblematic cessations of the Hellenistic kingdoms and the beginning of the Roman Mediterranean world.

The most infamous of wartime extinctions was the destruction of Byzantine Constantinople on May 29, 1453, "Black Tuesday," the subject of chapter 3. While the Greek language and Orthodox Christian religion survived scattered in southern Europe and in the outlands of Asia after the fall of the Byzantine Empire, the millennium-long reality of an Eastern, Greek-speaking Roman Empire and attendant cult in Asia Minor disappeared—despite Russia's later claims of reestablishing a third Christian Rome. Constantinople had survived and more or less recovered from the brutal sack by Western knights of the Fourth Crusade in 1204. But it would not rebound from the far more ambitious agenda of Sultan Mehmet II, who would finish off Byzantine civilization, and appropriate and transform its renowned capital.

The Ottomans harbored a hatred of Christianity. They had assumed rightly that Constantinople was old and weak and mostly long abandoned by Western Christendom. After the end, Hagia Sophia, the largest Christian cathedral in the West for seven hundred years, became the greatest mosque of the Islamic world. There were never again to be Byzantines, the Greek city of Constantinople, or even the idea of any cohesive Christian, Greek-speaking Hellenic culture in Asia. The Greek shell of the sacked city remained, given its strategically invaluable site at the Bosporus. But now it was to be absorbed as the new dynamic capital Kostantiniyye of the ascendant Ottoman Empire, and in modern times renamed Istanbul.

From a global perspective, the fall of Constantinople marked the end of the Eastern Mediterranean–centered world, the transference of Hellenic power and influence to Renaissance Europe, and soon, the beginning of the Atlantic era. In 1444, a near decade before the city fell, Portuguese explorers, trying to find a maritime route around Ottoman control of the Mediterranean and the land routes to Asia, had already reached the westernmost point of Africa. Well south of the Sahara, they were beginning to circumvent Muslim control of trade with the African Gold Coast. By 1488, they had reached the Cape of Good Hope, ensuring Europeans soon had direct access to trade with Asia. In 1492, a mere thirty-nine years after the fall of Constantinople, Europeans discovered the New World.

Like "vandal," "Byzantine" as a living concept survives today only as an adjective. It is used inexactly and unfairly to convey the supposed inefficiency and intrigue of fossilized, bloated bureaucracies. Otherwise, the Byzantines receded into the collective Greek memory. The idea of a living Byzantium reemerged only once, as an ephemeral fantasy. After the dissolution of the Ottoman Empire in 1918, the Hellenic dream of the Μεγάλη Ιδέα (*Megali Idea* or "Great Idea") gained increased impetus, but then soon afterward died for good. This new incarnation of the Megali Idea had envisioned a twentieth-century Panhellenic Aegean, once more united by Greek-speakers in Asia Minor, the Greek mainland, the Islands, and the northern Egyptian coast. It was crushed by Turkish nationalist Mustafa Kemal Atatürk's army at the final conflagration in Smyrna (1922), and finished off by the nascent state of Turkey.[3]

The savage work of Hernán Cortés in destroying the Aztec Empire is the concern of chapter 4. When the siege of the city was finished in 1521, there was no longer a concept of an Aztec people or a majestic indigenous capital at Tenochtitlán, nor a Venice-like island city of canals. Indeed, there was little left except subsequent mythologies of a lost Aztlán homeland in the US Southwest, and enslaved laborers constructing the new Spanish capital of Mexico City, deliberately plopped down atop the site of the old. Like Carthage and Constantinople, Tenochtitlán had been the nerve center of a brittle empire, a single great city organizing thousands of square miles on its periphery.

Although they had become familiar with Aztec civilization over the prior two years, the Spanish almost immediately sought to obliterate its religion, race, and culture. In their view, they had more than enough reasons to destroy the Aztec Empire rather than just defeat the *Mexica* (the indigenous word for "Aztec"). As with Thebes, the destruction of Tenochtitlán and the Mexica empire did not just erase one state. The demise of the city marked the end of Central American *altepetl* ("city-state") civilization as a whole. When combined with the later Spanish conquest of the Inca Empire, indirectly inspired by Cortés, the city's death marked the collapse of the age of independent New World civilizations.

A brief epilogue charts a tragic but predictable scheme to all these geographically, ethnically, religiously, and chronologically different case studies. And the result offers timely warnings for us and our own future. Even as humanity supposedly becomes more uniform and interconnected, so too our world grows increasingly vulnerable and dangerous, as the margins of human error and misapprehension in conflict shrink—from Ukraine to Taiwan to the Middle East. We should remember that the world wars of the last century likely took more human life than all armed conflicts combined since the dawn of Western civilization twenty-five hundred years prior. And they did so with offensive weapons already obsolete, and all too familiar destructive agendas that persist today, unchanged since antiquity. As for the targets of aggression, the old mentalities and delusions that doomed the Thebans, the Carthaginians, the Byzantines, and the Aztecs are also still very much with us, especially the last thoughts of the slaughtered: "It cannot happen here."

1

HOPE, DANGER'S COMFORTER

The Obliteration of Classical Thebes
(December 335 BC)

Melians. But we know that the fortune of war is sometimes more impartial than the disproportion of numbers might lead one to suppose; to submit is to give ourselves over to despair, while action still preserves for us a hope that we may stand erect.

Athenians. Hope, danger's comforter, may be indulged in by those who have abundant resources, if not without loss at all events without ruin; but its nature is to be extravagant, and those who go so far as to put their all upon the venture see it in its true colours only when they are ruined.
　　—Thucydides, *The History of the Peloponnesian War*

COLLECTIVE NAÏVETÉ CAN get a vulnerable people killed. So it was with the classical Greek city-state of Thebes. In 335 BC, its leaders bet wrongly that revolting from the Macedonian empire of Alexander the Great would either succeed or, if not, at least result in its negotiated surrender and the continuance of its civilization. They were fatally wrong on both counts.

In the all-too-common miscalculations of the targeted, defiant Thebans looked to their impressive military, the justness of their cause, the sympathy of their allies, and their city's hallowed reputation as an icon of eternal Hellenic culture—but not to the ruthless

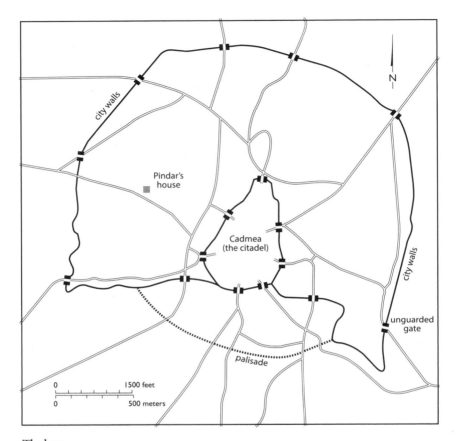

Thebes

record of Alexander the Great. They had forgotten the superiority of the Macedonian phalanx. And their leaders ignored the terror that the Macedonian occupation had instilled among some fifteen hundred conquered Greek city-states.

And so they died en masse.

One recurrent theme of the wartime extinction of civilizations is precisely this frequent naïveté of the targeted—a gullibility innate to humans in extremis, and especially unchecked by reality during the passions and hysteria released by war. Die-hard defenders understandably delude themselves into thinking that all others are idealists like themselves, or at least must be just as committed to the cause of their own survival. They tend to mock as traitors or appeasers any

Greece and Macedonia in the Fourth Century BC

realists in their ranks—with responsibilities to their families and homes that transcend collective idealism—who do the arithmetic of death and so assess their decisions solely by the chances of victory.

Shattered illusions awaited the trusting Theban envoys who traveled south to the Isthmus of Corinth to meet supposed savior allied armies arriving from southern Greece. Under their friends' sharp questioning, the Thebans had conceded that Alexander was nearby, loose in Boeotia close to their own walls. Almost immediately, the other would-be Panhellenic revolutionaries prudently expressed sympathy but decided to pass on any war against the feared Macedonians. They all quickly turned around and headed back home in shame—but alive. As a result, defiant Thebes was left alone to face the fatal consequences of its own idealism.

In their revolutionary zeal, the indomitable heavy infantrymen of the besieged Thebans confidently poured outside the walls of their surrounded ancient city to meet the invaders. These hoplite spearmen—citizen-soldiers in heavy bronze armor with large wooden shields—would not wait inside for the Macedonians to attack, despite the apparent wisdom of that course. They conceded that the famed walls of legendary "Seven-Gated Thebes" had plenty of vulnerable points that might never withstand the siegecraft of the master city-stormers, the Macedonians under Alexander the Great. So instead of just manning the ramparts, the Thebans were eager to rush out of the trapped city and keep the Macedonian besiegers from hauling their siege engines to the walls.

The Thebans were especially worried that the growing mass of Macedonian infantry outside the walls might be able to rescue their captive garrison guards inside the city. These were Macedonian troops trapped *inside* the fortified acropolis of the city known as the Cadmea. Unfortunately, unlike most acropolises, such as Athens's, which served as the center of the walled *poleis* ("city-states"), the Cadmea's fortifications on one side also served as the city's common circuit wall. So, unlike a protected medieval keep, the renowned citadel of Thebes was in part right atop the front line of a siege.

Why was the future Alexander the Great now parked outside a pre-eminent Greek city-state threatening to raze Thebes? The war had recently started as a purported Panhellenic rebellion against Macedonian occupation forces, following the death of King Philip II of Macedon and the ascension of his son and heir, Alexander. The Athenian firebrand politico Demosthenes had falsely claimed that Alexander had been killed in a campaign to suppress revolts in Illyria (modern-day Albania), far to the north. Once the Thebans heard this fable, rebellion broke out. As their first insurrectionary act, the Thebans attacked the local Macedonian occupation garrison, apparently on the presumption that other Greek city-states would emulate their lead. Remarkably, the Thebans in short order had managed to fence in Alexander's men on the Cadmea, in a somewhat humiliating fashion, given the supposedly ironclad Macedonian subjugation of Greece.

But now it seemed that Alexander was not dead after all. In fact, in response to these rumors of his demise, he had marched his army three hundred miles in just two weeks from Illyria to Thebes in central Greece—at an astonishing rate of over twenty miles a day. So there was an unexpected fresh force of Macedonians arriving outside the walls, while their occupying brethren were locked inside above the ramparts, and the Thebans in their own city were stuck in between.

For three years most of Greece had been more or less pacified by Macedon, until the unexpected assassination of its conqueror, Philip II. Soon his twenty-one-year-old son liquidated his rivals, and marched his late father's army down to Thebes. What followed was a standoff between Thebes, iconic site of Greek mythology and home to classical Greece's most accomplished army, and an untried Macedonian boy-king leading a feared pack of veteran professional killers. Earlier, while a teen, Alexander had led the left wing of his father's army at the nearby battlefield of Chaeronea (338 BC); there his decisive action helped break the multistate "coalition" army of Greece. But in Greek eyes Alexander was still no Philip II, the one-eyed monster who for twenty years had revolutionized Hellenic warfare and finally accomplished what no Persian king had ever pulled off—the complete subjugation of the free Greek city-states.

But now the Thebans imagined that their unexpected and rather easy capture of the Macedonian garrison would further arouse other Greek city-states to flock once again to their assistance. Indeed, the reputation of the Theban army and its declaration that it would fight for the return of a free Hellas would surely prompt a Panhellenic uprising against the Macedonians. Together, the Greek city-states would no doubt mass at the gates of Thebes and crush the invading Macedonian phalanx. Wild rumors already had spread that several of the best Peloponnesian armies of free Greeks—especially the Aetolians, Arcadians, and Eleans—were marshaling not far away at the Isthmus of Corinth, in expectation of joining the mounting insurrection. For a brief moment, many Greeks thought this resistance might have included Athens and Sparta. Even if Alexander the Great was not dead as rumored, the insurrectionists assumed he was likely too young to hold together the Macedonian army of his late father and his old-guard generals.

Yet the besieged Thebans waited for help in vain. Apparently, once the allied armies of the south had marched out, it soon became evident that none of their generals had any exact picture of what they were all getting into, especially concerning the size of the Macedonian invading force, much less where and when a very much alive Alexander planned to march. Instead, each Greek army calculated that while in theory all the city-states together could defeat Alexander and his Macedonians, if left alone any polis would be wiped out by him. And so all now determined not to be that lone city-state.

Alexander was already ratcheting up the pressure on the suddenly isolated city. As the first-century historian Diodorus put it, most in Greece on news of the revolt were sincerely worried about the Thebans. But their sympathy was not the same as their succor. The other Greek city-states not only assumed that Alexander would likely put down without mercy the rebellion, but also rationalized their inaction by correctly claiming that their would-be liberators, the Thebans, were too reckless and unpredictable. In fact, the timid allies advanced all sorts of flimsy excuses why discretion was the better part of valor, claiming that a century and a half earlier the Thebans had helped the Persian invaders and thus were unworthy of the sacrifice of their brethren.[1]

Nonetheless, the abandoned Thebans went ahead with plans for a pitched battle. The mystique of the Theban phalanx, the envy of all fourth-century Greeks, was something like the interwar reputation of the supposedly indomitable French army of World War I—an ideal based on hope from the past rather than a reality grounded in current experience. In 1916, *l'armée de terre française* had miraculously stopped the Germans at Verdun with the cry of *"Ils ne passeront pas!"*—"They shall not pass!" During the interwar 1930s, most Western Europeans and the British still assumed this huge force, the former bulwark of the West, would once again bend, but likewise would never break. No doubt, its one million soldiers in the field, with five million more in reserve, would stop Hitler's Wehrmacht just as the army had once stalled the Kaiser's invading legions. Beginning in May 1940, that dream dissipated in six weeks.

Like the hidden fissures within the French army, the decline of Thebes, from its once preeminent role in Greece to an unpopular head of a shaky democratic Boeotian federation, ensured the erosion of the legendary phalanx of their earlier renowned general and leader Epaminondas (ca. 419/411–362 BC). The current Theban army had already been crushed just three years earlier by the Macedonians at the battle of Chaeronea. There, in an hour or so, the vaunted Sacred Band of 150 paired lovers was wiped out to the last man. Most likely deployed on the right side of the Greek army, the Thebans had found themselves facing off against Alexander himself, who was leading the Macedonian left. The Theban wing was routed. The legendary Sacred Band now lay buried under the battlefield of Chaeronea. In modern times, most of their remains, which had been lying under a majestic stone commemorative lion, have been unearthed. The survivors of that battle likely remained traumatized by their unaccustomed defeat, flight, losses, and subsequent months under Macedonian occupation.[2]

Nonetheless, three years later, here they were in their armor, facing the same army and the same leader that had destroyed their army. And they soon discovered just how massive was the Macedonian army at their gates. Alexander had arrayed well over thirty thousand phalangites, or pike-bearing, infantrymen equipped with long sixteen-foot sarissas. Included among their foot soldiers on the flanks were smaller contingents of shield-carrying hypaspists, armed more like Greek hoplites in full armor, with large shields and shorter spears. Another three thousand veteran horsemen, plus missile- and light-armed troops, were arranged along and to the rear of the battle line to exploit and expand any weaknesses and gaps in the Thebans' front.

In other words, the new Macedonian army created by the late Philip II was a symphony of killers. And it was now augmented by thousands of nearby rural Boeotians hostile to their shared capital at Thebes. Each Macedonian battle contingent enhanced the others, each with its particular complementary role, time, and place of attack—quite in contrast to the one-dimensional hoplite phalanxes of old. Ironically, the supposedly half-civilized Macedonians had first learned of the power of phalanxes of spearmen from the classical Greeks. But then, unlike their ossified mentors, they vastly expanded and improved upon the idea of a mass column of spearmen by lengthening spears into pikes. They added a variety of fighters to complement the one-dimensional phalanx, fielding both light and heavy cavalry, infantry, and missile troops with a variety of weapons and body protection.

A patient Alexander had been waiting for three days outside the walls, in hopes that the sheer spectacle of his forces would erode Theban morale and force a submission. Would they not come to their senses and remember that he, as a mere eighteen-year-old, had smashed the Theban contingent at Chaeronea? But just in case of Theban recalcitrance, Alexander's siege-engineers were busy preparing to conduct a protracted assault, even as he sent envoys to broker a negotiated, and not humiliating, surrender. The Macedonians' relatively lenient terms revealed an eagerness to end the rebellion peacefully. Alexander had even offered amnesty to all the Theban firebrands if they just turned over the rebellion's ringleaders, Prosthytes and Phoenix.

Nonetheless, the Theban rebels were hardly impressed with Alexander's moderate terms. They naïvely believed their infantry phalanx could fight far better outside their walls, in part because they had put up makeshift field palisades, fronted with recently dug trenches. These forward field fortifications outside the city also prevented the attackers from easily storming the vulnerable Cadmean wall and liberating the hostage Macedonians. Again, the defect of the Theban fortifications had always been a weak spot where the city's circuit wall also served double duty as the outer wall of the inner citadel.[3]

The Thebans apparently had more confidence in their army in the field than in the city's mobilized population on the ramparts. For nearly a century until Chaeronea, glorious Theban hoplites had crushed all comers. Victorious in the Peloponnesian War under the legendary Pagondas, they had routed the Athenians at the battle of Delium (424 BC) and sent thousands—except for doughty middle-aged Athenian hoplite Socrates and his coterie—running for their lives back into Attica. Later, led by the emancipator Epaminondas, the Thebans had all but destroyed the Spartan army at Leuctra (371 BC). Within just months of that victory, they overran the Spartans' homeland itself—the first invaders, according to legend, to enter sacred Laconia in nearly seven hundred years. Even in defeat at Chaeronea, the Thebans for a moment had nearly turned the Macedonians, before being routed by Philip II and Alexander.

In some sense, the Thebans' inability to draw lessons from their pivotal recent defeat at Chaeronea was similar to die-hard American Civil War Confederates' adherence to a mystical "lost cause." The Thebans apparently believed that the catastrophe at Chaeronea, perhaps like the pivotal Southern loss at Shiloh, was not an unequivocal referendum on—or warning of—their innately inferior military strength. Rather the quirky defeat was attributable merely to chance, bad luck, and the untimely deaths or blunders of their own commanders.[4]

Still, even in its twilight, the classical Theban phalanx remained an offensive army, famed for its bodily strength and audacity. In extremis, the realists in command at least thought it better to die in open battle than to be slaughtered in twos and threes in their streets. It was characteristic of the Thebans to attack in great depth and advance often obliquely—impossible tactics inside the walls of the city. The brute Herakles, the demigod hero who typified super-human strength and was in some myths born at Thebes, was their city's patron god. And his rough-hewn club remained emblazoned on their shields. Most in the army were not about to surrender.

More importantly, fourth-century Thebes prided itself as the incubator of revolution. Once it had become democratic earlier under Epaminondas and Pelopidas, the city had turned Greece upside down. The Theban nation in arms had once emasculated Sparta, reconfigured the entire political status of the Peloponnese, freed the Messenian helots, and later anchored the Greek resistance at Chaeronea. Thebes was rebranded as a moral force as well, as the liberator Epaminondas had not ordered mass executions or enslave-ments of the defeated. Had he not been killed at the battle of Man-tinea (362 BC), Epaminondas may even have aimed at a federalized, democratic, and Panhellenic nation. It was no surprise, then, that the Thebans once again bragged to the Greeks that their polis would oversee the spiritual rebirth of the city-states. They would arise, phoenix-like, from their subjugation once again to overthrow the status quo of an occupied and humiliated Greece.[5]

Alexander took no chances about this first and most powerful of what in theory could become a wave of rebellious cities at precisely the moment he was planning to invade Asia. The young king there-fore had decided to deploy his entire Macedonian army, a muster nearly the same size as the force that within four years would wreck three Persian armies at the climactic battles of Granicus, Issus, and Gaugamela, thereby destroying the world's greatest empire.

Indeed, the Thebans had not seen such a huge enemy outside their famed seven gates in nearly a century and a half—likely not since 479 BC, when the polis had turned traitor by joining the

Persian enemy. Then as quislings the Thebans had gone down to defeat at the battle of Plataea alongside their allied Persian invaders. In shame, Thebes ended up surrounded and besieged by outraged fellow Greeks. The city was forced to surrender, in humiliation begging for mercy from the victorious and vengeful city-states. That ancient stain upon the Thebans was still a frequent propaganda point of its enemies. And Alexander now once again invoked it to dissuade any other would-be rebellious Hellenic city-states from joining such dubious insurrectionists.

In purely military terms, the old-fashioned farmer hoplites of Thebes were vastly outnumbered by Alexander's professionals, by perhaps as much as three to one in the field. For all their Panhellenic renown as tough physical brawlers, the Thebans, like all Greek armies, remained a one-dimensional militia. The phalanx fought without closely integrated contingents of light-armed and missile troops, without heavy cavalry comparable to that of the Macedonians, without reserves, and without a general anywhere near the equal of Alexander. There was no longer any general of the caliber of an Epaminondas or Pelopidas of past glories to lead them. There were no new tactics, no new equipment, no new musters in the three years since the disaster of Chaeronea. To paraphrase the assessment of Arthur Wellesley, Duke of Wellington, concerning Napoleon's defeated army at the Battle of Waterloo, the Thebans came on in the same old way and the Macedonians would defeat them in the same old way.[6]

In the past, the Thebans had built palisades around their farmland to keep out the Spartans, and integrated such obstacles into a fluid defense in the field. That habit and expertise may also explain why the Thebans once more relied on field fortifications to protect their acropolis from the enemy below. Their defense in depth, then, was twofold. Aside from the main phalanx that marched out to fight beneath the city walls, a second extramural contingent was stationed nearby; outside the walls and behind the palisades, it would sally forth from its cover and ensure no Macedonians would break into the rampart beneath the Cadmea. Alexander reacted by dividing his army into threes: his chief force was to hit the main Theban phalanx; a second would storm the outer palisade and drive through the Thebans beneath the acropolis; and a third was held in reserve.

Almost immediately, the two armies were deadlocked beneath the walls of the city. The desperate hedgehog of the Thebans' protruding eight-foot-long spears was soon stopped—but not broken—by the larger mass of pike-bearing Macedonian phalangites. Alexander's infantrymen had the advantage of stabbing with far longer sarissas of some sixteen feet, nearly twice the length of the old Theban hoplite spears. The sarissas' sheer size and weight required both hands just to wield them. As a result, in the initial clash the Thebans were hit by Alexander's first five ranks—two more rows of spearpoints than could be reached by the shorter spears of the Theban hoplites. Soon thousands of Macedonian reserves were also sent into the fray to swell their mass. The exhausted and outnumbered Thebans were continuously struck by yet another wall of fresh pikemen. We do not know whether Alexander had intended to prompt a collision in the field with the Theban phalanx, or whether his subordinate Perdiccas simply had preempted his king to force the issue. In any case, the Macedonian army, whether in pitched battles or attacking the walls, was larger and more experienced than the city's defenders.

The Roman-era historian Diodorus, drawing on earlier and now lost contemporary Greek sources, detailed the resulting fury outside the walls of the city and how the battle quickly turned to hand-to-hand fighting:

> Once they all resorted to the use of the sword at close quarters, a tremendous struggle ensued. The Macedonians enjoyed greater force, because of the numbers of their men and the weight of their phalanx. Yet the Thebans remained superior in their bodily strength and in their endless athletic training. Still more so, they were of unconquerable spirits and thereby became dismissive of dangers. Thus, on both sides, many were wounded, and plenty were falling after taking frontal blows. There arose mixed-up sounds of moaning, shouting, and rallying cries from the melee of the dense

struggle. As for the Macedonians, they were intent on not falling short of their prior battle courage, while the Thebans could not forget their children and wives and parents who were now threatened with enslavement, as every native house was open to the fury of the Macedonians. And they were to remember the battles of Leuctra and of Mantinea and those illustrious deeds that were now common knowledge throughout Greece. So, for a long time the battle remained evenly fought.[7]

The Thebans would win or die—all of them, soldiers, slaves, and civilians. After their spear shafts were shattered and their order lost, the defenders degenerated into a mob of free-for-all individual fighters. They were battling as free men for their homes and families, their kin now only a few hundred yards behind them within the city. For that desperate reason alone, they remained confident in their famed physical superiority, even over the better-equipped professional Macedonians.

Yet endless streams of enemy reserves continued to pour into the battle. Diodorus continues his description with the wearied Thebans' desperate final efforts to overcome Macedonian numbers and professionalism:

The Thebans did not concede the victory, but just the opposite: inspired by the will to win, they now dismissed all dangers. So much were they emboldened by their courage that they shouted out that even the Macedonians themselves now agreed that they were their inferiors. When an enemy sends in fresh reserves, it is customary for all soldiers to fear these infusions of reinforcements. But the Thebans alone met these dangers ever more boldly, even as the enemy sent in against them new troops to supplement those struggling from battle weariness.[8]

It is doubtful that the Thebans' boasts and taunts could be heard over the din of battle. Few on a losing side ever view the enemy's use of reinforcements as reason for optimism. In truth, the defenders' fate grew steadily bleaker. Minute by minute, they became more tired and isolated. Desperate hopes for reinforcements from the city or allies from the south perished. Any retreat of the Thebans would bring the battle inside the fortifications—and might entail not just defeat, but the immediate slaughter of their families. Finally, the sheer numbers of Alexander's phalangites tore apart all semblance of order among the Thebans. Macedonians at last broke through the defenders and headed toward the city walls.

Because the exterior palisades and ditches beneath the Cadmea had been thrown up and dug hastily, they were now easily knocked over and crossed. Suddenly a detachment of northerners under Perdiccas, one of the inner circle of Macedonian generals, spotted an unguarded and mysteriously open gate to the city itself—the proverbial lapse in famous sieges, whether due to treachery or incompetence, that undermines an otherwise spirited defense. Perdiccas, apparently on his own initiative, immediately ordered hundreds to divert through the unforeseen entrance. That ad hoc decision led to the breakthrough into Thebes itself. Most of the city's gates were now presumably thrown open from the inside. At this point, all plans for a formal siege gave way to open fighting within the streets of the city.

General terror spread among the citizenry. Any surviving Theban hoplites outside the walls turned around and likewise rushed back to help save women, children, the elderly, and their servants. A few of the slaves and older men feebly tried to bar the entry of more Macedonian mercenaries. But more often they too fled into the narrow, winding streets to escape the intruders. "Every man for himself" during sieges proceeds like depositors panicking during bank runs, when naïve trust in the integrity of the status quo can ensure being left the most imperiled. Each defender who forsakes the walls becomes a force multiplier of the collective collapse of those who remain.

That Theban design flaw—the old citadel of the Cadmea sharing the main wall of the city—meant, first, that the trapped Macedonian garrison inside the city was right on top of their brethren just beneath the walls. And, second, any breach would mean not just an entrance into the city, but a route right into the high point and last redoubt of Thebes. In comparison with other, younger cities such as the Peloponnesian fortresses at Mantinea, Messene, and Megalopolis—many of them built just decades earlier with help from Theban architects, ironically enough—the ancestral parapets of Thebes were vastly overrated.

In truth, the legendary reputation of the city's circuit wall had derived from the huge stone blocks of earlier Mycenaean fortifications, mythologized centuries later during the dark age and archaic period as constructed by the monstrous Cyclopes. Classical Thebans could gaze every day upon the sizable foundational stones left by their ancestors near or inside the later classical city. They also prided themselves on a massive update of their fortifications in the mid fifth century, perhaps completing a second circuit around the old city. Still, there was no sign that they ever accomplished anything comparable to the Long Walls at Athens or the circuits of the Theban-inspired megacities to the south. And walls that might have withstood the earlier siegecraft of the city-states simply were no protection against sophisticated Macedonian besiegers.[9]

Classical Theban defense strategy for over a century had remained both expeditionary and preemptive: to use the Thebans' excellent cavalry and superb infantry to fight at a distance from the city and, if possible, near the frontier or even in the homeland of the enemy. The fields of Boeotia—the political and geographical region surrounding the capital at Thebes—were feared by all Greeks as the "dancing floor of war." The epithet was deserved. Dozens of battlefields dotted the Boeotian landscape, except around the walls of Thebes itself. But now the traditional Theban battle space had been reduced to just a few acres in and outside the city itself.[10]

During the rout, pockets of the retreating Theban hoplites were tangled up and battered by their own confused horsemen, as some of the braver Theban cavalry likewise had raced to the rear to save their families inside the walls. The jumble of mounted men mixed in with infantry made even chaotic resistance almost impossible. To make matters even worse, suddenly the once-trapped Macedonian garrison in the Cadmea broke out from the inner city. The result was that the doomed defenders were soon squeezed between a hammer and anvil of Macedonians. Diodorus even notes that the Thebans were often trampled by their own cavalry and speared by their weapons:

> But during these operations, the retreating Thebans' cavalry galloped alongside the infantry into the city. And many trampled—and then killed—lots of their own men. In their own abject disorder, they kept fleeing into the city in disorder. But then they became mired among a maze of alleys and trenches, lost their footing, tripped, and kept being killed by their own weapons. Just at that moment, the Macedonian garrison in the Cadmea burst out of the citadel, engaged the Thebans, and in their confusion made a great slaughter of them.[11]

The killing spree did not cease until nightfall. Calm came only with the virtual annihilation of the Theban military and the end of all resistance from noncombatants, many of whom were simply murdered in their homes. Alexander had by design unleashed zealots from the surrounding Boeotian towns, especially the notorious Theban-haters of the smaller cities of Plataea, Thespiae, and Orchomenos. All would be richly rewarded after the Theban defeat; they were given a major say in the fate of the captives, and remunerated handsomely when put in charge of the redistribution and appropriation of Theban farmland and the sale of enslaved Thebans.

Most of these satellite-townsmen were the historical enemies of Thebes. Yet they remained a minority in the Theban-led Boeotian confederacy, and earlier had once eagerly joined the agendas of the great liberator of the Messenian helots, Epaminondas. They were now seen by the Macedonians as ideal successors to the rebellious Thebans, and might act as Vichy-like collaborators once the yoke of their capital of Boeotia at Thebes was broken. The vengeance of these gangs of apostate Boeotians served as an accelerant to the growing hatred spawned by the Macedonians' mounting losses, and their furor that the Thebans had dared revolt against the young king. The resulting combined frenzy sealed the fate of the trapped survivors.[12]

Nearly five hundred years after the destruction of Thebes, the Roman historian Arrian gave a vivid description of the last hours of the hallowed city. Like the earlier Diodorus, he drew on lost contemporary Greek historians, in this case especially Ptolemy, a Macedonian general and comrade of Alexander. Thus, Arrian's account is likely to be reasonably accurate, if drawn almost exclusively from the Macedonian side. He confirmed that local Boeotians, even more so than the Macedonians, were responsible for much of the opportunistic bloodletting once organized Theban resistance ceased. Often the besiegers of an iconic city incorporated as allies local and indigenous people—the Balkan Christians among Mehmet II's invaders, the Numidian cavalry who aided Scipio Aemilianus at Carthage, or the Tlaxcalans who joined Cortés's conquistadors. Such opportunistic states either chafed under the imperialism of a hegemonic city or knew best the opportunities for plunder if the rich mother city fell. So now they calculated that the invaders indeed were likely to succeed, and they wanted to end up on the winning side.

One reason that Alexander apparently had outsourced the final mop-up dirty work to local rival Greeks was to ensure Greek-on-Greek carnage. That pretense of an internal Greek civil war might lessen his own culpability and help Macedonian propaganda that Greeks, not Macedonians, had brutally dealt with their own renegade city:

> Then the furor arose not so much on the part of the Macedonians as among the Phocians, Plataeans and the other Boeotians. In reckless fashion they cut down the Thebans who offered no resistance. They even fell upon some in their houses, where they had sought a way to defend themselves. They spared no others who were praying for salvation to the gods in their temples, and neither the women nor the children.[13]

Such hatred was abhorrent. But it was somewhat understandable. The Thebans in the past had razed the neighboring Boeotian cities of Orchomenos, Plataea, and Thespiae. The offspring of any survivors of those mini-holocausts now repaid the descendants of the perpetrators in kind. Diodorus provides an even more horrific final scene than Arrian, as he focuses on the Macedonians' unambiguous role in the murdering of civilians:

> As the Macedonians shouted threats, they further pressed themselves on the forlorn people, killing all whom they encountered, without sparing any. The Thebans, for their part, still desperately counted on their vanishing hope of victory. They so judged their lives as nothing that when they met any enemy, they swarmed him and endured his attacks. Once the city was captured, no one of the Thebans was seen begging the Macedonians to spare his life. Nor did any in cowardly fashion fall and grab on to the knees of the victors. But neither did the agony of their bravery earn any pity from their enemies nor did the day's length satiate the savagery of their revenge. Instead, the entire city was ransacked. Everywhere both boys and girls were bound into captivity even as they pathetically cried out the names of their mothers.[14]

The Thebans were within a single day completely defeated. Their army was routed and erased from history. But what were the victors to do with the more than thirty thousand residents still alive, captives trapped inside what was now their own prison? Were all the Thebans to be seen as collectively guilty of the rebellion? In one sense, the Thebans had a consensual government and thus the proverbial people had voted in their *ecclesia* ("political assembly") to revolt. On the other hand, were there any surviving Theban collaborationists or supporters of Alexander's vision of a new Panhellenic anti-Persian coalition who would deserve exemption from punishment?[15]

Such particulars mostly proved irrelevant, at least in the general street-by-street rampage. Instead, what followed the cessation of fighting was the summary execution of most surviving adult males, at least the majority who were not priests or could not prove any Macedonian ties. The killing was accompanied by the mass enslavement of thousands of young, old, and female Thebans. A complete razing of the physical infrastructure of the city ensued. In other words, both the material "Thebes" and the idea of ethnically, linguistically, and politically distinct "Thebans" living there, for all practical purposes, ceased to exist.

Ancient historical accounts and popular belief agreed that the destruction was total, absolute, and ruthless. Plutarch adds additional information that the battle ceased only when the last survivors of the Theban army had made a desperate last stand in the city, between Alexander's attackers and the Macedonian garrison that had sortied out of the Cadmea. Otherwise, Plutarch matter-of-factly confirms the trapped and surrounded were killed where they stood, thus ensuring the city was "captured, plundered, and razed." Although Plutarch wrote 450 years after the end of the city, he lived at Chaeronea, a mere thirty miles from Thebes, and thus was probably familiar with now lost contemporary local Boeotian historians, monuments, and inscriptions.[16]

There are no accurate figures of the size of the population of Thebes in 335 BC. Scholarly estimates put the total inside and near the walls somewhere around 30,000–50,000 residents—one of the larger Greek urban cores, but still far smaller than the populations of the three largest ancient Greek cities: Athens (ca. 150,000), Corinth (ca. 90,000), and Syracuse (ca. 100,000). Consequently, Thebes was an easier target for extinction than the more populous Greek metropolises, especially because it was landlocked and could neither be supplied by sea nor send survivors to safety in ships. Typically, ancient accounts do not separate combat from civilian deaths. In addition to the difficulty of discovering the accurate number of survivors, it is also almost impossible to determine exactly how many Thebans died in battle per se. All that said, we have enough consistent and exact numbers of general deaths and enslavements to appreciate the totality of Alexander's carnage.[17]

Plutarch wrote unambiguously that there were only a few small categories of residents who escaped execution or slavery: "After separating out the priests, and all those who were on friendly terms with the Macedonians, and those who were descendants of Pindar (the legendary early fifth-century BC lyric poet) and those who had voted against the rebellion, he sold all the rest into slavery—and they numbered more than 20,000, while those who had been slain were more than six thousand."

Plutarch also relates a human-interest tale of one of the rare survivors, the noblewoman Timocleia, widow of Theagenes, who had heroically perished at the head of the Sacred Band at Chaeronea. Once Alexander's Thracian contingents were let loose, some broke into Timocleia's house and stripped it. Their leader raped her. Then after he threatened to kill her unless she produced more gold and silver, Timocleia pointed to the house well, the proverbial household safe place in times of war. As their commander peered in, she pushed him down the hole then stoned the trapped Thracian until he died.

The dead commander's thugs bound and brought Timocleia to Alexander for execution. In supposedly typical Alexandrian heroic fashion, he was more impressed by the details of her spunk and courage than concerned about the murder of one of his more savage and expendable barbarian henchmen. So he released her and her children to safety. We have no idea how many, if any, more elite Thebans were given amnesty by the unpredictable Alexander.[18]

Plutarch apparently included this anecdote not so much to emphasize Alexander's mercurial magnanimity, as both to illustrate the fanatical level of civilian resistance to the victors, and to suggest the real barbarity was due to freelancing foreign auxiliaries rather than the Macedonian army on direct orders from Alexander himself. In this regard, we should also remember Thucydides's earlier story of the sickening slaughter of schoolboys at the nearby Theban town of Mycalessos during the Peloponnesian War. That ancient war crime was also perpetrated by similar roving Thracian gangs, an apparent stereotype of wartime barbarism in Greek historical literature. In 413 BC, the Thracian mercenaries had gone on to slaughter every man, woman, and child in the small city, effectively wiping out Mycalessos. So the Thracian role in destroying Thebes also provided an opportunity for the Boeotian Plutarch to emphasize the sad fates of Boeotian cities and their defense of civilization beset by northern, non-Hellenic barbarism.[19]

Except for his smaller number of the enslaved, Plutarch's totals of the combat losses are roughly echoed by Arrian. Both again probably drew on many of the same lost sources. Arrian also concurs with Plutarch in his generalization that "more than 500 Macedonians were killed," as well as 6,000 Theban fatalities. But like Diodorus he reports a greater, and more likely, figure for the enslaved—some "30,000 sold into slavery."

Diodorus added final summaries about Macedonian dead and the Theban property that was plundered: "Over six thousand Thebans perished, more than 30,000 were captured, and the amount of property plundered was unbelievable. The king gave burial to the Macedonian dead, more than five hundred in number."[20]

The general numbers who perished at Thebes are clear enough. Some six thousand Thebans likely were killed in the fighting and during the murders and executions that followed. That was a ghastly figure by the standards of the usual battles between Greek city-states, which, remember, on average were smaller than Roman or later European cities. The sum might have included all the infantrymen and horsemen lost in the fighting, all the civilians who resisted and were murdered in the streets, and a few surviving adult males executed in the aftermath.

We have some contemporary context for the number of dead from the fatalities three years earlier at the climactic pitched battle of Chaeronea, where Philip II finally destroyed organized Greek resistance. There the total number of actual combatants was far greater (ca. 60,000–70,000). Yet the routed Athenians and Thebans suffered together only around 2,000 deaths, the Macedonians less than 150. Indeed, even at the ferocious battle of Leuctra (371 BC), the losing Spartans suffered only 1,000 dead. So we can assume that the very idea of 6,000 slain Thebans was an extraordinary loss for a classical Greek city-state and again reflects the absolute obliteration of the Theban army and the slaughter inside the city that ensued.[21]

Arrian notes that Alexander sold "into slavery the women and children, and as many of the males as survived." Like Plutarch he noted exceptions to the mass executions and enslavement, such as "those who were priests or priestesses, and who were guest-friends bound to Philip or Alexander or had been public agents of the

Macedonians. They say that Alexander preserved the house and the descendants of the poet Pindar, out of respect for his memory."[22]

The aggregate number of exempted clerics, pro-Macedonian operatives, descendants of Pindar, and various Theban turncoats could not have been large. When the dead are combined with the thirty thousand slaves, we should assume that the majorities of those Thebans alive when Alexander arrived at the city within twenty-four hours either perished or were enslaved.

We are also told that the slave-sellers who auctioned off the thirty thousand Theban men, women, and children made a profit of some 440 talents, or 2,640,000 drachmas. That sum amounts to about 88 drachmas per head, an extraordinary figure for such a quick and mass sale of thousands. In general, the price of a slave varied widely throughout the Greek world across time and space. It was often set by the supply and demand of war, especially in cases where thousands from a defeated city were put on the market all at once by the money-strapped victors. Our late source for the Theban slave sale, the historian Justin, also claimed that one selling point was sheer hatred of the Thebans by the neighboring Boeotian purchasers—as if witnessing their continued torment as slaves was an added incentive for the buyers. Such enmity apparently helped to drive up the price of the enslaved survivors.

One drachma a day was considered a classical Greek daily wage for labor, so the price per enslaved was about the equivalent of eighty-eight days' worth of labor, or about a quarter of the average Greek's annual income. Among the newly enslaved were also the existing slaves of the Thebans. They simply changed their masters and were sold off along with their previously free owners.[23]

The enslaved were branded and then likely either resold for higher prices in the years following the end of Thebes, or were worked to death given the great number of aged and infirm. Their fate depended somewhat on their skills, age, and sex. Educated older Thebans might become household slaves, doing everything from domestic chores to tutoring. Younger females might be sold off as prostitutes, mistresses, household workers, weavers, or wet nurses. Most younger males, however, would likely end up in harsher conditions as farm workers and field hands, or resold across the border to work in the Athenian silver mines.

We have no figures for how many civilians, like Timocleia, had either been exempted by Alexander, fled the city during the early days of the resistance before the arrival of Alexander, or snuck out from the walls in the three days between Alexander's arrival and the destruction of the city. Several sources speak of Theban "exiles," yet we have no idea whether they were mostly prior refugees who had earlier fled the subjugated Thebes, or a few survivors of the rebellion against Alexander.

Even here Alexander's wrath was not quenched by mass death and enslavement. He issued an edict to all the Greek city-states that any of the Theban exiles living in their environs were to be expelled, either to wander stateless or to be turned over to the Macedonians. The decree in part reflected Alexander's anger at how the previously docile Thebans were said to have been goaded to revolt by the arrival of once-exiled Theban agitators who had returned to the city to foment rebellion.

After the city's destruction, the Athenian firebrands made peace with Alexander. Their orators pleaded on behalf of the few Thebans who abroad had survived the extermination of their city. Eventually, under changed conditions, some of the exiles apparently survived and were given refuge by individual city-states. A very few may have participated in later Macedonian efforts to build a smaller new Thebes on the rubble of the old.[24]

So what exactly was the fate of the physical city, the infrastructure of Thebes itself? After all, our sources variously talk of finality, of Thebes "razed to the ground" (*kataskapsai es edaphos*), with the exception of the poet Pindar's house and sacred precincts and temples. Were such vivid descriptions and exaggerations similar to ancient accounts of farmland being "destroyed" or "cut down" or "burnt" by enemy ravagers that in fact rarely resulted in total losses?

Perhaps not. Whereas the farmland of Boeotia likely covered some twelve hundred square miles, and agricultural devastation conducted during active wartime conditions was often contested and limited in duration by the brief campaigning season, the Macedonians now faced no such inherent obstacles or resistance. The size of the urban core of Thebes proper was only a few hundred acres. Thebes was no Carthage or Constantinople. The Macedonian army and its Boeotian henchmen constituted a huge labor force of destruction. No doubt the thirty thousand enslaved Theban survivors were pressed into the humiliating work of leveling their own homes and city.[25]

So a total annihilation of Thebes was certainly likely. It was seen so by contemporary observers who mourned Thebes's final disappearance.

Yet in a world of human and animal muscular labor such destruction was no easy task. Despite the incorporation of noninflammable stone foundations, mudbrick walls, and tile roofs, ancient houses could be torched by igniting wooden rafters and supporting lumber to cause a general collapse. Clay roof tiles and dressed stone were valuable commodities in the ancient Greek world. So, we should assume that, as in the case of the sale of slaves, peddlers swarmed the desolate site and auctioned off stones, bricks, and tiles to the surrounding Boeotians.

The task of carting away salvageable building materials would have taken months, if not years. Indeed, contemporary extant inscriptions on stone reveal that the pro-Macedonian Boeotians who helped raze the city were using the spoils—such as gold, silver, bronze, and iron utensils and salvageable wooden furniture—to endow shrines and buildings for years to come. The urban core and the surrounding farmland of Theban families were sold off as well at property auctions, or divided up among the Boeotians who had joined the Macedonians in the fighting.[26]

The historian Arrian ends his sad account by remarking that locals were left to finish the auction of spoils and guard the desolation:

Alexander allotted the final settlement of Theban matters to the allies who had a share in the action. They found it wise to secure the Cadmea with a garrison; to raze the city to the ground; to redistribute among themselves all the lands, except what was consecrated to the gods; and to sell into slavery the women and children, and as many of the men who had thus far survived.[27]

In sum, on the first day of the siege, the city of Thebes was as it had always been for the prior 350 years. Within days, there were neither Thebans nor a Thebes at all. At the conclusion of the battle, Alexander momentarily was unsure, or feigned uncertainty, about the eventual fate of the survivors. The politics were tricky, aside from the more immediate logistical challenges of providing for a sizable surviving Greek population of thirty thousand or more without means of support.

On the one hand, Thebes was the most hallowed of the city-states, the mythical home of Panhellenic heroes and gods like Herakles and the god Dionysus. The most renowned of Greece's tragic archetypes—Antigone, Cadmus, Oedipus, Pentheus, Teiresias, and Semele—were synonymous with Theban lore. The city and its environs had produced some of the greatest names in Greek poetry, such as Hesiod and Pindar, and their repute apparently remained dear to Alexander and the Macedonians.

The followers of Pythagoras had enjoyed a large cult in Thebes. There was also a Socratic philosophical following in the city. The Theban philosophers Simmias and Cebes appear or are mentioned in Socratic discourse in both Plato and Xenophon. Crates, the Theban Cynic, was at the time a student of Diogenes of Athens. The Theban and Pythagorean Epaminondas, just three decades after his death, was by popular consent considered the greatest man Greece had produced. The Roman Cicero three centuries later would still proclaim him *Princeps Graecae* ("First Man of Greece"). So did Alexander really wish to exterminate the home of such a rich philosophical and cultural tradition?[28]

More germanely, if Alexander razed the city and killed or enslaved the surviving population, he still could not be sure of the reaction from the other fifteen hundred or so Greek city-states. True, in the numerous wars of the Greeks, there were plenty of occasions when the losing poleis were leveled. But neither an obliterated tiny Melos nor Plataea approached the area or population of classical Thebes.

Other cities, such as Athens and Sparta, had been defeated, and their victorious enemies either occupied their city centers or had reached their suburbs, but both survived intact defeats in 403 and 369, respectively. The squabbling city-states in general did not wish to see their major poleis, such as Athens, Sparta—or Thebes—razed to the ground.

So there were some reasons for leniency. Alexander was a student of his late father's Macedonian propaganda. Philip II had disingenuously preached for two decades that the monarchy simply wished to unite the perennially squabbling and self-destructive city-states into a Panhellenic coalition. Then, as an indivisible Greek-speaking people, all the city-states under Macedonian leadership would in unison invade Asia. They would liberate the fellow Greeks of Asia Minor. They would pay back the Persians for nearly two centuries of interference in Hellenic affairs, including two invasions of the Greek mainland. And more practically, they would all become collectively rich by looting the cities and treasuries of the Achaemenid Empire. Slaughtering the unarmed inhabitants of one of the most renowned cities in Greece on the eve of such a project was likely not conducive to such an ecumenical narrative.[29]

Thebes, along with Sparta, Athens, and Corinth, had traditionally formed a tetrad of the most prestigious, powerful, and influential of the Greek mainland states, perhaps analogous to the preeminence of the early nineteenth-century American cities of Boston, New York, Philadelphia, and Washington. There was a tradition that while the tetrad fought each other in shifting alliances, and the victors often *threatened* the extinction of the defeated, such obliteration of major cities had *never* yet occurred.

On the other hand, there were even more realist arguments for Macedonian severity. Alexander was only twenty-one. He was untested. His kingship was the freak result of the assassination of his father, who should have been king for at least another decade or two. The murder of this forty-six-year-old military genius had immediately prompted numerous coup attempts against Alexander from prominent, older, and established claimants to the throne. Assassination plots were still rife. There remained potential rebellions of subject cities to the north throughout the Macedonian empire.

To exterminate the Thebans, then, would serve several purposes. Most importantly, it would signal any would-be Macedonian rivals to the throne that Alexander was ruthless, and recklessly and unpredictably so. If he was not afraid to wipe out the most legendary of Greek cities, then certainly he would deal with Macedonian court conspirators even more harshly.

Next, the ruins of Thebes would warn the Greeks of the wages of rebellion. Post facto, it did just that. Would-be allied polis revolutionaries not only ceased their agitation on rumors of his invasion but also, within days of Alexander's arrival at Thebes, they were rooting out any of his pro-Theban opponents within their own cities. At the same time, the city-states were sending obsequious delegations professing their unlimited support.

Annihilation would immediately remove the final obstacles to the impending invasion of Asia Minor, whose planning and preparations had been started under Philip II in Asia Minor itself the year prior. Alexander was especially infuriated by the Persian hiring of Greek mercenaries. He assumed that the extermination of Thebes would send a message that Greek soldiers for Persian hire might consider the fate of their Theban brethren. Yet even after the leveling of the city, thousands of Greeks, both in Greece and Asia Minor, enlisted in the service of the Persians to stop Alexander. Perhaps some twenty thousand would fight against him in his first great battle at Granicus (334 BC), and Greek mercenaries continued to be hired by the Persians at Issus (333 BC).[30]

There were already reports from Asia Minor of growing resistance to preliminary preparations by Alexander's generals. They urged him to settle the Greek home front as quickly and permanently as possible. In a cynical sense, Alexander realized that his severity at Thebes would prompt calls for Greek unity under

Macedonian leadership, and that any clemency would embolden talk of Panhellenic resistance to foreign tyranny.

Moreover, young Alexander had tried to follow his late father's carrot-and-stick lead in strategic thinking, especially in responses to insurgency. Philip in 348 BC, just thirteen years prior, had dealt in existential fashion with the rebellious and influential northern Greek city-state Olynthus on the Chalcidian peninsula. He quickly conducted a short and successful occupation of the historic capital of a thirty-two-city-state league. After he oversaw the enslavement and sale of the surviving population, the entire city was razed. Such ruthlessness was followed by immediate gestures of goodwill toward Macedon from most terrified northern Greek cities.

Apparently, neither Philip nor Alexander worried that their respective annihilations of two great Greek cities, Olynthus and Thebes, might boomerang back on their legacies as monstrous and illustrative of half-civilized Macedonians to be fought to the death rather than appeased.[31]

Alexander and Philip also likely had personal reasons for feeling a particular animosity toward Thebes. As a boy, Philip had greatly admired Epaminondas, the great Theban general who ended Spartan power. Indeed, he had spent several years as a hostage (ca. 368–365 BC) in Thebes during his own father's reign, apparently absorbing military strategy and diplomacy from Epaminondas himself. When he became king, he adopted Theban infantry protocols along with his own tactical innovations. Yet Thebes did not return the admiration, and in fact led the opposition to Philip.

There were other reasons to end Thebes and massacre Thebans. Alexander sensed that Thebes was also deeply hated by its Boeotian neighbors for a variety of reasons, some quite warranted. The Theban hegemony (371–362 BC) traditionally had forced satellite city-states to remain subordinates rather than ascend to partnership with Thebes. The capital had always dealt harshly with any polis in the Boeotian league suspected of foreign intrigue. Indeed, as we have seen, the chief reason there were Plataeans, Thespians, and Orchomenians murdering Thebans in the streets was because Thebes at various times had razed all three of these neighboring cities and enslaved their populations. Their neighbors, the Phocians, likewise shared prior grievances and were eager for Thebes's destruction. Some of our sources mention additional "other" Boeotians of unnamed city-states who also loathed the Thebans and participated in the rampage.

Thebes was also still scorned for siding with the Persians during the Persian War of the early fifth century BC. While Sparta and Athens were earning undying glory at Thermopylae and Salamis, and leading a grand coalition to final victory at the climactic battle of Plataea, Thebes, to its eternal infamy, in 480 BC had allied itself with the Persian invaders.

While Theban myths were dramatic Panhellenic boilerplate, they were also grotesque reminders of something creepy and perverse about the Greek past, and in particular of eerie events in the city beneath the shadows of Mount Cithaeron. Greeks noted that all the worst pathologies of the Athenian tragic stage—the supposed "ancient infamy" of the "old crimes" of incest, patricide, fratricide, filicide, matricide, beheading, self-mutilation, orgiastic excess—characterized the Theban houses of Oedipus and Cadmus. The horrific tales of mythological characters such as Eteocles and Polynices, Laius, Jocasta and Oedipus, and Pentheus and Agave seemed properly representative of Thebes. These old stories were popularly reenacted in the theater of Dionysus at Athens, traditionally Thebes's most proximate enemy. Justin noted that this theme was central in the arguments for destroying Thebes: "They also brought forward the fabulous accounts of their old crimes, with which they had filled every theater, to make them odious not only for their recent perfidy, but for their ancient infamy."[32]

The Macedonians also benefited by wiping out the putative strategic and military leader of the Greek city-states. Before the catastrophic Greek defeat at the battle of Chaeronea, a unified Boeotia under Thebes had led the Greek resistance to Macedon. Destroying Thebes weakened the unity of Boeotia and thus a nexus of anti-Macedonian resistance. Boeotia, itself without a large capital, was no longer to be feared. Its leadership would be fragmented and dispersed. The Boeotians would be left squabbling among their small cities in a new world while the old giants Athens and Sparta, once fearsome military powers, were reduced to empty megaphones.[33]

Moreover, Macedonians were Greek-like rather than considered true Hellenes. They spoke a closely related but still somewhat different language that was only partially understandable to Greeks of the south. In addition to linguistic and ethnic differences, they were wedded to anti-Hellenic traditions of monarchy and political agendas that precluded free and autonomous city-states.

The half-Greek, half-Macedonian Alexander, for all his pious later regrets about leveling Thebes, and Panhellenic blather about the "freedom of the Greeks," characteristically showed little empathy for any who crossed him, whether individuals or collective peoples. He certainly did not bequeath democratic ideals to his dictatorial successors in the Hellenistic world. The list of his razed cities, enslaved peoples, and slaughtered friends and enemies would only grow over the next decade in Asia.[34]

Alexander elicited the views of the conquered and emasculated Greek states only if and when he assumed they would dovetail with his own wishes. Only in that context did he formally put the fate of the Thebans to the League of Corinth, Philip's servile council of Greek city-states—with special deference to those poleis that had participated in the recent battle—in a faux-display of democratic concern. He played the role of the later Pontius Pilate, in simulating a reluctant concession to the harsh verdict of his allies.

In truth, Alexander knew instinctively that the toady Greek representatives among the League of Corinth would surely call for the harshest of penalties against Thebes, if only to avoid the now idle Macedonian military marching on their own walls. So Alexander welcomed the airing of Boeotian demands for no mercy due to centuries of alleged Theban sins. He was not disappointed. The list of pent-up grievances from venomous anti-Theban Boeotian states ranged back even to mythical times. The historian Justin reviewed the laundry list of Theban transgressions:

> In the deliberations about the destruction of the city, the Phocians, Plataeans, Thespians, and Orchomenians—allies of Alexander and

participants in his battle victory—kept emphasizing the destruction of their own cities and the cruelty of the Thebans. They railed against them, not only because of their present, but also their past aid to the Persians against the interests of the freedom of Greece. For that reason, they said, the city had become the object of general hatred, as was clear when all had given oaths to destroy Thebes once the Persians should be conquered.[35]

Cleadas, a Theban rhetorician and now a prisoner facing enslavement or death, begged the Macedonian victors to spare the captives and preserve the city. Cleadas cited legal, historical, and mythological grounds for leniency, guided by his own self-interest in living as a free man one more day. He argued perversely that the Thebans had technically revolted only upon the false rumors of Alexander's demise, as if such erroneous calculation was a principled decision. Cleadas apparently reasoned on behalf of the doomed that they did not know whether a supposedly deceased Alexander's Macedonian heirs would have abided by their late leader's arrangements with the Greeks. In legally reductionist terms, the Thebans were thus guilty only of wishing to rebel against a dead Alexander's killers, and thus could now logically become allies of the living Alexander. How the Thebans' current armed struggle against a young king, still very much alive, bolstered such a plea we cannot know.

In the end, the desperate Cleadas had the unfortunate task of convincing Alexander that his fellow Thebans were not opportunistic when they searched for any event that might weaken their overlords. Rather ingeniously, he portrayed Thebans as good lawyers who saw the would-be Macedonian claimants to the supposedly dead Alexander's throne as less trustworthy than their late king. In the end, no one bought such a ridiculous argument.

Cleadas, however, did add at least one logical and realistic point: that destroying Thebes was redundant. After all, its youth of military age were mostly already dead. Its military was nonexistent. The city was now largely the pitiful domain of the elderly, women, children, and the enfeebled. He then finished with an emotional appeal to the common mythological roots of Theban panhellenism, an allusion aimed directly at Alexander's celebrated worship of Herakles:

> He sought a reprieve from the king also on grounds of his superstitious affinity for Herakles, who had been born among the Thebans, and from whom the clan of the Aeacidae was descended, and also from awareness that the youth of his father Philip had been spent at Thebes. And so he begged to spare a city, one which had celebrated as gods some of Alexander's own ancestors who had been born in it, and had viewed others who had been raised there as kings of the greatest stature.[36]

As Arrian recorded the debate, the aggrieved pro-Macedonian Boeotians also reminded Alexander that the Thebans had not only betrayed the Greeks in 480 BC some 145 years prior, but also they had attacked nearby Plataea during the Peloponnesian War, precipitating a war in which the Thebans demanded and achieved the neighboring city-state's destruction. In addition, after the defeat of Athens in the Peloponnesian War (nearly seventy years earlier), the Thebans had in vain begged their allies, the occupying and victorious Spartans, to level Athens. That the Thebans had made even the Spartans appear lenient was a good argument in the present against showing leniency to them. In sum, Thebes had a long history of advocating and carrying out the destruction of quite a few city-states, and now the goddess Nemesis would have her way.[37]

Nor can we omit the role of the irrational. The Thebans had not just defied Alexander, but after refusing his terms had insulted his envoys. On the prompting of the Theban exiles who arrived back home before the siege, they had earlier murdered two of the Macedonian garrison's officers inside the city, along with a few prominent Thebans in Alexander's puppet government. In the battle, Theban hoplites had slain five hundred of his best troops. In other words, Alexander suffered more fatalities at Thebes than he had three years earlier at Chaeronea and would in six months in his initial great victory over the Persians at Granicus (May 334). Even at his masterpiece victory over the Persians at Gaugamela (331 BC), Alexander reportedly lost only five hundred infantrymen. For the Macedonians, the death at Thebes of five hundred professionals on the eve of invading Persia was a terrible—and unforgivable—loss.

Some scholars add still another motive, one more personal. Just as Alexander's father Philip II had razed Olynthus on the charge that the city-state's citizens preferred one of Philip's rival claimants to the Macedonian throne, so Alexander suspected the Thebans were not so much eager to throw off the Macedonian yoke as to replace his claim to Philip's throne with that of his rival Amyntas, a general deemed more favorable to the Greeks.[38]

Nonetheless, Alexander found a solution to his dilemma. By outsourcing the decision to a "majority vote" of his Greek allies representing the League of Corinth, Alexander would assuage some Boeotian hatred of Thebes. The Theban-haters would get their chance at revenge and profit. The Macedonian-haters could blame fellow Greeks rather than Alexander for the slaughter.

The unleashing of the vengeful Boeotians upon the helpless citizens of Thebes was in many ways analogous to Wehrmacht policies following the June 1941 invasion of the Soviet Union. The Nazis often contracted out some of their barbarity to local fascists in Eastern Europe and the Baltic states. Indeed, in this regard, two fatal weaknesses of the targeted are thematic in our study of doomed states. First, so often their supposed "friends" or allies either joined in the destruction, or carefully kept quiet at a safe distance. And second, on the eve of the invasion the defenders were often internally squabbling and fractious, and never could really unite in the face of a common enemy.

There was again the financial argument. Selling the entire surviving population to slave auctioneers earned Alexander, as mentioned, 440 talents. That sum was the equivalent of paying more than seven thousand of his soldiers together a year's worth of wages, apparently a far preferable proposition than providing sustenance for thousands of the helpless in the occupied city.[39]

In the end, Alexander also found a legalistic pretext for no mercy. His Greek surrogates judged the Thebans guilty of dishonoring the gods by having violated their sacred oaths as members of

Alexander's own stooge League of Corinth, namely, their prior pledge to unite in common cause under Macedonian leadership against the Persians. The so-called delegates ruled that the Thebans had betrayed not just Alexander, but also their fellow Hellenic states.[40]

How did contemporaries later explain the chain of disastrous Theban decisions that step by step led to the destruction of their culture, people, and city? At any given point in the fall and winter of 335 BC, a different choice, a demurral, a step back might have resulted in an occupied, but extant Thebes. The city might otherwise have been like the other cities that had remained unfree—but alive—under Macedonian stewardship. In short, how did the Thebans miscalculate so badly as to stage a doomed rebellion, and then allow a likely defeat to become a certain annihilation?

The Thebans' first decision, disastrous in retrospect, was a complete miscalculation of both their military power and their prestige and influence among the city-states. Their confidence in the Theban army was anachronistic, as if they were back thirty-five years earlier in the days of the Theban hegemony (371–362 BC). Moreover, for some reason the Thebans believed that if they alone dared defy Alexander, thousands of other Greeks would flock to their cause. Others well might have, but only if Thebes had first defeated the huge Macedonian army descending on it from the north.

The problem was not just that the Thebans had an antiquated or indeed romantic view of their own past. They also had never fully appreciated the military revolution brought about by Philip II and his once rustic and slighted Macedonians. His new army's use of the longer pike, or sarissa; a much better integrated use of larger contingents of heavy and light cavalry and assorted missile troops; the élan and drill of a professional phalanx; the key inspirational role of a mounted king at the head of his army—a force now much larger than the population of most city-states—all had rendered obsolete the old agrarian hoplite militias of the city-states.

The Theban failure to fully appreciate the consequences of Philip's military revolution was especially ironic, given that during young Philip's three critical years as a hostage (369–367 BC), he was under the custodianship of Pammenes, a leader of the Theban Sacred Band. The teenager, even if only fifteen to seventeen years old during these hostage years, knew Epaminondas and Pelopidas, both generals at the pinnacle of their military and political careers. Scholars have argued that many of the military reforms Philip enacted a decade later were drawn from his earlier firsthand observations or related accounts of the tactical and organizational genius of Epaminondas himself, particularly the Macedonian use of reserves, the oblique attack of a deepened phalanx, the synchronization of infantry and cavalry, and the use of an army as a tool of political ideology. Indeed, Philip had applied many of his earlier lessons learned at Thebes throughout some twenty years of conquest in which he conducted nearly thirty successful campaigns. His Macedonian military had successfully stormed over ten cities and captured another forty-four.[41]

The second baleful Theban choice was one widely shared by all the Greek city-states, namely, giving credence to empty rumors from the returning Theban exiles that Alexander had been assassinated in the north. It might have been a reasonable supposition, given that Alexander spent the months after his father's assassination liquidating rivals to his father's throne—many of them blood relations with better connections to the old guard of Macedonian generals—and in turn avoiding plots.

Many of our ancient sources cite this Theban delight at the very thought of a dead Alexander as the spark that ignited Theban passions. Again, an account found in Arrian explicitly blamed the Theban uprising on the return of self-interested Theban exiles who had earlier been banished by Philip and now saw their futures as free Thebans contingent on the defeat of the Macedonians.

Still, it seems incredible that the Thebans could have believed a so obviously self-interested rumor, spread by exiles whose lives and careers depended on the budding revolt against Macedon. So unhinged were the rebellious that they continued to lie that

Alexander could not possibly be at the head of the advancing army—until he showed up beneath their walls.

Note too this predictable, recurring human trait of trusting in hope, or "danger's comforter," as the historian Thucydides characterized such naïveté. Carthaginians would also want to believe like-minded Macedonian renegades had drawn off the power of Rome from Africa. Byzantines on the walls of Constantinople would cling to rumors that a Christian relief fleet was on its way to the Bosporus. The Aztecs numerous times would convince themselves that Cortés had been overwhelmed in battle and was dead.

Exiles had apparently scattered throughout the Greek city-states following the defeat at Chaeronea. Most were unable to return home, given the large Macedonian garrison on the Cadmea. The terrified puppet Theban government had barred them from even visiting their homes. Yet in Arrian's narrative, the arriving exiles not only introduced the lie that Alexander was dead, but also were immediately engaged in a veritable coup to displace the Vichy-like pro-Macedonian government of Thebes with a democratic substitute. He notes how easily they whipped up the Theban assembly with democratic sloganeering:

> At this time some of the exiles banished from Thebes who had entered the city by night, were escorted by those citizens planning a revolt . . . Once they had entered the assembly, they incited the Thebans to rebel from Alexander, by invoking ancient and noble slogans like "freedom" and "independence," and at last to free themselves from the oppression of the Macedonians. They seemed especially persuasive to the people by insisting that Alexander had died while among the Illyrians. The rumor was trafficked in by lots of people and gained credibility because Alexander had been absent for a long time, and no communications at all had arrived from him.[42]

Even if the exiles' rumors about the death of the twenty-one-year-old Alexander had been true, once again the Thebans had failed to ˙ te that his army was still led by Philip's surviving old guard ned generals, the professionals who had first created the

Macedonian military. Their reputation for institutionalized military superiority is why the rumors spread that the supposedly dead Alexander's subordinate Antipater was leading the march to Thebes. The Theban revolutionaries omitted the fact that the veterans of some twenty years of constant warring at the side of Philip meant that even without Alexander, battle-scarred killers like Antigonus, Antipater, Craterus, Eumenes, Parmenio, and Ptolemy were more than a match for any Greek city-state general and his army. On the mainland of Greece, they had no need for Alexander to instruct them in warcraft, diplomacy, or how to deal with rebellious cities.[43]

A third miscalculation was misplaced confidence in the power, prestige, and alliance of the noisy and self-important but now impotent Athenians. After the end of the Peloponnesian War, Thebes had soon triangulated with the defeated Athens to prevent an ascendant Spartan hegemony over Greece. That partnership had later failed at Chaeronea, but there were still strong ties between the once inimical rivals. The stalwart orator and arch-Macedonian-hater Demosthenes had not just stirred up Greek hatred of Alexander. He had also supplied money and arms to the Thebans, with the unrealistic expectation that Athenian troops might join once Thebes led a successful Panhellenic rebellion.[44]

Unfortunately for Thebes, Athens was governed not only by pragmatists, but also by some statesmen who genuinely supported the Macedonian cause, were bribed to do so, or were terrified into silence. Athens still had some luster as Pericles's "school of Hellas." Yet it was not merely naïve, but suicidal for Theban leaders to predicate the fate of thousands of noncombatants on the fickle revolutionary fervor of nearby Athenians in general, and in particular of Demosthenes, who reportedly had earlier tossed his shield and fled in panic as the Athenian army dissipated at Chaeronea.

Although the Athenians later offered sanctuary to any Theban refugees who had escaped the battle, upon the initial sight of a live Alexander heading their way, their revolutionary fervor simply vanished. Or as the historian Justin dryly put it, when the Athenians saw the Macedonian army in Attica: "The Athenians, just as they had been the first to rebel, so they were also the first to regret their

47

rebellion, as they turned their contempt for their enemy into near worship of him, admiring the once despised youthfulness of Alexander as superior to older leaders."

Plutarch remarked that Demosthenes had ensured arms for the Theban rebels who attacked the Macedonian occupying garrison. The orator had written letters to Persian generals in Asia to urge them to declare war on Alexander. Later he had aroused all Greeks to stand with Thebes. Yet once Alexander leveled Thebes, and then turned his gaze toward Athens and targeted Demosthenes, in Plutarch's words, "Demosthenes withered."[45]

A fourth Theban blunder was the venom with which their leaders gratuitously insulted the Macedonian king, turning a political or even ideological revolt into a matter of personal honor and revenge for the young, mercurial Alexander. The Thebans had begun their rebellion by murdering two Macedonian overseers, Amyntas and Timolaüs, who apparently in peacetime had been walking the streets of Thebes without any fear of violence.

When Alexander arrived at the walls, the Thebans not only rejected his terms of capitulation—a rather lenient status quo ante bellum, albeit with surrender of the instigators—but also mocked Alexander in the process. Their defiance was understandably aimed at fueling popular furor at the enemy at their gates. But Theban derision, allegedly incited again by exiles, also helped to ensure that the city's annihilation, rather than its mere defeat, would alone assuage Alexander's sense of honor.

The historian Diodorus offers a good picture of the unreality at Thebes. Despite the lack of wherewithal to stop the greatest army the classical world produced, the Thebans nonetheless pressed on to revile the most dangerous man alive:

> At first, the king kept quiet, allowing the Thebans some time to change their views, and believing that just a single city would never even dare to face in battle with such an army. . . . If the Thebans had given in to the situation and had negotiated with the Macedonians for peace and an alliance, then the king would have accepted their requests with pleasure. And he would have agreed to everything

they had asked, given that he was quite anxious to be free of these disturbances in Greece and that way he might be able to conduct the war against Persia without distraction. Finally, however, once he fathomed that he was hated by the Thebans, he grew intent on destroying the city. Through such terror, he would crush the zeal of those daring to revolt against him.

Alexander in vain offered the defiant Thebans one last chance to capitulate and save their lives and those of their families:

After he prepared his forces for battle, he then sent a herald to proclaim that any of the Thebans who wanted, could come join him and thereby enjoy the peace common to all the Greeks. In reply, the Theban heralds from a high tower in the city, answered in their confidence that anyone who wanted to join the Great King [the Persian king] and Thebes to liberate the Greeks and to destroy the tyrant of Greece should come join them. Alexander grew irate at that slur and became so enraged that he now decided to inflict upon the Thebans every sort of punishment. Still furious, he set to work building siege engines and preparing everything else necessary for the impending battle.[46]

In the years after Alexander was done, what was known or left of the physical city, other than a handful of abandoned religious precincts and the supposed historical home and descendants of Pindar the poet? Remember that Thebes was a city-state, not part of a nation of the Boeotians. The so-called Boeotian federation was only a loose alliance of surrounding and smaller city-states that shared a similar dialect, history, cults, and ethnic commonality. But, again, they were not a country. Alexander knew that to decapitate Thebes and its federation, he simply had to eliminate all Thebans inside the city, leaving only a few exiles scattered about Greece.

The point is that Thebes was not a Carthage or Constantinople, cities that had overseen a once huge empire. Unlike a parochial Thebes, both Carthage and Constantinople at their zeniths mustered manpower and money well beyond their walls. Even in their decline, they still drew on natural resources of timber, farmland, and mines from their hinterlands. In contrast, Thebes, while important to the Boeotians, was not indispensable to Hellenic civilization. And such a small city-state ipso facto never had any realistic chance of survival against the greatest besieger of the ancient world once its Athenian-incited, dreamy Panhellenic rebellion fizzled into nothingness.

After the end of the city, hostile Boeotian neighbors farmed Theban land. Given that Thebes was not near stone and clay quarries, most of the roof tiles of buildings, stone foundations, and walls were valuable flotsam and jetsam, and thus carted off to neighboring towns. The leveling of the city and the continual reuse of any salvageable Theban stone and tile materials over the centuries, coupled with the fact that the modern city sits atop its ancient predecessors, explain why modern archaeologists have found few material traces of the Theban cataclysm of 335 BC.

The population, except for a few religious figures and the descendants of Pindar, was either dead or enslaved. In theory, there were now no free Theban citizens alive—except a few vestigial exiles in some cities who had not joined the original influx back into Thebes that had incited the revolt. Perhaps some had managed to buy their freedom or were emancipated by sympathetic masters. Names of a handful of Thebans survive. The Athenian orator Hyperides was said to have bought for an exorbitant price a young Theban captive, one Phila ("Beloved") who became his mistress. No doubt that was a common occurrence.[47]

There were a few Thebans, or at least a few Boeotian names, later mentioned during the Macedonian wars against the Persians in Asia. We have no idea who these survivors were among the few spared by Alexander: the pro-Macedonian agents and operators of Alexander; former members of the priestly castes; distant descendants of Pindar; or those resistance fighters enslaved in 335, who were later freed by their masters and trekked to Asia to join the Persian army.

Some have suggested that a few Thebans fighting outside the walls might have escaped the holocaust by fleeing to local ports on the Corinthian Gulf and taking to sea. Or perhaps some members of the defeated Theban cavalry took rare opportunities to ride to safety and did not reenter the city, seeking instead to flee from the losing battle. Arrian, for example, says of the Theban horsemen that they "filled up the plain" outside the city at one point. But again, Thebans mentioned later in Greek literature and history were mostly those few enslaved or spared citizens still alive at Thebes on the day after Alexander assaulted the city.[48]

Did the Greeks regret the loss of such an iconic city? At first, no. Alexander achieved his purposes of bullying any remaining revolutionary city into submission. For the next twelve years of Alexander's life, all Greeks under Macedonian rule either kept quiet about the fate of the Thebans, or rivaled one another to ingratiate themselves with the Macedonian occupiers.

But after Alexander's death in Babylon in 323 BC, and amid the various rivalries and wars among his many successors and would-be dynasts, restive, emboldened Greeks began canonizing the fallen Thebans as heroic resisters. Gradually, the extinction of Thebes was compared to the disappearance of the moon, or the greatest wordsmith of Greece going mute. Somehow the once "deserved" Theban fate was transmogrified into something more lamentable than a staged tragedy.

Indeed, "the sack of Thebes" became a topos of sorts for later Athenian orators like Aeschines and Dinarchus to outdo each other in praise of past Theban bravery, as if what Athenians would not do materially for Thebes while it existed, they would most eagerly do rhetorically after it vanished. Arrian compiled an entire catalog on how grievously the Greeks later bore the loss, albeit with him claiming that the destruction was due to divine anger rather than the furor of his hero Alexander. Indeed, writing five hundred years later, Arrian judged the destruction of Thebes as the greatest catastrophe in Greek history. Such crocodile tears are reminiscent of Western Christendom's "shock" on hearing the news of the Islamic sack of Constantinople, a siege that few in the West previously had felt merited substantial European aid to the Byzantines in extremis.[49]

After Alexander's death, the ever-warring, opportunistic successor Macedonian regents would on occasion encourage Panhellenic anger at the obliteration of the city. In such revisionism, some pro-Macedonian historians reminded the Greeks that Alexander himself later regretted his barbarity and had deliberately sought to make amends by helping any individual Theban he met.

In such an evolving revisionist climate, a new "Thebes" reappeared in the historical record some twenty years later, but only *after* the death of Alexander the Great. The Macedonian general and successor regent in Greece, Cassander, refounded a smaller, near-token version of the famous ancient city on the site, with a shorter circuit wall that encompassed just the old Theban urban core and the Cadmea acropolis.

Thebes 2.0 had arisen largely as a propaganda effort to appease subjugated Greeks. Cassander apparently thought he could instill goodwill by virtue signaling his Panhellenic sympathies; a part of this agenda was the ploy of restoring what the dead Alexander had taken, erasing the stain of the devastation of 335 BC. Some sources even suggested that Cassander's own widely acknowledged dislike of Alexander had fueled his effort to undo his former leader's legacy in Greece.

To remake something on the old Theban site, and provide a classical veneer to his new Thebes, Cassander apparently rounded up a few of the Theban exiles absent during the devastation and living abroad as stateless residents in various Greek cities. He may even have sought out survivors, either freed slaves or escapees, from the actual day of devastation, on the theory that they were now seen as patriotic rather than as insurrectionary, naïve, and foolish. Likewise, he persuaded any die-hard Theban-haters that it was in their interests to resurrect a city on the Cadmea, especially given that almost all of their old enemies were dead.[50]

Most Boeotians, as well as Greeks in general, welcomed the chance to wipe away at least symbolically the stain of Alexander and resurrect a replica of the ancient polis. Contemporary inscriptions on stone reveal widespread Panhellenic interest in either settling at Thebes or contributing funds for the rebuilding of the city and its walls, albeit on a far smaller scale. Visitors to the newly reduced Thebes a century later even noted its modern grid, quite unlike the older Greek cities of meandering narrow streets that lacked such urban planning.[51]

Still, the numbers of would-be colonists could not have been large, even if bolstered by any surviving enslaved Thebans from 335 BC who turned up or were now purchased or manumitted. Whether defined by demography or by the physical layout of the new city, this substitute was not Thebes at all. It was simply a place for mostly Boeotian but non-Theban people, with a far different government, occupying an old place with the same name as Thebes.

It was ironic that those who likely had joined in exterminating the Thebans years earlier may have been among the replacement "Thebans" of the new city. Those who did nothing to save classical Thebes may have contributed to the costs of resurrecting its linguistic avatar. It was also ironic that in Roman times the rebuilt Hellenistic Thebes would be razed and sacked at least twice: by the Roman general and city-destroyer Lucius Mummius in 146 BC, and then again by Lucius Cornelius Sulla (85 BC).[52]

The ersatz Thebes would eventually grow to about a quarter of the population of the old Thebes. Perhaps by imperial Roman times some ten thousand to fifteen thousand "Thebans" resided there, even as the urban core covered a fraction of the former city. Throughout later Hellenistic, Roman, Byzantine, Frankish, and Ottoman eras, the surrogate Thebes was known as a provincial backwater, noted for its weaving and silk industries. It remained a regional political nexus for the surrounding agrarian towns of Boeotia, but never again regained the stature, population, or influence of the Thebes of old.

Today, the name "Thebes" is almost entirely associated with the original, legendary city of Greece, not with the pale Hellenistic imitation. The modern city of nearly forty thousand residents sits atop the ruins of what Alexander destroyed and enjoys a robust agricultural and manufacturing economy. It is also aided by its status as a slight detour on the Athens-Delphi tourist route, in part because the famous battlefields of Chaeronea, Delium, Leuctra, Marathon, and Plataea are all nearby.

A theme of this book is that most razed cities are refounded or reoccupied by the conquerors. Walls fall, but the innate advantages of the natural sites remain. Most were chosen originally because of their commercial, military, political, or cultural advantages, predicated on unchanging geographical suitability, natural resources, or rich farmland.

In that context, the destruction of a major city, even if razed to the ground, does not mean the site itself ceased having such permanent potential for resettlement. Sometimes new people took over the rubble, whether or not the old walls were razed or partially left intact by the defeated and vanished. But again, this continuation of some sort of human habitation at a site hardly translates into the perpetuation of a vanquished people, the continuity of a consistent culture, or even a kindred civilization.

The word "nation" is a Latin derivative (*natio*). No Greek word existed for the admittedly foreign idea of such a multicity, singular, and all-encompassing political entity. Thus, there is no equivalent in classical Greek to *natio,* or "nationhood." *Ethnos* (ἔθνος/English "ethnic") refers to a people in racial or tribal rather than political terms.[53]

There were certainly leagues and federations of Greek city-states (known as *koina*), all of which roughly could share the same language, religion, and customs. Fifth-century Athens ruled by coercion over an "empire" (ἀρχή/*archê*) of subordinate city-states. But politically there was never a unified Hellenic commonwealth, at least until the on/off–again subjugation under the Macedonians and later the incorporation of Greece into the Roman Empire.

Instead, the some fifteen hundred autonomous Greek poleis, with the exceptions of the large city-states like Argos, Athens, Corinth, Sparta, and Thebes, were relatively modest, and thus always vulnerable. Few were home to populations of even ten thousand residents. Their city walls were not unassailable. Their armies seldom mustered over five hundred to a thousand hoplites.

Consequently, in a world of near-constant war, shifting alliances, and usually successful siegecraft, the obliteration of Greek city-states was not uncommon. The historian Thucydides pays special attention to the extinctions of the poleis Plataea, Scione, and Torone during the Peloponnesian War that predated the later fourth-century BC complete obliterations of the Boeotian towns of Thespiae and Orchomenos.[54]

The imperial Athenian destruction in 416 BC of the neutral city-state of Melos, an island in the Aegean, deserved the famous account by the historian Thucydides. In his "Melian Dialogue," a protracted back-and-forth negotiation over the city-state's fate conducted between its leaders and the invading Athenian envoys, Thucydides seems to use the tragic occasion to instruct his readers on the amoral use of overwhelming power against doomed and weaker adversaries.

The historian brilliantly captures the dire human predicament of the targeted. In their resistance, the Melians appeal to values and emotions such as honor and hope in reply to the Athenians' reminders that there is neither glory nor courage in waging a doomed war. In such dire straits, the ultimate stakes are not merely victory or defeat, or the display of courage or cowardice, but the absolute extinction of the Melians' very city.

Still, the islanders persist, citing further, mostly vain arguments such as the Greeks' sense of justice, or the message of brutality that their own destruction would send to others and thus discredit the Athenians. The Athenians famously answer that the Melians' reliance on hope is no substitute for a realistic appraisal of the asymmetry of their relative forces, and thus their principled but naïve resistance would prove catastrophically suicidal. The historian may be reminding his readership that resistance against overwhelming odds does not always lead to an incredible victory; that such defiance is perhaps not always noble, although the Athenian aggressors themselves had once chosen to fight when vastly outnumbered at Marathon and Salamis. Certainly, the glorious military defeat of three hundred Spartan soldiers at Thermopylae was nevertheless a military disaster that cost the life of their king Leonidas. The Athenian envoys to Melos assumed that few would either lament the fate of the dead, or challenge the power of the annihilators.

When the thin veneer of civilization is ripped off by unending conflict, where exactly does morality lie? With shameful survival that at least offers the weak, women and children, and the elderly some sort of continuation? Or in glorious principled resistance, despite faint hope of victory and the likelihood of extermination? At what golden moment does a civilization weigh the consequences of surrender when facing sure defeat against the glory of resistance that might offer even a small chance of triumph against bad odds?

Statesmen and revolutionaries alike have for twenty-five hundred years quoted or paraphrased the famous line of the wretched Io in Aeschylus's *Prometheus Bound*, who laments that "it is a better thing to die once than to suffer terribly all of one's days." The Mexican revolutionary Emiliano Zapata supposedly offered something similar in a military context—"It is better to die on your feet than to live on your knees"—a now common enough aphorism among wartime leaders. But however noble the sentiment, such courageous fatalism is often wise advice only to the strong, or to those at least with some confidence in victory. For the vulnerable, dying "once" on your feet can mean ensuring the torture, enslavement, or slaughter of the young who have not yet learned to walk.[55]

The fate of Thebes eventually horrified the Greeks, but also lowered the bar on what was deemed permissible in classical warfare. In his final assessment, Arrian compared the destruction to similar catastrophes suffered by Thebes's major rivals, Athens and Sparta. He concludes that not even the Athenian loss of the Peloponnesian War, marked by the destruction of its Long Walls and temporary surrender of its democracy, or Epaminondas's defeat of Sparta at Leuctra and Mantinea and the subsequent invasion of Laconia, marked a comparable disaster.

While there were certainly far greater deaths in cataclysmic defeats during the Peloponnesian War (such as the destruction of the imperial Athenian expeditionary forces of nearly forty thousand who rowed to Sicily in 415 BC), Arrian's point is still valid: no one in the past had obliterated such a large and legendary city as Thebes. And its complete destruction had a catastrophic political and psychological effect on the Greeks for decades to come.[56]

One significant consequence of the destruction of Thebes was appreciated much later. Alexander's razing, along with the battle of Chaeronea three years earlier, eventually was regarded as the iconic end of the civilization of the classical city-states—the so-called golden age of Hellenism—and the beginning of the Hellenistic era, of "Greek-like" culture spreading throughout the Eastern Mediterranean and Asia. Alexander's singular power, military dynamism, and ruthlessness were well beyond the ability and vision of earlier city-states, yet perhaps necessary to create an empire stretching to modern-day Pakistan. But what he destroyed when he focused this power on Thebes—the freedom of the Greeks—ensured that many in his new Hellenistic world of tyrants and strongmen would eventually lament what they had obliterated.

With Alexander's rampage into Asia would come the torching of Darius III's capital at Persepolis, and the annihilation of many unfortunate communities whose culpability was simply that they were in Alexander's path. Later the Romans would not hesitate to level the legendary Corinth in 146 BC. In the same year, they razed much more thoroughly an even larger Carthage, as we shall see in the next chapter.

It would be reassuring to believe in last-minute successful and glorious last stands of doomed idealistic cities and states. But usually the fate of the vanquished can be calculated in advance and more mundanely by their numerical or military inferiority, their prior and present naïveté, their long decline, their incompetence, or the sheer military genius and resources of their attackers.

With Carthage, the stakes were raised. Carthage was not a small city of fifty thousand, but ten times larger. Its walls were not of questionable strength, but among the most monumental in the ancient world. Its demise did not, as in the case of Thebes, result in the loss of a branch of a larger culture, but rather in the erasure of an entire civilization itself. But its conqueror, like all the others in our case studies, was as ruthless as Alexander, and yet similarly deemed himself a philosopher, a reluctant obliterator, and a "good" man.

2

THE WAGES OF VENGEANCE

The Destruction of Carthage and Punic Civilization in Africa (149–146 BC)

It is innate to human nature to hate
those whom you have injured.
(*Proprium humani ingenii est odisse quem laeseris.*)
—Tacitus, *Agricola*

NO GREAT CIVILIZATION, or so the Carthaginians must have thought, could have risen to preeminence on the primitive idea of savage revenge and genocide. Surely, the Romans knew that a twice defeated and reduced Carthage, a mere remnant of its former majesty, had been compliant to all their demands. The rational Romans must have also appreciated that even a dynamic mercantile rival could be a boon to the increasingly Roman-controlled Mediterranean trade. And as the republic expanded outside Italy, had not Rome incorporated and profited from, rather than exterminated, conquered peoples? Razing a huge, fortified city did not add up in any cost-benefit analysis so characteristic of the money-obsessed Romans. Whatever bitterness that still resided in Italy from two decades of Hannibal's prior swath of destruction must have long abated after a half century. So the confident Carthaginians discounted the idea of Roman ultimate vengeance, met all that the sober and judicious Roman Senate had demanded—and thereby found themselves trapped and surrounded in their city by a vengeful army bent on their final destruction.

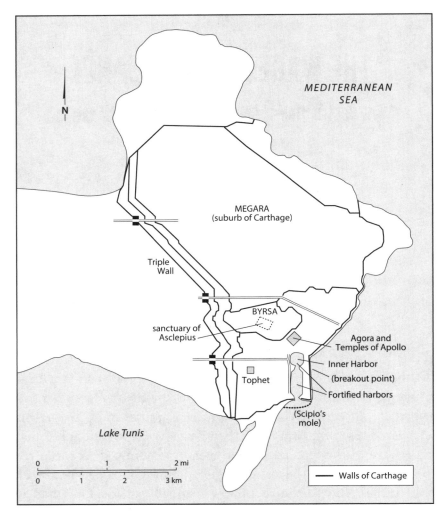

Carthage

In 146 BC, the Romans finally broke into the marketplace of Carthage after three years of besieging the Punic capital in modern-day Tunisia. Their sudden onslaught sent the survivors of the huge city fleeing up to the citadel, the legendary Byrsa. Here, near the end of their final six-day rampage through the city, the legionaries began to tighten their final ring around the last of the Carthaginians. Maybe some hundred thousand were still alive. Most had burrowed into their shrinking redoubt atop the city. All were in desperate shape,

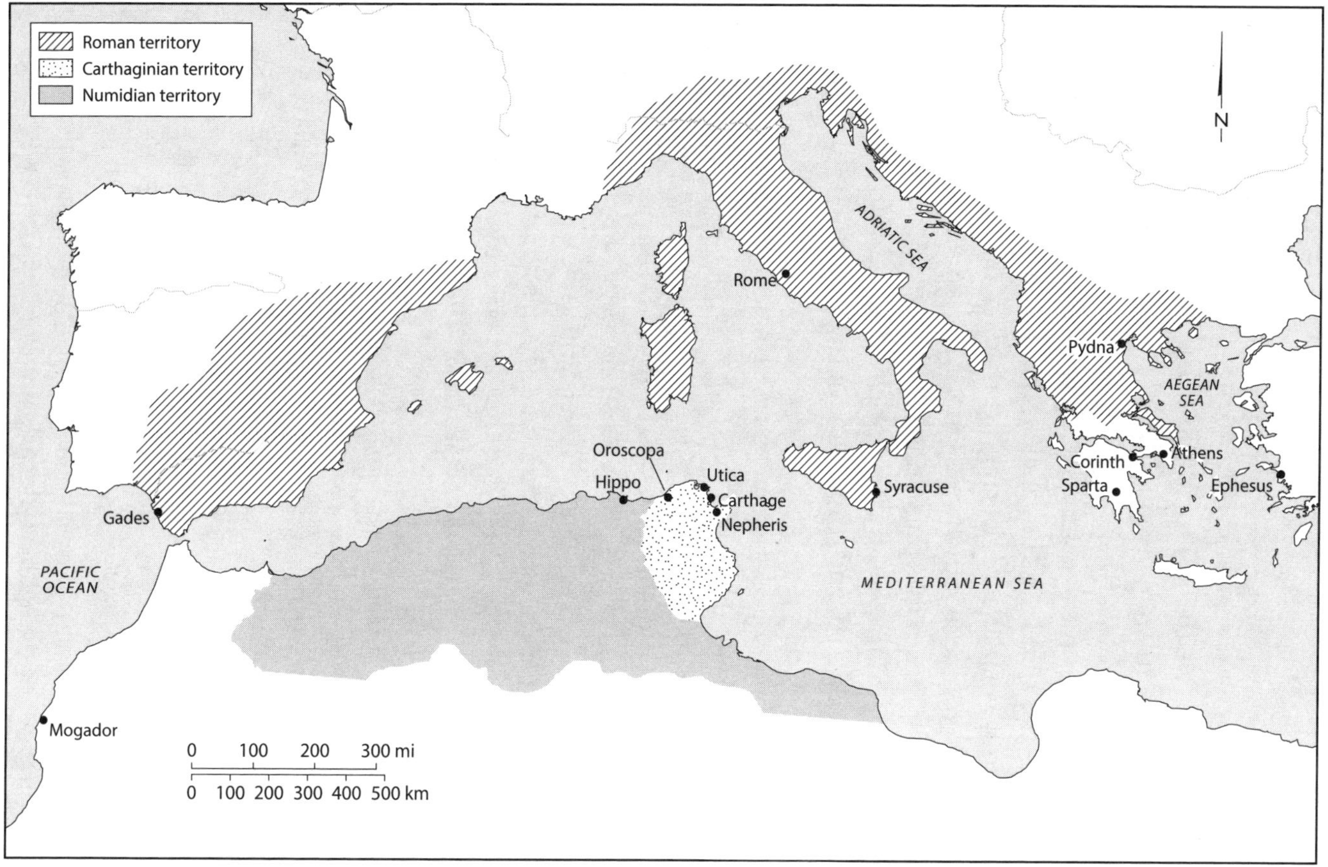
Roman territory
Carthaginian territory
Numidian territory
N
ADRIATIC SEA
Rome
Pydna
AEGEAN SEA
Corinth
Athens
Sparta
Ephesus
Syracuse
Oroscopa
Hippo
Utica
Carthage
Nepheris
Gades
PACIFIC OCEAN
MEDITERRANEAN SEA
Mogador
0 100 200 300 mi
0 100 200 300 400 500 km

The Roman and Carthaginian Empires in the Second Century BC

the last ragtag holdouts of the shattered defenses of the last three years.[1]

The defenders soon barricaded themselves in any houses still standing. Some were six stories high and offered ideal platforms for missile attacks on the advancing Romans below. The beleaguered had blocked the streets, thus forcing the Romans to begin demolishing what was left of Carthage block by block. There was some characteristic order in the Romans' steady progress among the growing chaos and the rubble of the citadel. The advance mop-up cohorts methodically went ahead, clearing the roads of bodies and the rooftops of fighters, hacking pathways among the corpses for the cavalry to follow. The historian Appian described the slaughter that ensued when the remaining stone and mudbrick buildings were torched and then finally collapsed, with thousands of the besieged inside them:

> So the crashing sounds became much greater, and many corpses fell *en masse* amid the stones. But there were some others still living, particularly the old men, women, and young children who had hidden themselves in the innermost recesses of the houses. Some of them were wounded; others were suffering major burns, and uttering heartbreaking cries. But there were still some others who had been pushed out and had fallen from the heights right along with the stones, timber, and fire. And they appeared torn apart in all manners of horror, smashed and mangled.

The killing required the exhausted legionaries to work in shifts. With such huge numbers of corpses, the mechanics of clearing the bodies from the narrow streets taxed the Romans and delayed the final conquest of the city:

> But this was not even the end of their miseries, given that the street cleaners were now trying to remove the mess with their hatchets, pickaxes, and pitchforks to make the roads accessible. They used their tools to throw the dead and the living together into hollows in the ground, dragging them along as if they were sticks and stones while flipping them over with their iron tools. Trenches were filled

with men. Some who had been thrown in headfirst, with their legs stuck out of the ground, kicked about for a long time. Others fell downward feet first, and their heads poked above ground. Horses now ran right over them—crushing their faces and skulls, not on purpose, but in their headlong hurry.[2]

When the Roman consul and general Scipio Aemilianus, who himself had prowled among the front ranks of the final assault, finally called off his troops, he found only fifty thousand surviving Carthaginians of an original population that three years earlier had been close to five hundred thousand. Nine out of ten Carthaginians alive at the beginning of the siege were likely now dead. But Scipio nonetheless spared the survivors, only to sell them into slavery.[3]

There was also a final, eerie pocket of resistance. Some nine hundred Roman legionaries who had earlier turned traitor had joined the Carthaginians still holed up in the sanctuary of the god Asclepius. Among those Carthaginians was Hasdrubal the Boetharch, the city's commander during the siege. His wife and their two boys were trapped in the sanctuary alongside him, and all were close to starvation.

The Roman traitors and the last of the Carthaginians were now perched on the roof of the temple. Earlier, Hasdrubal had secretly met with Scipio and obtained immunity—solely for himself. Upon learning of this treachery, the turncoat Romans and Hasdrubal's family lit the temple, and themselves, on fire. Ironically, Hasdrubal had previously been considered Carthage's greatest firebrand. His hatred of Rome had galvanized a half million Carthaginians to die on their feet rather than live on their knees as subordinates to Rome. Now he let his family be incinerated so he could live among his conquerors.

As his wife went up in flames, she screamed at her cowardly husband: "Defiler! Traitor! Most unmanly of men! This fire will bury me and my children. Will you, the 'leader' of great Carthage, adorn a Roman triumph?" In fact, yes, Hasdrubal would, but not in the fashion that his wife had hoped. He had already negotiated for himself a long and safe retirement in Italy, after being put on display in Rome.

Indeed, Hasdrubal was one of the few defeated nationalist leaders to be ceremoniously paraded before the Roman people and yet not quietly garroted following the public triumph. He would not die with his city in the fashion of Constantine XI in Constantinople or Montezuma at Tenochtitlán.[4]

In the last weeks of the city's survival, the Roman besiegers had systematically slaughtered without distinction tens of thousands of civilians, along with soldiers and freed slaves recruited into the army, thereby fulfilling their announced agenda to annihilate all human traces of the city. It is impossible to ascertain the exact population of ancient Carthage, much less its inflated size when rural people flocked into the city on the eve of the siege. But if there were five hundred thousand residents in 149, by the end of 146, 90 percent of them were likely dead, in what historians understandably sometimes call the "first genocide."[5]

After Scipio finished with the killing of the last pockets of Carthaginians and the Roman turncoats, he turned his men loose to loot whatever they wished in the city. But first the legions destroyed all the weapons they could find. Once the ravaging was complete, they demolished the huge ancient walls, toppled all the remaining buildings, and torched anything combustible—bringing to an end some seven hundred years of Punic civilization in Africa.

It was no easy thing in the ancient world, relying on muscular labor and hand tools, to reduce or even burn to ashes monumental buildings and stone ramparts. But Scipio and the Roman Senate were eager, whatever the time and cost, to ensure that no Roman would ever have to fight the Carthaginians a fourth time. Indeed, when the news of his destruction of Carthage first reached Rome, the people were incredulous—for only a moment, until they broke into mass celebrations, as if a chronic dread was now past. The instincts of the jubilant Roman crowds were prescient. The destruction of Carthage did mark the end of one age, and the beginning of a new epoch when Rome would no longer feel itself threatened by any rival Mediterranean power that might bring war home to Italy itself.

As seen earlier, after the destruction of Thebes, Alexander the Great went eastward to achieve immortality—invading, conquering, and destroying the Persian Empire, including Anatolia, Syria, Egypt, Mesopotamia, Persia itself, Afghanistan, and much of what is now Pakistan. He then died abruptly in Babylon at the age of thirty-three, the self-described missionary of Hellenism and lord of all he had seen. Alexander left no will, no blueprint for succession. So his surviving generals, the so-called *Diadochoi* ("Successors")—Antipater, Perdiccas, Ptolemy I, Seleucus I, Antigonus I, and Lysimachus—divvied up Alexander's empire among themselves. Amid nonstop war against foreign enemies and each other, they soon founded new Greek cities in Asia and North Africa, spreading both the Greek language and Hellenic culture throughout the East. As Macedonians, they inaugurated what is now called the Hellenistic ("Greek-like") world.

After several decades of Macedonian infighting for the spoils of Alexander's empire, the generals' smaller principalities eventually coalesced in the Eastern Mediterranean and Asia into a few powerful kingdoms. Alexander's birthplace in Macedonia was secured by the Antigonid dynasty that came to incorporate much of Greece itself. Pergamum in western Anatolia emerged as the capital of a rump state in Anatolia ruled by the Attalids. Syria and Mesopotamia comprised the core of the Seleucids' huge empire in the east. The richest of all provinces, Egypt, was rebooted as a center of Hellenism by Ptolemy. For the next three centuries, at their new cosmopolitan city of Alexandria on the Mediterranean, the Ptolemies would prosper as a relatively stable and rich hybrid Macedonian monarchy.

Yet the likely future ambitions of Alexander and his successors in the Western Mediterranean world had been abbreviated not only by his death, but also by the emergence of two dynamic states, Carthage and Rome. The emergence of a unified Italy and its transformation into an expansive Roman Republic resulted in endless wars of self-preservation that inevitably would conclude with Roman annexation of large swaths of what is now France, the Benelux countries, Spain, Sicily, and the Balkans. Yet the three-centuries-long growth of the republic was often stalled or checked by its formidable

Mediterranean rival, Punic Carthage. The latter's land empire on the North African coast soon expanded into Sicily and southern Spain. Moreover, a huge Carthaginian navy ensured maritime supremacy, enormous commercial wealth, and a check on Roman Mediterranean aggrandizement.

Like the earlier rivalry between democratic, naval, Ionian, cosmopolitan Athens and oligarchic, infantry-based, Doric, and tradition-bound Sparta, the competition between Rome and Carthage involved antithetical civilizations. Rome was an infantry power. After 275 BC, the Roman legions had unified most of Italy south of the Po River. Carthage dominated the Western Mediterranean by sea. Carthaginian allies and colonies were spread throughout Sicily, Sardinia, North Africa, and along the coast of Spain. They were all considered an eventual and intolerable barrier to Roman expansionism. During the contentious course of the third century BC, Rome and Carthage inevitably had collided in two long and brutal wars, now known formally as the First (264–241 BC) and Second (218–201 BC) Punic Wars.

The initial twenty-three-year-long conflict was fought primarily over Sicily and at sea. During the war's course, Rome built from nothing several successive galley fleets, despite knowing little about Mediterranean naval warfare. At the landmark sea battle of Cape Ecnomus off southern Sicily (256)—perhaps the largest maritime fight in history—Carthage somehow managed to send a fleet that outnumbered even Rome's new gargantuan navy of 140,000 sailors and soldiers. The climactic encounter that followed involved some 300,000 total combatants. While Rome won the hard-fought battle itself, in the following year it lost nearly its entire once-victorious fleet in a single day to storms on the Mediterranean, suffering perhaps 100,000 fatalities—likely the worst one-day military losses in naval history.[6]

Nonetheless, after this heroic effort to master warfare at sea, Rome emerged victorious from the First Punic War, in the characteristic Roman resilient style that would mark all three Punic Wars. In each of these conflicts, the republic somehow seemed to grow stronger after suffering grievous but temporary setbacks. As a result of its first defeat in 241 BC, a humiliated Carthage had no choice but to forfeit its possessions in Sicily and Sardinia. Both were then annexed as the first Roman provinces. An emboldened and grasping Rome grew confident that it could now prune away additional Carthaginian colonies that were closer to Europe than Africa; this strategy would eventually render Carthage itself far more vulnerable to foreign invasion than Rome's own Italian hinterlands. Yet in the two decades between the first and second wars, Carthage for its part was not idle. It too rebooted its empire, primarily by new acquisitions in Spain and North Africa. Indeed, despite losing the First Punic War, Carthage by the outbreak of the second round with Rome had reached the zenith of its strength in both manpower and resources.[7]

In 218 BC, the Second Punic War began with quite different agendas than the prior conflict. Almost immediately, the Carthaginian general Hannibal, one of history's authentic military geniuses, marched his army out of Spain. He traveled overland though Gaul, and then under great duress amid late autumn mountain snow and ice, and with considerable losses, crossed the Alps (famously along with his war elephants), and descended into Italy proper to at last bring the war home to the Romans. Once there, in a series of four sequential and brilliant victories at the Ticinus River, the Trebia River, Lake Trasimene, and Cannae, Hannibal obliterated every consular army the Romans threw against him, killing nearly a hundred thousand legionaries, capturing or wounding nearly as many, and rendering the shattered Roman army nearly combat ineffective.

Only after nearly two decades of costly battles of attrition did Publius Cornelius Scipio (later given the honorific "Africanus") manage to craft an innovative strategy to send the Carthaginians back to Africa. First, the Romans neutralized Carthaginian supply bases in Spain, cutting Hannibal off in Italy from any relief from Africa or help from defecting Roman cities. Then Scipio pressured him to leave Italy altogether to save his homeland by sending a Roman army to North Africa proper. The final battle, at Zama outside of Carthage, ended in a monumental Roman victory in 202 BC. Scipio forced a humiliating defeat upon Hannibal and the

Carthaginians, and thereby charted the future of unchecked Roman aggrandizement throughout the Western Mediterranean.

After the defeat of Hannibal in 202 BC, Carthage itself was stripped of her empire and reduced to city-state status, loosely retaining only a few local allies with common Phoenician ties of culture and language. Meanwhile, with its century-old western rival apparently neutered, Rome found itself drawn more and more into the affairs of the Greek Eastern Mediterranean through a seemingly endless series of conflicts among the Hellenistic kingdoms in Macedonia, Greece, and adjacent parts of Asia Minor.

While the Senate let an inert Carthage be for a half century, Rome's legions kept fighting in four major wars against Macedon, and one against Seleucid Syria, usually in support of one of its quasi-allies, Pergamum and Ptolemaic Egypt. Even as it besieged Carthage in the Third Punic War, the Romans also fought and vanquished the Achaean League, a confederation of Greek city-states banded together to offset the Hellenistic superpowers. After the consolidation of Greece and Asia Minor, the Romans on a multitude of theaters defeated almost all of their Eastern Mediterranean enemies and forced these decaying kingdoms and states into humiliating concessions. As its expansion, east and west, continued, the Romans characteristically dropped prior pretenses of victimization and stopped being pushed into defensive wars by aggressive, older powers. Instead, the republic began to see preemptive wars as a transformational means of destroying all its rivals in the Mediterranean world while becoming far richer and globally preeminent in the process.

Finally, by the mid second century, Rome at last turned its attention to its old enemy and provoked the Third Punic War with Carthage, while almost simultaneously settling final accounts in the Fourth Macedonian War and an additional finale with the Achaeans. A usually astute Carthage had failed to understand fully that the Rome its ancestors had gone to war against in 264 BC now bore little resemblance to the stronger, more aggressive, and ultimately more ruthless power that would demand its obliteration in 149.

The Latin-derived "Punic" (Poenus/Punicus) was borrowed from the Greeks' term for Phoenician (Phoinix/Phoinikes). The adjective usually designated the culture of the western Phoenicians of North Africa. By the time of its first war with Rome, Carthage had grown to dominate some three hundred Phoenician colonies and had expanded well beyond its original coastal domain in modern-day Tunisia. The city was acclaimed as founded by the legendary Phoenician queen Dido in the early ninth century, supposedly in the exact year 814 BC. The queen, according to foundational myths surviving most famously in Vergil's *Aeneid*, led the Phoenician colonists of Tyre to the North African city site, nearly seven hundred years prior to its destruction. Ironically, the founding of Carthage was roughly simultaneous with the mythical origins of Rome itself in 753 BC, adding to the paradox of the likely oldest Phoenician colony in the West pitted against the most ancient of the Latin-speaking cities of Italy.[8]

Rome and Carthage differed in fundamental areas of culture, language, history, and economics. Yet they shared a few similarities in their respective spectacular growth and ascendance. In their own unique fashion, both represented a Western Mediterranean antithesis to the all-embracing, all-powerful Hellenistic world to the east. Rome drew strength and confidence from its larger environs of Latium, expanding the use of the Latin language and codifying Roman deities. Yet the Romans were also influenced by their quite different Etruscan neighbors across the Tiber, from whom they drew several of their political institutions and religious practices that incorporated some, but also were distinct from, Hellenic cultural influences.

Carthage's social identity was also not wholly dominated by the influence of Hellenism, but rather influenced as well by its mother country Phoenicia, especially its Semitic language, religious pantheon, and retention of the rites of child sacrifice. Finally, Carthage, the ancient Phoenician colony in North Africa, drew on native Berber tribal society, especially given that the indigenous tribes vastly outnumbered early arriving Phoenician colonists.

Along with their near-contemporaneous rise, Rome and Carthage were also considered somewhat politically similar. Both drew upon Greek political antecedents through their mutual contacts with scattered early Greek colonists in Sicily, North Africa, Spain, and Southern France. As a result, ancient observers argued that both cities had enjoyed the similar advantages of a Hellenic-inspired "mixed" constitution, often known in shorthand as a "polity" (πολιτεία). In antiquity, that was a formal term to denote the careful republican balance between the executive, legislative, and judicial branches of power within a single government, and championed by both Plato and Aristotle. In the eyes of Greek and Roman observers, this common borrowing of elements of Greek constitutional government ensured the two respective states unusual prosperity, stability, legitimacy, and unity—the ingredients for dynamic expansion.

Aristotle, for example, in the fourth century had praised Carthage's tripartite system of government. He logically compared it to the earlier and similarly stable Spartan constitution that included two chief executives (kings), a legislative assembly of all citizens (the Spartiates), a senior law-making body (the Gerousia), and a judiciary (ephors who served as magistrates). Spartan government had also allegedly proved a model of checks and balances for the later Roman state of consuls, the Senate and assemblies, and praetors. The historian Polybius agreed and likewise favorably noted the Carthaginian constitutional system. He equally argued that Rome's similar constitutional balance between executive, legislative, and judicial power ensured the aristocracy of the Roman Senate would not descend into oligarchic dominance. Nor would the tribal assembly result in a popular mobocracy, nor consular power descend into despotism.[9]

The internal political stability and efficiency of Rome and Carthage explain both how they outdistanced their respective tribal, monarchial, and autocratic rivals, and why the two were headed toward a catastrophic confrontation to settle control of the West and ultimately the entire Mediterranean. That both Carthage and Rome were consensual societies did not prevent contention and rivalry between them. In the ancient world, constitutional states often attacked other similar governments. The modern shibboleth that democracies do not war with other democracies would have been seen in antiquity as odd—especially at the near beginning of written history, when the two largest democracies of the classical Greek world, Syracuse and Athens, had fought a bitter two-year battle over the fate of Sicily (415–413).

———————

By the time of the Punic Wars (264 BC–146 BC), Carthage's hegemony had grown westward from Leptis Magna on the central Libyan coast to Mogador beyond the Strait of Gibraltar on the Atlantic seaboard in modern Morocco. Carthage by the third century had created a maritime domain of colonies and loosely aligned Punic-speaking port cities, much like the later Republic of Venice's sixteenth-century empire that ranged down the coast of Dalmatia, included Greece, and extended to Crete and Cyprus in the Eastern Mediterranean. Indeed, prior to the Second Punic War, the Punic stamp of a palm tree was as ubiquitous a trademark and coin imprint in the Western Mediterranean as the later Renaissance brand of a winged lion of Saint Mark in the Eastern Mediterranean.[10]

What had terrified republican Rome in the third century was an all too familiar Carthaginian colonization across the Mediterranean into Europe. The Roman Senate finally concluded that Carthage was aiming at incorporating Spain and Sardinia to the west of Italy, and Sicily to the south. The Senate feared this was part of a larger project to box Rome within Italy proper and create a hostile Punic culture in Sicily, a mere two miles from Italy. Rome was not necessarily paranoid in its chronic fears of a Punic Mediterranean. At the outbreak of the First Punic War, Carthage's confederacy was perhaps nearly double the population of Roman Italy.

By any fair measure, Carthage's enormous wealth from its Mediterranean-wide fleet made Rome's own contemporary maritime ambitions appear pathetic in comparison. Both Carthage and Rome could draw on substantial populations. Yet the city of Carthage itself was nearly twice the size of Rome proper. And during the Second Punic War, Carthage had been able to put into the field, throughout the various theaters of the conflict at any given time, about fifty thousand more soldiers than Rome could.

Greek observers also noticed major differences between the militaries of the two states. In particular, the Carthaginians relied more on mercenary infantry, whereas Rome mustered levies of citizen soldiers. Carthage, in contrast, usually sought to recruit citizens only in its navy. The historian Polybius, who accompanied Scipio Aemilianus to Carthage, took pains to emphasize the differing profiles of both militaries.

> For a naval expedition the Carthaginians are the better trained and prepared—as is only natural with a people for whom it has been hereditary for many generations to practice this craft, and to follow the seaman's trade above all nations in the world—yet, in regard to military service on land, the Romans train themselves to a much higher pitch than the Carthaginians. The former bestow their whole attention upon this department: whereas the Carthaginians wholly neglect their infantry, though they do take some slight interest in the cavalry. The reason for this is that they employ foreign mercenaries, the Romans native and citizen levies.[11]

One of the oddest and most repugnant features of Carthaginian culture, at least to Hellenistic Greeks but also to the Romans, was the Punic institution of child sacrifice. The practice was considered pre-civilizational, and was unusual elsewhere in classical antiquity. Nevertheless, the sacrificing of children is well attested for Carthage in both archaeology and ancient literary sources. Archaeologists have noted that the prevalence of *tophets,* sanctuaries used for child sacrifice, increased during the fourth through second centuries BC. They speculate that precisely this form of sacrifice became a marker in the contemporary Mediterranean of a distinctively "Carthaginian" identity, separate from most religious practices of the general Hellenistic world.[12]

Greeks found the notion of killing children repugnant. The fourth-century historian Cleitarchus, for example, was quoted in a fragment of his lost history emphasizing the gruesome nature of the practice:

> And Kleitarchos says the Phoenicians, and above all the Carthaginians, venerating Kronos, whenever they were eager for a great thing to succeed, made a vow by one of their children. If they would receive the desired things, they would sacrifice it to the god. A bronze Kronos, having been erected by them, stretched out upturned hands over a bronze oven to burn the child. The flame of the burning child reached its body until, the limbs having shriveled up and the smiling mouth appearing to be almost laughing, it would slip into the oven. Therefore the grin is called "sardonic laughter," since they die laughing.[13]

Despite these existential differences, after the first two Punic Wars there was no call at Rome to level a defeated Carthage. Instead, like the conclusions of almost all Rome's prior wars, the Second Punic War ended with a formal treaty, specifically the settlement of 201 BC between a victorious Rome and the defeated but *not* destitute Carthage. This time the Carthaginians were forced to surrender all their possessions beyond a few near Carthage itself, pay an enormous indemnity to Rome, and ask Rome's permission to engage in any border war in Africa. Over the next fifty years, Carthage paid off the indemnity (completed by 151 BC) ahead of schedule and prospered commercially even without its empire (one might compare it to a resurgent, nonimperial Japan after World War II).

The ostensible reason prompting the Third Punic War was a disagreement over the provision of the treaty relating to war in Africa. The contentious issue was Carthage's longtime rivalry with its nearby North African neighbor and former vassal, the kingdom of Numidia, which had revolted against Carthage in the last years of the Second Punic war and then allied with Rome. The Numidian king who led the revolt, Masinissa, remained king in 151 (incredibly, he was ninety years old and still led his armies). Masinissa repeatedly ordered attacks on Carthage's allies and picked off its possessions in North Africa. Yet whenever Carthage petitioned the Roman Senate to be allowed to strike back, Rome refused.

In 151 BC, after a particularly injurious Numidian raid, Carthage raised a large army and, without Rome's permission, retaliated. Perhaps finally paying off their indemnities to Rome had emboldened the Carthaginians. Nonetheless, this counterattack proved a complete tactical failure for Carthage, and after its strategic defeat at the battle of Oroscopa nearly the entire Carthaginian army surrendered to the Numidians. The campaign, conducted without Roman permission, became the trigger for the Third Punic War.

After the failure of this military expedition, Carthage sent a series of diplomatic missions to Rome to try to explain and justify to the Senate why it had finally resorted to an armed response to serial Numidian aggression. The exasperated envoys pointed to the continuous Numidian raids that had never been answered. They argued that no matter what the text of the treaty said, did not every state surely have a right of self-defense? They pressed their case forcefully, but the senators, always fixated on the slightest sign of Punic resurgence and not unhappy with the Numidian aggression, were adamant that some sort of punishment was required. The Carthaginian ambassadors then requested at least a clear statement of Rome's demands. Yet the Romans were unwilling to state what they had in mind and obfuscated their intentions—an eerie portent that a fixed Roman agenda predated the counterstrike against the Numidians. Eventually, the Carthaginians agreed to meet with Roman envoys in Africa and reach a final accord.

Instead, in the year 149 BC a large Roman army and fleet, commanded by both consuls for that year, arrived at the nearby North African harbor city of Utica to complete the "negotiations." The initial and practical obstacle to any Roman use of military force against Carthage had been finding a port near Carthage to land and marshal thousands of assault troops. That problem was solved well before the Roman arrival, when Utica wisely defected to Rome on promises of its survival as a Roman client.

The invading Roman army and navy that had first marshaled on Sicily and now landed at Utica was enormous. A fleet of some 150 large galleys, four thousand horsemen, and reportedly a core of eighty thousand legionaries marked perhaps the largest amphibious force seen in the ancient world since the 480 BC invasion of Greece by Xerxes. The Roman force was likely larger than the American contingent that landed in France on D-Day, June 6, 1944.

The two consuls divided responsibility for the siege, with Manius Manilius in charge of the army and Lucius Censorinus acting as admiral. From the outset the seemingly nonchalant consuls proceeded as if the surrender of Carthage was a fait accompli. Indeed, if the historian Appian is correct about the size of the expeditionary force, then the Roman multitude proved about double the size of Scipio Africanus's army that had landed at Utica fifty-four years earlier and then the next year had crushed Hannibal's army at Zama.[14]

The terms of the Romans' ultimata to Carthage at their meeting in Utica by design kept incrementally being upped. Apparently, the consuls assumed that their own excessive demands either would guarantee a much desired war, or were so punitive that a compliant and humiliated Carthage would be easily emasculated. At first, the Romans mandated three hundred hostages during negotiations. They demanded the Carthaginians cease the acquisition and use of elephants which, ironically, were as feared in the ancient world as they were often uncontrollable on the battlefield.

The Romans further required the surrender of all Carthaginian weapons—eventually some two hundred thousand suits of armor, two thousand catapult bolts, and all offensive arms. They ordered the destruction of nearly all the Carthaginian fleet. Yet the frightened Carthaginians agreed to *all* the stated terms, and then promptly carried them out to the letter.

At this point, with the Roman force having landed at Utica, Rome and Carthage were not yet actively engaged in their third and final war. Of course, the sheer size of the expeditionary armada, along with the presence of Rome's two highest officials, were at first aimed at intimidating the Carthaginians into immediate submission. But curiously, the actual details of carrying out the Roman Senate's directives to the fleet at Utica were still somewhat confused and fluid. Ostensibly the two commanders were there to implement what were already assumed to be the final—and mostly accepted—terms of Carthaginian surrender. And indeed those stipulations had now all been met. Still, the seemingly abject Punic capitulation perplexed the consuls about what to do next with their large invasion force.

In a moving plea for moderation and appeal to justice—reminiscent of the desperate arguments in the historian Thucydides's account of the doomed Melians—the Carthaginian envoys reminded the invaders that they had now met every Roman requirement. In a note of pathos unusual in such high-stakes negotiations, they also noted that Carthaginians had suffered terribly in the wars of the past. And they now simply wished to live in peace:

> We have been robbed of our leadership on land and sea; we gave over our ships to you, and we have not obtained others; we have restrained ourselves from hunting or possessing elephants. We have handed over to you, both in the past and now, our noblest as hostages, and we have paid our tribute to you regularly, we who had always been used to receiving it from others. These things pleased your fathers, with whom we fought. They concluded treaties with us that we should be both friends and allies, and the same oath stands for both parties to observe that pact. And they, with whom we had battled, later remained faithful to their word.

The Punic envoys seemed flummoxed. It was obvious to them that no more of their own concessions were either possible or sufficient. Thus, the huge Roman army at Utica logically had no ostensible reason to march on Carthage other than as part of a long-planned agenda of simply leveling the city. Yet the desperate Carthaginians continued their sad recital:

> But you, with whom we have never fought—what part of the treaty do you claim that we have violated, that so abruptly you have voted to go to war and march out against us without even a formal declaration? Did we not pay you the tribute? Do we possess any ships, or any detested elephants? Were we not faithful to you from that time

to the present? Are we not deserving of pity for the recent loss of 50,000 men to famine?[15]

Yet once the Carthaginians had been tricked into disarming, they appeared to the Romans to have forfeited any real chance of resistance. The hoodwinked heralds at last fully learned to their horror of the consul Censorinus's apparently preplanned, additional, and final senatorial demand: a surreal order requiring nearly half a million Carthaginians to vacate and destroy their ancient harbor city of seven hundred years. Adding insult to injury, Censorinus breezily noted that the maritime Carthaginians surely could found a new capital anywhere they pleased—if the new site was safely *at least ten miles from the sea*. After all, was not Rome itself twelve miles from the Italian coast? The historian Appian gives us some idea of the smug arrogance of the Roman consuls:

> We praise both your obedience and attitude up to this point, Carthaginians, in this issue of both the hostages and the arms. But in matters of necessity, it is vital to talk bluntly: Bear up nobly to the remaining demand of the Senate. Yield Carthage to us. Take up residence wherever you wish within your own territory—at least at a distance of at least ten miles from the sea, for it has been decided by us to raze your city to the ground.[16]

The demand has been described as one of "collective suicide," an erasure of Punic civilization in North Africa by destroying its traditional hub at Carthage. In truth, Rome by now wanted only war and answered back to the pleas for leniency by peppering the naïve envoys with a variety of half truths, trumped-up charges, and grievances from Roman special interests. For weeks, Rome had been simply maneuvering to weaken its enemy and find the proper casus belli to begin the siege—and the anticipated easy leveling—of the city. What was unspoken was an undying hatred of Carthage and an insatiable desire for vengeance on the part of Romans to pay back the now vulnerable old enemy for more than a century of hot and cold wars.

Both Rome's penultimate demands, and Carthage's initial submissive acceptance of them, were uncannily similar to Hitler's various ultimata between 1936 and 1939 and his long-planned and successful invasions of the Western European democracies that followed, as well as the appeasing responses from allied democracies so desperate to do almost anything but fight Germany again. The results, initially at least, also were identical: prior Carthaginian appeasement had guaranteed that the inevitable war was to be waged by a fully mobilized state against credulous and stunned opponents now rueful over prior near-disarmament.[17]

The shocked and terrified Carthaginian emissaries headed the short distance home from Utica. The envoys were frightened of what awaited them inside the walls. But they were also ashamed that they had been played for weeks by false promises from both the Senate at Rome and the conniving consular generals marshaling nearby at Utica.

By fulfilling the Roman demand to hand over all their arms, the Carthaginians had just ensured that they were almost defenseless. Worse in a way, they had also shocked and frightened the Romans by the sheer amount of sophisticated weaponry they actually surrendered. The trove had the odd effect of confirming the senior Roman senator Cato's often shrill warnings to the Senate that an intractable, resourceful, and resilient Carthage would always pose a military threat. The Carthaginians only at the eleventh hour grasped the ironies of their self-destructive past policies. Their failed response to Numidian aggression had paradoxically angered and encouraged Rome, given both the city's violation of the treaty and the unexpected dismal failure of the Punic attack. So too the surrender of the Carthaginians' gigantic arsenal pleased the consuls, but also abetted the Roman desire to extinguish such a resilient and previously well-prepared enemy.

Nonetheless, the embarrassed returning Carthaginian ambassadors related the latest and seemingly unhinged Roman demands to a huge crowd thronging the council meeting. Predictable bedlam followed. Some of the envoys were caught and dragged through the streets. Others were stoned. Both hawks and doves who had previously been praised for advocating grudging acceptance of the initial harsh Roman terms—no doubt warning about what the Romans had done in similar conditions when they sacked and nearly destroyed a defiant Sicilian Syracuse sixty-three years prior—were hunted down. Throngs further went after any Italian traders they could spot in the city, killing as many as they found.

Mothers wept for the fate of the three hundred hostages, mostly children, who had been earlier handed over to the Romans as guarantors of the peace, and were now seen as forever forfeited. Some even shouted out the names of their beloved elephants they had stupidly released to the Romans at Utica. In sum, on the eve of the siege, the defenders were as divided as the besiegers were united in their aim to take the city.[18]

As war loomed, the once shunned Punic firebrands, previously deemed too incendiary for their firm rejection of the escalating Roman ultimata, were now canonized as prescient. Upon learning of these final and unexpected demands from the Roman invaders, the volatile crowds, understandably suddenly as bellicose as they were earlier acquiescent, demanded that all the war hawks be released from jail or recalled from exile.

Among them was the impulsive but otherwise undistinguished general Hasdrubal the Boetharch. On his arrival from exile and pardoned from a prior death sentence, he almost immediately sought to muster at least thirty thousand troops. He also called on some of the neighboring Numidian tribes, historical enemies of Carthage and its Punic cities, to consider flipping their allegiances, and instead honor their blood ties to his wife by sending aid. In addition, at least for the first two years of the siege, and except for four or five large cities, most of the Punic allies of the Carthaginian confederation, despite their greater vulnerability to enemy attack, would stand fast with Carthage, or at least stay neutral. The initial loyalty of their allies, especially the Punic cities of Libya, would ensure that the half million in the city itself did not starve due to the initial siege and blockade.[19]

All the slaves in Carthage were freed on promises of taking up arms against the Romans. Miners brought into the city metalliferous ores from the still-open countryside, and new weapons were frantically produced in the city's forges—all to replace those foolishly surrendered to the Romans just days earlier. Women collected all their gold jewelry and cut their tresses for ropes to supply newly constructed torsion catapults. Workshops turned out a reported hundred shields, five hundred hand-held missiles, and a thousand catapult missiles *each day*—and would soon nearly match the weapon arsenal that was forfeited earlier. Once the desperate situation was fully understood, the trapped Carthaginians ceased attacking the messengers. They channeled their fury into rearming and preparing for an existential war against Rome, the clear aggressor.[20]

The Roman consuls were apparently somewhat startled by these unexpected acts of Punic defiance. Again, they had assumed an automatic surrender, given the intimidating size of their forces and the previous docility and obsequiousness of the frightened Carthaginian envoys. In Roman eyes, the toadyish Punic ambassadors had seemed a far cry from their own grandparents' scary folktales about fierce Carthaginians, who fifty years earlier had brought their Punic war home to the Romans and for nearly two decades run wild in Italy under Hannibal.

Yet the duped Carthaginians now finally grasped that a vengeful Rome had welcomed Carthaginian resistance to local Numidian attacks as a way of greenlighting the complete destruction of Punic civilization in the Western Mediterranean, while claiming a defensive war against "treaty breakers." Or was it worse still—that Rome wished to make a Mediterranean-wide example of Carthage by unleashing a policy of sheer terror to teach any other neutral or hostile power the horrific wages of resistance to Roman imperialism? As the harshness and the malign intent of the serial Roman ultimata finally sunk in, the Romans initially achieved the opposite effect of what they intended. Given the notion that submission meant a veritable end to Carthage itself, and resistance at least for a while a continuation of their freedom, both the leaders of the city's oligarchic Council of 104 and the Carthaginian masses united and agreed to fight.

As the siege of 149 BC began, the attackers knew that in some 115 years of prior on-and-off warring, no Roman force had ever breached the formidable walls of Carthage. Then again, no Roman expeditionary force in either the First or Second Punic War had even tried. For a city that relied on its navy for preemptive defense, its circuit was nonetheless vast, running some twenty-three miles. In places the walls were thirty feet thick. They rose over forty feet in height, buttressed with even taller parapets and towers. The Carthaginian ramparts likely marked the greatest fortifications of the ancient world until the founding of Constantinople a half millennium later, with its impregnable Theodosian walls. But compared to the final and doomed defense of the Byzantine ramparts in 1453, Carthage had ten times the population to defend its walls.

So Carthage certainly enjoyed some advantages even in extremis. The indomitable nature of its fortifications might stymie even Roman siege engineers. And Carthage still had some open supply lines by land and sea, in contrast to the Roman besiegers' need to either win over the Punic countryside or ensure reliable logistical support from Sicily. So why did the Carthaginian envoys, and indeed much of the city, initially equate the Roman ultimata with their own likely destruction? Why the pessimism?

Most likely, the city had believed initially that it could not replace all the quantity of weapons and war materiel it had just handed over to the consuls in vain hopes of avoiding a war. Moreover, the strength of Carthage in the prior two wars had rested upon four givens: the Carthaginian navy was traditionally equal to or superior to Rome's fleet; Carthaginian and allied cavalry were traditionally far more skilled than Roman horsemen; mercenary infantry recruits, mostly from allied Punic cities in Africa, had often fought the legions to a standstill; and Carthaginian elephants were still considered formidable weapons of war.

Yet the challenge in 149 was not just that these advantages had waned over the last half century since Hannibal's final defeat, or that Carthage had foolishly turned over its arsenal to the Roman consuls at Utica. The problem was that the Third Punic War would hinge on the siege of a great imperial city without an empire. Carthage could not build and man enough new ships to break open the blockade and fight Roman ships on the Mediterranean. Its horsemen could not easily engage in climactic pitched battles outside the walls, and were likely outnumbered by the huge Roman cavalry of some four thousand mounts. Allies themselves were either under threat from Rome, had already flipped to the enemy, or were cut off from the city and thus could no longer furnish sufficient paid infantrymen or steady supplies. Even if Carthage had not surrendered her elephants as demanded, there was little role anyway for such beasts during a siege.[21]

Yet the Roman besiegers had their own problems, given that Carthage at its founding had been ideally located on a defensible peninsula. The city was joined to the African mainland along a protected three-mile-wide isthmus. Carthage's design of defense had also focused on redundant logistics: supplies from the Mediterranean via its well-protected harbors, and overland via its fortified isthmus to the African hinterland.[22]

What followed, at least for the next thirty months, bore out the initial confidence of the Carthaginians, the folly and poor intelligence of the Romans, and the innate difficulty of any expeditionary force far from home attempting to storm a city whose population had swelled to over five times the size of the attacking force—and with far better shelter and protection than Roman would-be conquerors in the field. Moreover, the Carthaginians felt they possessed the moral high ground, given that they fought on the defensive for their homes and beside their own families, and had obeyed to the letter the prior treaty with the Roman Senate. The Romans in contrast chose an optional and preemptive war of imperialist aggression, far from Italy and largely for loot.

The consular mediocrities Manlius and Censorinus assumed the siege would be short. The critical barometers of success—cutting off all Carthaginian supply lines both by sea and from the Numidian interior—were supposedly already assured, with the self-destruction of the Punic fleet, the control of the key port at Utica, and their fickle but for now ostensible Numidian ally Masinissa's dominance of the North African interior.

Yet for the first few months the Romans met with failure. Their serial defeats were largely due to the hubris of the two Roman consular generals. Again, both approached the siege as a brief interlude before capitulation. Meanwhile, Carthage ramped up sorties from the city that denied Romans access to the timber necessary for the construction of their siege engines. Attempts to climb over the walls with ladders against the mainland and seaside ramparts likewise met with predictable defeat.

Moreover, the morale of the newly armed citizenry soared with each repulse. The shocked Romans became further disheartened by their own hundreds of dead and wounded from these serial skirmishes outside the walls. As in every case when the weaker belligerent gains a victory and some tactical success over the dominant aggressor, and thus believes the unexpected feat presages final strategic success, so too the Carthaginians began to believe that while they lacked a fleet or army large enough to defeat the Romans in pitched battle, the invaders in turn had lost the ability to take their majestic city fortress. Historically, the longer a siege continued without progress, the more the besiegers had to worry about their own supplies, shelter in winter, disease, and an increasingly hostile environment outside the walls. Regional neutrals always watched the pulse of the battle to calculate which side would likely prevail and thus was safer to support or attack.

An emboldened though once despised Hasdrubal, now enjoying near absolute power as general, roamed even farther from the city into the interior and along the coast with his army. He hoped to encircle the encamped Romans and squeeze them between his army, the sea, and the city walls. In concert, his subordinate and more brilliant cavalry commander Himilco Phameas raided the Roman camps directly with hit-and-run mounted sorties. Hasdrubal may have been no Hannibal, but certainly the two Roman consuls proved even more wanting in comparison to the legendary Scipio Africanus, hero of the Second Punic War.

Since in these first few months of the siege the Romans could neither mount the great land walls nor build engines to knock them down, and given that sorties of Carthaginians roamed almost unchecked about the Romans' camps, the exasperated invaders began to change course. They now unwisely sought to force the issue with brute frontal assaults. The Romans hoped that their two huge battering rams, each manned by some six thousand legionaries, could blast apart the city gates or any perceived weak spot in the walls. Yet neither engine could create a large enough fissure to prompt a full-scale entry. Small Roman contingents for a time did break through a few small breaches, but were quickly isolated and repulsed. Meanwhile, the Carthaginians inside sought to wall off any of the Romans' initial entries, and then sent sorties out to break up the rams.[23]

So back and forth the Romans and Carthaginians fought over fissures and ad hoc counter walls, while the defenders made constant sorties to dismantle siege engines. A few months after the invasion, the siege was bogged down because the Romans could not prevent either the entry or exit of the Carthaginians and their allies. By late summer and early fall of the first year, 149, the poor morale and declining readiness of the legionaries, the mediocre generalship of the consuls, the unreliable supply train from Sicily, and the unhealthy environs and poor defenses of Censorinus's camp on Lake Tunis about twelve miles distant from the city all combined to stalemate Roman efforts. The soldiers were increasingly hungry, sick, and listless. They had become so disheartened that even when they punched an entryway into the city's massive walls, they were unable to exploit the opening, and were pushed back with considerable losses.

Both ancient historians and modern scholars have often cited Thucydides's "Melian Dialogue" to parallel the tragic dilemma of the Carthaginians. And indeed, as veritable Melians they were now facing extinction from Roman realists playing the role of ruthless Athenian imperialists. But after a near-year of failure, the better comparison might have seemed the disastrous and ultimately failed 415–413 Athenian siege of far-off Syracuse, some two centuries before the Romans obliterated the Sicilian city in the Second Punic War.

The incompetence of the Roman command and the ensuing stalled siege before Carthage were beginning to resemble just that iconic Athenian misadventure. The failed siege of Syracuse had led to the near total annihilation of the invaders and a subsequent revolution back home at Athens—and made it unlikely that Athens could any longer win its long war with Sparta. Thucydides recorded the Sicilian disaster in tragic fashion:

> Of all the Greek events that occurred in the war, or rather, it seems to me, of all Greek events that we know of, this action was the greatest: both the most illustrious to the winners, and the most catastrophic to the losers. For they were entirely and in every aspect defeated, and their miseries proved completely unimaginable. Both their ships and their infantry fully perished from the face of the earth; and there was nothing that was not destroyed. Of the many who had gone out, few made it home. So ended the Sicilian expedition.[24]

As the first siege year came to a close, a now stymied Censorinus had been called back to Rome. An eroding army solely under the command of the even less talented and lame-duck Manilius was forced to forage for food farther out into the countryside, even as it sought in vain to cut off new food trains from entering and supplying the city. The Romans managed to do neither well.

In contrast, the trapped Carthaginians proved increasingly ingenious and recovered their spirits. They kept torching any new or repaired Roman siege engines. They sent wind-aided fireboats out of their harbor into the anchored Roman fleet and almost incinerated it. They filled in the ditches and toppled the palisades of the Roman besiegers' camps, and unleashed the redoubtable Phameas's cavalry to pick off Roman foragers. For a moment at least, the Carthaginians were buoyed into thinking they could win—as were the earlier Thebans who initially repulsed the Macedonians from their city, as would be the Byzantines of Constantinople who for weeks beat back the Ottomans, and as would be the Aztecs after La Noche Triste who believed they could continue to decimate the Spanish besiegers.

Indeed, for a while the defensive fighting even turned away from the city to constant offensive Punic skirmishing in the plains. Unfortunately for the Romans, the first year also revealed the continued incompetence of the consul Manilius. He was repeatedly baited, ambushed, and cut off by roving Carthaginian cavalrymen under Phameas, as well as by the risk-taking main forces under Hasdrubal. By the year's end, the Roman attackers had lost thousands of wounded and dead. And they were clearly no closer to storming the walled and expansive city.[25]

In contrast, Carthage for the first year of the siege remained well fed, rearmed, and supplied from the hinterlands. Most crucially, native Numidian cavalry, historically at odds with Carthage and allied with Rome, often stayed neutral, waiting to see how the siege progressed. Soon both humiliated Roman consuls had finished their tenures and were back in Rome. Neither would return. Ironically, the end of their disastrous assignments proved unfortunate for the Carthaginians, who up to now had humiliated the entire mediocre Roman consular command.

Amid this vacuum of Roman leadership, only one high-level officer, the legate Scipio Aemilianus, had displayed leadership qualities. When asked about Scipio during the first year of the siege, the cranky, aged Cato back in the Roman Senate paraphrased Homer in his praise: "He alone still thinks, the others flit about as shadows." Through a series of rescue operations of his superiors' bungled Roman frontal assaults, Scipio had managed to keep the siege viable, at least until reinforcements arrived and there was a change in supreme command.

Scipio himself was the fourth son of the famous victorious Roman general Lucius Aemilius Paulus, who was the brilliant conqueror of the Macedonian king Perseus at the battle of Pydna (168). And, in the aftermath of that victory, Aemilius became infamous for the mass slaughter of the conquered Epirotes of northern Greece, along with the unprecedented enslavement of 150,000 civilians who survived the complete erasure of seventy cities of Epirus. But perhaps more importantly Scipio Aemilianus was also the adopted grandson of Hannibal's own conqueror, Scipio Africanus. If nothing else, the mere name of Scipio brought fear to the Carthaginians and hope to the legions.

Moreover, the younger Scipio was a shrewd diplomat and strategist. In the absence of competent supreme commanders, he now freelanced and systematically traveled the hinterlands around the city and inspected the supply routes into it. As his retinue entered Carthage's allied towns and hamlets still loyal to their capital, Scipio showed magnanimity, while eroding their support for the trapped Carthaginians. Word spread that any African ally of Carthage who now surrendered to Scipio's men would be treated strictly according to the conditions under which he had surrendered—an act interpreted as notable leniency. Most importantly, Scipio considered as enemies only those who took up arms against Rome; this left open the chance for opportunistic or frightened neutrals later to join what he hoped would soon be the winning Roman side, with appropriately allotted spoils to come.[26]

As the siege entered its second year, the younger subordinate Scipio—he was only thirty-seven years old in 148 BC—was increasingly seen as a kind of Roman fireman, who rushed to put out the conflagrations ignited by his incompetent superiors. Given the alternatives, he was certainly the only Roman with enough prestige, political clout, and proven military acumen to salvage the misadventure. Scipio's record of alleviating much of the quagmire became immediately obvious to Roman senatorial inspectors sent to autopsy the disastrously stalled siege. On their return to Rome, they ensured that the full dimensions of the sorry debacle were known to the Roman Senate and people at large.

Rome needed a stimulant, given that more news now depressed even the war party of the Senate. The elder Cato, who had supported Scipio's military appointments both before and during his initial assignment to Carthage—and whose annual monotonous demands for Carthage's destruction had helped to launch this apparently ill-considered Third Punic War—had finally died at age eighty-five in 149. Meanwhile, Rome's staunchest friend and ally in Africa, the ninety-year-old Numidian king Masinissa, had likewise passed away not much later in January 148. Roman confidence in the siege was reaching a new low.

Consular incompetence, the deaths of Cato and Masinissa, and the continuing stasis of the siege were turning the war into an open Roman sore without immediate hope of resolution. Scipio had no consular power to change either Roman tactics or strategy. The Carthaginians grew even more confident of success under the aggressive integrated leadership of Hasdrubal and Phameas. The two now became even bolder than before in their foraging and raiding sorties beyond the walls of the city. In response, despite Scipio's good-will missions canvasing Carthaginian towns, the Romans became more directionless. The new consular replacement Calpurnius Piso was as unexceptional as his predecessors. His admiral, the legate Lucius Mancinus, proved even more second rate. Both Carthaginians and Romans slowly began to accept that the war would de facto be decided only by the fate of Scipio. In short, if Scipio returned to the two-year-old siege as consul and savior general with powers of supreme command, then the city's days were likely numbered. If not, then Rome would soon be facing an ancient version of a Dunkirk or Gallipoli.

Scipio had initially returned to Rome in 148, ostensibly hoping to be elected aedile, an important office responsible for maintaining public buildings and auditing state functions. But he brought with him the brilliant Carthaginian cavalry commander Phameas; he had flipped and joined the Romans with his twenty-two hundred cavalrymen, due mostly to the Carthaginians' admiration for the skill and leadership of Scipio, and his ample bribes. Still, the Roman masses were disgruntled by the terrible news that had filtered back across the Mediterranean about the stalled siege. The people demanded Scipio forget about the aedileship and instead be elected consul to salvage the debacle at Carthage, with exemptions granted the young legate for not yet being the required consular age of forty-two.

During Scipio's absence at Rome, back at Carthage the consul Piso, appointed to remedy the mistakes of the prior two consuls, had repeatedly failed to cut off the city from its subject cities in the interior—always the key to winning the siege. In fact, nearly eight hundred Numidian cavalry had recently defected from Piso and joined Hasdrubal. It did not escape Roman notice that the current consul had lost allied horsemen through defections to the Carthaginians, while his former subordinate Scipio had earlier won over far more Carthaginian cavalry under Phameas to join Rome.[27]

Given his remarkable successes, Hasdrubal had all but dispensed with Carthage's civilian government and increasingly commanded the city as an absolute ruler. There were even hopes inside Carthage that Rome might be compelled to draw off besieging forces, to stop the rebellion on a distant front of war with the would-be Macedonian liberator and pretender to the throne of Macedon, Andriskos. The upstart had already destroyed a Roman occupying legion and ignited a fourth Macedonian war for independence from Rome. The aim of every enemy of Rome, or so Carthage now calculated, was to find a kindred ally on a distant Roman front, and to force the legions to fight in multiple theaters without being able to concentrate fully on any.[28]

Yet once he was made consul in early 147 and returned to North Africa that spring, Scipio began to change the course of the stagnant siege. He quickly set sail and stopped at Sicily to muster reinforcements. There he took on thousands of new recruits to replace the army lost in the first two years. Then, accompanied by Phameas, he headed straight to Utica to bail out Piso and Mancinus before the cause was lost altogether. The historian Appian noted that during Scipio's absence, and given the ineptitude of Piso, the Carthaginians had been routinely roaming the countryside, easily finding supplies. At the same time they were trying to bring back into the fold fence-sitting and defecting Punic cities, as their envoys continued to lodge "insulting diatribes against the Romans among the town assemblies." Apparently, the Romans had lost all ability to control traffic in and out of the walled city.[29]

Hasdrubal's strategy was often offensive: keeping Romans away from the walls, isolating them from their own supplies in the interior, joining both Numidian and Carthaginian cities to the resistance against Rome, and hoping unforeseen developments such as the deaths of anti-Carthaginian zealots like Masinissa and Cato the Elder might lead to some sort of armistice. In other words, the Third Punic War was always a contest of attrition—the Carthaginians still tried to prove to the Romans that the decision to destroy their city was a correctable mistake, one that would hurt them far more than had they just allowed Carthage to remain independent and neutral.

On his arrival with reinforcements, Scipio almost immediately moved to save a trapped Mancinus. The consul, who thought he had found a seam in the Carthaginian defense, had become the first Roman to enter the city. But he was quickly cut off and surrounded in the vast expanse within the walls, and was facing annihilation without Scipio's relief efforts. No wonder that within weeks the supreme command of the siege was solely in Scipio's hands. Piso and Mancinus, like their failed predecessors Manilius and Censorinus, returned in humiliation to Rome. The ossifying siege was yet another reminder that elected Roman consuls were rarely military geniuses. The careers of consular supreme commanders of the caliber of Fabius Maximus, the Scipios, Flamininus, Aemilius Paulus, Pompey, and Julius Caesar were always the exceptions.

The change in command gave the young consul Scipio a rare occasion to reboot the undisciplined and eroding Roman army. He offered the legions promises of rich rewards—but only after the city was taken. (Note that booty was always a necessary incentive for even well-trained legions.) That remodeling of the army was an impossible feat without far greater discipline and constant drilling, and plenty of expulsions from the camp. Or as the new consul in carrot-and-stick fashion warned his army of demoralized, greedy, and raggedy besiegers:

> You are more thieves than fighters. You are deserters rather than defenders of our camp. You are more like banqueteers than success-ful besiegers. You want luxuries even while you are fighting instead of waiting until you have won. For this very reason, an enemy that had no hope and was weak when I left him, has risen to great power. And so your task has now become far harder due to your sheer lazi-ness. If I should have felt that you were to blame for this laxity, then

I would punish you now. But since I put the blame on another, I am willing to overlook all that has happened up to now.

Scipio then reminded the legionaries that he was not a robber—at least not yet—but first a conqueror:

I for my part have come here not to rob, but to conquer, and not to worry about money before victory, but first to beat down the enemy. Now, all of you who are not soldiers must leave our camp today— except those who have my prior permission to stay . . . But for you, soldiers, I set one model, to be in force in all situations: my own habits and my own industriousness. If you can observe that one command, you will neither fall short of your duty nor you will lack any reward. Indeed, now it is necessary to work hard while we are still in danger. Loot and the soft life we must postpone to their proper time. This is what I and what the law commands. And for those who obey, it will bring great rewards; but for those who disobey, only sore regret.[30]

With morale and order gradually restored and the army cleansed of riffraff during the spring of 147, Scipio felt secure enough to attack Megara, a sprawling Carthaginian suburb of cultivated fields inside the city walls. From there, hundreds of Romans under cover of darkness began to consolidate their positions and hoped to spread over the outlying districts of the rambling city itself. However, after finding the suburbs crisscrossed with orchards, brambles, ditches, and hedges, the confused Romans backed out of the city. But at least they had demonstrated that much of Carthage outside the inner citadel was now porous.

Scipio's sortie enraged the Carthaginian command and worried the city. And so a turning point in the entire war came when a furious Hasdrubal abruptly mutilated and slaughtered on the walls all the Roman prisoners in his hands who had not gone over to the Carthaginian side. His sheer barbarity, or so he thought, would so incite the Romans that his own desperate people would finally accept there could be no quarter given from the now infuriated legions—and thus no chance of survival except to fight on with increased desperation. Appian relates the gory details:

> When sunrise came, Hasdrubal, desperate and despondent by the attack upon Megara, collected all the Roman prisoners in his possession, and brought them atop the walls. In full view of their Roman comrades, he had their eyes, tongues, tendons, and private parts torn out with iron hooks. On some he cut out the soles of their feet. On others he chopped off their fingers. And some more he skinned alive. Any who were still breathing after these tortures he threw down from the top of the walls.

Whatever Hasdrubal's actual motivations, the Romans—like the later enraged conquistadors of Cortés who watched Aztec priests on the great pyramid of Tenochtitlán tear out the hearts of their captured comrades—wanted to fight and kill even more, while his own disgusted Carthaginian people may have wished to resist somewhat less:

> The result proved the very opposite of his intention. Instead, the Carthaginians, given these unholy crimes, became terrified rather than defiant. And they now despised Hasdrubal for robbing them of any hope of Roman mercy. Their own Senate denounced him for committing these savage and unnatural cruelties, amid so many of their other domestic disasters. Nevertheless, Hasdrubal rounded up some of the outspoken senators and executed them. Afterwards he made it clear in every respect that he was a tyrant rather than a general, and so felt himself safe only if he were an object of sheer terror to them. And in this way he would become immune from danger.[31]

As Appian described it, the gory spectacle harmed Carthaginian morale and rendered Hasdrubal little more than a thug in the eyes of his desperate people. Yet the Roman reaction, now and in the future, was cruelly paradoxical, since the savage Hasdrubal would prove to be the sole Carthaginian leader able to negotiate from the Romans his own safe conduct to a quiet retirement in Italy. On the other hand, his own people, who were outraged by the cruelty of their leader, were to be butchered or enslaved nearly to the last person by the Romans.

In a radical reversal of fortunes, it was now the defenders who began to suffer from terrible leadership and collective depression. In contrast, as the third year of the siege began, the Romans had dismissed their sorry commanders and turned the assault over to one of the authentic tactical geniuses of his age, even as the once dynamic Hasdrubal descended into megalomaniacal savagery and near madness.

In reaction to the horror, Scipio dispatched more troops throughout the countryside that had continued through the entire siege to send in supplies to the beleaguered city. The Romans systematically began to cut off all entries and exits to the city, by land and sea—an old mission that finally became viable, given that the surrounding towns and farms had learned that the winning Romans had been able to enter the suburbs of the huge city. Even more effectively, Scipio focused on isolating Carthage entirely from its rural districts by digging fortified ditches across the isthmus approach to the city. He could now ensure that supplies would not enter the city from any direction from the African hinterlands, nor could they be rerouted by sea and brought in by night to the city harbor. The result was mounting hunger inside the still-crowded city.[32]

Scipio, unlike his predecessors, had never underestimated the valor, resiliency, and ingenuity of his half million trapped enemies. Indeed, throughout the back-and-forth brawling over the walls, and despite their anger at Hasdrubal, the Carthaginians had so far harbored no thought of giving up, no desire to negotiate terms. Instead, they had somehow managed in secret to build a small fleet and were intent on attacking the Romans from the sea and reopening supply routes by water.

Appian describes the near fanatical efforts of the Carthaginians to relieve pressure on the city and stop Scipio's engineers from blocking them from their harbor and its lifeline to the city. He notes that the Carthaginians somehow dug another entrance at the opposite end of the harbor, thanks to the labor of the city's noncombatants. And, simultaneously, the Carthaginians in secret built a small fleet of triremes and quinqueremes by scavenging and reusing old wood. Despite the noise of the construction, the usually astute Scipio and his command apparently were completely unaware of this ad hoc replacement Carthaginian navy inside the fortified harbor—up to the very moment the ships emerged: "Finally, now all the work was finished, the Carthaginians opened their new entrance to the harbor about dawn, and sailed out with fifty triremes, but also with less impressive warships, boats, and even smaller craft still—all outfitted in a manner to instill fear."[33]

Such an enterprise might well have reversed the course of the siege, had the Carthaginians only been well led. Yet the disgraced Hasdrubal and his officers never capitalized on this moment of complete surprise to the Roman besiegers, who on the verge of victory were witnessing a mysterious fleet emerging from a supposedly surrounded and doomed city.

Yet once more Hasdrubal the Boetharch proved that he was no Hannibal, and so the courage of the doomed was mostly wasted:

> Both the sudden appearance of this entrance, and an entire fleet sailing from it, so shocked the Romans that had the Carthaginians immediately attacked their ships—then in the disorder from the ongoing fighting over of the walls, and the fact that there were neither any sailors nor rowers on duty—they might have conquered the entire Roman fleet. But given that it was fated that Carthage should be destroyed, the new fleet only sailed out to make a demonstration, and having embarrassed the enemy in such a glaring fashion, they simply turned back into the harbor.

It was another irony of the siege that those in greatest danger proved more nonchalant than Scipio's men who had brought them such peril:

> On the third day after this display, they finally sailed out again for a naval battle. The Romans, after preparing their ships and all their

equipment, advanced against them. Loud shouting arose from both sides with accompanying cheering from the rowers, pilots, and marines. The Carthaginians invested their final hope of salvation in this last battle while the Romans were hoping to turn the fight into their definitive victory.

After fighting for hours, the exhausted Carthaginians returned to their new harbor entrance. But its very unfamiliarity led to chaos. There was not enough room for the entire fleet to enter the harbor safely, and many ships were simply moored in the water and left vulnerable to the next day's Roman counterattack. In a brief moment of reprieve, the Carthaginians discovered that the larger Roman triremes had advanced too far into the narrow channel, stalled, and then proved easy static targets for the sudden counterattacks of the Carthaginian fleet.[34]

Finally, the Romans and their allied ships from Asia Minor returned and managed their own counterattack, blocking the Carthaginian advance. The defenders had already lost one fleet handed over to the consuls in 146. Now its replacement was all but sunk. They were unable to build a third. Winter was approaching, making sea fighting problematic. Moreover, Scipio had finally captured Nepheris, the last and most important Carthaginian allied town outside the wall, which had long been a key supply depot and camp for Carthaginian sorties against the besiegers. The Romans now planned to build on that momentum and storm the inner harbor. That combined effort might ensure that the trapped Carthaginians would have no source of food at all.

In early winter, at the end of the year 147, the Romans were preempted by yet another gallant and unforeseen desperate gambit of the defenders. Appian relates how for the last time the attacked became the attackers:

The Carthaginians, although they were beset by hunger and afflictions of all kinds, sallied forth by night to attack the Roman siege engines. Yet they did not advance by land, for there was no pathway out. Nor could they go out in ships, given the seawater was too shallow. Instead, they jumped into the sea naked with their torches not yet lit, so that they would not be seen from a distance. So, at a point no one would have expected, they entered the water and crossed over. Some of them waded up to their chests, others were swimming. When they reached the Roman engines they now lit their torches, and became visible. And since they were naked, they suffered terribly from wounds. Yet they returned the blows. Although they were hit constantly with barbed arrows and spear-points pierced their chests and faces, they did not relent. Instead they kept going forward, despite their injuries as if they were wild beasts—until they had torched the siege engines and sent the Romans fleeing in disorder. . . . Scipio, in shock at this reversal, charged out with some horsemen and commanded his orderlies to kill all those who would not stop fleeing. Indeed, he killed some of them himself . . . But the enemy, once they burned the engines, swam back home.[35]

———

With the end of that last courageous Carthaginian effort, all that was left for the Romans was to reenter the suburbs, march on the inner citadel of the city, and kill off thousands of its surviving defenders. Despite continued resistance, they soon stormed the walls and drove toward the Byrsa redoubt, systematically demolishing the old city and killing the inhabitants. When Scipio was finished with Carthage, there would be little if anything left. Almost all the Punic-speaking inhabitants, free and formerly servile, who may have flocked into the city and once numbered some five hundred thousand at the start of hostilities in 149, had either died of disease or famine, committed suicide, or were killed in battle—save a final fifty thousand who were now captured and enslaved.

Most of the city's walls and buildings were leveled. The site of the city was ordered abandoned. Satellite Punic cities and towns were stormed. Only a few were given exemptions for having earlier professed fealty to Rome. While later stories of Romans salting the soil of Carthage to make it forever uninhabitable are modern folktales expanding upon ancient myths, the site may have been ritually plowed under and cursed. In any case, the location was largely abandoned as polluted or only haphazardly reoccupied, until the founding of the new Roman city of Carthage on or near the old Punic spot. Appian describes the final scenes when Scipio unleashed his troops to plunder whatever they could find among the ruins, while he formally burned all the weapons of the dead:

> Scipio allotted the soldiers a certain number of days to plunder everything they could except the gold, silver, and temple offerings. After this, he gave numerous prizes to all who had shown themselves brave—except any who had defiled the precinct of Apollo. He then dispatched a fast ship, loaded down with plunder, to Rome to announce his victory. Scipio also sent word to Sicily that whatever collective temple properties they could identify as stolen from them by the Carthaginians in past wars, all these they now might come and take back. In this way, he made himself popular to the people, as one who had joined generosity with authority. He then sold off the remaining plunder, and, in sacrificial fashion, he burned up the arms, engines, and useless ships as offerings to Ares and Athena, all according to Roman customs.[36]

When exactly the decision had been taken to destroy *all* of Carthage after the surrender of the last enclave of resistance in the Byrsa remains somewhat unclear. During the three-year siege and after the final effort of Scipio that wiped out all the final defenders and enslaved the rest, much of the city had been physically destroyed—but apparently not entirely.

So back in Rome a final debate quickly ensued over what Scipio was to do with what was left of Carthage, and presumably any survivors he had captured or had missed in or outside the walls. In reaction, the senators quickly voted to send envoys with strict orders to end the very idea of Carthage, both abstractly and concretely. That rapid response to Scipio's good news suggests that the decision to obliterate rather than merely defeat Carthage was pro forma. It apparently had been implicit three years earlier when Rome had warned the Carthaginians either to move their city inland or face annihilation. So the historian Dio Cassius concluded of Scipio's strict adherence to the senatorial communiqué on the future of the site: "The entire city was thus completely erased, and it was further decreed that if anyone were to settle upon the old site, that act should be considered accursed."[37]

Historians, ancient and modern, have often defended many of the Roman Republic's wars, not just its earlier defensive efforts, but also some of its later preemptive and imperial aggressions far abroad. But almost no ancient observer—contemporary Roman writers included—and few modern historians have justified Rome's Third Punic War. Most have condemned the Senate for instigating an unnecessary conflict of aggression against a diminished enemy, one that had been clearly willing to meet all of Rome's demands to avoid yet another conflict and to accept a permanently inferior, indeed impotent, status.

For example, the historian Polybius himself, although he was a friend of Scipio, nevertheless concluded that all the "reasons" the Romans gave for the war were simply pretexts:

> Long ago having made up their minds in these matters to act thus, they were seeking the suitable occasion and a viable pretext for outside observers. For the Romans especially showed great concern to this matter and rightly so, since just as Demetrius says, when the justification for starting a war appears just, it makes the victory greater and the misadventure less dangerous, while on the other hand, if it is thought to be dishonorable and fallacious, the very opposite effect ensues. So, on this occasion, given their disputes with one other about the effect on outside opinion, they nearly pulled back from entering the war.[38]

Carthage, as stated, had complied with all the old conditions following its humiliating defeat in the Second Punic War a half century earlier. By 149, it possessed no real ability to harm Rome or its interests abroad. Instead, Carthage had welcomed Romans into the city for decades to trade and prosper. Moreover, Rome was still a consensual republic, not formally an empire, much less a dictatorship. Its foreign policy was not the sole decision of a megalomaniacal strongman. Consensus was usually worked out by an aristocratic Senate, which traditionally had been sensitive to Rome's image abroad and the cost-benefit analyses of expeditionary efforts. What then can explain Rome's unalterable decision yet again to fight Carthage, to defeat it a third time, and finally to obliterate all traces of its civilization? To answer that question is to understand how strange the Third Punic War had become.[39]

The siege of Carthage between 149 and 146 was hardly a war, at least in comparison to the multifaceted theaters of the First (twenty-three years) and Second Punic Wars (seventeen years)—and for a variety of reasons. Unlike the prior two wars, other than skirmishing and raiding, there was no major fighting either in pitched infantry battles or by sea on the Mediterranean, in Europe, or on and around Sicily. Carthage no longer had any ability to project power beyond its hinterlands. It had no capacity to organize, train, and field an army capable of meeting the Romans face to face outside the walls in one dramatic showdown to decide the fate of the city, at least in the manner of the failed effort a half century earlier at nearby Zama. Except for efforts to cut off Carthage from its interior and ports, and a few maritime encounters near the shore, the war was synonymous with a siege of the city itself.

Unlike the two earlier conflicts, the sides were no longer even remotely matched in power and wealth. In the fashion of a vastly diminished fifteenth-century Byzantine Constantinople, the formerly large Punic Empire had for a half century consisted only of Carthage itself and a few Numidian and Punic cities only loosely supportive of the capital. In contrast, Rome was becoming a truly Mediterranean empire stretching from Spain to Macedonia, and from the Alps to Sicily.

There were no major territorial disputes of the sort that had triggered the past two wars. The First Punic War was fought mostly in a radius around Sicily. The second was over Carthaginian colonies in Spain, again in Sicily, and in Sardinia—and over the future of Italy itself. But in 149, Carthage had sought no territory that Rome had claimed either as its own, or as belonging to its sphere of influence. Indeed, in the years leading up to the final siege Rome freely conceded that its opportunistic ally, the wily and aged Numidian Masinissa, was methodically carving off chunks of Carthage's interior domains guided by his correct belief that his Roman patrons always would prevent any serious Punic pushback.[40]

There was also no grassroots, popular Carthaginian demand for war with Rome; no one like Hannibal Barca swearing since childhood to avenge prior defeat. Given Carthage's earlier two disastrous defeats, its people had reconciled themselves to inferior status vis-à-vis Rome, and were terrified of yet another war with the legions. Even in the last days before the siege, Carthaginians had accepted all but one or two of the humiliating ultimata and were convinced there was no reason for Rome to attack. For a half century before the city's end, there had been no serious calls to overturn the treaty that had ended the Second Punic War and to instigate a third conflict. In sum, the bellicosity was all on Rome's part, and so recognized even by prominent Roman statesmen unapologetic about the unfettered use of terror to punish the conquered and to deter others, what the historian Polybius dubbed the "Roman custom" (*to ethos*) of war.[41]

Although Semitic Punic culture and religion were markedly different from their Roman counterparts, there were not existential structural or cultural variances between the two states that made war inevitable. Other than the contentious issue of child sacrifice, which was seen as a precivilizational anathema to classical culture, Carthage, like Rome, drew on a number of shared Hellenic precedents.

A century after the destruction of Carthage, Virgil could devote the entire fourth book of his monumental epic poem the *Aeneid* to the mythical passionate love affair between the two respective founders of Rome and Punic Carthage, Aeneas and Dido. If anything, Carthage and Rome were more integrated following the Second Punic War than they ever had been before the First Punic War. There were numerous Italian traders based in second-century defeated Carthage, and frequent travel of Carthaginians to Italy. For example, the Roman comic playwright Terence (ca. 195–159 BC) may have been born in or near Carthage, have come to Rome as a slave to a Roman noble, and then have been freed. This assimilationist trend would accelerate under the late republic and empire, with prominent North African writers such as Fronto and Apuleius.

However, unlike in the two earlier wars, from the outset Roman strategy ensured the ultimate outcome: any defeat of Carthage would become synonymous with the cessation of Punic civilization in North Africa. In the two earlier conflicts both Rome and Carthage, nearly evenly matched, had no preset aim other than victory. The conditions of an eventual peace were fluid, and entirely predicated on the ebb and flow of the multiyear wars.

So, again, *why* did Rome in 149 decide to attack Carthage in the first place? Ancient and modern military historians have often followed the prompt of the historian Thucydides's timeless lessons about conflict from his analysis of the origins of the Peloponnesian War. Accordingly, they often separated the "real" cause (*aitia*) of the Third Punic War from the alleged cause of, or stated pretext (*prophasis*) for, the war. Such duplicity seems especially common in the case of constitutional systems and democracies, as Appian implied of Rome. Such governments appear more likely to preface their aggressions with moral justifications that reflect legal pretensions, government consensus, and public support. In the case of the Roman Republic, the pretext was usually defined as the "just" reason to excuse instigating a "necessary" war of aggrandizement, itself usually passed off as a preemptive reaction to impending enemy "aggression."[42]

As for the actual causes of the Third Punic War, they are to be found in both long- and short-term contexts. Ancient historians often emphasized the fixations of the octogenarian Marcus Porcius Cato ("Cato the Elder") on Carthage in the last five or so years before the outbreak of the war, given his purported and now famous pro forma epilogue to speeches in the Senate: *"Carthago delenda est!"* ("Carthage must be destroyed!").[43]

Cato also added occasional melodramatic reminders of the supposed existential threat posed by Carthage. For example, he famously once displayed still-fresh figs in the folds of his toga to his Senate colleagues, claiming they had been picked just three days prior in Carthage. Cato's skit thereby reminded the Senate—successfully we are told—of the dangerous proximity of the Punic city to a vulnerable Rome (ca. 370 miles to Rome by most combined sea and land routes).[44]

For Cato and his elder generation who still had firsthand memories of the Second Punic War—Hannibal had been the first foreign enemy in memory to ravage the countryside of Italy—disappointment steadily grew that a recovering Carthage had not been destroyed after its loss to Rome in 202. In the mere two years from 218 to 216, the Romans had lost over a hundred thousand legionaries in a series of four crippling defeats inside Italy (Ticinus, Trebia, Trasimene, and Cannae, the latter battle alone nearly accounting for half of those deaths). During the remainder of the war, Rome suffered another two hundred thousand deaths in subsequent battles. As a result, its manpower reserves were nearly nonexistent. For the old survivors of those disasters, Cato among them, no Italian would be safe until Carthage itself was leveled. *"Hannibal ad portas!"*— "Hannibal at the gates!"—had become a traditional parental warning to scare Roman children into obedience over the following centuries.[45]

Generations of Romans were convinced, rightly or wrongly, that the resources of their Carthaginian enemy were timeless and endless. So there could be no such thing as a sufficiently diminished and quiescent Carthage. For all the ostensible Carthaginian good will, Cato and most of his cohort suspected that hereditary Punic hatred of Rome simmered among the entire Carthaginian population, ready to ignite the moment another Hannibal appeared. This paranoia existed even among the postwar generation of Romans, who knew nothing of Hannibal firsthand, grew up during the republic's recovery and ascendance, and had no inkling of the true power a vastly diminished Carthage had once possessed, or how close Rome had come to defeat. But despite such ignorance, they did inherit an elemental loathing of Carthage and an almost institutionalized zeal for vengeance. The adopted great-grandfather of Scipio Aemilianus, Lucius Cornelius Scipio, had held an important command in the

First Punic War. In the Second Punic War, Scipio Aemilianus's famous adopted grandfather, the conqueror Scipio Africanus, had fought the Punic invader for nearly two decades. And Scipio Aemilianus's real grandfather, Lucius Aemilius Paulus, had been killed earlier in the infamous slaughter at Cannae (216) while serving as both consul and general.

This century-long history of violence and distrust reached a crescendo after Cato and other envoys, in 153 on the eve of the Third Punic War, had returned from an effort to negotiate an armistice between Carthage and Rome's ally Numidia. While the trip was a diplomatic failure, Cato and his fellow senators had an opportunity to visit the landscape surrounding Carthage and the city itself.

The general lushness, given that most North African coastal soils were even richer than those of Italy, certainly did not appear to the inspectors to represent a struggling state impoverished by two long and unsuccessful wars with Rome. Once inside the walls, Cato's senatorial delegation grew even further exasperated at the urban prosperity, wealth—and confidence—of a supposedly defeated people. To these Roman envoys, the city seemed as affluent as Rome. They privately wondered what Carthage would become, once freed of the postwar treaty restraints of the last half century, while Rome was bogged down in dirty wars in Spain and Greece. And paradoxically, the more Roman grandees became convinced that a revived Carthage was fabulously wealthy, the more some in the Senate saw great profits to be had from its obliteration. None of the Roman envoys made the connection that the loss of the Punic Empire and a recalibration toward peacetime commercial maritime investment might have explained the affluence of a pacifistic Carthage, now shorn of its naval costs, imperial ambitions and burdens, and colonial expenses abroad.

Appian captures this astonishment and nervousness that arose among the Roman ambassadors once they visited a lush Carthaginian landscape:

> They carefully surveyed the countryside, noting how intensively it was developed, and the vast infrastructure that was impressive.

They then entered and viewed the city, especially how magnificently it had increased its power and its population since its wastage by Scipio [Africanus] not long before. When the ambassadors returned to Rome they announced that Carthage seemed to them more worthy of fear rather than of envy, given the city was so ill-intended, so close to them, and so rapidly expanding. Cato especially declared that even the very liberty of Rome could never be ensured until Rome eliminated Carthage.[46]

There were still wider reasons why in 149 Rome landed a huge army at Utica. The catchphrase *mare nostrum* ("our sea") may have been rarely used formally by Romans themselves. But by 149, Rome was fighting a war in the Western Mediterranean against Carthage and one in the Eastern Mediterranean against Macedonia and the Greek Achaean League. Rome had naturally come to believe that the entire Mediterranean properly was "our sea," given that it had the will and increasingly the ability to sweep the sea and coasts of its enemies.

More importantly, even small transgressions, such as Hasdrubal's response to Numidian assaults, were no longer considered tolerable for a would-be world power. Rome had apparently decided that any small concession anywhere in its growing domain would hardly be considered benevolence to be reciprocated by the offender, but instead seen as vulnerability to be further developed. The appearance of fragility became a fatal condition for an ascendant imperial hegemon such as Rome, whose currency was unambiguous deterrence and automatic, disproportionate reprisals to even the suggestion of disobedience. As Voltaire famously described, the British "from time to time hang an admiral," in efforts "*pour encourager les autres*"—that is, to deter any naval officer from believing there were no capital consequences for failure.[47]

In the modern post–World War II era, the Allies rejected the "Carthaginian" solution to a perennially aggressive Germany proposed by American secretary of the treasury Henry Morgenthau. He had in vain lobbied to turn Germans into the fragmented, pastoralized, and deindustrialized people of centuries past. But that said, the ious Allies—the Soviets, French, British, and Americans—still ended the idea of a prewar imperial Germany, as it had been known since 1871, by ceding former German territories to Poland in the east and France to the west. The Western powers for their part consolidated their three zones of occupation and installed a constitutional democracy. More than seventy-five years after the end of World War II, a reunited Germany—still 24 percent smaller in size than it had been in 1938—remains the economic engine that drives European Union prosperity, and yet is not the perennial military bully that once so frequently invaded the borders of its neighbors.

The eternal lesson is perhaps that accusations of war guilt and harsh reparations accompanied by feeble enforcement, as occurred at the end of World War I, can ensure another war with an insulted but newly resurgent enemy. In contrast, quiet magnanimity backed by unyielding force and confidence in enforcing a tough postwar settlement, as occurred after World War II, can guarantee lasting peace. In Rome's case, it had acted harshly after its victory in the First Punic War. But that sternness was not always backed by unyielding Roman force, as a wily and opportunistic Hannibal soon discovered. In reaction to that subsequent bloody second chapter in the hundred-year Rome-Punic conflict, Rome was determined to be inflexible and punitive. As part of its deterrent policy, Rome gave Carthaginians no exemption for engaging in an understandable retaliatory war with Numidia, one that nevertheless was seen as a conflict in violation of the terms of their long-standing treaty with Rome. Romans in retrospect had viewed their prior peace settlements of 241 and 201 as too conciliatory, without having earned Romans any acknowledgment as magnanimous victors. Thus, provocative Roman belligerence not backed by actual deterrence may have been responsible for a resurgent Carthage in the wars' aftermaths. So, both before and after the Third Punic War, Romans were determined not to experience a fourth Punic war at any cost.[48]

Yet Rome's third successful war against Carthage did not necessarily have to be synonymous with destroying Punic civilization. After all, at the end of the First Punic War, a triumphant Rome did not level Carthage in 241. Nor did it obliterate the city after its second victory in 201, even when arguably the Carthaginians had prompted the conflict. Why then did the Romans envision their own Third Punic War of naked aggression, either at the outset or during the three-year-long siege, as an effort to annihilate the capital and all things Carthaginian?

"Annihilate" is the proper verb to describe the true mission of the Roman expeditionary force's landing at Utica. The demands that the Carthaginians disarm—to destroy their machines of war, their fleet, and individual arms—and then to demolish their own city and move it ten miles from the sea, were understood as either ending old Carthage outright, or creating the conditions by which its people would resist and then could be easily and justifiably destroyed. From ancient descriptions of the aftermath of the war, Scipio Aemilianus, with additional prompts from the Roman Senate, carried out those orders to the letter. That he had torched and devastated much of the city well before receiving a command to do so from the Senate on news of his victory suggests Carthage's destruction was implicit from the beginning of the siege.

So, again, why level Carthage? Rome was probably guided by several concerns.

Many Romans had wanted to destroy Carthage after the victory in the Second Punic War, but an exhausted Rome lacked the resources to actually do it, just as it did not have the wherewithal to finish off the great city after the First Punic War. After the second war Rome rightly feared a serious war looming with the Macedonian king Philip V, which in fact broke out the year after the Carthaginians surrendered. Rome in 202 was no more able to undertake a multiyear siege of Carthage than it had been in 241.

Unlike at the end of these prior two exhausting wars, the Roman military in 146 during the last days of the siege was more formidable than at any time in the previous century. Despite earlier setbacks, Scipio felt he at last had the money, the manpower, and the leadership ability to annihilate rather than defeat and occupy Carthage. And so, what Rome *could* now do to Carthage, it did.

In addition, Rome had grown tired of the very idea of Carthage, what some historians have occasionally called "historical impatience." After 117 years of nonstop rivalry with Carthage, it felt that the Punic cities and empire—and its agendas—had been so antithetical to Roman traditions, customs, and policies that endless war was inevitable. We might call Roman existential hatred a "psychological" cause of the war.

The *metus Punicus*, "dread of the Carthaginian," had long ingrained in the Roman people a loathing of the city, and eventually a paranoia about what even a vastly diminished Carthage might again do to Rome. The destruction and death that Hannibal had caused in Italy for nearly fifteen years (218–203) was never forgotten. Aside from Hannibal's initial four victories at Ticinus, Trebia, Trasimene, and Cannae, the Carthaginians in Italy had continued to destroy a series of Roman consular forces at Silarus (212), Herdonia (212), and Petelia (208). In between his victories, Hannibal systematically carried out a scorched-earth strategy to denude the Italian countryside of crops, infrastructure, and people. It was not just the Senate, but the Roman people who wished vengeance on the Carthaginians.[49]

Occasionally in the ancient world we hear of two wars between indomitable rivals, but rarely three. An initial negotiated armistice prevents a lasting solution to conflict. Eventually, such an ad hoc hiatus prompts a second all-out war in which one side is clearly defeated, humiliated, and ceases to be a belligerent. For example, the failed first Persian invasion of Greece by Darius was followed by the complete defeat and humiliation of his son Xerxes—and so not by a third Persian invasion. There were First and Second Peloponnesian Wars between Sparta and Athens, but by 403 a surrendered Athens was in no condition to wage a third war. Usually, the far more violent rematch ended the rivalry, and thereby precluded a third. The same pattern held for World Wars I and II; the second was existential in the way even the murderous first was not, and so a third did not break out.

Moreover, in the exception that proves the rule, Rome between 149 and 146 was also fighting a fourth Macedonian war (150–148), because it had failed to make the third one (171–168) th ˙
new lesson to Roman expansionism seemed to be "Ens
rent war is the final one." Additionally, this final strike

was seen, a half century after the Second Punic War, as the proper corrective to what was increasingly viewed as a too lenient treaty of 201. The second war's indemnities and restrictions on warring now appeared insufficient to ensure that Carthage would never again be able to war with Rome.

There are, of course, other theories for why Carthage was annihilated rather than merely defeated. Some have argued that Rome feared a rising Pan-Africanism that might unite Masinissa's expanding kingdom of Numidia with Punic North Africa, thus creating a superstate with a population and territory larger than Romanized Italy. Yet one constant in Rome's long subjugation of what are now Morocco, Algeria, and Libya was its ability over three centuries to play off local tribes against one another, and to ensure that Numidia and Carthage did not weld into an anti-Roman pancontinental alliance. During the Third Punic War that strategy of dividing African tribes and states was continued by adroit Roman diplomacy.[50]

Others, perhaps less persuasively, have argued that Carthage was increasingly becoming democratic in the radical sense of the word. In the ancient world "democracy" usually meant that the proverbial vox populi of the assembly of the masses was gaining the upper hand over the senior and smaller council of mostly oligarchs and aristocrats, as well as over strongman generals. The aristocratic Roman Senate, in this view, wanted to nip in the bud foreign insurrectionists before they contaminated the shores of the Mediterranean with their radical democratic and redistributionist agendas.[51]

Profit, of course, was always a Roman motive during the gradual transition from republic to empire. Carthage was a storehouse of wealth. Even in their reduced state, the Carthaginians had paid off their indemnities and yet still recovered enough to resume their former position as one of the most successful and richest commercial cities on the Mediterranean coast. Appropriating all the city's wealth and enslaving tens of thousands of its citizens was seen as yet another incentive. Plutarch records a famous anecdote concerning the supposedly upright and parsimonious Scipio Africanus that may illustrate how gaining foreign loot also incited both the Senate and Roman elites to demand a final solution:

After being appointed censor, he [Scipio Aemilianus] confiscated the horse of a young cavalryman, when they were waging the war against Carthage. The youth had put on a lavish dinner and ordered for the event a honey-cake to be baked in the form of the city. And calling the desert "Carthage," he served it to the guests for them to "plunder." So when the young man asked why he had his horse taken away, Scipio answered, "Because you plundered Carthage before I did!"

Such anecdotes assume a profit motive to imperialism, where making money from Roman wars came to be so commonplace an aim as to become noncontroversial. The Roman comic playwright Plautus (254–184 BC), a rough contemporary of the Second Punic War, has one of his characters matter-of-factly, albeit sarcastically, state: "I shall now summon a meeting of my mental Senate to take counsel on financial questions, against whom it is best to declare war, and where to steal some money."[52]

The radical agrarian reformer and tribune Gaius Gracchus (154 BC–121 BC), a quarter century after the destruction of the city, attempted—and failed—to found a viable Roman city on the deserted site of Carthage in 122. The fact that Julius Caesar eventually succeeded in doing so in 46, a century after the city's destruction, illustrates that the Punic North African corridor had always been seen as ripe for Roman colonization. The site of Carthage was the closest point in Africa to Roman Sicily. A new city there would be much nearer to Rome itself than either Roman ports at Piraeus or Corinth, and thus give the growing republic readier access to the wealth of the North African interior and the Mediterranean west to Gibraltar.

Advocates of such economic motivations for the Third Punic War variously point to the nonending ambitions of the senatorial class to acquire wealth, power, and influence by conquests; to the landed aristocracy's ambition to acquire slaves; to the Roman commercial class's desire to eliminate competition from Carthaginian traders; to the Roman people's desire for bread-and-circus distributions from the great wealth of the vanquished city; and to the republic's long-term agendas to colonize the North African corridor and redistribute its rich farmlands to Roman citizens and veterans. Yet these were always generic reasons for Roman imperialism per se that did not inevitably guarantee particular optional wars, much less the erasure of foreign civilizations.[53]

Rome had allowed client kingdoms all over Asia Minor, and for a time in Numidia, to survive and direct their own internal policies. It was a paradigm it had once found more profitable in a cost-to-benefit sense than simply erasing an enemy off the face of the earth. But by the outbreak of the Third Punic War in 149, the feeling in the Roman Senate may have shifted. Unlike rival interior kingdoms in Asia or Spain, Punic civilization was too proximate to southern Italy, too burdened by over a century of enmity to Rome to ever become a predictable satellite, much less a reliable client, and always too liable to become once again a formidable sea power.

Carthage's obliteration was one of the first steps in what would develop as an expansive idea of the new Roman province of "Africa" that was one day to encompass modern-day northeastern Algeria, Tunisia, and western Libya along the Gulf of Sirte. Stretching from the Red Sea to the Atlantic, Roman North Africa as a whole, including the additional provinces of Egypt and "Mauritania" (western Algeria and eastern Morocco), would ensure Roman control over some of the richest farmland in the ancient world and a number of geostrategic harbors.

———

The Carthaginians were quite willing to disarm as demanded, even after paying off their prior war indemnities. But they were unwilling to dismantle their ancient city and move inland, and therefore by default they had no choice but to resist a siege. That decision did not spring necessarily from confidence in arms, given that they had already lost two Punic wars, and had recently lost an entire army to the Numidians. What, then, were they thinking?

Some of Carthage's leaders, at least, were surely apprised of Rome's true intentions, given their knowledge of the prior four years' senatorial ranting from the elder Cato and his anti-Carthaginian supporters. They were certainly cognizant that a dreaded new Scipio was on the horizon, even if initially without consular command, and that he was an intimate of their archenemy Cato the Elder and his war party. Scipio Aemilianus would likely wish to match his adopted grandfather's legacy by completing what the family had apparently left unfinished at Carthage. And the Carthaginians also knew well the legendary terror that Scipio's real father, Aemilius Paulus, had unleashed upon the conquered Epirotes—a campaign in which Scipio himself had fought and so witnessed the destruction firsthand.

Carthage's naïveté may have arisen from hopes that it had friends of sorts in Rome. There was a large Roman faction that did not want war, much less the destruction of Carthage. It was led by the renowned Publius Cornelius Scipio Nasica Corculum, one of the most distinguished men of the republic. Also born into the aristocratic Scipionic family, hero at the battle of Pydna (168), and twice consul, Scipio Nasica was every bit as influential as Cato, and a rival to the old senator and to his own cousin Scipio Aemilianus.

The clout of Nasica in the Senate and his stature among the public (he was the son-in-law of the famous Scipio Africanus) perhaps explain why the Carthaginians apparently had enough confidence in Nasica's influence that they felt they could risk a retaliatory war against the Numidians, without endangering the terms of the 201 treaty that had guaranteed Carthage's continued existence.

For every saber-rattling speech of Cato, Scipio Nasica answered the war party in the Senate with several counterarguments. In all his replies, Nasica opposed Cato not on grounds of humanitarianism or even the shame of Rome starting an optional, immoral, and mostly unnecessary war. Instead, he appealed to Rome's collective self-interest in a manner that may seem odd to the modern mind: the idea of an elemental enemy Carthage, even in a reduced state, was important to an ascendant Italy. Its potential threat provided a constant warning to Romans to remain armed, and especially for Roman youth to prepare for military service. In contrast, the demise of Carthage would mean the erosion of any need for deterrence, replaced by the enervating enjoyment of the riches of the defeated.

Nasica's worry over the deleterious calm of peace should not be discounted. It was not an uncommon Roman idea. This notion that prolonged tranquility arising from an assured peace is enervating recalls the later poet Catullus's (84–54 BC) confession that "idleness has destroyed both kings and blessed cities before" (*otium et reges prius et beatas perdidit urbes*). Indeed, Roman apprehensions over the enfeebling effects of lacking an existential enemy were commonplace during periods of long peace, especially during later imperial times. Or as the satirist Juvenal put it at the end of the first century AD, "Now we are suffering the evils of a long peace; a luxury crueler than wars hangs over us and takes its revenge on a conquered world" (*Nunc patimur longae pacis mala, saevior armis/ luxuria incubuit victumque ulciscitur orbem*).[54]

Indeed, Scipio Nasica supposedly ended his speeches with his own riposte to Cato's inevitable chant, employing a similar gerundive phrase: "*Carthago servanda est!*" ("Carthage must be saved!"). Some 145 years later, the late-Republican historian Sallust, perhaps drawing on traditions of Nasica's apprehension, believed that the destruction of Carthage marked the apex of the republic. Thus, the end of the Third Punic War supposedly ushered in a rapid descent into decadence, given the absence of Rome's ancient and existential enemy Carthage and the booty that ensued:

> In truth, until the destruction of Carthage, the Senate and Roman people conducted the affairs of the republic with shared calmness and restraint. There were no rivalries among the citizenry for either glory or dominance. Instead, a fear of the enemy kept the state in good order. But when that anxiety was absent from their considerations, then decadence and hubris—the natural dividends of prosperity—began to dominate. Consequently, the very calm that they had once so eagerly sought in their times of trial, proved, later when they had obtained it, to be far more injurious and dangerous than the adversity itself.[55]

Unfortunately for Carthage, a series of events weakened the influence of Scipio Nasica's noninterventionist policy. In the year following Cato's own visit to Carthage, in 152, Nasica was sent to settle the growing Carthaginian-Numidian tensions. Yet, after some brief successes, he was unable to restrain his Carthaginian clients from retaliating against Masinissa and thus technically violating the treaty with Rome. That setback perhaps eroded Nasica's own senatorial influence. His antiwar ally Marcus Aemilius Lepidus was another of the most distinguished and charismatic Roman aristocrats of his time. Both as *pontifex maximus* ("supreme pontiff") and *princeps senatus* ("leader of the senate"), Lepidus was accordingly chief priest at Rome and first man of the Roman Senate. Unfortunately again for the noninterventionist bloc, Lepidus died in 152. His departure left Scipio Nasica without a strong ally at precisely the time Carthage was understandably but unwisely preparing for the war it would lose with its Numidian neighbors.

Worse still for Carthage, Scipio Nasica was given a command in Greece on the eve of the Fourth Macedonian War (149–148) to put down the upstart Andriskos, the Macedonian renegade and would-be Macedonian king. That assignment conveniently shuttled him far away from the Senate debate over Carthage. No doubt his deployment abroad was pushed by Cato and the consuls to dispose of one of the last major senatorial defenders of Carthaginian autonomy.

In sum, by 149 Carthage was targeted for harsh treatment and likely doomed, even if the city believed otherwise and even if some Romans had not yet a clear idea of turning such a huge metropolis into rubble. But a subsequent perfect storm of unfortunate events gave it very few options to escape from its rendezvous with annihilation. Carthage had de jure broken the peace by raising an army to stop the endless aggression of Masinissa—only to see some thirty thousand of its key defenders destroyed in the failed effort. The war party at Rome was now firmly in control of senatorial policy toward Africa. Carthage's two advocates, Lepidus and Scipio Nasica, were neutered: the former dead, the latter far away in Greece. Moreover,

Scipio Aemilianus was friendly with Cato's war party, and in any given war would likely land an important appointment commensurate with his lineage and military genius.

In general, it is mostly foolhardy for a belligerent to believe at the outset of hostilities that his opponent may call off a war because of a "peace" party, either sympathetic to the enemy or not convinced an ongoing war is in its country's national interest. Once a war starts and intensifies, the pulse of the battlefield usually adjudicates whether a peace party exists and grows, rather than any innate sympathy for the enemy or prior antiwar ideology. Carthage's gallant first eighteen months of resistance clearly rattled the Roman Senate. Yet its reaction was not to offer concessions, but rather to call in Scipio and give him a veritable blank check to finish the war and rid Rome of Carthage for good.

By the time of the Second Punic War, Roman armies had begun to destroy rather than merely retake besieged cities and points of resistance. In 212, for example, Romans did not just storm Sicily's most hallowed city, Syracuse—they demolished it. The legions slaughtered thousands of the resisters and enslaved the survivors. Epirus was not so much subdued but de-peopled by Aemilius Paulus in 167.

The destruction of Carthage and the near-simultaneous ruination of Corinth by the consul Gaius Mummius near the close of the Fourth Macedonian in 148 BC and Achaean Wars in 146 BC can in retrospect also mark the end of the Hellenistic age. Carthage, an independent Macedonia, and the Achaean League had ceased to exist; the Roman provinces of Africa, Macedonia, and Achaea were to emerge in their places. Seleucid Syria and Ptolemaic Egypt were eroding, as Rome prepared for them to fall into its lap.

The Hellenistic world is usually defined as ending with the Roman defeat of Cleopatra and her Egyptian forces at the battle of Actium in 31 BC. In fact, the destruction of Carthage plausibly soon ushered in the subsequent collapse as well of the older, Greek-dominated world of the Eastern Mediterranean. The republic at Rome, after ending Carthage and thus any further challenge to its dominance in the Western Mediterranean, was now free to consolidate the entire ancient Mediterranean world, east and west. It was not just that the older Hellenistic kingdoms had no answer to the republic's more dynamic constitution and politics, war-making, economic practices, culture, and new notion of total war that often resulted in the annihilation rather than the defeat of the enemy. Rome, after obliterating Carthage, had changed from a power that perceived itself as on the defensive; it was now a blatantly aggressive, unrepentant imperial juggernaut, bent on incorporating all of the Mediterranean and the East under its rule, in a manner atypical of even the autocratic and brutal Hellenistic kingdoms. Such unapologetic imperialism of the Roman Senate was justified not merely by the profit and power it earned, but also by the presumed benefits of its civilization for the supposedly less-civilized abroad that it conquered. And integral to this new self-confidence was a growing appreciation that Senate-mandated terror—the ability and willingness to annihilate any state that offered resistance to the imperial agenda—was both an acceptable and effective way of growing an empire.

Until Rome's emergence from the Punic Wars, it was not clear whether Greek-speakers in the East would continue using their cultural influence and military power to assume that they would alone define Western civilization, or whether Carthage would impede or even destroy its rival Italian upstart. After 146 Rome never looked back, and saw its rivals and enemies, whether kingdoms in the East or tribal peoples in Northern and Western Europe, as mere speed bumps on the way to global domination. Ruthlessly wiping out Carthage convinced Rome that it not only had the power and a formula to obliterate entire hallowed civilizations, but also had a moral right to do whatever it pleased. And so from then on it did just that.

Once a state's inferior status was established by Rome, either through military force or diplomacy, the relationship was considered sacrosanct and unalterable. No disobedience was tolerated. It was the general opinion in the ancient world that while Rome had been magnanimous to the defeated when it was striving for Mediterranean-wide power, once it gained superiority over almost all its rivals, it proved ruthless. The maintenance of empire is so often more taxing and bloodier than its acquisition.[56]

More than two centuries after the end of Punic Carthage, the Scottish rebel Calgacus, as famously quoted in Tacitus's *Agricola*, gave a long critique of the violence and terror inherent to Rome. He finished his broadside against the institutionalized Roman way of annihilating the loser with a now iconic summation: "They make a desert and call it peace" (*Ubi solitudinem faciunt pacem appellant*).[57]

Again, the same year that Carthage was obliterated, the consul Gaius Mummius ended the Achaean war and the last resistance of the Greek city-states by razing the historic city of Corinth. The legions killed almost all the active Greek defenders. They enslaved the women and children, destroyed many of the finest monuments of the ancient world and looted the rest, then flattened much of the city. Somewhat like the fate of Carthage, the site of Corinth would remain mostly deserted for over a century, until Julius Caesar refounded the city in 44, just two years after his own establishment of Roman Carthage. We rarely equate the dictator Caesar with restoring cities that his republican predecessors had obliterated.

Given its strategic location, the new Roman Corinth quickly became one of the major imperial cities in Greece. But unlike vanquished Punic Carthage, the end of Greek Corinth did *not* become synonymous with the evaporation of Hellenic civilization, although Greece was conquered and occupied by Rome. Corinth, both old and new, Greek and Roman, remained just one of many larger Greek-speaking cities. Greece would continue to be ruled by Rome and then Constantinople for a millennium and a half, even as Greek culture continued to master Rome. Note also that Punic culture per se was not the trigger that ignited Roman vengeance, although the Romans occasionally expressed shock at the Carthaginians' child sacrifice. Rome equally wiped out Greek cities, whose cultures they emulated.[58]

However, what made the end of the Third Punic War different from almost all of Rome's prior obliterations was that a once great civilization by 146 had shrunk to little more than its magnificent capital and its environs. Consequently, the leveling of the city could become synonymous with the end of everything Carthaginian—in modern-day terms, Carthage had become reduced to a "one bomb state." A theme of wartime genocide is the disparity between a target in civilizational decline, and its aggressor in ascendance.

It was also characteristic of conquering Roman generals both to unleash the legions to murder, loot, and destroy once the walls were breached, and later to express regret for the ensuing carnage and the end of a once majestic city or civilization. That sort of transitory pseudo-remorse was expressed as well by Alexander the Great over ruined Thebes, by Mehmet after the sack of Constantinople, and by Cortés following the leveling of Tenochtitlán. The crocodile tears shed by the killer Scipio Aemilianus over what he had wrought were no exception. They did not mask his willingness to exterminate entire peoples to end Rome's wars. Scipio, remember, prior to his obliteration of Carthage, had served as a teenager under his father in the aftermath of the battle of Pydna, when the legions wiped out vast swaths of the population of Epirus (167). In Spain (151–150), Scipio had been attached to the corrupt and ruthless Lucullus, who in the so-called Numantine War as a matter of policy leveled Celti-berian towns and murdered the inhabitants. After the destruction of Carthage, Scipio returned to finish the twenty-year-long Numan-tine War by starving the city of Numantia, prompting many of the residents to commit suicide, and then enslaving all the surviving residents (133). So we must put the legendary refinement and phil-hellenism of Scipio into the wider context of his often brutal service in advancing Roman imperialism. Nonetheless, Appian, again drawing on the lost narrative of Polybius, offers a melodramatic scene of near regret on the part of Scipio:

> Scipio was gazing out at this city that had flourished for 700 years from its foundation, and had ruled over so many lands, so many islands and seas, and so richly endowed with arms and ships, and elephants and money, equal to the greatest ancient empires but far surpassing them all in daring and spirit. And indeed, stripped of its ships and all its arms, and amid famine, it had held out in a nonstop war for three years—and now it had come to its end in destruction. It is said that Scipio, taking all this in, cried openly and grieved over the fate of his enemies. And after thinking to himself for a long

time and contemplating on the rise and fall of cities, nations, and empires, as well as of people, and on all the things that Ilium [Troy] had suffered, that once blessed city, and as well on the sufferings of the Assyrians, of the Medes, and of the Persians, the greatest empire of all, and then, more recently, the glorious Macedonian empire, either willingly or perhaps the words themselves of the poet escaped from his mouth:

"There will come a day when sacred Ilium shall perish,
And Priam, and the people of Priam of the strong ash spear."

And when Polybius asked him casually—and Polybius had been his teacher—what exactly his rambling alluded to, Scipio replied that he did not hesitate to name explicitly his own country, for on its behalf he feared whenever he contemplated the mutability of all things human.[59]

Scipio was prescient. The Vandals under Gaiseric looted, destroyed, and reoccupied Roman Carthage in AD 439. And then they went on to build a navy and sack Rome itself in AD 455, some 601 years after Scipio's prediction.

––––––

Obviously, Rome did not wipe out every Carthaginian vestige in just the last days of the Third Punic War in 146. In some classical texts, mention of survivors from the final days of Carthage occasionally appears. The Carthaginian-born philosopher and head of the Platonic Academy at Athens, Hasdrubal Cleitomachus, purportedly wrote a later book (now lost) of consolation to his former fellow Carthaginians recently taken prisoner by the Romans, suggesting that philosophy might offer some consolation for the loss of their city. We do not know whether Cleitomachus, an ethnic Greek born at Carthage and writing at a great distance from the fallen city, was ignorant of the finality of Scipio's carnage, or if he had some information that there were surviving captive Greek-literate Carthaginians. Nonetheless, the

Roman statesman and author Cicero, writing about a century after the end of Carthage, also confirmed that Cleitomachus's lost work assumed some number of surviving Carthaginians: "I have read a book of Cleitomachus, which after the destruction of Carthage he sent to comfort his fellow-citizens who were prisoners."[60]

As for other Punic cities, once Carthage was obliterated in 146, Carthaginian satellite communities in North Africa beyond the rubble of the capital became inert. Most were either destroyed or, more often, subjected to Rome. Indeed, many Punic cities had made prior deals with the Romans, gauging correctly that Carthage would fall. Those few communities were left alone as legally free cities in the new Roman province of Africa, and gradually Romanized during the imperial period. In any case, the Roman people equated the end of Carthage with the end of their Punic North African nemesis altogether, regardless of whether there were semiautonomous Punic small towns and isolated settlements largely left alone in western North Africa.

Back in Rome, Appian describes the Roman popular reaction to the ship sent by Scipio with the first announcement that he had finally defeated and then destroyed Carthage—prompting both wild jubilation and yet bewilderment that their century-long and most feared enemy was now truly obliterated:

When the people of Rome both saw the ship and learned of the victory in the early evening, they rushed out into the streets and spent the entire night with one another, both celebrating and hugging each other, like those who had just now been liberated from their fears—given they were now assured of their global dominance, and were convinced that their own city was finally secure, and had won such a victory like no other before. In the past they had rejoiced at the many brilliant achievements of their own generation, and even many more of their ancestors, both in Macedonia and Iberia and recently against Antiochus the Great, and in Italy itself. Yet they had never been so terrified by any other war fought on their own doorstep as the Punic wars, due to their enemy's courage, foresight, and daring—as well as its dangerous duplicity.

In addition, when news of the destruction of Carthage quickly reached a still paranoid Rome, the Senate, in its customary oversight role, dispatched ten auditors to guarantee that Scipio had in fact demolished all the towns that had remained loyal to Carthage, as it insisted on beating a dead horse. Scipio was also to authenticate to his overseers that the site of the capital itself was completely leveled, and to ensure that it would remain uninhabitable. He was additionally to warn locals that any who might ignore the senatorial edicts were subject to the maximum punishments. Yet as for those loyal allies of Rome, the envoys were to ensure that they too received their promised spoils of war:

> To all those who had helped the Romans, the auditors gave each some of the lands they had conquered. To the Uticans foremost, they bequeathed the territory of Carthage itself, all the way to Hippo. But as for all the rest, the Romans levied a tribute, both a land tax and a personal tax, and on their men and women alike. And they decreed that a general should be sent from Rome annually to oversee them. After they had established these arrangements, they sailed back to Rome. Meanwhile, Scipio completed all their mandates, and conducted sacrifices and honorific games for the victory. When all these matters were finished, Scipio too sailed for home. He was accorded the most splendid triumph of any known—one gold-studded and loaded with the statues and votive offerings that the Carthaginians had from time immemorial gathered from every part of the world and brought back to Africa as the fruit of their countless victories.[61]

Nearby Utica, which had wisely flipped to the Roman side and facilitated the invasion of 149 with its key harbor, now replaced the demolished capital as a nexus of trans-Mediterranean trade. In the aftermath of the war, Roman efforts to rebuild a colony of superannuated Roman legionaries on the strategically located site eventually failed, most notably an attempt a mere twenty-four years later by the radical reformer Gaius Gracchus.

Gracchus had naïvely envisioned a new Roman Carthage (*Colonia Junonia*) as the ideal second start for some six thousand impoverished Roman farmers and veterans displaced by the rising slave-worked vast estates (*latifundia*) that would soon turn Italy from an agrarian republic into the center of a corporate empire. The aristocratic Senate, however, wanted no such Gracchan agrarian scheme replacing its vanquished Carthaginian rivals. If the Senate had once feared a democratically run, radical Carthage, it surely was not going to replace a foreign revolutionary regime with a city founded by its own Roman redistributionist reformers, especially at such an ill-omened location. So the Senate withdrew most of its Roman subsidies and support for Colonia Junonia, and the colony withered away after a brief thirty years.[62]

There were never any Punic efforts to reoccupy the site, not only because it was forbidden by Rome, but also because there were too few scattered Carthaginians left alive to found any major city. Instead, some hundred years after the outbreak of the Third Punic War, as earlier mentioned, Julius Caesar between 49 and 44 poured money and manpower into the desolate site. In a richer, more expansive Roman Empire, the dictator launched a new Carthage that grew spectacularly ex nihilo. It was soon to become the second-largest Roman city in the West, as it took advantage of its proximity to Italy and the perennial natural bounty of climate, soil, water, and minerals that had once helped to explain the Punic miracle. Eventually, this Roman Carthage would become perhaps the fourth or fifth most important city of the entire empire, along with Rome, Alexandria, Ephesus, and Antioch. By AD 100 Roman Carthage was as least as large as its Punic predecessor. So occasionally the conquerors' replacement cities—Kostantiniyye and later Istanbul for Constantinople, Mexico City for Tenochtitlán—became wealthier and larger than the vanquished originals.

The Punic language continued to be spoken in the rural parts of what are now Libya, Tunisia, and Algeria. With the steady growth of the Roman presence in North Africa, a Latinized Punic alphabet appeared. Indeed, hundreds of Punic inscriptions date from the destruction of Carthage well into the late Roman period, suggesting that, for some, Punic, not Latin or indigenous Berber, for a while remained their first language.

Yet references in Latin literature following the Third Punic War to "Punic" do not necessarily equate to large numbers of survivors of the vaporization of the Carthaginian empire. "Punic" became a vague Latin generalization, often used in disparagement, for almost anyone of non-Italian pedigree who resided in North Africa in Roman times. In general, in the ancient world, subsequent residents in the environs of a vanquished city often self-identified with the renowned name of the vanished, without any indication of a continuity of culture.[63]

As a Romanized Berber, the early Christian theologian and church father Augustine of Hippo (AD 354–430) referred to Punic-only local speakers, Punic proper names, and the need for Latin translators for non-Latin local languages. The survival of these scattered Punic speakers for centuries is analogous to the continuity of the Nahuatl language in pockets of rural Mexico for some five hundred years after the destruction of Tenochtitlán—a language mostly long-orphaned from the vanquished culture of its birth.[64]

While Roman rule had later accommodated the Punic language and local Punic political institutions, such as the office of the *suffete* ("magistrate"), it had no official tolerance for Carthaginian child sacrifice. Nevertheless, the practice did continue in semisecret in North Africa for generations. Indeed *tophets*, or child sacrifice sanctuaries, are attested archaeologically throughout Punic history well into late Roman times. So both the public and private practice of killing young children to appease gods did not cease completely in the countryside with the destruction of the city in 146, but continued on a vastly smaller scale for centuries despite both Roman and Christian prohibitions.

As for the phases of habitation on the site itself, the destruction over a millennium of a sequence of cities called "Carthage" would become synonymous with the end of a succession of civilizations in North Africa: Roman Carthage (destroyed AD 439), Vandal Carthage (destroyed AD 534), and Byzantine Carthage (destroyed AD 695). In all these cases, sequential invaders and occupiers of Carthage's North African nearby realm were never completely successful in assimilating the majority of the native Numidians and Berbers.[65]

Both *Romanitas* ("Roman-ness") and Christianity, if not as relentlessly effective as a later Islam, were nonetheless creeds that could appeal to peoples quite distinct from either the religion's Jewish origins in the Middle East or Rome's birth in Italy. By the middle and late Roman Empire (AD 100 to 400), present-day Libya, Tunisia, and Algeria were some of the most dynamic centers of Westernized culture in the empire.

The south shore of the Mediterranean continued to grow in religious importance, as exemplified by the enormously influential Augustine, who was born in the Berber town of Thagaste in present-day Algeria, but became bishop of the old Roman colony of Hippo Regius, two hundred miles to the west of Carthage. Augustine died at seventy-five years of age, trapped inside Hippo by the besieging Vandal armies that had swept out of Eastern Europe into Roman North Africa and would establish a capital at Carthage after the storming of the Roman city (439).

Yet the tribal Vandals' African rule, which at one point extended to Sicily and southern Italy, was doomed after little more than a century, destroyed by the brilliant Byzantine general Belisarius, who retook Carthage in 533. He all but ended Vandal culture, initially a northern European incursion that had preyed on the decaying flesh of a dying fifth-century AD Roman Empire. After clearing the Vandals from North Africa, Belisarius beefed up old Roman forts and garrisons along the coast, and then retook Sicily and southern Italy for Constantinople. Yet despite the irredentist visions of the later Byzantine emperor Justinian (482–565), his dream of dispatching Belisarius to permanently restore a Roman North Africa would last only about 162 years.[66]

Islam finally proved a far more successful and viable occupying foreign presence. Not until the arrival of Muslim Arab conquerors and settlers in the seventh and eighth centuries did there emerge, through both proselytization and coercion, a religiously harmonious Tunisian population. It would gradually become culturally homogenized as well (although in the wider North African world of today, the Berbers are still not completely ethnically and linguistically assimilated).

More specifically, in 695 an Islamic army of the Umayyad Caliphate led by Hassan ibn al-Nu'man stormed Carthage and overran what might be called the Byzantines' Roman restoration of North Africa, centered on its capital at Carthage. The outnumbered Byzantines for a moment retook the city, but by 698 had found its occupation too costly, and soon retired for good from most of the continent. In response to their departure, Hassan leveled Byzantine Carthage—the old Roman Carthage—and once more tore down its buildings and walls. In the same way that Scipio 841 years earlier once feared that a spared city infrastructure might rebirth Punic culture, so too Hassan ibn al-Nu'man took no chances that a Christianized Carthage could anchor an anti-Islamic empire. So he ensured the choice site of ancient Carthage was once again made uninhabitable and rebuilt his new city of Tunis about ten miles away.

The subsequent Arab invasions and Islamization of North Africa ended European settlements for over a millennium, at least until the relatively brief and unsustainable nineteenth- and twentieth-century colonization efforts of Britain, France, and Italy that spread a Western veneer from Egypt to Morocco. That Western colonial presence in turn ended shortly after World War II during the period of global European decolonization and North African wars of independence.

Still, the romance and tug of a vanquished and near-mythical Carthage remain strong even in the modern Arab world. Just as Lebanon has often adopted "Phoenicianism"—accentuating its ancient Phoenician rather than strictly Arab heritage—so too has the contemporary Maghreb of North Africa adopted a nostalgic "Carthaginianism." The former long-standing dictator of Libya, General Muammar Gaddafi, named his fifth son Hannibal and commissioned a yacht called the *Phoenicia*. When Arab nationalist Habib Bourguiba became the first postcolonial president of Tunisia in 1957, he deliberately focused on reimagining Tunisians' hallowed heritage, not primarily as Muslims or Arabs, but rather as the indigenous Berber and Phoenician heirs of Punic Carthage.

Bourguiba's capital of Tunis (the name is derived from either a Berber or a Punic source) was transmogrified in official government narratives into the successor city of ancient Carthage (now a suburb of Tunis). The new Tunisian nation claimed a majestic North African civilizational pedigree, to remind the world that North Africans had once invaded and colonized Europe itself rather than perennially being colonized by it. Bourguiba's successor, Zine El-Abedine Ben Ali, constructed a "Carthageland" theme park and named the country's first commercial television channel Hannibal TV.[67]

In the next chapter, another great but declining civilization and its majestic walled city likewise sought to avoid the wrath of a rival, ascendant, and antithetical civilization. In their last weeks, the Byzantines too chose to resist from the vast and supposedly invincible walls of Constantinople, and were similarly forced to decide between resistance and oblivion, or submission and survival of a sort. Constantinople too hoped to find salvation in sworn allies, in third parties who shared an antipathy to Islam, in its own skilled diplomacy, in its appeals to its attackers for compassion and reason, and in its confidence that it was not as weak or its enemies as strong as generally believed. And so, as with Carthage, the civilization of Constantinople and the age it had created would cease to exist.

3

DEADLY DELUSIONS

The Fall of Constantinople and the
End of the Byzantines (Spring 1453)

We all live on the past, and through the past are destroyed.
(*Wir alle leben von der Vergangenheit
und werden durch die Vergangenheit zerstört.*)
—**Goethe,** *The Maxims and Reflections, Life and Character*

IGNORE THE TALK of civilizational decline. Forget the dreaded violence of the Janissaries. Discount the imperial domains devoured by the Ottoman juggernaut. Surely, a millennium of Byzantine civilization could not, would not, now vanish in a few days?

Look instead to the majesty of Hagia Sophia, a cathedral unrivaled in size and beauty in the world, or the walls of Theodosius, the most impressive urban fortifications ever raised. Gaze out at the city of Justinian, savior of Romanitas in the East, that had withstood countless past assaults, as it somehow must survive the latest—and last. Christendom whether East or West would rally to save its center.

Thus the emperor, his counselors, and the people of Constantinople in spring 1453 knew the incomprehensible realities of the huge Islamic army massed beneath their ancient walls and their pitiful force atop them, but their own mythologies of the eternal city were proving far stronger. So no one in the city, indeed in all of Europe, could imagine that the mystical fortress could now fall. What European minds knew was predetermined, their hearts insisted was unthinkable. So for far too long Constantinople had looked to its glorious past more than to the awful present, now manifested outside its walls.

The historian Edward Gibbon recorded that even in the last hours of Constantinople, as Ottomans poured over the ramparts and thousands of Byzantines flocked in terror into Hagia Sophia, the greatest church in Eastern Christendom, the doomed never gave up hope that their god would intervene, as he had for over a thousand years, to save his majestic earthly city. In one of his most moving passages in *The History of the Decline and Fall of the Roman Empire*, Gibbon chronicled the attempted escape of the Greeks targeted by pursuing Ottoman besiegers who, breaching the great walls of the city, were racing toward the cathedral in search of booty, slaves, and wealthy captives to ransom. And yet surely God would not allow his city to fall to Islam:

> From every part of the capital, they flowed into the church of St. Sophia: in the space of an hour, the sanctuary, the choir, the nave, the upper and lower galleries were filled with the priests, monks, and religious virgins; the doors were barred on the inside and they sought protection from the sacred dome. . . . Their confidence was founded on the prophecy of an enthusiast or imposter, that one day the Turks would enter Constantinople, and pursue the Romans as far as the column of Constantine in the square before St. Sophia; that this would be the term of their calamities; that an angel would descend from heaven, with a sword in his hand, and would deliver the empire, with that celestial weapon, to a poor man seated at the foot of the column. "Take this sword," would he say, "and avenge the people of the Lord." At these animating words, the Turks would instantly fly, and the virtuous Romans would drive them from the West, and from Anatolia, as far as the frontiers of Persia. . . . While they expected the descent of the tardy angel, the doors were broken with axes; and, as the Turks encountered no resistance, their bloodless hands were employed in selecting and securing the multitude of their prisoners. Youth, beauty, and the appearance of wealth attracted their choice.[1]

The entire fate of Constantinople had always hinged on the protection of just a few small and vulnerable sections of the Theodosian Walls, the massive rampart that guarded the land approaches to the capital and had never yet been penetrated. The two weakest areas were at a low spot in the Lykos riverbed at the center of the outer wall—the so-called *Mesoteikhion* ("the middle of the wall")—and at the section of the wall abutting the Blachernae Palace, a weak point similar to the Cadmea section of the wall of Thebes. It was at these sections of the wall where the sultan, as expected, on May 29 had massed his final attack and targeted the formidable Genoese contingents and the emperor Constantine and his guard.

Two successive waves, first forcibly conscripted Balkan Christians and then Turkish rank and file, had advanced against these soft spots. The outnumbered defenders on the walls easily slaughtered the first assault, and with some difficulty beat back the second. Even the third wave of elite Ottoman soldiers began to slow down under a shower of missiles, and stagnate beneath the towering ramparts. At that moment, it seemed to some of the Greek and Italian defenders that after almost eight weeks of fighting, the city would in fact finally hold. It was also rumored that the sultan's third wave was to be the last-ditch attempt of his fresh Janissaries to take the wall or go home. Mehmet was reportedly increasingly demoralized, especially by the presence of the ubiquitous gallant Italians on the walls, whom he thought had saved the city from what was supposed to be certain defeat.

Had the weeks-long siege, then, collapsed? Almost.

But then suddenly, Genoese leader Giovanni Giustiniani, the irreplaceable hero of the prior two-month defense, was severely wounded under a hail of Ottoman small-cannon fire and swarms of arrows. He was carried away from his critical post. Conflicting reports from contemporary sources suggest that Giustiniani was likely struck by a bullet from a primitive firearm (*sclopus*), or perhaps an arrow that entered his cuirass though an armhole.

Giustiniani may have been additionally wounded in his feet or legs. Yet for some strange reason, the Italian *condottiero* ("mercenary captain") was not treated for his wounds on the walls. Even more mysteriously, his mostly intact Genoese contingent ceased its heretofore successful resistance, just hours away from beating off the last thrust of the sultan. Even worse still, almost all of the Genoese panicked at the sight of their severely wounded captain and obeyed his orders to carry him far from the fray. That decision entailed the abandonment of their key positions at the very focus of the final Ottoman attack. Apparently, the maddened Genoese felt that without their famed leader on the walls the city would be lost, and so they were hoping to find safety for themselves in their ships in the harbor and a sea escape out the Dardanelles. Whatever the cause of the mass flight at that moment, the calamity was compounded by the final push of the crack Janissaries who swarmed the now vacated section of the ramparts. For the first time in weeks, the Ottomans easily scaled it with their ladders.

This general collapse of the defenses on the land walls that followed seemed as much psychological as physical, and yet it rippled throughout the entire city. Contemporaries rightly or wrongly felt the serious wounding of just one man caused the withdrawal of hundreds, whose flight in turn collapsed the resistance of thousands— and the end of over a millennium of Byzantine civilization in the East. Yet the even stouter and taller inner walls were certainly still defensible. But in their frenzy to abandon the outer ramparts, the crazed defenders tried to escape piecemeal across the intervening open spaces or the pavilion between the walls, making their haphazard way through the massive gates of the inner walls into the city to reach their families. Unfortunately, the Greeks formed no coherent rear guard. Much less was there a systematic and collective effort of the defenders to march in order, close the gates behind them, and reconstitute their defenses. Instead, in the utter chaos individual fighters trampled each other to reach the supposed protection of the inner wall—or more likely to flee well beyond it to the other side of the city in hopes of finding a galley docked in the Golden Horn.

The Ottoman firebrand Zaganos, who was instrumental in persuading Mehmet not to give up the siege, reportedly had led this final successful assault. As word went out that the city was all but lost, hundreds of Ottoman banners were seen raised from the walls and towers. In turn, once the sultan saw Turkish flags atop the city, he ordered his entire army to swarm up the ladders of the Janissaries and on into the vast expanse of the now defenseless city itself.

Later, rumor arose that the emperor Constantine tore off his imperial insignia, charged the incoming horde, and was killed along with the last contingents of Byzantine guards. His head was cut off and brought to the sultan as a trophy. So ended the mystical city and the empire it had created.

Constantinople fell to Ottoman attackers under Sultan Mehmet II on the afternoon of Tuesday, May 29, 1453, some 1,123 years after the Byzantine capital's founding. The fortress city had been birthed in 330, during the crisis years of the Roman Empire. The new city had been fully populated within just six years by its founder, the Roman emperor Constantine the Great.[2]

Somehow, the beleaguered Eastern Romans, who not until the nineteenth century would be commonly renamed in Western historiography as "Byzantines," had lasted some 977 years after the capture of Rome and the demise of its Western empire. That baffling fact has prompted endless speculations over how the Greek-speaking half of the empire survived for a near-millennium when its original Latinate core in the West had collapsed.[3]

An obvious theme was Eastern unity versus Western fragmentation. Those in the predominantly Greek-speaking East gradually developed a cohesive national character when such accord was disintegrating in the West. Greeks in Constantinople and its eastern imperial domains shared a tripartite identity. First, they were foremost *Romaioi*, or proud emissaries of the true Roman Empire, the only ones left after the late fifth-century disintegration of the West. Second, they were proud speakers of the Greek language and inheritors and advocates of Hellenism, the brilliance and achievements of classical Greece. Third, they saw themselves as the true Christians, even before the Great Schism of 1054, when Greek Orthodoxy formally broke with Roman Catholicism, the climax of a division as old as the 400s, beginning with Eastern disagreements over Augustinian theology and papal supremacy.[4]

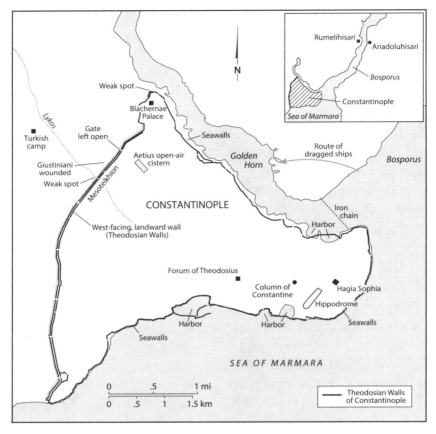

Constantinople

But more specifically, given the equally hostile landscape of Asia, what had the Eastern empire done that the Western could not? And what had changed a millennium later by 1453? How had the once indomitable East been reduced to seeking salvation from a resurgent West that for centuries had struggled to arise from the detritus of the Western Roman Empire? Scholars, mostly from Western Europe and the United States, long attributed the Byzantines' longevity to geography and Constantinople's brilliant structural adaptations to its natural environs. Bryan Ward-Perkins, one of the most gifted recent historians of Rome's fall, characterized the paradox in almost reductionist geographical fashion:

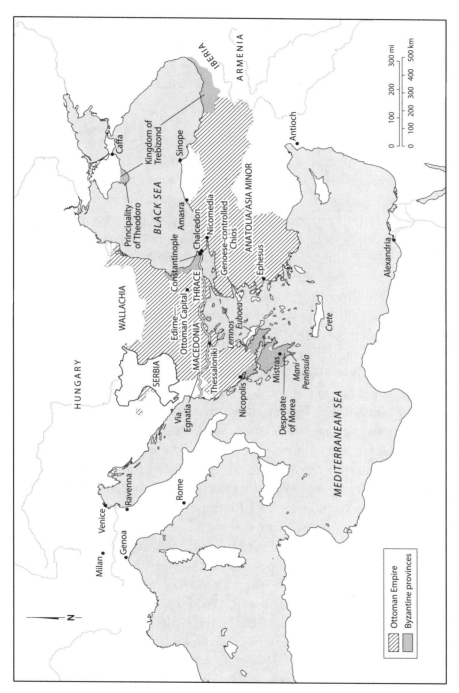

The Byzantine and Ottoman Empires in the Fifteenth Century

HUNGARY

WALLACHIA

SERBIA

Milan

Genoa

Venice

Ravenna

Rome

Via Egnatia

Nicopolis

Thessaloniki

MACEDONIA

THRACE

Edirne
Ottoman Capital

Constantinople

Lemnos

Euboea

Mistras
Mani Peninsula

Despotate of Morea

Crete

MEDITERRANEAN SEA

Principality of Theodoro

Caffa

BLACK SEA

Kingdom of Trebizond

Sinope

Amasra

Amasra

Chalcedon

Nicomedia

Genoese-controlled Chios

Ephesus

ANATOLIA/ASIA MINOR

IBERIA

ARMENIA

Antioch

Alexandria

Ottoman Empire

Byzantine provinces

N

0   100   200   300 mi
0 100 200 300 400 500 km

The decisive factor that weighed in favor of the East was not the greater power of its armies and their consequent greater success in battle, but a single chance of geography—a thin band of sea (the Bosporus, Sea of Marmara, and Dardanelles), in places less than 700 meters wide, that separates Asia from Europe.[5]

Ward-Perkins's "thin band of sea" was not everywhere so narrow, given the vast expanses of the Black Sea and Sea of Marmara. But what he meant more specifically was that the northern maritime doorway into the former, the Bosporus strait, and the southern hallway into the latter, the Hellespont or Dardanelles passage, were constricted bottlenecks where the centrally positioned city's navy could block sea raiders, pirates, and enemy fleets. Both straits—one protecting the city from the north, the other from the south—were impediments to invading armies and could be defended by land far more effectively than the Western empire's exposed capitals (Rome, then Milan, then Ravenna) could keep out its northern European tribal enemies of the fifth century. In this regard, the failure of Britain's massive World War I amphibious landing at Gallipoli in 1915–1916 remains a modern reminder of the near impossibility of landing in the Dardanelles with the intent to march on to Constantinople.

Constantinople was also better positioned overall for survival than was the far older Rome. Of course, Rome's central position in Italy, with a port on the Tyrrhenian Sea, suited the earlier Italian republic, with its largely West Mediterranean concerns, far better than it would serve the later vast Roman imperial domain of some one million square miles of territory and seventy million people, largely concentrated in the East. In contrast, Constantinople far more effectively worked as a pivotal city between East and West, at least initially when it had the wherewithal to deter a variety of enemies in Anatolia and the Balkans. Rarely did invasions aimed at the capital arrive simultaneously from several directions, in part also due to the adroit realist diplomacy and sophisticated military of Constantinople. The city for centuries was prepared to send its armies and navies from east to west and vice versa in order to meet single-front threats.

Moreover, the wandering tribes of Central and Eastern Europe were not sea peoples. They found it difficult to navigate Byzantine waters to cross into the eastern Asiatic realm. Likewise, invaders from the east had first to achieve maritime supremacy, if not storm Constantinople itself, to descend into the European part of the empire.

Just as importantly, the city was also situated on the nexus of the two great ancient roads that connected the Roman west with its eastern provinces. Constantinople was the last stop on the seven-hundred-mile Via Egnatia that led westward to the Adriatic Coast via Thessaloniki. And in Asia Minor, the city was the starting point of the main route through Anatolia linking Chalcedon and Nicomedia, important commercial centers of the empire.

Economically, by 330 the Eastern Roman Empire had grown far more intertwined with the natural wealth of Asia and Egypt than had Rome. Its new capital near the Bosporus was more suitably located to capitalize on East-West trade over both land and sea. By the late imperial period, the wealthiest provinces of the old empire were not Spain or Gaul, but rather Asia Minor, Egypt, and Syria; and Constantinople was far better positioned than Rome to trade with and dominate all their opulent cities. It was roughly 500 miles closer than Rome to either Alexandria or Ephesus, some 650 miles closer to Antioch, and 300 miles closer to Thessaloniki. Even more importantly, until the beginning of transatlantic navigation, much of the western trade from what is now Russia, Persia, and points farther east found its way through the Black Sea to Constantinople. The accruing profits from these nodes of commercial wealth would allow Constantinople not just to field better armies and build secure forts and garrisons, but to pay off and divide potential enemies through its near limitless largesse.[6]

Among ancient historians and religious figures, East and West, there was also a contemporary debate in the fifth and sixth centuries over why Constantinople had thrived while Rome, the center of the empire, suffered constant attacks until finally imploding—sacked in 410 by Visigoths under Alaric, in 455 by the Vandal king Gaiseric, and a final time in 472 by Ricimer's Germanic coalition.

Ecclesiastical historians claimed that paganism and religious schisms had divided and weakened Western Roman military cohesion and resolve. By contrast, the East solidified more quickly and readily into a monolithic state religion and undivided military. The result was a more confident, unified Christian East that believed its piety and orthodoxy had led to earthly successes and galvanized its armed forces. That confidence in turn strengthened further religiosity.

Indeed, one of the key differences between Eastern and Western Christendom was precisely the Byzantines' stronger fusion of the state with the church, in contrast with the West. There a multiplicity of warring kingdoms competed for the favors of an occasionally quasi-deified pope. Or as Anthony, the Patriarch of Constantinople, in a 1393 letter put it to Basil I, grand prince of Moscow:

> My son, it is not possible for Christians to have a Church and not have an empire. Church and empire have a great unity and community. It is not possible for them to be separated from one another. For the holy emperor is not as other rulers and the governors of other regions are.[7]

Such natural, cultural, and religious advantages may explain why Byzantium's capital remained fixed at Constantinople for over a millennium. In contrast, by later imperial times Western emperors had moved the capital in 286 from Rome to Mediolanum (Milan), to Constantinople in 330, and then again in 402 to Ravenna. Yet the West found it impossible to sustain an effective capital when these two substitutes in Italy were no longer the economically or culturally preeminent cities of the empire.

For some idea of the relative permanence of Byzantium and its capital at Constantinople, moderns might reflect that the city and empire survived over four and a half times longer than the current lifespan of the United States. In part, such longevity was also due to intangibles such as the majesty, beauty, and even mystique of Constantine's famous city on the Bosporus, and the foundational stability of its government and codified set of laws. Indeed, everything about imperial Constantinople in its first centuries exuded near-celestial grandeur; it earned a millennium of envy mixed with occasional hatred from its later Western peers, while being an object of desire, emulation, and dreams of conquest for its Eastern enemies.

By late Roman antiquity, Hellenic learning, anchored in Greece, Egypt, and Asia Minor, had reasserted its scientific, mathematical, and engineering superiority over its Latin counterpart. Throughout the late Roman Republic and Empire, the giants of Roman applied and theoretical science—such as Galen (Ephesus), Hero (Alexandria), Posidonius (Apamea, Syria), Ptolemy (Alexandria), and Theon (Alexandria)—wrote in Greek and were born and usually worked outside of Rome.[8]

Byzantium adroitly capitalized on this legacy, and for a millennium established itself as the preeminent scientific research center of the Mediterranean world. In terms of military technology, vital to the survival of the empire, the traditions of Hellenic engineering and science produced weaponry such as Greek fire, pressurized flamethrowers, counterweight trebuchets, and ceramic fire grenades. Such technology became essential to ensure military parity for an empire usually vastly outnumbered by its many enemies.

Under its fabled emperor Justinian the Great (482–565), Constantinople had continued to codify Roman law that would become the foundation of all later European jurisprudence, and created a haven for scholarship, research, and applied science. Architecturally, Anthemius of Tralles and Isidore of Miletus applied their mathematical genius to design the great cathedral of Hagia Sophia that dwarfed all contemporary religious buildings. In addition, not all of Byzantium's later scientific superiority was due to its Hellenic resonance and inheritance. The city's position as an East-West gateway had by the eighth century also made it a rich depository of some key Islamic and Jewish translations of lost Greek works in ways not true of either its Eastern enemies or Western rivals.[9]

The city itself in the era of Justinian's near-four-decade rule (527–565) had grown to well over five hundred thousand residents. It was larger than any metropolis of the then vanquished Western Roman Empire. And by the twelfth century the city may have exceeded eight hundred thousand residents. Constantinople soon became to the ancient world what London was to the early nineteenth century, or New York to the twentieth in terms of wealth, population, and influence. The urban area alone covered some thirty-five hundred acres—about the size of old Rome within the Aurelian Walls. Hagia Sophia, the massive cathedral of the Holy Wisdom, finished by Justinian in 537, would remain the world's largest church for a thousand years until the construction of the sixteenth-century Cathedral of Saint Mary of the See in Seville, Spain. It still contains the second-largest brick dome in existence. And the forum of Theodosius was the most expansive municipal square in the ancient world.

The outdoor hippodrome was likewise the greatest racetrack of its kind, at its height seating more than eighty thousand (thirty thousand more than the Colosseum at Rome), and often serving as a political rallying arena. The cisterns of the city—well over two hundred—allowed a stored water reserve unmatched by any urban areas of the preindustrial world. One of the largest, the Aetius open-air cistern (currently the site of a soccer field), held over forty million gallons of potable water, most of it transported by a network of some 350 miles of aqueducts, ranging as far as 90 miles away in Thrace.[10]

Constantinople was even more famous for its magnificent fortifications that brilliantly had been fitted to the city's natural contours. Triangular in shape, the layout of the capital was protected on two sides by formidable seawalls, in some places nearly embedded into cliffs—to the east above the legendary estuary of the Golden Horn, and to the south facing the vast Sea of Marmara. Even to attempt an attack here required unquestioned naval superiority, which was impossible for any enemy for most of the life of the city, at least until the detour of the Fourth Crusade when Western European Venetians, who dominated the sea, finally breached a small section of the seawall to enter from the Golden Horn.[11]

The third side, protected by the city's west-facing landward wall of some three and a half miles, was in theory the place most vulnerable to attack, and therefore the most impressively fortified section of the entire thirteen-mile city circuit. Yet *never* were these so-called Theodosian Walls permanently breached by attackers until the last day of the city's life. Indeed, there was no other example in ancient or modern fortifications of such a massive tripartite bulwark: moat and mound, pavilion and outer wall, and a second pavilion and inner wall.[12]

After the reconstruction and expansion of the Constantinian circuit by the emperor Theodosius II (401–450), most subsequent invaders for a near millennium conceded that a landward attack against the city was futile, even though the alternative of storming the city's cliffs and single high seawall above them was nearly as impossible, at least if the fortifications were adequately manned and maintained.

The Theodosian land walls were not just invulnerable, but had been designed to become for invaders lethal killing zones of entrapment. They were stone snares for any attackers foolish enough to be lured in to assault the city by land. Indeed, the fortifications were conceived as an intricate, unified system in which outer and inner walls, terraces, towers and a moat conspired to enmesh, paralyze, and destroy would-be besiegers. Should the moat and outer wall be crossed, the defenders were trained how to retreat in order from the outer wall through the intervening pavilion to the gates of the inner wall, without allowing entry to a pursuing enemy.[13]

The inner wall alone was reinforced by ninety-six towers; in some sections these turrets rose more than sixty feet. These ramparts on the walls were nearly fifteen feet thick, with limestone blocks and interiors filled by brick, and reached in many places forty feet above the level of the city.

The less imposing outer wall was still impressive in its own right—six to eight feet in width and in some places more than twenty-five to thirty feet high. Beneath it, there was yet another outer terrace of stone pavement whose size allowed no cover for the attackers, while serving as a line of retreat or advance for troops who had sortied from a first line of walled defense beyond the outer wall. Finally, the outer moat, at some points some seventy feet wide and twenty-three feet deep, was itself protected on the far bank by a wide berm, with a short wall on its inner side. Until the final death throes of the city, it was no wonder that no attacker had ever successfully breached the outer or inner walls.[14]

Yet there were two vulnerabilities inherent in these brilliantly designed fortifications. First, such a complex required constant maintenance, especially along the several gates of the land wall. But the investment involved in upkeep proved at times almost financially impossible for a beleaguered late empire. Second, to work as designed, the walls required sufficient defenders to man simultaneously both the higher inner wall and the lower outer wall. In 1453, however, prior earthquakes, assaults, and natural aging of the millennium-old stones had resulted in fissures that required more, not fewer defenders. Envision the Byzantines' fifteenth-century capital of Constantinople as akin to an English heir of limited resources who inherited a majestic but aging mansion, but without the necessary capital and income to maintain properly its vastness.

A dearth of manpower prompted the city's scarce defenders to choose between either positioning limited forces on the smaller outer wall to stop all attackers, or ceding to the enemy the moat and outer wall in hopes of concentrating defenders on the higher, more defensible inner wall—the last fortification between the enemy and the people of the city.

As we shall see, Constantine XI and his Genoese and Venetian allies may have understandably wished to grant no entrance or protective cover at all to the Ottomans by manning in most places only the outer wall. Or they preferred to keep the option open of conducting sorties from the outer wall opposite the Turkish camps. But in hindsight it would have proven perhaps wiser to begin by marshaling the limited number of troops on the more defensible and higher inner wall. One eyewitness to the siege, Leonardo of Chios, certainly felt it had been a mistake to post the defenders on the outer wall. He alleged the blunder was due to the emperors' laxity in not repairing and maintaining the more impressive inner rampart, or an undue confidence in the outer-wall defenses with which the Byzantines had successfully repelled an earlier Ottoman siege in 1422. That effective resistance three decades earlier may have somehow misled the later defenders into thinking that such a successful defense could be replicated in 1453, with even fewer resources against a greater number of attackers.[15]

As the Western empire collapsed, the Eastern Romans realized that if their capital city were to endure, then so too would its empire. The vastness of the walls, like the iconic buildings of the city itself, was designed to signal to friends and allies that Constantinople was an enduring symbol of Romanitas, both secular and religious, and thus forever worth defending. Given the final destruction of Constantinople, it is often common to refer to Byzantium and decline as if they were synonymous. But no civilization shows symptoms of "decline" at its inception, much less "declines" for over a millennium. Nor was Constantinople's "Byzantine" bureaucracy any more convoluted, corrupt, or conspiratorial than contemporary equivalents in the West.

"Byzantine" as a pejorative adjective seems to have risen mostly in modern twentieth-century English-language usage. It perhaps drew on the general caricatures and stereotypes of the Byzantines earlier in the histories of Edward Gibbon ("a tedious and uniform tale of misery and monotony") and the monumental German philosopher Georg Hegel ("a thousand-year-long series of uninterrupted crimes, weaknesses, basenesses, and lack of character, a most repulsive and consequently a most uninteresting picture"). Both may have overly relied on the widely read and influential sixth-century *Secret History* of Procopius, a lurid chronicle of sexual deviance and material excess at Justinian's court. But the empire's stereotypical "Byzantine" behavior more likely reflects the need for intrigue, espionage, stealth, and conspiracies as adjuncts to force, given that eventually Constantinople simply did not have the manpower or wealth to defeat decisively and permanently a host of hostile and powerful enemies. It is best then to envision Byzantine civilization as a brilliantly adoptive system of religious governance whose dynamic culture and civilization so often nullified the vast numbers of a series of existential challengers.[16]

More specifically, Constantinople faced three constant vulnerabilities that it struggled to overcome: religious disunity with the Catholic West; serial conflict with Islamic powers; and the logistical and public health difficulties of managing an enormous city.

After the Great Schism of 1054 and for the next four hundred years, Byzantine and Western Christians were never able permanently to reunite, at least in the formal sense of a union of government grandees and religious elites. Nor in their separation could East and West at least permanently agree to an alliance of need against the rising common enemy of Islam. That religious schism grew inseparable from the political realm. Such discord helps explain both the later catastrophe of the Fourth Crusade (1204), and the subsequent disastrous Frankish and Venetian hijacking of vast swaths of the Byzantine empire.

In some regions of the lost realm, the ensuing *Frankokratia* and *Venetokratia* spanned nearly six centuries of Western European absorption of rich Byzantine provinces, most prominently by the Franks and Venetians. The East-West split continued to be expressed in relative Western indifference to Constantinople's growing fifteenth-century vulnerabilities to the Ottoman juggernaut. The tension illustrates the lack of gratitude for both Byzantium's role as a shield against the East and its seminal influence on the budding Renaissance, as hundreds of Greek scholars with thousands of texts sought refuge in Italy from the incoming Ottoman wave. That divide helps to explain why thousands of Christian Europeans were in the sultan's besieging force of 1453—sometimes because they were coerced as subjects of the sultans, or were opportunists who had capitalized on the divide, but also often due to their own suspicions of Orthodoxy. Only in the last months before the siege were there frantic but ultimately impotent efforts to unite the Eastern and Western Christian churches to ensure aid from the West and marshal a common defense. If in theory there was an agreement of unification, in fact few abided by it and fewer sent help to the beleaguered.[17]

In addition, after the traumatic seventh-century loss of the Byzantine Levant, Maghreb, and Egypt to various Muslim forces, the Byzantines were mired in a near-constant cycle of war, reprieve, truce, and renewed hostility with Islamic regimes. The nonstop fighting was characterized both by battles outside the very walls of Constantinople, and theater conflicts in distant Anatolia, Armenia, the Balkans, and the Middle East. Given the proselytizing success and popular growth of Islam, and the Byzantines' own demographic disadvantages, Constantinople at best learned to divide its Islamic enemies to mitigate these Eastern threats. But it was never able to neutralize them, at least in the way it had dealt with dangerous and warlike earlier Persian and Vandal enemies.

The East remained dangerous to the Byzantine Empire for a millennium, but after the seventh century, Islam became a force multiplier of the empire's intrinsic vulnerabilities. This constant vigilance against a dynamic and ecumenical religion that could unite even disparate enemies explains why so much of Byzantine labor and capital became invested in recruitment and deployment of troops, in military technology, fortification, and in hiring mercenaries—and why in the last two hundred years of the city's life it lost tribute-paying productive croplands and mercantile centers to the Ottomans in Anatolia, the Aegean, and Eastern Europe. The Islamic challenge had grown far more dangerous in the tenth to twelfth centuries with the arrival of Seljuk Turkish tribes in Anatolia itself, given that the prior Islamic invasions had been anchored not in the Byzantine hinterlands but rather more distantly in the Arab Middle East and Maghreb.[18]

If Westerners could boast that the European Renaissance emerged from the post-Roman dark and medieval ages to outpace the brilliance of a supposedly fossilized and continuous thousand-year Constantinople, the Byzantines might have retorted that after the seventh century their endless work in retarding Islamic imperialism provided Europe some security for its reawakening after the calamity of Rome's fall.

Finally, at critical junctures in the long history of Byzantium, the empire contracted to become not much larger than the city and its suburbs, even if only temporarily when an enemy incursion broke through border defenses and approached the Theodosian Walls. At such times the number of residents and refugees inside the walls may have soared to nearly a million people. Even in peacetime, the city's huge population depended on massive imports of grain from all over the empire, while city officials always worried about the ability and safety of its aqueducts and cisterns, vast as the latter were, to ensure sufficient potable water.

Constantinople's opportune location as a nexus of sea and land travel and commerce between Asia and Europe nevertheless had drawbacks in terms of public health. The cosmopolitan nature of its multiethnic merchants, traders, and shippers acted as a sort of municipal petri dish, ensuring the city was eventually vulnerable to even distant outbreaks of deadly diseases in a way perhaps less true of its many enemies.

The great bubonic plague of Justinian (541–549) was believed by contemporaries to have swept in on grain ships from Egypt, and perhaps also arrived simultaneously with traders from Central Asia via the Black Sea. The flea-transmitted disease may have eventually killed 40 percent of the Byzantine population. And the death toll tragically rose at precisely the moment when the emperor Justinian, who himself nearly died of the plague, was well on his way to reestablishing the Western Empire by retaking the Maghreb, Sicily, and much of Italy through three decades of warring under his masterful generals Belisarius and Narses. The pandemic, which may have peaked at killing five to ten thousand a day in Constantinople, probably cost the manpower-short empire over a million lives. The pandemic abruptly curtailed the dream of reclaiming the lost Western provinces of the Roman Empire in modern-day France and Spain, given that the disease swept through the city, the countryside, and Byzantine armies in the field.[19]

Even more grievous was a series of outbreaks that returned to a much diminished city eight hundred years later in 1347, during an era of catastrophic Western European losses to the Black Death. The plague once again over a few years likely killed over half of Constantinople's population. This time around, the city never recovered its former size. At least ten subsequent waves of bubonic plague over the next decades rippled throughout the empire, hitting especially hard Byzantine Thessaloniki, the islands of Lemnos, Euboea, and Crete, as well as Trebizond and areas of the Peloponnese.[20]

Of course, pandemics also hurt the enemies of Byzantium. But what made the outbreaks particularly devastating to the Byzantines in comparison to the Ottomans and others was their far smaller, more vulnerable population base, their reliance on far-flung maritime trade that facilitated constant reinfections, and their large and cramped cities such as Constantinople and Thessaloniki. The cities of Turkish Anatolia were mostly smaller than their European counterparts, the populations more rural, and their lands less visited by global travelers and merchants.

By the time Sultan Mehmet II's besiegers arrived in early April 1453, the once bustling city of a half million had dwindled to a mere fifty thousand or so residents. The reduction was in part due to the prior century's plague losses and the mass exodus of terrified citizens to the perceived safety of the distant countryside, or westward to the Mediterranean islands and Europe. Most Greeks remaining in those outlands lost to Ottoman rule either had forcibly been converted to Islam, or were living as second-class Orthodox residents in Muslim Anatolia, or had intermarried among the Turkish population and become fully assimilated, at least linguistically and religiously.[21]

For much of the Byzantine Empire's existence, all these chronic challenges to the Byzantines were manageable and usually not occurring simultaneously. But by the city's last decades, the dangers were lethally coalescing, and multiplied even further by a series of decades-long dynastic civil wars in the early fourteenth century. Much of Byzantium's recent history prior to 1453 comprised religious and political dissension, occasional betrayal or attacks by the West, steady erosion of both European and Asian imperial territory, and a somewhat lonely confrontation with a maturing and robust Ottomanism.[22]

Given such dangers and limited resources, the empire's millennium of survival hinged on pragmatic Byzantine grand strategy. Constantinople accepted that enemies usually had far greater manpower reserves and were more intent on destroying the Byzantines than the latter were on starting wars with their enemies. Whatever its technological brilliance and excellence of commanders, ultimately the empire's survival hinged on its adroit diplomacy. Byzantium carefully avoided long campaigns of attrition. It maintained deterrence by constant preemptive patrolling and the avoidance of full mobilizations.[23]

Byzantine realpolitik was characterized by ensuring above all the safety of the iconic capital by keeping the seawall, along with the complex Theodosian land wall, repaired and adequately manned, especially in the thirteenth and fourteenth centuries as the borders of the empire collapsed to nearly the immediate environs of the city. Whenever possible, endless wars were avoided through the habit of constantly shifting alliances without losing deterrence. Optional military engagements with little chance of a decisive result were avoided. The military was imbued with the idea that it was the tool of God and the Church, surrounded by enemies of different faiths and non-Greek heritages, and used mostly to fend off various infidels bent on wiping out a powerful Western Christian empire in Asia Minor and Syria.[24]

Additionally, the Byzantines ingeniously arranged dynastic marriages with both hostile and friendly Anatolian and Balkan monarchies. Indeed, the twice widowed Constantine XI desperately sought a third opportune dynastic union in the years leading up to the siege. Otherwise, they counted on bribes and tribute to deter their more powerful enemies. Despite Byzantium's role as a cultural and religious outpost of Romanitas and Christianity, there were no such things as permanent Byzantine friends and enemies—only transient imperial interests. To avoid war on unfavorable terms, Constantinople was perfectly willing to temporarily negotiate and ally with Arabs, Bulgars, Genoese, Ottomans, Persians, Rus, Serbians, and Venetians in a manner that saw former friends become sudden enemies and vice versa.

Along with Byzantium's diplomatic skills, not since the army of Julius Caesar had an ancient military fielded such diverse, well-trained, and highly specialized forces. A number of detailed Byzantine military handbooks survive detailing armament, operational theory, recruitment, and logistics. What emerges from these treatises and from the narratives of contemporary historians is a picture of a highly trained rapid-response force of specialized contingents. The sixth-century *Strategikon* of the emperor Maurice (491–518), and its tenth-century adaptation and expansion in the *Tactica* of the emperor Leo VI (895–908), as well as dozens of other handbooks—often based on Greek military strategists of the Roman imperial period such as Aelian, Arrian, and Onasander—reveal a scientific approach to war, emphasizing state-of-the-art weaponry, strict discipline, and logistics to offset chronic manpower disadvantages and campaigning often distant from the capital.[25]

The core of the Byzantine military in its prime had always been its heavy infantry, an inheritance from both Hellenic hoplite and Roman legionary traditions. Foot soldiers were equipped with spears of some ten feet or more, secondary swords, heavy mail armor, and kite- or almond-shaped wooden shields. They were often arranged in masses and advanced as a neophalanx, again as reflected in Byzantine manuals derived from Hellenistic and Roman tacticians writing about the challenges of ancient Macedonian phalangites. They were often protected on the flanks by light-armed skirmishers, both javelin throwers and bowmen, along with cavalry contingents, both light and heavy.

Byzantine heavy cavalry later evolved into true cataphracts that often invoked terror among the empire's enemies. These heavily armored lancers rode larger warhorses protected with thick cloth armor. As shock troops they were sent in to exploit fissures in the enemy line or outflank an opposing battle line. Often cataphracts charged less well-equipped enemies head on and, if protected on the flanks, were unstoppable when mowing down retreating enemies. In contrast, the light cavalry was used as skirmishers and in pursuit of the defeated. They usually wore lighter chain mail and were armed with javelins, swords, axes, or bows. In Anatolia the Byzantines enlisted *akritoi*, usually Greeks living along the empire's border, who as militia would join the regular army in regional campaigns as lightly armed skirmishers, outfitted with bows and javelins.[26]

––––––––––

The vanguards of the enemy that ultimately defeated the Byzantines appeared on their horizon in the eleventh century, with the advance of Turkish tribes into Anatolia. The first of these Turkish migrants were the Seljuks, who inflicted an iconic and devastating defeat on the Byzantines at the battle of Manzikert (1071) in eastern present-day Turkey. The catastrophe saw the capture of the emperor Romanos IV, the general collapse of an entire Byzantine army, an ensuing Byzantine civil war, and the eventual loss of much of Anatolia.

The Seljuks originally had been one of many nomadic Islamic tribes of Central Asia who beginning in that century swept into Anatolia, drove out Arab-controlled dynasties, and soon after Manzikert began expropriating much of the old Byzantine realm in Asia Minor and the Middle East—at least until their absorption by and evolution into the even more formidable kindred Ottoman Turks of the thirteenth century.

The Ottomans marked a challenge to Byzantine power not seen in prior centuries, since they were able to unite disparate enemies of Constantinople under their growing Islamic suzerainty, while successfully drawing on European arms and technology in a way past Eastern enemies had not. The Ottoman sultans, perhaps even more pragmatic than the later Byzantine emperors, adopted ecumenical policies of allowing subjugated Christians and Jews to live relatively safely under Islamic laws—*if* they accepted an inferior social status, greater taxation, and subjection to the levies of the *devshirme* (forced conscription of Christian youth) and harem. It was Byzantium's misfortune to be suffering from the sack of the Fourth Crusade, the plague, and dynastic civil wars at precisely the time of the growing challenge of the Ottomans and their effort to absorb most of what was left of its imperial territory in Anatolia.[27]

By the 1200s the Byzantines were facing existential threats from the Ottomans well beyond those posed earlier by Turkish tribes and the Arab Muslim armies. Increasingly, Ottomans were annexing Byzantine territory in the Balkans, resulting in at least half of their subject population now being composed of conquered Christian Greeks—along with their rich farmlands. The relationship of the Ottomans with their supposed archenemy eventually became somewhat ambiguous, as the Ottomans often borrowed Byzantine ship designs, and, via Constantinople, Western metallurgy, ballistics, and engineering. The Turks were even granted mercantile enclaves inside Constantinople to take advantage of the city's ties with Italian traders.

In the last two centuries before the conquest of the city, the East-West, Muslim-Christian dichotomy somehow became even more complicated. Many conquered Christian communities in the Levant and Anatolia claimed there was less-burdensome government and lower taxes under the sultan than under the old emperors. Some Jews may have felt less persecuted in Ottoman communities than in Christian-controlled ones. Indeed, many Jewish refugees from Spain during the Inquisition would later flee to Islamic Constantinople. Genoese and Venetians enjoyed concessions in the city proper and its suburbs across the Golden Horn from both Ottomans and Byzantines, and seemed almost to favor the former over the latter.

Like the Arabs far earlier, the fourteenth- and fifteenth-century Ottomans remained fixated on Constantinople, or what they termed the "red apple," the final goal of Asian conquests. They assumed they were fated at the opportune time to inherit the famous city, whose transliterated Greek name they would keep until 1923. The city's beauty and history mesmerized the Ottomans even as they grew irate that such a purportedly weak people as the late Byzantines should continue to enjoy such a capital.

The father of Mehmet the Conqueror, Murad II, in 1422 had given up storming Constantinople after a costly siege, once dynastic rivals threatened to challenge his rule. Moreover, Murad assessed that Constantinople was becoming more and more dependent on the Ottomans, yet remained more or less impregnable. Rather than stage another siege, he adopted a strategic policy of steady strangulation. In a cost-benefit analysis, Murad wagered that this compromised window on the West brought profit to the Ottoman Empire, was a treasured conduit of scientific expertise, and no longer posed a serious roadblock to the steady expansion of an Islamic empire westward. Thus, its future capture, at a date suitable to the Ottomans, was supposedly assured by the city's steady decline.

Throughout the fifteenth century, a common theme within Christendom was the haunting fear of the Turk, a terror that transcended all other formidable enemies in Europe and Asia. Part of the apprehension is easily explicable by the rapid conquests of the Ottomans, and their apparent intent to conquer and convert all of Eastern Europe as a prelude to absorbing large swaths of current Central and Western Europe as well. But more importantly, the Ottomans, in battle and especially after victory, were seen as notoriously cruel—although many historians point out that in 1453 they were not necessarily any more savage than were the victorious Christian Franks and Venetians who had sacked Constantinople in 1204 during the misadventure of the Fourth Crusade.

Nonetheless, the horrific defeat of Western Crusaders at Nicopolis in 1396, and subsequent humiliating Crusader losses at Varna (1444) and at the second battle of Kosovo (1448), cost the Europeans anywhere between 45,000 and 60,000 dead. These consecutive disasters ended assumptions that polyglot European Crusaders still possessed the religious unity, ethnic cohesiveness, superior technology, and sheer manpower to mount a sustained rollback of the Ottoman advance. After the infamous disaster at Nicopolis, almost all the captured Europeans were systematically beheaded, mutilated, or died in forced marches back to Ottoman territory. These three humiliating defeats, the horrific losses incurred during the actual battles, and the savage treatment of prisoners and stragglers traumatized Europeans, and mostly ended outright the centuries-old idea of further serious crusading—on the eve of the siege of Constantinople.[28]

Yet it was not just the cruelty and ferocity of the Ottomans that made them objects of loathing and fright in the minds of their Christian enemies. At least part of the fear was due to various Ottoman institutions that seemed entirely alien to the Europeans, if not surreal—and that aimed at instilling horror as a force multiplier of military prowess. Indeed, the proverbial Turk made the same nightmarish impression on Crusaders that Aztec religious sacrifice and ceremonial dismemberment would later have on the otherwise unshakeable Spanish conquistadors.

Take the devshirme, the institution of forcibly drafting into Ottoman diplomatic and military service the young children (ages six to fourteen) of conquered Christians, mostly from the Balkans and Greece. From the Turkish perspective, there were a variety of reasons, both macabre and pragmatic, for the strange practice. The Turkish government lacked the manpower necessary to fight its way through to Western Europe. Forcible recruitment of conquered subjects at an early age helped solve that problem, albeit in an unsettling fashion. The devshirme especially was widely hated among the conquered Christian communities, even though the Ottomans were careful to limit the number of the kidnapped to usually no more than one child per family. And they reminded the victimized parents that due to their lost children's immersion in Islamic doctrine and military and bureaucratic training, their former Christian children could rise to be among the highest officials in the army and government, in which a near majority of elites was comprised of European forced converts. Moreover, it is also not altogether clear that children always forgot their Christian parentage. Those forcibly recruited in their late teens as Janissaries and bureaucrats sometimes sought to do favors for their former Christian villages and families.

Indeed, many of the grand viziers who ran the daily business of the empire for the sultans were themselves European-born. At the siege, most of the chief lieutenants of Mehmet II were also of European ancestry. The admiral of the Ottoman navy during the attack, Baltaoglu Suleyman Bey, had been conscripted as a Bulgarian prisoner of war. The firebrand Zaganos Pasha, the most adamant in advising the sultan not to give up on the siege, was an Albanian who had been enslaved and brought into the Ottoman military through the devshirme. The sultan's secretary and personal diplomat, Demetrios Apokaukos ("Kyritzes"), was a Greek. Mehmet II himself was of half-European Christian lineage through his mother Hüma Hatun, the harem concubine of his father Sultan Murad II. She was variously said to be of Italian, Jewish, Serbian, or Greek origin.[29]

The Ottoman sultans, of course, saw a number of advantages in the advancement of Christian European children into the highest echelons of the Ottoman state. These converts could serve as a check on the power of clannish Turkish noble families and their threat to the sultan's monopoly on violence. Indoctrinated since childhood in both the Islamic faith and Ottomanism, the orphaned graduates of the devshirme often proved the most loyal of Ottoman subjects and the most fanatical, especially as they made up the vast majority of the feared Janissary corps. Indeed, by the sultanate of Mehmet, there was growing anger and jealousy among the empire's Turkish subjects over the elite billets and offices reserved for European converts. The exalted status of the mostly foreign-born Janissaries over native Turkish contingents also bothered many in the military.

The presence of so many ex-Christians at the highest levels of the Ottoman bureaucracy and military also had a disturbing effect on Christian enemies, as well as a possible enticement for them to reconsider their loyalties given the obvious manifestations of Ottoman meritocracy. Given that Christian-born viziers, ambassadors, advisors, generals, and admirals had no Ottoman familial advocates, their ascensions were often due to talent and the fact they harbored no loyalties to particular Turkish clans, instead recognizing that their existences hinged only on continued featly to the sultan.[30]

Rebellious Ottoman Christian subjects were often intimidated by the appearance of formidable Janissaries—European and Christian to the eye, but among the fiercest killers of their own. They may have been formally slaves, but they usually enjoyed privileges well beyond those of most Turkish subjects, and barracked and associated exclusively with each other. In theory, Janissaries were akin to the Roman praetorian guard that had protected the emperor, or perhaps the Byzantines' own Varangian guard, an ax-wielding elite mercenary "barbarian" force recruited from northern Europe and Scandinavia that had been phased out by the time of the siege of 1453.[31]

The red-turbaned Janissaries added to their terrifying reputation by charging into battle with a cacophony of castanets, trumpets, drums, and tambourines. They were the first Ottoman troops to be equipped with firearms and were famed for not leaving any of their dead on the battlefield. The Janissaries constituted the third and final wave of Turkish assaulters on May 29, 1453, and were the first to break into the city, despite suffering terribly from a hail of stones and arrows from the walls.[32]

Other male captive Christian children were castrated and sent as eunuchs to the harem along with young girls. Inside the harem, the same bizarre mix of savagery and enticement was at play, given that the ecumenical Ottoman government in theory treated Muslims of all ethnicities similarly. It was always possible for a male Christian captive and convert to become prominent in the harem, either as a consort of the aristocracy or through a liaison with the sultan himself. Fortunate Christian-born female concubines could become the mothers of future sultans. Indeed, the sultans themselves were usually the products of the harem. The would-be successor to the sultanate often ensured his ascension to power by liquidating scores of his half-brothers along with their mothers, but nonetheless honoring and elevating his own often European mother.

Usually, the sultan's mother became the head of the harem, with power to arrange dynastic marriages, influence emancipations, and put down conspiracies. Strangely, for much of the expansionary period of Ottoman history, about 75 percent of the sultans had mothers of European descent. There is evidence that such matrilineal influence somewhat reduced the sultan's frequency of war-making against European Christian states. In any case, the strange idea that the Ottomans were waging a holy war against Christendom, spearheaded on the battlefield by formerly Christian children together with assimilated Ottoman Greeks, advised often by a European-born grand vizier, and led by a sultan with a European-born mother, created an eeriness to the Ottoman Empire every bit as scarifying to its enemies as Turkish military prowess.[33]

By the 1400s Constantinople was not properly an empire at all, but a commercial city-state whose destruction even to its enemies might have seemed as unprofitable as it was unnecessary. Moreover, no

Islamic army had ever yet figured out how to storm the vast Theodosian Walls of the city, much less how to conduct an amphibious assault on the seaward ramparts over the Bosporus and Golden Horn. In this sense, Constantinople in its last years was analogous to Carthage at the time of the Third Punic War. It too was a once vast empire reduced to its capital, a doomed target for decades left to itself as not worth the cost of an expensive siege, since massive walls made an assault by its ascendant rival nearly impossible.

The new aptly named Byzantine emperor, Constantine XI, had himself been born in Constantinople. At seventeen, Constantine had witnessed the failed siege of Mehmet's father, Murad II, in 1422. As the former despot of Morea, the Byzantine province in the Greek Peloponnese, Constantine over two decades of constant fighting had mostly freed the Peloponnese from Ottoman incursions. By the time of his death, the forty-eight-year-old emperor had served in almost every major Christian battle of the last three decades, and at great personal cost and effort. He was twice widowed, without children, and in his brief tenure as emperor leading up to the siege was looking for a dynastic bride whose family alliance might bolster the defenses of the city. Having seen Byzantine victories in the Balkans and the failed earlier siege, Constantine thus was convinced that the Ottomans could not prevail, and might even not attempt another assault. His chief challenge was persuading the complacent Byzantine elite—and himself—that the ascension of the young Mehmet II marked a new chapter in Ottoman bellicosity and a near guarantee that the teenaged sultan would inaugurate his tenure with an attack on Constantinople.[34]

An unfortunate naïveté had plagued the preceding emperors of Constantinople during the entire century before the fall. Increasingly and dangerously, they had convinced themselves that the sultans still believed that a nominally free Christian Constantinople—and the slivers of its empire left in Greece, Thrace, Macedonia, and along the Black Sea and Dardanelles—posed little serious threat to the now expansive Ottoman empire. But given the reality that the Anatolian populations of the once vast and now lost Byzantine Empire were still mostly ethnically Greek, albeit under Turkish rule, many in

Constantinople wisely feared that such growing familiarity with Ottomanism made it a more, not less, dangerous rival.

Sultan Mehmet II came to power at the age of eighteen in 1451 on the death of his father Murad II, after a brief prior and aborted sultanic tenure when he was a mere twelve years old. The teen's ascension unfortunately raised false hopes among the worried Byzantines. They had always intently watched Ottoman successions for any clues to the temperament of the new sultan, which increasingly might determine their own survival. In 1451 the Byzantine nomenklatura naively thought that the young Ottoman ruler believed with his late father that for now it was still wiser to trade with and profit from a near vassal Constantinople than to attempt to storm and expropriate the impregnable fortress.

But Mehmet quickly proved a different sort of sultan, in ways well beyond his ruthless liquidation of rival claimants and siblings. He interpreted Byzantine magnanimity as weakness to be exploited rather than as favors to be reciprocated. The effect on the Byzantines was again a sort of schizophrenia, as they swayed wildly between righteous fury and shaken timidity. When told that the sultan was routinely breaking the peace and had slaughtered Greek farmers in their fields near the city, Constantine in retaliation rounded up all the Turks in the city of Constantinople and imprisoned them—only then to release them in fear of the consequences.[35]

Even in the months leading up to the 1453 siege, when there could be no doubt of the intention of Mehmet to storm the capital, the emperor Constantine sent him numerous letters and envoys whining about the Ottoman construction of the Rumelihisari fortress on the European north side of the Bosporus. Worse, he sought leverage over the sultan by implying that the Byzantines could stir up trouble among claimants to the Ottoman throne, or craft together a grand Christian alliance, or at least prompt a civil war among the Ottoman provinces. In all these surreal exchanges between the desperate emperor and the brash teenaged sultan, there is a note of pathos in Constantine's assumption that his once grand empire, now almost reduced to an underpopulated city-state, could ever negotiate as an equal with young Mehmet concerning the Ottomans' aggressive global agenda.

Sultan Mehmet now reminded Constantine of the imbalance in relative power when he snapped back to the Byzantine envoys in one of their last exchanges before the end of the city:

> The whole country is in my power. I hold the forts on the Anatolian side of the straits, and Turks are inhabiting them, and the untenanted land on the western side is mine, since the Greeks are too insecure to be able to live there . . . Can I not do as I wish in my own dominions? Go, tell your Emperor that this ruler is not like his predecessors. What they were powerless to achieve is within his grasp and easy of accomplishment for him; and he is both willing and eager to do what they would not ever attempt.[36]

Even with warning by the sultan of his intended plans for Constantinople, Byzantine mastery of the use of dynastic intrigue, bribes, tribute, and concessions still gave the Greeks a false sense of confidence that the emperor could in the eleventh hour finesse a new sultan into leaving the waning empire alone. At times, Byzantine emperors had harbored would-be rival claimants to the Ottoman throne to encourage civil war among their enemies, most famously orchestrated by the Byzantine emperor John VIII Palaiologos. John had induced Sultan Murad II's rival and younger brother Mustafa to lead successful revolts behind the besieging force of 1422. The same Byzantine strategies of stirring up internal and external opposition against a besieging sultan had earlier worked off and on between 1394 and 1402. Then the blockading Ottoman ships and encamped land forces had finally given up in order to turn their attention to threats from European invaders and Iranian Sunni Muslim forces of the Timurid dynasty.

Despite his resolve and experience, Constantine had from the outset misjudged the new eighteen-year-old sultan, especially when he had asked Mehmet for double the annual Ottoman subsidy that went to Constantinople for the upkeep of Orhan, a hostage earlier sent to the Byzantines. Orhan, in fact, was the sultan's second cousin, rival to the throne, and incessant plotter who had been under a sort of lavish house arrest, or preventative detention, among the Byzantines. That Byzantine demand for more money, of course, had the opposite effect. It enraged the sultan and embarrassed the pro-Byzantine Halil Pasha—formally known as Çandarli Halil Pasha the Younger—the grand vizier and "moderate" who had advised the sultan against attacking the city. Or as the exasperated Halil put it to the emperor's naïve Byzantine envoys:

> You ignorant and foolish Greeks! I have been aware for a long time of your villainous tricks. You must change your ways. The previous Sultan had a gentle nature, was genuinely friendly to all and most conscientious in his dealings. But our present Sultan Mehmet is not the kind of man you think he is, and if Constantinople escapes from his grasp—and I know the boldness and wild impetuosity of which his nature is capable—then I shall know indeed that God is still overlooking your plots and wicked games.[37]

The subtext of Halil's diatribe was that the Byzantines had undercut his own court position with the sultan as a temporizer and thus endangered his life, while enhancing rival bellicose viziers and firebrand generals intent on storming Constantinople. Indeed, the second and third viziers, the Greek-born Zaganos Pasha and the Georgian-born eunuch Shihab al-Din Pasha, would soon eclipse Halil with their prescient advice to the sultan that with enough besiegers Constantinople could at last fall. Halil would indeed soon be executed—the first grand vizier to suffer capital punishment—after the fall of Constantinople, ostensibly for his gloomy and ultimately wrong counsel, and charges of bribery, treason, and intimacy with the enemy.

Halil Pasha had been a realist. As foreign minister for some thirty years under both Murad and Mehmet, he had advised father and son to wait patiently as Constantinople irreversibly fell into decline and one day dropped into their lap. He argued that it would be more profitable to continue Ottoman domination of the eroding Byzantine Empire through asymmetrical agreements, tributes, and alliances. In a less charitable narrative, rumors had reached the sultan that Halil had long taken large bribes from Byzantines for his advice against storming Constantinople.[38]

Almost immediately upon coming to power in 1451, Mehmet II began making preparations to seize Constantinople and end outright the Byzantine Empire. Meanwhile, he insisted to the emperor Constantine and his advisors that he had no desire to attack the city or go to war against the Byzantines, whether in their capital or the remnant provinces on the Black Sea, the Aegean, or the Peloponnese.

At the same time, the duplicitous new sultan likewise deceived Western European emissaries who flocked to his court at Edirne— the former ancient Roman eponymous city of Hadrianopolis, captured and renamed by the Ottomans in 1369, and a mere 150 or so miles west from Constantinople. Mehmet claimed to the relieved envoys that he had no ambitions to extend Ottoman dominance much into Eastern Europe. Nor should they worry that he would seek the end of Christendom in the East.

Yet privately, the sultan calculated that his empire deserved a more majestic city than Edirne as its capital. Or as Mehmet put it shortly after assuming power: "The ghaza [holy war] is our basic duty as it was in the case of our fathers. Constantinople, situated in the middle of our domains, protects our enemies and incites them against us. The conquest of this city is, therefore, essential to the future and safety of the Ottoman state."[39]

In fact, Mehmet upon ascension to the sultanate carefully mobilized his forces for the largest siege attempt against Constantinople in the city's eleven-hundred-year history. He marshalled somewhere between 100,000 and 200,000 men, including sailors, attendants, teamsters, day laborers, slaves, personal servants, camp followers, and a besieging force of some 80,000 soldiers. In the past, there had been many attempts on the city: the failed attack by Avars and Persians (626), the two Arab sieges of 674–678 and 717–718, the Bulgar invasion of 813, the siege of 860 by the Rus, a brief and half-hearted attempt in 1097 by some knights of the First Crusade, and the 1422 failure of Mehmet's father, Murad II. Despite the advantages of manpower, all these besiegers—except the combined Venetian and

Frankish armies that had broken through the seawalls and captured the city in 1203 during their detour from the Fourth Crusade—had failed for several key reasons.[40]

The Byzantine navy usually controlled the sea approaches to the city, both southward from the Black Sea through the Bosporus strait, and northward up through the Dardanelles to the Sea of Marmara. Such accustomed naval supremacy usually denied the attackers critical supplies while obstructing attempts by sea to blockade the city. In fact, throughout the siege of 1453, vastly outnumbered Venetian, Genoese, and Greek galleys often defeated their Turkish counterparts in sea battles, checked ambitious attacks on the seawalls of the city, and were able to break out through the Dardanelles before, during, and after the actual siege.[41]

The Byzantines were also able either to encourage foreign attacks on their enemies or to foment internal divisions over succession. As mentioned, worry about his renegade little brother Mustafa had forced Sultan Murad II in 1422 to break off the siege of the city to address the rebellion and fragmentation of his forces to his rear. As it happened, in 1453 Mehmet II's troublesome rival cousin Orhan (Durgano) would be on the walls fighting alongside the Byzantines against the Ottomans.

In extremis, the city usually was also able to enlist or hire at least some help either from Europe, despite the historic schism between Eastern and Western Christianity, or from the outlands of the Byzantine empire. Moreover, most besiegers, often suffering from poor logistics and planning, had not been able to break into the city before they themselves began to suffer diseases, the befouling of their camps, insufficient food supplies, and shortages of clean water, especially as spring encampments lengthened into the hot summers.

Finally, the traditions of Byzantine science and research often translated directly to superior weaponry, at least until the final siege. In the age before widespread use of gunpowder, the outnumbered Byzantines usually enjoyed technological advantages from their monopolies on Greek fire and pressurized flame throwers, and superior catapults, trebuchets, heavy cavalry, infantry equipment, and sophisticated tactics.[42]

Most of these obstacles were known to the Ottomans by the mid-fifteenth century and explain why the city so far had survived even while much of its empire had not. As a result, Mehmet's enormous forces streaming in below the walls of the city after April 2, 1453, were prepared to overcome all of them. The besiegers had carefully worked for two years to ensure what the sultan surmised would be naval superiority, at least measured by the overwhelming number of Turkish galleys. They were mostly united, without worry over revolts to the rear. The sultan remained confident that he had ensured little help would reach the city in time from the West or from the Byzantines in Greece or the Black Sea.

The Ottoman army was supplied by skilled logisticians who in the year prior had acquired enough sources of water and food for a lengthy siege. Mehmet had purchased European-designed cannon that were larger and far more numerous than those found on the wall and towers of the city. He stocked far more gunpowder than was found inside the ramparts.

One of Mehmet's first steps before mustering his huge throng had been to ensure that at last both sides of the Bosporus were fortified and occupied by permanent Ottoman garrisons. He planned to complement the prior Ottoman fortress of Anadoluhisari ("Anatolian fortress") on the Asian side of the strait, built by his great-grandfather Bayezid I, with an even more impressive twin, Rumelihisari, on the European opposite shore.

Construction on the citadel started a year before the siege and was finished just months before the attack begin. These complementary artillery batteries of the two forts facing each other made it difficult for any galley to safely enter or exit the Black Sea. Consequently, during the siege it became nearly impossible for Genoese-controlled cities on the Black Sea such as Caffa, Sinope, and Amasra, or the Byzantine-affiliated kingdom of Trebizond, to send help or receive refugees.

Later, after the fall, surviving Christians blamed the various outposts of the empire for not sending succor to the mother city. But the real cause of the reluctance of the Black Sea mini-kingdoms was the fear of dispatching their ships past the twin Ottoman bases on the

Bosporus and the superior size of the Ottoman fleet in the Sea of Marmara. Despite some occasional Venetian success in skillfully evading the forts, few ship captains possessed the skill to reach Constantinople from the Black Sea. As a result, Rumelihisari would soon be known as the "Throat Cutter," inasmuch as the sultan could figuratively slice the neck of all Bosporus traffic.[43]

Just as importantly, in the autumn prior to the siege, Mehmet had sent a substantial army under his old general Turahan Bey to raid the Peloponnese and cut off and isolate Byzantine Morea from the north. That successful effort precluded help from Byzantine Mystras, the small but influential cultural and political capital of the Morea. The emperor Constantine's two squabbling brothers, Thomas and Demetrios, were blocked from leading relief columns before or during the nearly two-month-long siege. This general inability of Byzantine Greece to offer any help to its mother city—either out of fear of Ottoman reprisals, or an inability to break out and march to Constantinople—would become an object of shame for centuries.

The historian Sphrantzes also bitterly noted that the Hungarian Christians were too terrified of Mehmet to send troops. But in the aftermath of Constantinople's fall, he perhaps reserved his greatest disdain for the Christians of the Black Sea regions and along the Danube: "Which of the Christians, the Trebizondian emperor [on the Black Sea], the lords of Wallachia [on the lower Danube], or the Iberian king [in Christian Georgia in the Caucasus] contributed a single penny or a single soldier to our defense, openly or secretly?"[44]

In the prior two years, Mehmet had amassed a fleet of 320 war galleys and supply ships. While they were not always comparable in quality to either Byzantine or Italian galleys, their sheer numbers in theory ensured naval dominance for the besiegers, especially by deploying fleets to swarm simultaneously the Golden Horn, the Bosporus, the Sea of Marmara, and the Dardanelles. In the case of the Golden Horn estuary, midway through the siege the Ottomans dragged their ships overland in a historic detour to circumvent the famous Byzantine iron chain that had traditionally blocked hostile entrance into the inlet from the Bosporus.[45]

In the end, the Ottoman plans of attack were simple and sufficient. Mehmet's navy would blockade the city, probe the seawalls, feign maritime landings, and force Constantine to use his scarce defenders—no more than sixty-five hundred to eight thousand active soldiers in a city population reduced to about fifty thousand—to defend the seawalls above both the Golden Horn and the Sea of Marmara. Just the presence of such a vast enemy fleet would ensure that the land wall, the focus of the siege, would be short of defenders.[46]

Meanwhile, the Ottoman land forces would camp outside the Theodosian Walls and with impunity unleash artillery barrages against the famed bulwark. The plan was to thin out the Byzantine defenders on the outer wall and blast holes in the fortifications. These volleys would either eventually exhaust the herculean efforts of the defenders to plug up gaps through frantic nocturnal reconstruction efforts, or create wide enough openings that the Ottomans could storm through the breaches.

Mehmet famously brought in an array of huge siege cannons. Among them was the dreaded giant bombard (dubbed the "Basilic" cannon) designed by the infamous Orban (known also as Urban), the Transylvanian or Hungarian engineer who contracted to build the monster for the sultan after having offered his services to the impoverished Byzantines, who could not afford his price.

Known to the Byzantines as a "monster" (*teras*), the bombard was some twenty-four feet long and two and a half feet in diameter. It was forged of expensive bronze. The monster required two hundred men, thirty wagons yoked to sixty oxen, and nearly three months to transport it the 150 miles to Constantinople. When properly loaded and operated, the barrel reportedly could shoot a twelve-hundred-pound stone ball a mile.

Yet for all its notoriety, the cannon remained problematic, given that it could usually be fired only four or five times a day. The barrel required careful attention to keep the surface cool enough to prevent cracking and warping. For the nearly two months of the siege, despite the localized destruction it wrought on the walls, the gun was unable to sustain the rate of fire necessary to nullify the efforts of the skilled nighttime civilian Byzantine work crews patching up the damage.

Mehmet, in addition, collected an entire arsenal of various smaller cannon. Yet their barrages also never brought down the massive walls. These cannons, too, were also slow-firing, inaccurate, poorly deployed, and often lacked the velocity to break apart the Theodosian Walls without sustained and concentrated fire.

Contemporary reports suggest that some of the guns, including the monstrous bombard, may have cracked or blown up during the siege. Rather than the destruction of the walls, perhaps the chief value of Ottoman artillery was tying down thousands of Byzantine civilian workers who nightly packed stone and brick into the day's new fissures, and consequently were unable either to fight from the walls or to fully support the Byzantine defenders.[47]

Yet whether the aged and weakened fortress, and its vastly out-numbered defenders, would survive yet another siege ultimately hinged on the West—specifically, on whether Pope Nicholas V could marshal a Western crusade to sail up the Dardanelles and free the city from the blockade; on whether an independent German or French monarch would send an army; on whether Hungarians and other Eastern Europeans would join Constantinople; and on whether enough Venetian, Genoese, Cretan, or Spanish mercenaries, traders, and volunteers could reach Constantinople in time on news of an impending siege.

In the end, and unfortunately for Constantinople, only about two thousand Western Europeans from Italy, Venetian Crete, and Spain would heed the emperor's desperate calls over the prior two years to save the city and with it the Christian empire in the East. Yet among those who did arrive, especially the Genoese, were some of the most experienced and professional soldiers and sailors in Europe, long-time veterans of conducting and resisting sieges. Contemporaries noted that despite their small numbers, the Italian volunteer contingents were superbly equipped and deployed constantly on the walls or protecting the harbor—and perhaps were more effective soldiers than the Greek defenders. The quality of their armor was especially noted and made the Genoese, for example, almost immune to arrows and sword thrusts. Unlike their Byzantine counterparts, most of the Westerners had no families inside the city and therefore had no need to leave their posts periodically to check on the security of their wives and children.[48]

Most notable of all was the famed Genoese Giovanni Giustiniani, one of the most renowned Italian soldiers of his age. Luckily for the defenders, Giustiniani, "the guardian of all our fortunes," arrived three months before the siege with two ships full of supplies and weapons, four hundred veterans from Genoa, and another three hundred condottieri from Chios. The Genoese were also aided by perhaps eight hundred Venetians who had arrived in two large ships. Despite a papal call to all Christians to aid Constantinople, in the end few Westerners came, variously pleading poverty, domestic problems, and an inability to reach the city in time. But mostly they were terrified of fighting the Ottomans on their home turf. In fact, at about the time Giustiniani arrived, some seven hundred Cretans and Italians under Pietro Davanzo had abandoned the city with six valuable ships. That loss of roughly 25 percent of the foreign contingents that were expected to be assigned to the walls may have proven disastrous for the city.[49]

Tragically for the defenders, more Christians—hired, willingly, coerced, or enslaved—would fight on the side of the sultan than were fighting on the walls. With the sultan were Hungarian horseman, German and Serbian sappers, and various foot soldiers from the Balkans. On the other side, the Greeks had a contingent of about six hundred Turkish soldiers loyal to Orhan, known as Durgano, a cousin of Mehmet and a lifelong claimant to the Turkish throne. The wannabe sultan had lived most of his life in Constantinople as part of a convenient Byzantine bargain with Mehmet, who paid the emperor to keep the aspiring sultan confined in subsidized affluence and unable to intrigue for the throne. Orhan had no choice but to join his "captors" since he realized he would be summarily executed by his rival cousin the moment the city fell.

Western Christians in the end were too disunited and squabbling to save Byzantium. Religious differences also played a role. Moreover, the ongoing Hundred Years' War was still dragging on in

Western Europe, despite having exhausted Europe's two most powerful kingdoms, France and England. And most Europeans held a legitimate fear of Islamic armies, especially the Ottomans, and were not eager to fight them on the distant frontiers of Europe.

In addition, too many Westerners concluded that the city was likely to fall anyway and was no longer needed as a bulwark. Indeed, stalwart Eastern Europeans, the Hungarians especially, were now seen as far more important frontline garrison states against the Turks. The irony, of course, was that the later heroic efforts of Giustiniani and his tiny contingent of seven hundred condottieri, recruited mostly from Genoa and Genoese-controlled Chios, in hindsight proved that it would not have taken too many more Western Europeans to have saved the city.[50]

In the final months before the Ottomans arrived, Constantine's efforts to flatter the sultan and offer increased tribute failed. Greek envoys sent to Edirne were butchered. Constantine may have seen keeping secure the sultan's rival distant cousin Orhan as a token of his fealty to Mehmet but, as noted earlier, his recent request for increased financial assistance to support the confinement of the Ottoman insurrectionists under his control only further incited Mehmet.

Constantine at least took the extraordinary but wise step of placing the foreigner Giustiniani in charge as *protostrator* (senior military overseer) of the overall land defenses of the city. He allowed Giustiniani and his Genoese retinue, in the weeks before the Ottoman arrival, to assign troops to the critical sectors of the Theodosian Walls, with special attention to the two notorious weak spots: a low area at the Lykos riverbed, and the junction with the seawalls along the Golden Horn.

The Byzantines were additionally fortunate that Constantine had proven to be an especially competent and popular emperor, who was determined to save the ancient city or die trying. For that effort, he had enlisted over half the dwindling population of the city, with perhaps as many as thirty-five thousand semi-armed civilians. Most of them worked at night repairing the damaged fortifications and, at least before the heavier bombardments, during the day served as auxiliaries on the walls. The sixty-five hundred to eight thousand defenders on the outer ramparts were well armored with breastplates that turned away arrows and sword thrusts. Most were outfitted with pikes and swords. They were supported by some cannon, crossbowmen, and archers. All in all, even the muster of such a relatively small number of defenders was astonishing, given the common perception that the city was finished, and the reality that the emperor was too poor to hire many mercenaries.

Despite shortages of gunpowder and artillery, the Byzantine forces had plenty of stones, pressurized Greek-fire throwers, sulfur, and oil—all of which for the nearly eight weeks of the siege took a frightful toll on the Turks, who were repeatedly trapped between the moat wall and the outer wall. While it is true that Constantinople was a shadow of its former glory, and weeds grew in the empty suburbs amid a greatly reduced population, nonetheless the most formidable municipal fortress in the world still mustered well over thirty thousand soldiers and civilians to help with the defense, in a fashion few European cities could match.[51]

If perhaps six thousand of some eight thousand active defenders of the city were arrayed along the three-and-a-half-mile Theodosian outer wall, the nexus of the siege, then there was likely one soldier stationed on the rampart every three feet. The emperor and Giustiniani had also cobbled together two contingents of strategic reserves. The megadux ("grand duke"), Loukas Notaras, a controversial figure in Constantinople, added a mobile reinforcement of one hundred horsemen.[52]

Two narratives still persist about the siege and the future of the city: the dominant one of fatalism and the other of some legitimate hopes for success. The pessimistic theme can be summed up as "If not taken in 1453, then the city would have inevitably fallen anyway a few years soon thereafter," given the loss of most of its provinces, the eternal court squabbling and intrigues at Constantinople, the religious rivalries, and the opportunistic freelancing of Europeans in league with the sultan. Or as Steven Runciman famously concluded of the abrupt but supposedly fated end of Constantinople: "It is easy to maintain that in the broad sweep of history the year 1453 stands for very little. The Byzantine Empire was already doomed. Diminished, underpopulated and impoverished, it was bound to perish whenever the Turks chose to move in to make the kill."[53]

Yet there is also the rival narrative, one arguing that the city, even at its nadir, came within days of surviving the greatest siege in its eleven-hundred-year history. Until May 29, when the Turkish forces finally breached the outer and inner walls—due both to the discovery of an opened gate or gates in the inner wall, and to the wounding and retirement of Giustiniani and his Genoese contingent—many of the sultan's advisors were concluding that the course of battle had turned against the Ottomans, perhaps in the fashion that Murad II had failed in 1422. The weather was growing warmer, raising the specter of disease and the need for increased supplies of potable water. The attackers' provisions were beginning to run out. Thousands of Turkish soldiers were dead or wounded—eventually over twenty thousand in total. The supposedly decisive bombard, along with the sultan's congeries of lesser artillery, still had not broken apart the fortifications.

Moreover, there was mounting fear that belated help from Italy would arrive any day, and a fleet would break through the Dardanelles. Even if such aid had amounted to a mere thousand or so additional troops, the boost might have been decisive, given the example of how Giustiniani's tiny band of seven hundred had so far saved the city.

And then there was the long history of outnumbered Christian defenders successfully resisting overwhelming numbers of Ottoman besiegers. At the famous great siege of Malta in 1565, a mere five hundred to six hundred Knights Hospitaller, along with an ad hoc force of five thousand European volunteers, mercenaries, civilians, and slaves, would for over four months successfully repulse a huge amphibious force of forty thousand Ottoman attackers—and keep the island permanently in the hands of Christian forces. Some 230 years after the fall of Constantinople, during the siege of Vienna in 1683, the European defenders would face a larger and better armed besieging force. Yet a vastly outnumbered Austrian defense of a mere eleven thousand soldiers and less than five thousand volunteers successfully beat off continuous Ottoman attacks. They successfully held the city for over two months until the arrival of relief forces. It was never predestined that the outnumbered Byzantine defenders of 1453, manning the greatest fortifications of the age, were doomed to defeat.

Most importantly, despite the ingenuity of overcoming the chained entrance to the Golden Horn, the huge Turkish fleet had performed poorly. It was never able to pose a serious threat to the two great seawalls of the city, or even to ensure that Constantinople was completely blockaded before and during the siege. Just as Constantinople had been safe for a generation after the failed siege of 1422, perhaps an even greater Ottoman setback in 1453 might have given it still more breathing room.[54]

So, despite the conventional historical assessment that the city was done for, it is just as likely that if the sultan's assault, two years in the planning, had collapsed, Constantinople would have been empowered and continued its successful diplomatic efforts to cobble together allies and sow dissension among its enemies. Perhaps a successful resistance might have gained the city a status like that of a twentieth-century autonomous Singapore or Hong Kong. There were sultans before Mehmet II who did not feel storming Constantinople was worth the effort—and there would have been plenty such realists after him as well, had he failed in 1453.

In contrast, the victory of Mehmet II, thereafter to be named "the Conqueror," radically changed the trajectory of the Ottomans' rise to dominance—post facto proof that Constantinople had inhibited, both materially and psychologically, Ottoman expansionism. Enemies and neutrals quickly began to make amends to and alliances with what they now felt was an irrevocably ascendant sultan.

When Mehmet's huge forces arrived before the Theodosian Walls, and his fleet blocked the Bosporus and Golden Horn, despair spread well beyond the outnumbered defenders on the city's walls. The Ottoman navy had also gained control of the Dardanelles and would soon begin absorbing key Greek islands at the channel's mouth in the Aegean. Any help from the Mediterranean would have to fight its way in or slip in at night. Never before had the Greeks seen the full strength of the Ottoman Empire now assembled before their walls. There were over eighty thousand soldiers below them, just yards from the outer moat, arrayed with banners, tents, and horns, and perhaps an equal number of auxiliaries, servants, and camp followers.

The sultan's strategies to take the city were flexible and multifaceted, and evolved in succession, as each attempt failed and was replaced by another method until the decisive and successful final attack of May 29. In the first weeks, the Ottomans believed their large bombards and numerous cannons could do what traditional battering rams, catapults, and trebuchets had never accomplished: break down the massive, complex Theodosian system of walls and gates. But the artillery never created permanent gaps sufficient to exploit with infantry.

By early May the Ottomans' artillery corps, more wisely, began concentrating their fire by arranging several cannons to focus and shoot in unison at vulnerable spots on the walls. Yet this improved effort mostly failed as well, in the similar sense that it did not result in exploitable fissures in the ramparts, although the fusillades further taxed the defenders to repair the mounting daily damage.

Finally, the sultan reverted to the time-tested approaches of using mobile towers, mining under the foundations of the walls, and sending in successive waves of attackers equipped with scaling ladders. All these efforts likewise came to naught. Yet like the early barrages, the assaults wore down the city's limited number of defenders on the walls and the repair crews. They also demoralized the civilian population, already worn out by the constant din of the Ottoman bombards. The Byzantines looked in vain for relief fleets from the West to end what seemed like unrelenting violence and impending doom.[55]

On April 5 the sultan himself had arrived from Edirne with his final contingent, and his troops spent the next day positioning their artillery and surveying the points of attack against the Theodosian Walls for the formal assaults that began between April 6 and 7. The Turkish camp was about two to three miles distant from the land wall, arrayed parallel to its entire length. The undermanned defenders were atop the lower outer wall and had ceded nothing to the attackers—no doubt on the directives of Giustiniani, who determined that the only hope for the city was to stop the assault outright the moment the attackers cleared the moat. Or perhaps he intended to draw the Ottoman cannon fire first toward the outer wall, keeping the larger inner wall as a redoubt, although it may have been in a greater state of disrepair. In any case, in the first few days the confident Genoese made several bold sorties beyond the outer wall, until they learned that even successful punitive raids were not worth the cost in scarce manpower.[56]

Contingents of Genoese, some Venetians, and Constantine's best troops were arrayed in succession along the Theodosian Walls. Venetian galleys kept the Turks away from the seawalls. Despite having few cannons comparable to the batteries of the enemy, for the next eight weeks the Byzantine forces unleashed steady volleys from bows, crossbows, small cannon, Greek fire, and handheld missiles to repel every sort of frontal assault. The Byzantines exploited the innate advantage of the besieged as they targeted the Ottomans massing under the outer wall, aiming downward from high above, while in contrast the Turks had to shoot arrows upward against scattered individuals well protected by stone and brick ramparts.[57]

The Turks were unable to scale the walls with ladders, or batter down the gates with rams, or advance close enough with wheeled towers and protected carts. In between the major massed assaults on the Theodosian Walls, during almost every day of the fifty-five-day siege the large Turkish cannons battered the walls, the Ottoman fleet sought to approach the maritime walls and draw off Byzantine manpower, and miners worked underground in a series of tunnels.

Despite some five thousand shots and the consumption of fifty-five thousand pounds of gunpowder, the besiegers never blasted permanent holes large enough to allow the Janissaries to pour through the fissures. The Turks' constant subterranean efforts to undermine the foundations of the walls equally led to their continual defeat and losses, given sophisticated Byzantine countermining.[58]

At sea, the vastly outnumbered Christians were able to beat back the Turkish fleet, given their superior seamanship, better commanders, and more battleworthy ships. Usually, the larger, higher-decked Genoese and Venetian galleys, outfitted with ample catapults and cannons, had little trouble targeting the smaller, densely packed Ottoman ships. The Byzantines still deployed a credible fleet of some twenty-six galleys, the majority from their Western allies. For a while they could contest almost all the attacks from the Sea of Marmara and the Golden Horn against the maritime walls.[59]

On May 21, thousands of Ottoman dead later, the exasperated sultan sent envoys to the emperor with an offer: hand over the city, and the Ottomans would offer Constantine three concessions. First, all Greeks could leave Constantinople with their property; second, the emperor could leave to govern the Peloponnese unharmed; and third, any Byzantines who wished to remain in the city under new Ottoman rule would be left alone after swearing an oath of fealty and paying the infidel tax. Constantine, with public support, rejected all the terms and vowed to continue fighting in defense of the city unto death. After the fall of the fortress, the sultan more or less revealed that, in fact, he had little intention of allowing the Peloponnese to remain autonomous. Instead, he conquered it within seven years. Had Constantine surrendered, it was unlikely that any of the Ottoman terms would have been honored.[60]

The Byzantine rejection of the Ottoman final offer after weeks of attacks was inevitable. As the near-contemporary chronicler Michael Doukas rhetorically declared: "It was quite impossible to take the city which belonged to the Greeks and give it to the Turks. If this were done, where could they go? What place could the Greeks dwell in, what Christian city where they would not be spat upon, and held in loathing and contempt?" One might compare the Ottoman offer with Rome's equally impossible and duplicitous demand that the Carthaginians abandon their city and move elsewhere, far from the sea.[61]

In frustration over their weeks of failure and the seeming obstinacy of the emperor, on May 28 the sultan's advisors urged a final, full assault to storm the land walls, given that the only alternative was to call off the siege. Despite nearly two months of serial frustrations and the mostly intact Byzantine forces on the walls, most of the

Ottoman commanders remained eager to try one last push into the city.

The Janissaries especially pressed for the attack, given the promises from their sultan that all who made it inside the walls would be unleashed for three days of plunder, murder, and rape. Mehmet, moreover, might have feared the continuing stalemate would soon prompt dissension in his own territories. On the eve of his final assault he sent envoys one last time to the city, offering safe passage under terms of surrender—if Constantinople was now immediately handed over. Constantine offered a last defiant rejection: "The city is not mine to give you, nor has anyone who lives in it the right to do so. We are all determined to choose death rather than surrender, and we shall not hesitate to give our lives to this cause."[62]

The sultan's pro-peace grand vizier Halil once again urged caution, offering pessimistic appraisals of the chances of a Turkish victory to an increasingly worried Mehmet:

> You see how strongly the city is defended and how impossible it is to storm it; in fact, the more men you send to attack it, the more are left lying there, and those who manage to scale the wall are beaten back and killed. Your ancestors never got as far as this, or even expected to. It is to your great glory and honor that you have done so much, and this should satisfy you, without your wishing to destroy the whole of your forces in the way.[63]

Mehmet once more ignored his old advisor's nagging and instead took counsel from his most aggressive commander and convert, Zaganos Pasha, who begged for one last day of collective effort: "Give us the chance of making one short sharp general assault, and if we fail, we shall afterwards do whatever you think best." The sultan then pledged to his enthused soldiers that their ruler and his state wanted only the city, the walls, and its buildings. For three days, everything else in Constantinople—money, people, property—was theirs to do with and profit from as they pleased.

The uncertainty on both sides about the course of the siege was not resolved immediately even on the last day of the Byzantine

Empire. In the words of Nicolò Barbaro, who witnessed the repulse of the first two waves of attackers massed below the outer wall on the last day of the siege, "Our crossbows and cannon kept on firing into their camp at this time and killed an incredible number of Turks." Another contemporary account noted that when the Turks began to fill in the moat and mass below the outer wall, they proved easy targets and were mostly slaughtered:

> Then with the object of filling in the ditch so as to facilitate an easy entrance through the breaches already made, under cover of bombardment and skirmishes, they threw earth and branches and other materials into the fosse; some even threw in their own tents. The sight was terrible to behold; many of them fell down owing to the fact that they were so many moving in such a restricted space, and those who followed behind them throwing in the earth and branches, buried alive those who had fallen, sending them to a pitiful death. Others, the strongest, impelled by the urge for speed, voluntarily seized the weaker and threw them pitilessly into the fosse instead of earth and branches. But they paid the price for their horrible actions and many of them were killed by the cannon and arrows from the crossbows and heavy stones flung by the catapults, and many others were wounded, while we also suffered some casualties.[64]

Yet the point of the sultan's initial attacks using expendable impressed Christians and Turkish peasants had been to wear down the defenders, and perhaps even give the Turkish artillery one last chance to blast holes for the subsequent main force of Janissaries and the sultan's other elite contingents. Now perhaps some ten thousand of the best in the Turkish army, spearheaded by the crack Janissaries, followed the initial two repulsed waves in a third and final make-or-break assault—hoping either to scale the walls with their ladders at the now undermanned areas, or to find cannon holes in the ramparts.

As mentioned, once Giustiniani was seriously wounded, by either a bullet or an arrow, and his troops carried him off the wall, the entire Genoese contingent panicked at the sight of their severely wounded captain:

> At this moment, such was the city's misfortune, Giovanni Giustiniani was struck by an arrow in the armpit. Like a boy unused to war, he trembled at the sight of his own blood, and feared for his life. In order not to dishearten his soldiers, who did not yet know that he had been wounded, he left the ranks with the intention of seeking a physician in secret. And if he had appointed a substitute to take his place the city would not have been lost. The battle was still raging furiously when the Emperor noticed that Giustiniani was missing, and went in great distress to see where he had gone. When our soldiers saw that they were without a leader, they began to retreat from their positions. At this point the fury of the Turkish attack increased while our own troops were filled with dread.[65]

The fleeing defenders were in such a panic that they did not even secure the closing of all the gates of the inner wall as they sought to pass through them, given the confusion of the melee and the frenzied Janissaries interspersed among them killing Christians. The final irony was that the departure of the wounded Giustiniani and his men did not just leave the targeted section of the wall unprotected. His absence as protostrator also proved even more catastrophic; only Giustiniani might have been able to fashion a coherent and defensible retreat to the inner walls after the failure of the outer wall defenses, and from their much higher ramparts reconstitute a successful resistance.

Later and bitter controversies arose over the final disaster. Greek accounts blamed the supposedly cowardly Giustiniani for losing his nerve, especially given that the Genoese did manage to reach their ships and break out of the Golden Horn, making it through the Dardanelles into the safety of the Aegean. Italian sources stress instead Giustiniani's mortal wounds and his subsequent death shortly after reaching Chios. There is no modern consensus on exactly how or where he was wounded; whether *all* the Genoese left en masse; or whether Giustiniani ordered a general withdrawal or his men simply lost heart at his collapse and spontaneously chose to save the contingent. There are even a few wild suggestions in the sources that Giustiniani may have been shot from behind by fifth-columnists, given that he had endured fifty-five days of hard fighting without being wounded, and happened to be struck for the first time just minutes before the defenses collapsed. In addition, Giustiniani had had a prior violent argument over strategy with a number of jealous Byzantines, most notably the megadux Notaras.[66]

So the defenses of nearly two months unexpectedly collapsed in minutes. Suddenly any defenders who stayed to fight on the outer wall or were caught retreating in the pavilion between the inner walls—and there were still some resolute pockets of Byzantines on the land walls, and Catalans and Cretans dispersed along the seawall—were enveloped by hundreds of Janissaries.

A witness to the battle, Leonardo of Chios, melodramatically confirms that after the failure of the first two assaults, the final thrust of the Turkish elite corps was likewise failing—and along with it the siege itself. Leonardo quotes the emperor: "Ah! . . . My brave soldiers, the enemy's attack is growing weaker, and the crown of victory is securely in our grasp. God is on our side; fight on!" Then followed the wounding of Giustiniani, the retreat of the Genoese, the collapse of the defense of the city, and the end of the Byzantines.[67]

The collapse of the city and the rest of the empire proceeded through three sequential and savage stages. First was the immediate fate of the Byzantines still battling on the ramparts; they became surrounded when the walls were transmogrified from a bulwark to first a killing ground, then an internment camp, and finally an execution yard. Second, after the fall of the city, there would follow a systematic, decade-long mop-up of all Byzantine lands in Greece, the Aegean, and the Black Sea. Third came a series of edicts and laws that turned any remnant Greek-speakers of the former empire into second-class citizens within vestigial pockets of beleaguered Hellenism.

In the short term, however, once resistance collapsed, chaos ensued. Yet for a brief period the epidemic of Turkish looting, slaughter, and vandalism allowed some of the armed defenders and their families to escape. They forced their way through the city to the

Golden Horn and the Venetian, Genoese, and Byzantine galleys in the harbor, thereby breaking out into the Sea of Marmara and through the Dardanelles to escape into the Aegean. In these first hours of the rampage, most of the victors were too busy looting the homes of the opulent, ransacking churches, rounding up choice slaves for sale (particularly young boys and girls), and carrying off booty to bother contesting the escape of the armed. Such looting and the realization that live hostages paid more than corpses explained why the Byzantine death count on the last day of the city was likely between four thousand and five thousand civilians and soldiers, while nearly fifty thousand of the rest were initially enslaved.

A historic moment, as Gibbon recognized, one that symbolized the end of both Orthodoxy and Romanitas in Asia, was the assault of the Janissaries on the inner sanctum of Hagia Sophia. Almost immediately upon breaching the walls, the Turks had targeted the cathedral where they knew some of the most prominent and richest of the city's clergy and nobles had assembled hoping for the appearance of a savior archangel.

After breaking down the ancient bronze doors, the Turks burst in, executing the old and infirm, looting the cathedral, and carrying off the survivors as slaves. Turks fought among themselves over the more attractive boys and young women, often binding them for later enjoyment, enslavement, or offers of ransom, then moving on to fight over additional captives. Within hours the church was completely ransacked, as even the floors and walls were smashed in search of treasure. Soon, Mehmet himself dramatically rode into the church, chastised those destroying valuable parts of his soon to be national mosque, and had his men deal with looters of what was apparently already Ottoman state property.[68]

What of the fate of the emperor in the general slaughter? The near-contemporary historian Michael Doukas, collating the narratives of earlier chroniclers, wrote that a soldier reported to the sultan that his contingent had swarmed Constantine and killed him:

"My Lord, I killed him; and then I was carried onward in the rush of men seeking booty, and left him lying dead." The other man claimed that he was the one who had struck the first blow. The Sultan then sent both to bring back the head. So they ran to find the body, cut off its head and brought it to their leader. Mehmet then said to the Megadux, "Tell me the truth. Is this the head of your Emperor?" Notaras inspected it, and replied, "My lord, it is." Others also saw the head and identified it. Then they nailed it to the column in the Augusteum, where it stayed until evening. After this the skin was stripped from the skull and stuffed with bran, and it was sent as a symbol of the victory to the governors of Persia and Arabia, and elsewhere in the Turkish empire.[69]

Contemporary witnesses and later accounts described the often mercurial fashion in which Italian and Greek survivors were variously allowed to be ransomed, enslaved, or executed, the decision depending on what particular information reached the volatile Mehmet, and his mood and sobriety at the time. Eyewitness Nicolò Barbaro noted of the first waves of Turkish soldiers and sailors who stormed into the city once they saw Ottoman flags flying from the ramparts:

They were all running furiously like dogs into the city to seek out gold, jewels, and other treasure, and to take the merchants prisoner. They sought out the monasteries, and all the nuns were led to the fleet and ravished and then sold for whatever they would fetch, although some of them preferred to cast themselves into the wells and drown rather than fall into the hands of the Turks, as did a number of married women also.[70]

A horrific story that swept the West after the fall of the city concerned the eminent Loukas Notaras himself, the megadux of the city, and the fate of his influential family. At first Mehmet assured the megadux that he and at least two of his sons, and perhaps a son-in-law as well, would not only be protected, but also were needed as new vassals of the Ottomans to help run the city. But after these assurances, the sultan had second thoughts at his banquet, and either driven by pederastic lust and drink, or following his deliberate plan all along to decapitate the Notaras family, ordered Notaras "to send your younger son to the banquet." After the megadux sent back his refusal, the sultan became enraged and demanded that the megadux and the surviving male members of his family appear immediately for their collective executions:

> The executioner took their heads and went back and showed them to that savage beast his master, as he made merry; the bodies were left there unburied, after they had been robbed of their clothing. Mehmet also sent the executioner to put to death all the nobles and high officials of the palace whom he had bought from their capture, while from their wives and children, the fairest women and most handsome youth were selected, and handed over into the custody of the Chief Eunuch.[71]

According to some accounts, the many executions created ill will among the surviving conquered. Perhaps such barbarity proved one reason why so many surviving Westerners fled the city—a fact that a supposedly remorseful Mehmet later sought to rectify by offering new concessions to attract Greeks and Italians back into Constantinople.[72]

By week's end, the Islamification of the city was in full force. Underway were not only the ad hoc conversion of churches to mosques but also the issuing of orders and protocols by which any free surviving Greek residents—many of whom possessed expertise as to the inner workings of municipal water, sewage, and storage infrastructure—could continue to occupy the city. Within days the Hagia Sophia cathedral had become the largest mosque in the Islamic world, as its famous frescos were whitewashed away. Within decades it would be refitted with minarets, obliterating for subsequent generations of Ottomans any memory or knowledge of its prior 916 years as the most revered church in Christendom.

News of the iconic city's finale arrived weeks later in Western Europe, followed by periodic reports of the subsequent ongoing demise of what was left of the Byzantine Empire in Asia Minor. The disaster was, of course, long feared, given the radical diminution in the size and wealth of the once Mediterranean-spanning Byzantine Empire. Nevertheless, the city's abrupt end shook all of Christendom. If the protective role of Constantinople was insufficiently appreciated by its beneficiaries in Western Europe during its long life, the city as eternal bulwark against the East was finally lamented after its death. No wonder some contemporaries found these post facto Western lamentations over the demise of Constantinople hypocritical. The Western Church and squabbling European fiefdoms had done little earlier to aid a beleaguered Orthodox Byzantine Empire when the capital's doom was by no means assured. But in fact, Western Europeans had apparently assumed that even the ossified fifteenth-century fortress city remained spiritually protected by God and was materially impregnable.[73]

Two general reactions to the fall occurred in the West. First, Western Christian outrage grew over the city's fall and the destruction of the free Greek population, with vows to launch a crusading fleet up the Dardanelles. Apocalyptic stories of the city's last day were accompanied by gruesome tales of the rape and murder of the trapped citizens, especially the fate of the megadux Loukas Notaras, the beheading of Constantine, and the taxidermy of his head. But if the pope and the Italian city-states for months talked of liberating the city, they soon thought better of it. Their more immediate worry was not so much over the Greeks' loss of Constantinople, but an even more aggressive and unchecked Ottoman sultan. And they now feared the fate of the various Italian trading concessionary enclaves in and around Constantinople, and ultimately the key Venetian fortresses in the Aegean, Greece, and the Eastern Mediterranean.

The second European response to the city's fall was calmer and less heroic, but equally predictable. By autumn 1453, "Mehmet the Conqueror" was swarmed by a host of Western envoys, variously pleading to ransom their relatives and grandees caught in the city and in trading enclaves across the Golden Horn. Official embassies from Italy immediately angled for a brokered peace, and perhaps even the continuance of Ottoman concessions to replace the now-lost trading posts, or negotiations for some sort of exemption from impending conquests.

As far as future conquests went, Western Europeans had long ago ironically jump-started the Ottoman gunpowder industry in the late thirteenth and fourteenth centuries. The Venetians especially had sold to the Ottomans finished cannons as well as strategic metallurgy and smelting expertise. Given their far greater resources and money, the Ottomans were soon able to buy foreign help to create their own foundries. At some East-West encounters in the Balkans over the next two centuries, the sultans' armies fielded more artillery than their enemies, even if not always equipped with qualitatively superior guns. Perhaps what eventually caused Ottoman technological competitiveness to stagnate by the latter sixteenth and seventeenth centuries was the Ottoman Empire's distance from the Atlantic, and thus from the continued European breakthroughs in transoceanic navigation, shipbuilding, and armaments.[74]

After the initial bloodletting, looting, and enslavement, the conquering Sultan Mehmet was confronted with owning a majestic but largely deserted metropolis. Its houses and stores were ransacked, and its population mostly killed, enslaved, or in hiding. Many of the Byzantine elite needed to operate the city's daily functions were either dead, taken hostage, or in flight to the West. The effort to repopulate the city, whose lifeblood had been commerce, forced the sultan within weeks to stop the executions of hostages and instead craft plans to entice his own subjects into the city and to invite back Greek and Western European traders, especially the Genoese and Venetians, a source of the city's historic wealth. Paradoxically, even as the Ottomans began to move on Venetian and Genoese possessions in the Aegean, they allowed Italian merchants to reboot their businesses in and around Constantinople.[75]

In truth, most of history's obliterators were not completely nihilistic. They usually refounded or rebuilt what they had destroyed, both because the sites of their conquests remained choice locations across time and space, regardless of the civilization that occupied them, and because greater glory accrued to the conqueror if his own culture absorbed and trumped the vanquished iconic imperial city of his enemies. In Mehmet's case, the sultan wanted the shell of

Constantinople intact, so that he could inherit and reinvent it as the largest, best fortified, and most dynamic Islamic city in the world.[76]

As for the Byzantines in the aftermath of the defeat, as noted, most of the forty thousand to fifty thousand surviving Greeks still inside the walls were either killed, enslaved, or allowed to live under carefully prescribed conditions per Sharia law. Those of noble birth were held for ransom for months, especially the prized Venetians and Genoese who would earn the greatest payments. All the Greek suburban towns and outlying cities still free along the Dardanelles were quickly overrun in the months following the fall of the city.[77]

Within a decade, most of the Greek-speaking vestigial lands of the Byzantines were conquered or surrendered, including the despotate of the Morea in the Greek-held Peloponnese, which fell in 1460. Its majestic but small capital at Mystras—controlled by the two brothers of the dead emperor, Thomas Palaiologos and Demetrios Palaiologos—was captured seven years to the day after the fall of Constantinople. A few holdout sanctuaries in the Mani Peninsula of the Peloponnese lasted for months afterward before being evacuated or overwhelmed.

On the Black Sea, the autonomous Greek-speaking empire of Trebizond, which had divorced itself from direct control of Constantinople during the aftermath of the disaster of the Fourth Crusade, was targeted and stormed in August 1461, as part of Mehmet's systematic cleanup of the vestigial fragments of the Byzantine Empire. The even more remote so-called Principality of Theodoro in the Crimea—a Greek-speaking, Orthodox principality dangerously tucked in between Venetian-controlled trading cities and the Turkic Khanate of Crimea—lasted the longest of the Byzantine remnants. It finally fell to the Ottomans in December 1475, some twenty-two years after the end of Christian Constantinople. The principality's lord, Alexander, was beheaded, his children converted to Islam, and his daughters sent to the harem. Of the capitulations of these very last holdout Byzantine mini-kingdoms in Europe, Asia, and the Aegean, Steven Runciman once concluded: "It was the end of the free Greek world."[78]

The orphaned Byzantine monarchy became merely nominal after the fall. Like Russia's Romanovs nearly five hundred years later, who for years traveled throughout Europe, the various surviving branches of the stateless and itinerant Palaiologos family were sometimes courted in the West by monarchs and given audiences with the pope as the true rulers of a lost empire. In return, they perpetually cajoled and promised to lead a great crusade to recover Constantinople. For example, Andreas Palaiologos, the eldest nephew of the deceased last emperor, Constantine XI, carved out a brief but occasionally remunerative career in Rome as the supposed true "Emperor of Constantinople." Andreas was often entertained in the papal states, before selling his title and succession rights to a nonexistent empire to Charles VIII of France—titles and privileges that he subsequently reclaimed and deeded to various other European monarchs.

Renaissance Italians finally tired of the visiting stateless Byzantine royals looking for armies and weapons to reclaim their lost lands, as well as of the itinerant Greek scholars peddling old manuscripts and seeking out patrons. As one modern historian put it, "As these state visits became more frequent and the accompanying requests for aid multiplied, the begging Greeks were viewed increasingly as pests rather than as dignified emissaries of an ancient culture that they were seeking so desperately to preserve"—rather like White Russian aristocratic refugees in Paris during the 1920s.[79]

Constantinople itself had contributed to the budding Renaissance with its introduction and translation of new Greek texts, many of them missing from or even unknown by Western centers of learning. The Italian scholar Aeneas Silvius Piccolomini, who would become Pope Pius II (1458–1464) after the fall of Constantinople, lamented the loss of just such a key role as the city had played in training Renaissance humanists in ancient Greek and introducing them to previously unknown classical authors and texts: "No Latin could ever be considered educated, unless he had studied in Constantinople. The famous name that Athens enjoyed when Rome flourished was held by Constantinople in our age."

The future pope would see immediately the consequences of the 1453 loss to the Ottomans of the Greek center of learning: "What am

I to say about the innumerable books that were there, still unknown to the Latins. Alas, will the name of such great men perish now? This is the second death of Homer, the second passing of Plato. Where shall we seek philosophical and poetical genius? The Fountain of the Muses has run dry."[80]

Among the many myths that surrounded the city's fall, the most famous concerned the dead and beheaded emperor Constantine XI. A legend grew that he had not died at all, much less been overwhelmed while fighting under a sea of enemies, his corpse decapitated on the last day of the city, and his preserved head put on display. Instead, he had been divinely marbleized and preserved in suspended animation by an archangel, who then deposited the "Marble Emperor" under the Golden Gate—the monumental gate to the city in the Theodosian Walls dedicated by the founder of the city Constantine the Great—whence to arise when the moment came for the Greeks to recapture Constantinople for Hellenism.[81]

As for the ascendant Ottoman Empire, it would not just expand by its incorporation of Byzantine lands. Psychologically, if not in actuality, it now loomed over all of Central Europe, which was soon to be further torn apart by new Reformation-era infighting between Protestants and Catholics. With the last Byzantine obstacles removed, and the Ottoman absorption of most of the Balkans, in subsequent decades Eastern Europe would be in its greatest peril ever from a sultan.

As for the city, Mehmet moved his capital from Edirne to Constantinople in 1457. Within thirty years he had been able to raise the population of the city to nearly seventy thousand residents. His successors, for a time and in their own interests, mostly honored their commercial concessions to Europeans, and allowed the few remaining Greeks to pay infidel fees and worship largely unmolested as second-class citizens. The Ottomans continued to incentivize Turkish immigration into the city, which itself underwent a centuries-long and massive architectural renaissance. A century and a half later, by 1600 Constantinople had grown to over a half million residents with thousands of new homes, mosques, and municipal buildings.

The natural advantages of the site transcended the nature of its occupants. Even today, they explain in part the geostrategic and commercial advantages of modern Turkey. The contemporary site of Istanbul capitalizes, in ancestral fashion, on being the sole guardian of entry into and exit from the Black Sea—to the chagrin of the Russian Federation. Today, Istanbul is the largest city in Europe at nearly sixteen million residents, even as Turkish president Recep Erdoğan's policies reflect the centuries-old duality of affinity for, and distrust of, historically Christian Europe. Turkey remains a nominal NATO member even as Erdoğan opportunistically both bullies and distances himself from his European NATO allies. Erdoğan proclaims modern and increasingly Islamist Turkey as the natural successor to the Ottoman Empire, rather than to Kemal Ataturk's secular and nationalist Westernized Turkey.[82]

The Greek population in Istanbul has been reduced to a mere two thousand residents, and perhaps another two thousand self-identifying as Greeks are dispersed throughout Turkey. Most are careful to avoid politics, curb their public use of the Greek language, and carefully watch for tensions between Turkey and Greece or Christian Armenia that might bode ill for their own security—in a way more reminiscent of the nineteenth rather than twenty-first century.[83]

In the immediate decades that followed the fall of Constantinople and its empire, Orthodox Christians viewed the disaster not as due to a failure to accept last-minute, pragmatic accords with Rome to unify against the Ottomans, but rather as an expression of God's displeasure at the supposed laxity and decadence that had rendered them so vulnerable to extinction. Ironically, the end of Constantinople created a new resoluteness among the dispersed and orphaned subjects of Byzantium, whose religiosity grew all the more embattled and zealous as they lived under the sultans. Most vestigial Orthodox Christians in Asia Minor survived in scattered settlements, but within decades of the Islamic takeover some had established distinctively Greek quarters even inside Constantinople itself.[84]

Nonetheless, Greek survivors, both immediately and for centuries after, later blamed in part Western Catholicism for the fall. They fixated on the irrevocable damage done to Byzantium by the Fourth Crusade. They cited the obstinacy of the popes in demanding unreasonable concessions for a belated union of Eastern and Western Christendom. And, most frequently, they faulted the failure of the West to send credible forces to save the city in its final defense.

Some Byzantines had before the siege naïvely assumed that a likely defeat under the Ottomans would in fact be preferable to survival in perpetual debt to Rome. Or as the doomed Loukas Notaras, the megadux of the city, was rumored to have sighed in the weeks before the attack, "Better the Turkish turban than the Papal tiara"—a quip he would live to regret. That much quoted aphorism could mean either that he preferred living under Ottoman rule to surviving with Orthodoxy inevitably absorbed into Catholicism—or that he saw an uncompromised Constantinople defiant to the end as a better fate than a humiliating subservience to Rome. In any case, the memory of the wealthy and internationally well-connected Notaras became controversial in the years after the city's fall and his own beheading, as he was often damned by the Italians who fought for the city for either his incompetence or triangulation with the enemy.[85]

With the destruction of all the institutions of formal Byzantine civilization, both Hellenic society and state Orthodoxy, and with the flight of hundreds of thousands of Greek-speakers from Asia to Europe, what was the ultimate fate of some two million orphaned Byzantines at the time of the fall? As far as Greece proper, former Byzantine subjects there would prove the most resistant of all occupied Balkan peoples to Islamic conversion. For the next 360 years, the second-class Greek-speakers of Ottoman-occupied Greece were able to retain a cohesive Hellenic culture, preserve the Greek language, and cultivate a vibrant Orthodoxy, albeit often by abandoning the major cities and the rich farmlands of the lowlands to Ottoman occupiers, and retreating to nearly inaccessible mountain villages.

As noted, after the conquest, Mehmet continually claimed that he wished to retain or even enlarge the Greek-speaking population of Constantinople. Indeed, within weeks of the fall, the sultan resettled his one-fifth share of the enslaved population—perhaps as many as ten thousand Greeks—in Constantinople. Still, for the next four centuries the Greek population would be subject to limitations placed on its religious observance, politics, and lifestyle, and would, under later sultans, struggle to survive occasional pogroms and atrocities.

Indeed, Mehmet himself was later criticized as being too tolerant of the conquered Greeks by needlessly incentivizing their return, through returning property and offering up vacant homes, while punishing the advisors of his inner circle who had persuaded him to execute high officials of Constantinople. It remained yet another paradox that a few Greek Christians, after the first few weeks of the often horrific takeover of their city, were treated in the subsequent years of the conqueror Mehmet's reign perhaps better than their descendants ever would be in later centuries under subsequent and far harsher Ottoman sultans.

Yet it is not quite accurate to suggest that Mehmet was innately more tolerant than his successors. After capturing the city, he had little choice in the immediate aftermath but to retain as many Greeks as possible to keep the infrastructure of Constantinople from collapsing, given his grand plans eventually to remake the city as his new capital of a global Ottoman empire.[86]

After the conquest of 1453, the subsequent sultans took to calling themselves caesars, as if they—not the ghosts of the Byzantines—were to be seen as the true heirs and successors to the Roman Empire and its majestic capital. But as memory of a Byzantine Constantinople faded under the later sultans, so too did recognition that the Eastern Romans had marked a cultural continuation of some three millennia of Hellenism.

It slowly was forgotten in the centuries after 1453 that the oldest and richest settlements of archaic and classical Greek civilization had arisen in Asia Minor. Accordingly, lands around the Bosporus, parts of Anatolia and the Black Sea coasts, and the islands of the eastern Aegean had all been Greek-speaking since at least the tenth century BC, and perhaps even centuries earlier. Despite the constant threats and subjugations by Lydians and Persians, Ionia—the Aegean coastal lands of modern Turkey—birthed the seventh- to fifth-century BC pre-Socratic philosophical tradition best exemplified by the Milesian school of Thales, Anaximander, and Anaximenes. The greatest of the early Greek lyric poets—Alcaeus, Anacreon, Archilochus, Sappho, and Simonides—were all born on the coast of Asia Minor or on the nearby Aegean islands that fell to the fifteenth-century Ottomans. Homer, the bard of the *Iliad* and *Odyssey*, was an Ionian. In legend, he was born somewhere in the eastern Aegean or on the central coast of Ionia. Many prominent Ionian Greeks later had played prominent roles in the campaigns and administration of Alexander the Great. And during the six centuries of Roman rule, Ionia saw its thriving commercial centers at Miletus and later Ephesus become some of the richest cities in the Roman Empire.

In sum, western "Asia" Minor had never really been Asian at all until the Ottoman conquest. The last of the hallowed political institutions that had protected and nourished this ancient legacy of Hellenism in Asia for centuries under different regimes—first Hellenic city-states, then Hellenistic monarchs, then the Roman Empire—was extinguished for good in 1453. In this regard, the Roman poet Horace could famously write near the end of the Roman Republic of the dominant influence of conquered Hellenism upon Rome: "A conquered Greece took captive its savage conqueror and brought its arts to rustic Latium" (*Epistles* 1.156–7). But fifteen hundred years later, a subjugated Hellenism had no such cultural dominance over its Islamic Ottoman vanquishers, despite the fables that Mehmet likened himself to Roman emperors and Alexander the Great, and saw his storming of Constantinople as a sort of belated payback for the Greek sacking of Asian Troy. When Mehmet supposedly viewed the legendary site of Troy, he was reported to have claimed ties to the mythical enemies of the Greeks: "After the passage of so many years, God appointed me to be the avenger of this city, of its inhabitants." That fantasy payback theme was oddly embraced by a few contrarian Italian humanists, who following Virgil had connected Romanitas to the survival and flight westward of the defeated Trojan Aeneas. In such thinking, they also argued that the sack of Troy had been finally and properly avenged by Mehmet—as if Turkish Muslims were somehow more Latinate than Westernized Byzantine Christian Greeks.[87]

In terms of population after the fall, again we do not know how many Byzantines remained in the countryside along the Dardanelles and Bosporus, or in enclaves on the Black Sea. The population of the entire Byzantine Empire on both sides of the Aegean had fallen from its sixth-century acme of some twenty million residents to less than two million by the time of the siege of Constantinople. The vast majority of that surviving population likely either fled to seek safety in the Aegean and Mediterranean islands, the Peloponnese or Italy, or formally made arrangements to continue in Anatolia as second-class citizens in close-knit Greek communities. Many converted to Islam. Others retreated to the mountains of Anatolia beyond the daily reach of Ottoman tax collectors and the agents of the devshirme. Over the next half millennium, a residual population of perhaps a million descendants of the Byzantines survived as Greek-speakers and Orthodox Christians scattered throughout Asia Minor. An Ottoman-approved patriarch in Constantinople continued as the nominal head of the Greek Orthodox Church.[88]

Yet in a strange twist of demographics, a recent DNA survey of the current Turkish population allegedly revealed that the majority has predominantly Anatolian Greek ancestry, rather than a genetic inheritance from the arriving Turkish tribes that eventually aggregated into the Ottomans. The study has evoked outrage in the contemporary Turkish government, given its efforts to account for current Turkish antipathy toward modern Greece in the Ottoman notion that, historically and presently Hellenism had no legitimate claim in either the eastern Aegean or Anatolia. Nonetheless, if accurate, DNA studies suggest that while the Byzantine Empire receded before and was absorbed by the Seljuk Turks, millions of the ensuing conquered indigenous populations remained ethnically Greek, and eventually became culturally indistinguishable from the later Ottomans.

cally, after the fall the Turks had kept the name of the gh transliterated into Turkish as *Kostantiniyye*. That was to endure officially until 1923, when the new Turkish government formally rebranded the city as Istanbul (a corruption of the Greek "into the city"/εἰς τὴν Πόλιν/eis tên polin). That belated change was gradually accepted internationally over the next few years. Note that it was the more secular nationalist government of Mustafa Kemal Atatürk, not the Ottoman Muslims, that finally insisted on the name change and the end of any reference to the great Greek city.[89]

There is a final modern footnote to the end of the Byzantines. In the mid– and late–nineteenth century, in the waning decades of the enfeebled Ottoman Empire, there was a resurgent Greek presence in Anatolia. Opportunistic reverse Greek migration into the more developed central coast of Asia Minor had been encouraged by the start of the Greek revolution against Ottoman rule in 1821, and the subsequent relaxed immigration laws of the fading Ottoman government. The result was that Greek immigrants began swelling the existing remnant population of the ancestral Greek minority communities on the coast of Asia Minor. By the early twentieth century, Greeks may have again formed a near majority of the population of the historically Greek city Smyrna, renamed the current Izmir in 1930.

As a result of these dynamic mass migrations, the vestigial Greek-speaking population of the new Turkish state rebounded to over one million, especially among the central coastal Ionian cities and along the Black Sea coast. After the defeat of the Central Powers and their ally Turkey in World War I, the old dream of resurrecting a Greek-speaking Byzantine Empire rearose, now to be known under the irredentist slogan of the "Great Idea," or Megali Idea. Energized by a new zeal for empire, what the Greeks lacked in manpower vis-à-vis the new post-imperial Turkey, they felt they more than made up for by having been an ally to Britain and France on the right side of the recent war. It was almost as if the marbleized emperor Constantine XI at last might spring from his centuries-old walled confinement and welcome in the new Byzantines to his lost city.

The zenith of Greek Byzantinist fervor came in June 1921 with the visit to western Anatolia of the appropriately named modern Greek king Constantine, now to be referred to as "Emperor-Designate of Constantinople and Commander of the Anglo-Greek Forces in the

Near East." As a recent scholar noted: "King Constantine was the first Christian king to land on Anatolian soil since the Crusades."[90]

Yet the Greek attempt to implement the Great Idea by incorporating into the new Byzantium all of Cyprus, much of the central Aegean coast of Anatolia, and the city of Constantinople—to round out prior additions to the Greek nation in the north, the Aegean Islands, and in the Ionian Sea—only inflamed already ascendant Turkish nationalism. Once the fight started, inevitably Greece's Great Power friends abandoned the Hellenic cause as too radical and dangerous, and thus the Greek expeditionary forces as expendable.

The tragic result was a violent Turkish national reaction that ended the Greco-Turkish war of 1919–1922 with the final defeat and expulsion of the Greeks in Asia Minor. The horrific burning and ethnic cleansing of Greek Smyrna followed. As part of the Greco-Turkish war's settlement, Greece ceded to the new Turkish nation *all* of its recently acquired Anatolian territories and historic claims on Constantinople. Such was the finale to the old idea that a reborn twentieth-century Greek Constantinople would reverse the verdict of 1453.

More population exchanges soon followed that eventually saw well over a million Greeks flee Turkey to Greece. Constantinople was almost completely ethnically cleansed of its historic Greek minority that had grown and numbered nearly a hundred thousand residents. The final population swaps ensured that by 1930 there was no real cohesive Greek community left in Asia.

So ended the entire Megali Idea and three millennia of Greek civilization in Asia Minor—the final footnote to the end of Byzantium.[91]

––––––––––

Just as Classical Thebes rearose as Macedonian Thebes, Punic Carthage reappeared as Roman Carthage, and Aztec Tenochtitlán was reborn as Spanish Mexico City, so Christian Constantinople was transformed under Mehmet into the capital of his Islamic empire. And just as the new Thebes had few if any classical Thebans, there was no Punic culture to speak of in Roman Carthage and, as we shall see, Mexico City bore no resemblance to the civilization of Tenochtitlán, so too Islamic Constantinople in the centuries after the fall of Byzantium was a decidedly different city. The former site of a seven-hundred-year resistance to Islam became the center of its greatest outward permanent expansion.

There was one difference, however. Whereas classical Thebes was leveled, Punic Carthage was razed, and Tenochtitlán was paved over, not so majestic Constantinople. Despite the deaths, the plundering, the destruction of Byzantine civilization, and the persecution of the vestigial population, and despite the Islamization of the city's religious centers, the city's infrastructure was simply too valuable and iconic, and thus was appropriated and largely remained intact.

In sum, despite the horrific final siege, Byzantium ended not with a bang, but a with a whimper. The Ottoman conqueror kept the corpse intact and reanimated it with a completely different spirit. That eerie conversion was another reason why contemporaries in Western Christendom were so horrified by the fate of the iconic city that after 1453 appeared superficially almost the same but was in fact most certainly not, as if the iconic buildings themselves had turned traitor. In sum, the bulwark of Christendom in Asia became the domain of its would-be destroyer.

Still, by the mid fifteenth century at the time of the fall of Constantinople, there were already subtle signs that the global future was not with Ottomanism. Future commercial wealth would no longer hinge so much on overland routes to the east, whether via Eastern Mediterranean ports, north to junctions with the old Via Egnatia, or through the Bosporus to the Black Sea. The Mediterranean naval powers of Venice and Genoa had long dominated these itineraries for centuries. But new vistas were opening up on the Atlantic.

In the last days of the empire, other Europeans—especially the Portuguese and Spanish—began to envision alternatives to the Eastern Mediterranean and Constantinople for their commercial routes. It was ironic that the rise of the Ottomans, and especially their capture of the city, only further accelerated the Western Europeans' ongoing efforts to find alternative passages to an increasingly hostile East.

Well before Columbus, the Atlantic coastal Europeans were already starting to master ocean sailing outside the Mediterranean, notably along the northern and western coast of Africa and the Canary and Azores Islands. Portuguese caravels by the early fifteenth century had already mapped out the beginnings of what would after the fall of Constantinople eventually become a rich maritime future of trade with China and India.[92]

May 29, 1453, also marked a great historical divide in which the ideas of "Asia" and "Europe" would permanently be delineated by Turkish Istanbul—on the premise that the Western city of Constantine was actually always on Asian soil and thus culturally and politically had returned to where it belonged. Any notion that Europeans would ever again claim as home the once Roman East was finished. In the Ottoman creed, Asia was to be for Asians—and eventually Europe as well. Ended too was any thought that Hellenism would supplant Latinate Western Europe, as it had done for centuries after the collapse of fifth-century Rome. The balance between a supposedly barbarous Latin West and a civilized Greek East was reversed.

Today, many of the areas fought over by Ottomans and Byzantines remain captives of memory. Much of the current twenty-first-century tensions between a stereotypically traditionalist, conservative, poor, and long-suffering Eastern Europe, and a liberal, wealthy, and freewheeling Western Europe arose after 1453. As Hellenism waned and the Byzantine brake on Ottoman expansion ended, Eastern Europeans felt they were abandoned to stop the Turk on their own, while a securer protected West was free to become rich.

Despite Muslim armies to come at the gates of Vienna in 1529 and 1683, there was a renewed and confident West on the horizon. Aside from the cultural and scientific breakthroughs of the Renaissance, Europe was soon to make a quantum leap forward in military arms and technology, and within a half century to obtain a virtual monopoly on transoceanic navigation that would bring the

Atlantic European monarchies untold riches from China, India, and the New World.

Western military and scientific dynamism would bring the emissaries of imperial Spain, just thirty years after the discovery of the New World, into the heartland of Mexico. There they encountered a wondrous empire—one confident, warlike, and antithetical to Catholic Spanish imperialism in almost every way imaginable. Yet Aztec Tenochtitlán, like its doomed predecessors, believed that its complex defenses, martial prowess, efforts to mollify, bribe, and bully the intruders—and its sense of divine right and demonstrable power—would ensure its eternal existence. Just as Thebans, Carthaginians, and Byzantines were not fully aware of either the strength of their attackers or the destructive genius of their enemies' leaders, so too the Aztecs could never fathom a man like Hernán Cortés, who was quite willing to annihilate them and would in just two years find the power to do just that.

4

IMPERIAL HUBRIS

The Annihilation of the Aztec Empire
(Summer 1521)

Trojans, trust not the horse.
Whatever it is, I fear the Greeks, even bringing gifts.
(*Equo ne credite, Teucri /*
quidquid id est, timeo Danaos et dona ferentis.)
—**Virgil,** *Aeneid*

The [Aztecs] no longer had nor could find any arrows, javelins, or
stones with which to attack us; and our allies fighting with us were
armed with swords and bucklers and slaughtered so many of them
on land and in the water that more than forty thousand were killed
or taken that day. So loud was the wailing of the women and children that there was not one man amongst us whose heart did not
bleed at the sound.[1]

So Hernán Cortés, the conqueror of New Spain, reported how he
had obliterated the Aztec capital of Tenochtitlán. If his lengthy
report in his third letter of 1521 to King Charles V—one of five written by Cortés to his Spanish king between 1519 and 1526, before,
during, and after the conquest—was mostly accurate, then the
details of the conquest he describes present a horrific picture. The
Spanish—empowered by their steel swords, crossbows, cannon, and
harquebuses—and their native allies may have killed twice as many
of the Mexica (as the Aztecs were generally known to themselves

and other tribes) in a single day of their final siege, as the British army of 1916 lost on the first day of the Somme.

As Cortés further wrote to his king, when the Spanish and their allies for a second time approached the city on Lake Texcoco, the war was assumed by all to be existential. The losers would be killed to the man and vanish from Mexico. The winners who survived would from then on do as they pleased. Like the Spartans and their allies at the battle of Thermopylae, Cortés's small band was outnumbered thousands of times over. But unlike Leonidas's Spartans and allies, Cortés won while on the offensive as an invader, rather than perishing on the defensive on his own soil, in one of the most astonishing victories and absolute annihilations of an opponent in military history.

Cortés may have later confessed to his king that his heart had bled at the sound of the slaughter of Aztec children who fell to his native allies. But the caudillo's victories would have been impossible without drafting into his army tens of thousands of fierce neighboring Tlaxcalan warriors. As frequent victims of Aztec human sacrifice, they detested the Aztecs more than they feared the Spanish, a fact essential to the strategy of Cortés. Indeed, that indigenous alliance, one that began with a series of bloody battles eventually lost to the Spanish by the Tlaxcalans, proved fortunate for the Spanish. The Tlaxcalans were acknowledged as the preeminent anti-Aztec warriors of central Mexico. Almost alone of Tenochtitlán's many enemies, they had found ways to ensure their autonomy through shifting alliances and extraordinary fierceness on the battlefield.

After their failed initial resistance to the Spanish, the Tlaxcalans had joined the Spaniards on sure promises of inflicting a final revenge on their Aztec tormentors. Over the next two years, of all Cortés's mercurial allies, it was the city of Tlaxcala that always proved the most reliable, the most competent, and the deadliest to the Aztecs. Tlaxcala was critical to Cortés's unlikely conquest, and to some extent to his later ability with small constabulary forces to control most of postwar central Mexico.[2]

To receive some idea of the ferocity of the Tlaxcalans and their loyalty to "the Captain" (Cortés), consider this Tlaxcalan song from the conquest:

You've arrived here in Tenochtitlán! Be strong, Tlaxcalans!
   Huexotzincans! And what will Nelpiloni be hearing from
   Lord Xicotencatl? Be strong! Hail!
Let's keep watch for the Captain's boats. And ah, his banner is just
   coming in from Tepepol. Beneath it the Mexican people are
   ravaged. Woe! Be strong! Hail!
Give aid to our lords! With iron weapons they're wrecking the city,
   they're wrecking the Mexican nation! Be strong! Hail!
Beat your drum and laugh loud, O Ixtlilxochitl! Dance at the Eagle
   Gate! Here! In Mexico! Your scarlet-plume shields are whirling
   at the round-stone. Be strong! Hail!
Meanwhile they sally forth and offer themselves. Oh, nephews!
   O Valiant Anahuacatl, and you, O Otomi Chief Tehuetzquiti,
   woe! Be strong! Hail![3]

The savvy invader knew that the Tlaxcalans, after suffering a century of forced contributions of their youth to the Aztecs' human sacrifice industry, would likely show no mercy during the final days of the hated city. Cortés accepted that his own small force had neither the numbers nor the means to stop the Tlaxcalans' retributory killing, even had he wanted to. At this risky moment in the streets of the Aztec capital he had no wish to restrain them, despite later avowals. The result was unending slaughter, a carnage that not only climaxed the defeat of the Aztecs but also ensured the eventual extinction of their civilization.

This surreal clash of cultures had all begun in November 1519, shortly after the Spanish landing on the eastern Mexican coast. Following rumors of a vast, rich city in the interior of the little-visited mainland, and after a series of battles with satellite Aztec subject cities, the Spanish contingent of roughly five hundred under Cortés made their way through the hinterland and entered Tenochtitlán. Yet after nine months of constant travel and serial fighting, an exhausted Cortés had finally reached the capital with a worn-out force that seemed to pose no threat to the vast Aztec Empire. But what they saw stunned—and excited—them. As they inventoried the riches of the island metropolis, noting the vast asymmetry between their small force and the expansive Aztec city, they yet grew confident that their innate military advantages would nullify their numerical inferiority.

Cortés's battle-hardened men had quickly surmised from their initial hazardous march inland from the Gulf Coast that, whether attacked or on the offensive, what the Spanish lacked in numbers might be partially offset by their cultural, political, and technological advantages. Just three decades after the discoveries of Columbus, Cortés had fathomed who and what the Aztecs were; in contrast, the Mexica at least at first were less sure about the nature of their intrusive guests. And they certainly had no inkling that the Spanish might desire, much less possess the ability, to destroy their immense empire in a matter of months.

Bernal Díaz del Castillo, veteran of the campaign and our most comprehensive contemporary historical source for the conquest, attributed in part the Spanish ability to obliterate Tenochtitlán to what is now sometimes described as "cultural confusion." This long-held explanation for Cortés's success assumed the Aztecs thought the Spaniards were gods. Thus, they not only backed off from initially attacking them, but also allowed the conquistadors to stay supplied within Tenochtitlán itself.

Still, there is a great deal of evidence that such existential puzzlement was not widespread, at least not for very long. In truth, Cortés never wrote that the Mexica or any other group thought he was a god. Instead, the earliest published eyewitness account mentioning the Spaniards as gods may have been that of Francisco de Aguilar, who eventually gave up his estates in Spanish Mexico, became a Dominican friar, and decades later in his eighties finally wrote a memoir of the violent conquest. "They regarded us," Aguilar later wrote, "as immortal men and called us *teules*, which means gods."[4]

Bernal Díaz, of course, agreed. In his comprehensive account of the initial encounters, he described the reactions of the local Mayans at Vera Cruz:

When they witnessed deeds so marvelous and of such importance to themselves, they said that no human beings would dare to do such things and that it was the work of *Teules*, for so they called the idols they worshiped, and for this reason from that time forth, they called us *Teules*, which is as much as to say that we were either gods or demons.[5]

Andrés de Tapia, another conquistador chronicler, detailed the first encounter between the Spaniards and the Tlaxcalans, showing again that at least some Nahua—generally the indigenous of Mexico— initially thought the newcomers might be divine:

Certain Indians had come to the camp bringing five other Indians to [Cortés], and saying to him: "If you be a god that eats meat and blood, eat these Indians and we shall bring you more. And if you be a kind god, here are plumes and incense. And if you be a man, here are turkeys and bread and cherries."[6]

As far as the Aztec religious hierarchy, the priests—part of the theocracy that was inseparable from the monarchy—supposedly concluded that the magical animals and weapons that Cortés brought with him to Tenochtitlán were confirmation of ancient prophecies. The feathered serpent and multifaceted god Quetzal-coatl was supposedly long expected to appear in the flesh—in the very year of the Spanish arrival—accompanied by a white-skinned, bearded retinue in human form.

Indeed, the Florentine Codex—a massive twenty-four-hundred-page illustrated cultural history of the Aztecs compiled from Nahua sources by Franciscan friar Bernardino de Sahagún decades after the conquest—lists a mishmash of natural phenomena that presaged a divine arrival. From lightning strikes to comets and magical appearances of strange beasts, such confused warnings grew of the impending arrival of the white-skinned strangers. As a result, the troubled Aztecs had some idea of unusually bad things on the horizon. Otherwise, they had no inkling of who or what Cortés was,

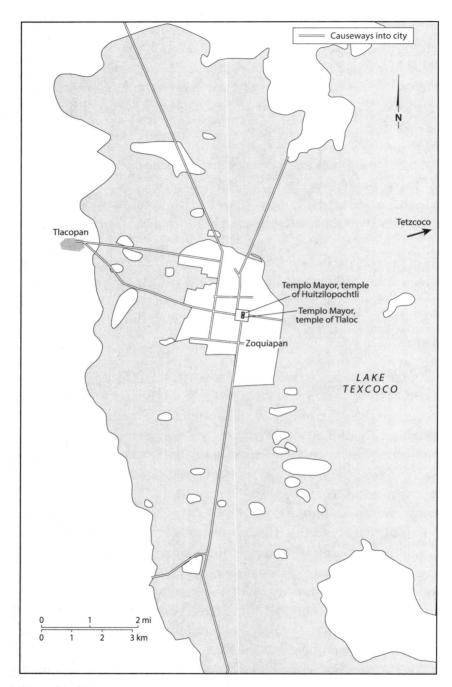

Tenochtitlán

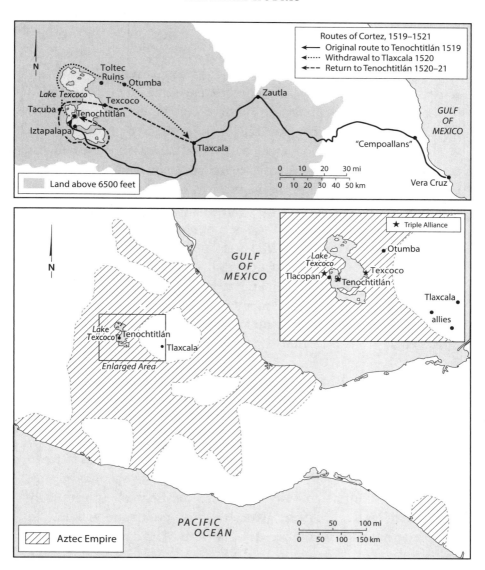

The Aztec Empire in the Sixteenth Century

much less the dangers in store for them, especially given the very different tactical and strategic protocols of European warfare: preference for decisive battle, reliance on superior technology, strict military discipline, logistics, and a comprehensive chain of command.[7]

Certainly, Cortés played on the fact that some Nahua religious leaders for a while had believed his men might be a part of a godly entourage of the divine Quetzalcoatl. Or at the least the messengers from coastal cities had initially related such supernatural suppositions to the spies and scouts of the ruling Aztec emperor Montezuma II—the ninth emperor and great-grandson of Montezuma I—shortly after the Spanish landing on the eastern coast.

Cortés further assumed that such fantasies were of enormous strategic importance, at least during his first visit to Tenochtitlán during the latter weeks of 1519 and early 1520. It may later have been equally convenient for Aztec survivors post facto to have confessed to the Spaniards that one reason for their own destruction was their priests' disastrous assertions that their warriors were dealing with immortal and near-invincible divine visitors. Whether or not the Aztec hierarchy ever really believed the Spanish to be divine, it mattered little after they failed to annihilate Cortés at his initial appearance while they still had a chance.[8]

Clearly, Montezuma II himself from their first meeting surmised that Cortés was human after all. In his October 1520 second letter to Charles V reviewing his experiences and outlining agendas, Cortés quotes Montezuma's first statements to the Spanish (presumably translated by La Malinche, Cortés's mistress, from Nahuatl to Mayan, and then by Francisco Aguilar from Mayan to Spanish):

"I also know that [your allies] have told you the walls of my houses are made of gold, and that the floor mats in my rooms and other things in my household are likewise of gold, and that I was, and claimed to be, a god, and many other things besides. The houses as you see are of stone and lime and clay." Then he raised his clothes and showed me his body, saying, as he grasped his arms and trunk with his hands, "See that I am of flesh and blood like you and all other men, and I am mortal and substantial."[9]

Much later, after the destruction of the city, the conquest was, of course, mythologized. Both the Spanish and survivors from the fall of Tenochtitlán spread the original idea that the Spanish cavalrymen were centaur-like demigods—part human, part bizarre four-legged beasts, and equipped with thunderous deadly firearms and sharp-edged weapons—who had confused the Aztecs into initial stasis. And perhaps some of the coastal Maya had initially believed Cortés's horses were dragons. They claimed they were especially frightened of their toothy and snarly mouths.

Yet scholars more recently have reminded us there are few pre-Spanish accounts that mention the mythical return of Quetzal-coatl in what would have been the year 1519. And even if Aztec religious grandees promulgated such a prophecy, the initial mystic shock of such discordant cultures soon wore off.[10]

Over the ensuing months the Aztec hosts noted how Cortés and his men bled. Their wounds confirmed some earlier conflicting rumors that had reached them about the Spanish from scouts and messengers from the coastal tribes. The Spanish also grew hungry. In petty human fashion, they squabbled. They haggled. They lusted for gold. They demanded sex from indigenous women. In the most ungodly furor, they tore down idols. They brazenly harangued their hosts about human sacrifice and cannibalism. Rather than being deities themselves, they proselytized the Mexica to accept as their savior their own deity Jesus Christ.

Most importantly, for all their magical weapons—horses, huge dogs, Spanish steel, cannon, harquebuses, and crossbows—these men of flesh were still outnumbered by some six to eight hundred to one. Later accounts compiled by Bernardino de Sahagún attested that even the temporizing Montezuma II remained adamant that his guests were not deities at all, much less well intended, but rather quite savage and dangerous humans with martial powers far beyond those of his own Aztec subjects:

Moctezuma wept, and [how] the Mexicans wept, when they knew that the Spaniards were very powerful. And Moctezuma loudly expressed his distress. He felt distress, he was terrified, he was astounded; he expressed his distress because of the city. And indeed, everyone was greatly terrified. There were terror, astonishment, expressions of distress, feelings of distress. There were consultations. There were formations of groups; there were assemblies of people. There was weeping—there was much weeping, there was weeping for others. There was only the hanging of heads, there was dejection. There were tearful greetings, there were tearful greetings given others.[11]

What ensued over the next eight months inside Tenochtitlán was a period of mutual fraternization and discovery, betrayals, revolts, civil wars, see-saw battles—and ultimately the near obliteration of the initial Spanish force. After just a few days inside Tenochtitlán, there was already growing confusion as to whether the tiny band of Spanish conquistadors were prisoners of hundreds of thousands of Aztecs, or if in fact they were in control of the city by virtue of holding their emperor Montezuma II as an implicit hostage. Indeed, just six days after their arrival on November 6, 1519, the Spanish had occupied and fortified Montezuma's imperial residence—with the emperor himself inside it. So both realities were true enough: the relatively few Spanish hostage takers in the imperial palace were also hostages themselves in the imperial city.

Soon, it seemed, most Aztec elites confirmed earlier rumors from the coast that the Spanish had arrived from great distances not as benefactors, gods, or even simple adventurers, but as human, gold-obsessed conquerors, and colonists determined to stay in Mexico. Growing Aztec familiarity with the Spanish over these months was also proving nearly disastrous for the often vain conquistadors, who as yet were almost oblivious to their growing peril. The always wily Cuitláhuac, brother of Montezuma II—and his soon-to-be replacement for a brief eighty days as emperor before succumbing to smallpox—increasingly had little doubt: the Spanish were criminals bent on theft, conquest, and Aztec ruin. Thus he advocated that they should be exterminated as quickly as possible before their numbers and power grew.[12]

From the moment the Spaniards first arrived at Tenochtitlán and asked for entry into the city, Cuitláhuac had seen them as existential threats. By contrast, Montezuma's nephew Cacama had urged that they be welcomed:

> Cacama [said] that it would show a want of courage to deny them entrance once they were at the gates. He added that it was not proper for a great lord like his uncle to turn away the ambassadors of another great prince. If the visitors made any demands which displeased Montezuma, he could punish their insolence by sending his hosts of brave warriors against them . . . Then Cuitláhuac warned him, "I pray to our gods that you will not let the strangers into your house. They will cast you out of it and overthrow your rule, and when you try to recover what you have lost, it will be too late."[13]

Unfortunately for Montezuma and his entire Aztec empire, he did not follow his brother's advice but instead agreed with his nephew and so let the Spaniards into the island city.

Amid these tensions of early November 1919, and after the initial six months of failed negotiations over the exact status and agendas of the Spanish occupiers, an unexpected development forced Cortés to divide his small force into even smaller contingents. He left the city accompanied by only 250–300 men, on news of a fresh Spanish force 250 miles to the east that had just landed near the new port at Vera Cruz. Upon arrival there, the outnumbered Cortés would learn that nine Spanish ships from Cuba had docked with more than eight hundred soldiers, twenty cannons, eighty horsemen, 120 crossbowmen, and eighty harquebusiers, all under command of his rival, the generally incompetent soldier of fortune Pánfilo de Narváez.

Cortés rightly suspected that these newcomers were not reinforcements so much as either usurpers or jailers. He would soon discover that these new conquistadors had been sent on orders from the governor of Cuba, Diego Velázquez de Cuéllar. The latter apparently had entertained second thoughts about his prior ad hoc authorization of Cortés's adventure. Now Velázquez sought to abort the effort of Cortés's uncontrollable Spanish freelancers, who apparently were planning to absorb what Velázquez had learned was in fact a huge and rich Mexican empire.

What followed was both a nightmare and a godsend. Unfortunately, Cortés had left only a skeleton force of conquistadors to hold Montezuma II as a de facto hostage back inside the Spanish redoubt in the capital. More disturbingly, he had placed the contingent under the command of his brilliant but mercurial and ruthless lieutenant, Pedro de Alvarado. Alvarado was the only conquistador leader with enough audacity and savvy to deter the opportunistic Aztecs in Cortés's absence. But he also was reckless enough in his tantrums and delusions to incite a general Aztec uprising. That was exactly what shortly followed Cortés's absence, once Alvarado claimed that he had discovered an apparent Mexica conspiracy to storm the tiny Spanish enclave and therefore had to preempt the suspected Aztec plot.

Or alternatively, Alvarado may have grown so enraged and terrified at ceremonial and ecstatic Aztec rituals that he foolishly murdered a throng of the assembled Aztec aristocratic and priestly classes. Or perhaps he simply saw the celebrants' rich displays of gold and jewelry and sought to both rob and destroy the ruling elite, given that for a brief time he was unfettered in Cortés's absence. Whatever the motives, the Spanish were perhaps no more than two hundred soldiers strong, and were now confronted by tens of thousands of furious Aztecs who were about to ensure their impending doom.

A Spanish soldier would later testify during Alvarado's subsequent trial that he saw pots, pans, and axes, and "heard the Indians say that all the above was for killing Spaniards, and cooking them, and eating them with garlic." Alvarado, understandably jittery at this point, also was disconcerted by a large figure of Huitzilopochtli built from amaranth seeds mixed with blood from captives who had just been sacrificed. It also seems likely that Alvarado derived most of his information about Aztec intentions from Tlaxcalans with an ulterior motive, or from Aztecs or their captives forced to say almost anything while under Spanish torture.[14]

Whatever his exact motivation—fear for his life, terror that the Spanish were to be expelled from the city, anxiety that he not fail the absent Cortés, fury that the Aztecs were desecrating their newly installed Christian images—Alvarado foolishly attacked the festivalgoers. An abject bloodbath followed. His band of well-armored Spanish lancers and their Tlaxcalan irregulars blocked all the exits of the temple courtyard. Then the tiny Spanish force charged in full armor, led by a few horsemen. In a fashion similar to the emperor Justinian's notorious slaughter of thousands of unarmed opponents assembled in the hippodrome at Byzantium amid the turmoil of the so-called Nika riots (AD 532), Alvarado and dozens of his mounted conquistadors mowed down hundreds of unarmed festivalgoers crammed together to worship their war god, Huitzilopochtli.[15]

> They attacked all the celebrants, stabbing them, spearing them from behind, and they fell instantly to the ground with their entrails hanging out. Others they beheaded: they cut off their heads or split their heads to pieces. They struck others in the shoulders, and their arms were torn from their bodies. They wounded some in the thigh and some in the calf. They slashed others in the abdomen, and their entrails all spilled to the ground. Some attempted to run away, but their intestines dragged as they ran; they seemed to tangle their feet in their own entrails.[16]

Meanwhile, an equally outnumbered Cortés at Vera Cruz proved far wiser than Alvarado had been in Tenochtitlán. Far from losing his command and being sent in chains by Pánfilo de Narváez to Cuba for treasonous insubordination, the mellifluous Cortés almost immediately sought to flip the soldiers of Narváez's constabulary mission, with his envoys promising easy riches that they too could share in at nearby Tenochtitlán. His serial offers of easy gold to Narváez's men, who were mostly young and without any experience with New World warfare, suggest that Cortés already had some vague plans of conquering the city upon his return to Tenochtitlán and dividing up its loot.

After protracted but failed negotiations, Cortés conducted a night attack, and following a brief skirmish imprisoned his would-be imprisoner, the hapless Narváez. In truth, most of Narváez's men were not fond of their imperious and incompetent commander. Many knew and respected Cortés—and liked even more his promises of quick riches to be had in the interior of Mexico. As a result, the battle was half hearted: Cortés lost only two men, Narváez a mere fifteen. The wounded and partially blind Narváez was left behind in custody; Cortés hijacked almost all of his force, which included critical supplies and trained doctors and notaries. Then Cortés and his vastly expanded army made their way back to Tenochtitlán. He had left the city with a paltry, ill-equipped force that had been reinforced and augmented en route to perhaps four hundred conquistadors. Yet he now returned after dispatching Narváez and appropriating his contingents with a huge, well-equipped army of somewhere between twelve and fifteen hundred soldiers. He would soon need them all.

Cortés found that Alvarado's equally risky gambit had gone terribly wrong, and his men were surrounded, half starved, and trapped in a makeshift fortified compound. Not surprisingly, the people of the city were in arms and ready to kill any Spaniard they could find.

Cortés reentered Tenochtitlán with much-needed resupplies of gunpowder, weapons, and horses. But if the Spanish were now in an ostensibly stronger tactical position, they were also far more strategically vulnerable, given the change in their hosts' attitudes during Cortés's absence.

Things soon got much worse. Amid the on-and-off fighting between the Spanish and Aztecs, sometime on June 30, 1519, Montezuma II was killed while in Spanish custody, apparently by a stone or missile. Later rumors claimed he had died by the hand of the conquistadors. No matter: his death marked a radical turning point in the now doomed Spanish effort to absorb the city without open warfare. The exact circumstances of his demise remain disputed some five hundred years later. Whoever the actual culprit, it was likely that both the Spanish and the Aztecs had come to see the increasingly incoherent and ineffectual king as irrelevant, or even a liability, and thus were not all that concerned to see him dead.

Nonetheless, the Spanish were viewed as culpable for killing an Aztec emperor, albeit one that thousands of the Mexica had already forsaken and come to see as an obstacle to killing off the conquistadors. At this juncture, the Spanish had little choice, when surrounded by a frenzied host, except to risk sneaking out of the capital with their entire newly augmented force—and all the gold the foolish, greedy, overburdened, and mailed conquistadors sought to carry out on their persons. If Cortés's original force of conquistadors had become acculturated to the Aztec way of war after the march into and occupation of the capital, Narváez's rookies had little idea of the dangers posed by swarms of Mexica warriors.

A heavy rain had rendered the causeways muddy and in places slick. On the night of the planned escape, far from darkness masking the flight of the conquistadors, the gloom and shadows only added to the thundering storm in confusing the Spanish far more than their pursuers. An Aztec lookout soon sent an early morning alarm that the Spanish were fleeing, plodding along Lake Texcoco's unfamiliar, dark, and slippery causeways.

Within minutes, hundreds of canoes appeared alongside the causeway exits, their occupants pelting the Spaniards with arrows and stones. Waves of foot soldiers from the city swarmed out to push the retreating armored men into the water. Many of Narváez's men, especially, had in their greed burdened themselves with sacks of gold, and so slipped or were pulled into the lake. There most either drowned or were fished out as later food for Huitzilopochtli. "So those who died, died rich, and their gold killed them," as a Spanish chronicler later recalled.

Still other Aztecs raced or paddled ahead to break up the causeways, cutting off retreat. The center and rear columns met the full brunt of the Aztec attack and mostly perished, while most of Cortés's men at the van were more fortunate. The debacle that followed would be immortalized by the Spanish as the legendary Noche Triste, or "Sorrowful Night." The later Florentine Codex described in gory detail the near-destruction of the Spanish column:[17]

When the Spaniards reached the Canal of the Toltecs, the Tlate-cayohuacan, they hurled themselves headlong into the water, as if they were jumping from a cliff. The Tlaxcaltecas, the allies from Tliliuhquitepec, the Spanish foot soldiers and horsemen, the few women who accompanied the army—all came to the brink and plunged over it. The canal was soon choked with the bodies of men and horses; they filled the gap in the causeway with their own drowned bodies. Those who followed crossed to the other side by walking on the corpses.[18]

Somewhere between four hundred and seven hundred conquista-dors were killed outright. Any left behind and alive were paraded up the steps of the Great Pyramid of Tenochtitlán to be sacrificed in the ensuing days. Cortés and his shattered force of fewer than eight hundred exhausted and wounded survivors scarcely reached the nearby plain of the town of Otumba, only to face a huge pursuing Aztec army of some twenty thousand warriors. Miraculously, a small band of mounted lancers had managed to survive and flee along the cause-ways. Now the constant charges of these mailed horsemen wisely focused on the pursuing Aztec elites. They finally speared enough of them at Otumba that on July 8, just over a week after the Noche Triste, the massive Aztec army gave up and marched home, in what would eventually prove to be a fatal mistake. It was not exactly clear why the Aztecs chose to attack the departing Spanish, although the proximate reasons—their abject thievery and murder of the festival goers, the death of Montezuma while in Spanish custody, and the fear they would return with greater forces—were causes enough to finish them off while the Aztecs still had the chance.[19]

Otumba marked for the invaders the low point of the Spanish conquest, except perhaps for indominable Cortés himself. True, he was now pursued by hordes of Aztecs and their allies. Most of his native allies had abruptly abandoned him on the assumption the Spanish remnants were doomed. The Mexican countryside was turning from support to hostility in fear of Aztec reprisals. Dissen-sion grew in the Spanish ranks. Half of his once proud and well-equipped new army was dead. Any other leader would have ordered an immediate fighting retreat to safety at the harbor of Vera Cruz. And yet things were to become only worse.

Cortés had to foil an assassination attempt, a harbinger of a likely general mutiny of the disaffected who claimed they simply wanted to march back to the coast, sail home, and put the nightmare of what they saw at the Templo Mayor—the Great Pyramid with its twin temples atop—behind them. His men screamed about Cortés: "Why does he want to keep us here to die the evil death? What has he got against us that he won't let us go? Our heads are broken, our bodies are rotting and covered with wounds and sores, bloodless, weak, and naked. . . . He [Cortés] does not consider the fact that he is without men, guns, arms, and horses (which bear the brunt of war), and has no provisions, which is the worst lack of all."[20]

Few even of Cortés's veterans wished ever to return to Tenochtitlán. Nearly all were at their wits' end over where they would find food, weapons, and ammunition. Most suffered from some sort of wound. All were not so afraid of death in battle, but after the mass captures of conquistadors in the lake and on the causeways, they were terrified of being bound, dragged up to the pyramid, and having their hearts ripped out by priests, their corpses flung down to the animals and starving masses to be devoured.

Yet Cortés almost alone kept his cool. A mere thirteen months after this disaster, Hernán Cortés with fewer than a thousand conquistadors, perhaps five hundred fewer than the army that fled on the Noche Triste, along with their Tlaxcalan allies, would destroy the Aztec empire. His reconstituted army would end up killing outright in battle perhaps over a hundred thousand warriors and far more residents of Tenochtitlán, while leveling the capital's iconic buildings and adobe homes of its inhabitants. Historians have argued for some five hundred years over the mystery of how such a tiny Spanish invasion force—at any given time never numbering more than fifteen hundred soldiers—beaten and near capitulation, rebuilt an extensive native alliance and returned to Tenochtitlán to obliterate an empire of four million subjects, ruled from a well-defended capital of hundreds of thousands of residents. And they did it all in less than two years.

When the Thebans revolted from Alexander the Great, they may have foreseen little chance against his crack Macedonian besiegers. Classical Thebes and its surrounding countryside numbered little more than a hundred thousand residents, the once indomitable Theban army perhaps no more than ten thousand strong. Alexander arrived with more than thirty thousand veteran soldiers and drew on thousands of anti-Theban Boeotians from Thebes's environs, who aided his siege. The soon to be surrounded Thebans understood all too well the reputation of the northern besiegers, the increasing odds against them, the savage Macedonian way of war under Alexander's late father Philip II, and the likelihood that a defeat would be synonymous with their subjugation—although perhaps not yet with their complete destruction. Nonetheless, they fought in part because the actual number of Alexander's besiegers was perhaps only twice the number of the Theban army and various civilian and slave defenders on the wall.

In contrast, when Montezuma II, grand ruler of the Aztec Empire, first welcomed Hernán Cortés into his capital city of Tenochtitlán, he had under his loose control three to four million imperial subjects of various statuses. He held sway over some 125,000 square miles in south central Mexico, an area almost as large as contemporary Castile itself without Granada—or roughly two-thirds of modern Spain. The sheer size of Montezuma II's domain seemingly made it unlikely that a few hundred Spanish soldiers could conquer it, much less occupy its territory and keep its population subdued. Rarely in the history of major sieges had such a small force as the Spanish and their Tlaxcalan allies taken such a large imperial capital.[21]

Tenochtitlán was a fairly young city, in its apogee in 1519 not more than two centuries old. It was also no parochial Thebes. The stunning metropolis of five square miles arose from a slightly elevated island in the center of the shallow Lake Texcoco. The floating city of somewhere between 200,000 and 400,000 permanent residents was interlaced over the marshes with a complex system of causeways. They connected the island with the surrounding mainland on almost all sides, like spokes emanating from a wheel hub. The access roads were part of a maze of canals, locks, and aqueducts that governed both the water level of the lake and access to and from the city. The ability to open and close off these lake exits and entries seemingly made the city almost impregnable. By modulation of the water levels of the lake, the city could quickly revert to a fortified island with channels on all sides, in a manner far more ingenious than a European medieval castle and moat.

After the Noche Triste, the Aztecs assumed the Spanish threat was mostly over. No doubt the beleaguered and defeated Spanish stragglers would be ambushed and picked off in the countryside by the empire's opportunistic subject states, now eager to ingratiate themselves to the new and far more bellicose emperor Cuitláhuac. Even when word came of the Spanish rebound, their subsequent mysterious construction of ships to be used on the lake, and the reformulation of the anti-Aztec alliance spearheaded by the indomitable Tlaxcalans, the Aztecs still had good reason to be confident. They had been reassured that the Spanish were still a tiny—and once-beaten—force.

The Aztecs also concluded, correctly, that the Noche Triste had represented the high-water mark of Spanish manpower and supply. They were not wrong in assuming that never again would Cortés lead so many well-supplied conquistadors against Tenochtitlán. As the Aztecs now turned from defense to offense, their immediate strategy was to chase Cortés to the coast, or at least to coerce subject cities to turn on and ambush him en route. Yet after the Aztec defeat at Otumba, there was a strange relaxation on the part of the Aztec hierarchy, as if the humiliated and defeated Cortés might never return, and the city was now safe.

In an odd way, the respective attitudes of victors and defeated resembled the paradoxical mentalities of the 1930s following World War I, when the defeated Germans were as eager for a replay of the war as the victorious French and British sought to avoid one, while confident that their forces could repel any German attack. So too Cortés was undaunted after his humiliating defeat and eager for a renewal of the conflict, while Cuauhtémoc, the next successor after

Cuitláhuac to the dead king Montezuma II, was even more self-assured that the resources and natural defenses of the city would once again repulse the invader. Hubris may have helped to destroy the Aztecs, but until their final end they had good reason to believe their numbers, allies, and wealth would prevail. They had no accurate idea from where exactly the Spanish had come, much less any knowledge concerning the population and resources of imperial Spain.

While the Spanish remained awed by the city's defenses, and stung by their defeat of July 1, 1520, they were far more repelled by the Aztecs' institutionalization of human sacrifice, especially the gory mechanics of the mass killing of victims and the feeding of the slain to the residents. Most all the indigenous peoples between Vera Cruz and Tenochtitlán, friend and foe of the Aztecs alike, practiced human sacrifice and cannibalism to some extent, but never on a mass scale approaching the industry of death inside Tenochtitlán, a killing machine that instilled fear and hatred throughout central Mexico.

So vengeance and a growing hatred of the Aztecs' cannibalism replaced the Spanish awe of the city. If anything, Cortés was even more determined to destroy the Aztecs because their sophistication and wealth were put in the service of mass murder on a scale completely repugnant to the Spanish, if not deemed by them as wholly satanic.

Modern scholars disagree about the numbers of Aztec victims sacrificed each year prior to the Spanish conquest. Some historians suggest anywhere between 20,000 and, less likely, 250,000 were annually butchered by the Aztecs alone, well apart from the toll in the satellite cities and towns of the four-million-person empire. Indeed, the enormous scale of Aztec human sacrifice—as presented, for example, in a pictographic commemoration stone from the actual dedication of the last rebuilding of the Templo Mayor in 1487—is nearly incomprehensible. The contemporary tabulations list 20,000 sacrificed at multiple altars during the four-day ceremony. ‾‾ ‾‾‾ mechanics of death needed to kill so many has led some :ators to argue that the numbers must be exaggerated.[22]

Besides the huge number of human victims, controversy arises also over the institutionalization of cannibalism following the sacrifices. It is sometimes argued that the absence of large native domesticated herbivores in Mexico resulted in a dearth of available animal protein. Thus, ritual and religion merely formalized the existential reality that other humans were the Aztecs' surrogate versions of cattle, pigs, goats, or sheep. Other scholars have seen human sacrifice and cannibalism as either reflecting the need to prevent overpopulation in a fragile landscape, or the practical value of terror and public spectacles of violence necessary for political control in such a complex, ranked system.

In any case, ending human sacrifice and cannibalism later became Spanish post facto justifications for the destruction of the Aztec Empire, as if the acquisition of gold, labor, and land were secondary considerations. Even during the final siege of the city and victory over the Aztecs, there were plenty of temporary setbacks, in which conquistadors were captured, bound, and sent up to the sacrificial tables atop the great pyramid—a fact that again both petrified and infuriated the Spanish even as they continually inched forward while leveling the city:

> One by one they were forced to climb to the temple platform where they were sacrificed by the priests. The Spaniards went first, then their allies, all were put to death. As soon as the sacrifices were finished, the Aztecs arranged the Spaniards' heads in rows on pikes. They also lined up their horses' heads. They placed the horses' heads at the bottom and the heads of the Spaniards above and arranged them all so that the faces were toward the sun.[23]

Twenty-two months after Cortés and his Spanish conquistadors and native allies had first entered Tenochtitlán, ostensibly coming in peace on November 8, 1519, they now returned for war in spring and summer 1521. This time around, they were determined to conquer and colonize—or destroy—the Aztecs. Much wiser now than during his first shocking visit to the city, Cortés fully grasped the dangers from tens of thousands of deadly Aztec warriors who had nearly obliterated his small army during the Noche Triste and afterward at Otumba.

In the months between the disaster and his return to exact revenge, Cortés had concluded that to storm this New World inland Venice on Lake Texcoco he would have to fight simultaneously by land and sea. One problem was conducting a full-fledged naval battle on an inland lake some 225 miles from the port at Vera Cruz. Cortés met this challenge by having his men design and then marshal his native allies to build thirteen brigantines—small sloops—overseen by his nautical engineering genius Martín López.

To prevent another disaster like the Noche Triste, the small lake armada planned to use its superior vessels and armament to beat back the furious attacks from some hundreds of Aztec canoes crisscrossing the marshy water. Then, freed from seaborne flank assaults, Cortés's mounted and mailed lancers and infantry could plough their way through lightly protected Aztec throngs onto the several wide causeways leading directly into the island city. In other words, all that had gone wrong on the Noche Triste would now be corrected to ensure a Spanish victory in the final assault.

Yet to acquire such an unlikely fleet required that the Spanish build their high-decked brigantines from native timber and power them by both sails and oars. Then such ad hoc ships had to be transported through often hostile territory—while disassembled in pieces—some eighty miles from their construction site at Tlaxcala to Lake Texcoco. Once there, the ships were to be reassembled at the shore and then launched through the marshes into the lake via a specially constructed canal. Only that way could the conquistadors and their allies blockade Tenochtitlán and then secure the causeways over the lake to batter their way into and capture the city.[24]

This feat of blockading an inland city by building and transporting an entire armada overland was unprecedented and a true mark of Cortés's military genius. A near-contemporary account from the Aztec side shows what a deadly impact this fleet made once it was launched in mid-April 1521:

The Spaniards now decided to attack Tenochtitlán and destroy its people. The cannons were mounted in the ships, the sails were raised, and the fleet moved out onto the lake. The flagship led the way, flying a great linen standard with Cortés' coat of arms. The soldiers beat their drums and blew their trumpets; they played their flutes and chirimias [oboes] and whistles. When the ships approached the Zoquiapan quarter, the common people were terrified at the sight. They gathered their children into the canoes and fled helter-skelter across the lake, moaning with fear and paddling as swiftly as they could. They left all their possessions behind and abandoned their little farms without looking back.[25]

By late May the Spaniards had succeeded in surrounding and blockading the city. They now faced the three-month-long horrors of capturing it block by block, given that there was no chance of a general surrender. Of course, Cortés had always professed that he had no desire to wreck the city. For two years Tenochtitlán had mesmerized him as a New World jewel. In size, the Spanish found it comparable with Cordoba or Seville, with an assured income of tribute from its empire. After nearly two years of on-and-off-again war, duplicitous negotiations, intrigue with and against the Aztecs and their allies, and internecine fights with his own Spanish adventurers, Cortés had radically altered his agenda, strategies, and tactics to reflect the pulse of the often bizarre and mercurial battlefield. Again, prior to the June 30, 1520, Noche Triste, Cortés perhaps had clung to the fantasy that annihilation might not be necessary if he decapitated the royal head of the Aztec serpent, rendering limp its imperial coils for hundreds of miles beyond Tenochtitlán.

Yet in the more than two years since he had landed on the eastern Mexican coast in March 1519, all his initial hopes of absorbing the huge empire into the Spanish domain by either coopting or liquidating the Aztec leadership and assuming control of the capital had slowly become an ungodly Spanish nightmare. Cortés's 1521 return to Tenochtitlán would preclude any Ottoman solution of simply changing the cultural DNA of the city while preserving its infrastructure, killing off or converting its elite, and transfiguring the rest to the victors' religion and politics.

In these last weeks of nonstop fighting in the aftermath of the Noche Triste, Cortés had seen from his camp too many of his captured hidalgos—the lower nobility of Spain—sacrificed to the Aztec gods on the city's high pyramid, their beating hearts torn out, parts of their painted corpses devoured by a hungry Aztec elite, and the leftovers thrown down to the dogs and carnivores of the royal zoo. An editor of Cortés's letters to Charles V once described the priestly practice in graphic detail that may explain in part the later Spanish merciless final attack on the city:

> Pronouncing the words of the ritual, he plunged a sharp knife, made of flint into the victim's breast, and, quickly thrusting his hand into the opening, tore out the beating heart, which he first elevated, and then deposited at the feet of the image of the god. Sometimes the heart was placed in a vase, and left standing on the altar, or it might be buried, or preserved with diverse ceremonies, as a relic, or it might be eaten by the priests; the fresh blood was smeared on the lips of the idols. If the victim were a prisoner taken in battle, his head was given to the priests, to be kept as a trophy, the entrails were fed to the dogs, and the other parts of the body were cooked with maize and offered in small pieces to the guests invited to partake by the giver of the sacrificial feast.[26]

Cortés's chief chronicler, Bernal Díaz, lamented the gruesome deaths of his captured fellow soldiers during the final siege of the city. Díaz himself was terrified that the Spanish would suffer another Noche Triste, but that this time around all the outnumbered conquistadors might have a rendezvous with the obsidian knives of the priests of Huitzilopochtli, the Aztec god of war:

> I must say that when I saw my comrades dragged up each day to the altar, and their chests struck open and their palpitating hearts drawn out, and when I saw the arms and legs of these sixty-two men cut off and eaten, I feared that one day or another they would

do the same to me. Twice already they had laid hands on me to drag me off, but it pleased God that I should escape from their clutches. When I remembered their hideous deaths, and the proverb that the little pitcher goes many times to the fountain, and so on, I came to fear death more than ever in the past.[27]

Much has been written about the horrors of Aztec human sacrifice, but little about its effect on horrifying, then enraging, and finally galvanizing the conquistadors to destroy the Aztec theocracy. It is also worth remembering that this type of human sacrifice was nearly universal throughout Mesoamerica. The Spaniard's Tlaxcalan allies were no exception. Cortés himself wrote to Charles V about the Tlaxcalans after a battle: "That night our allies supped well, because they cut up all those they had killed and captured to eat." Undoubtedly, the ubiquity of this practice helped motivate the Spaniards' later desire not just to destroy the Aztec Empire but to all but wipe out Mesoamerican civilization.[28]

When Cortés eventually returned to Lake Texcoco for what would turn out to be the final four-month siege of the capital from April to August 1521, the battle for Tenochtitlán devolved into a steady war of attrition and extinction as Cortés rooted out the city's diehard defenders. The Spanish attack was unlike traditional European sieges, since there were no massive fortress walls around the city with defenders on their ramparts, in the fashion of Carthage or Constantinople. The Aztecs instead used brilliantly their complex series of levies, causeways, and locks in the fashion of medieval Venice, which likewise had needed few walls given the protection of the surrounding lagoon and the Venetians' intimacy with the estuary's tides, currents, and man-made canals, channels, and docks.

As resistance increased over the summer of 1521, Cortés would gradually decide to destroy Tenochtitlán brick by brick, wiping out most of its aristocratic, political, and religious elites. As for the tens of thousands who lived in the lake city, he was prepared to starve, burn out, and kill off much of the desperate, sick, and starving population. Apparently, in his mind from that mini-holocaust would soon arise a phoenix civilization of "New Spain," composed of Spanish overlords and submissive indigenous peoples. The steady attrition of the Aztec elite meant not just certain conquest but also, without their presence, a more viable occupation and colonization of central Mexico.

The furious Spanish, thanks to their native allies, daily tightened their ring around the trapped capital. The current Aztec king, Cuauhtémoc (son-in-law and nephew of the deceased Montezuma II), who assumed rule after the brief reign of the firebrand Cuit-láhuac (brother of the late Montezuma II), understood too well that past Aztec naïveté about the Spanish threat was fatal. Instead, his people's only choice now was either to submit and join the Spanish, like the Tlaxcalans, or to resist the conquistadors to the end and kill them all.

After weeks of a virtually stalemated siege, by late July 1521 Cortés and his maritime besiegers had finally gained control of most of the shallow Lake Texcoco. That allowed the Spaniards to cut off most water, food, supplies, and transport to and from the besieged island city. Predictably, Cortés's once depleted coalition army suddenly revived on news of his surprising success. As he tightened his noose around Tenochtitlán, thousands of the Aztecs' long-suffering sub-jects returned to the Spanish ranks on the scent of victory, spoils— and revenge. Most importantly, three new developments had ensured that the final days of the siege would not end for the Spanish like the earlier ill-fated Noche Triste.

First, Cortés had been resupplied. After the Noche Triste retreat to Tlaxcala, Cortés had promised his discouraged troops that he would obtain for them new provisions and arms—critical since his vastly outnumbered troops relied on plentiful bolts for the cross-bows and gunpowder for the harquebuses, both of which could only be imported from the Caribbean coast and colonies. His secretary Francisco Gómara quoted him reassuring the troops:

"We shall soon have horses from the islands, and we shall bring up guns and arms from Vera Cruz, where there are plenty and near at hand. Have no fear or worry about provisions [from our allies], for I shall give you a great abundance, especially since they follow him who masters the country as we shall do with our horses" . . . With this speech and reply of Cortés, his men gave up the notion they had of leaving Tlaxcala and retreating to Vera Cruz.[29]

Then, prior to the arrival at Tenochtitlán in late 1519 and early 1521, supply ships actually arrived on the eastern coast of Mexico. The conquistador Bernal Díaz wrote:

> News now reached us that a large ship had arrived from Spain and the Canary Islands, laden with a great variety of merchandise, muskets, powder, crossbows and crossbow cords, and three horses, and other arms. Cortés sent envoys at once to buy all the arms and powder and everything else that she carried.[30]

Reports reached both Spanish authorities in the Caribbean and local Aztec agents that a reconstituted expeditionary army under Cortés had regrouped. His conquistadors were finally back on the offensive—now with a better chance of acquiring gold than of having their hearts ripped out at the Templo Mayor. As a result, some ships and their cargoes that had originally been intended for other Spanish colonists were redirected to Cortés. He was thus being resupplied adequately—if not at the level he had been on the eve of the Noche Triste, then at least enough to encourage his men and to demonstrate to his allies that he could likely capture Tenochtitlán.

During the final siege, thousands of indigenous allies came or left, predicated on savvy assessments of whether a vengeful Aztec emperor or an exhausted Cortés posed the greater danger to their nearby towns. Cortés pursued an adept carrot-and-stick strategy of severely punishing any ally that sent aid to Tenochtitlán, while offering to new allies amnesties and promises of lasting independence from both the Aztecs and the likely Spanish conquerors. Only Cortés possessed the diplomatic skill and cunning to keep enough indigenous forces in the fold to ensure victory.

Cortés had also managed to cobble together nearly a thousand Spanish troops. Most of the earlier inexperienced soldiers—largely those who had joined Cortés from the Narváez contingent of

1520—had been tragically lost during the Noche Triste. Cortés's remnants, however, were the battle-hardened veteran survivors from the last two years of near-constant fighting. All had gained invaluable experience of the Aztecs' eerie way of war, especially their emphasis on capturing rather than killing enemies and the vulnerabilities of their unarmored warriors to slashing Toledo steel swords.

Also, with reinforcements, Cortés had plenty of critical skilled specialists and horsemen. Indeed, over a third of Cortés's besieging forces were composed of heavily armed mounted lancers, experienced sailors, and veteran harquebusiers—foot soldiers equipped with primitive but still deadly muskets that at the time of Cortés's invasion had seen in Europe radical improvements in both their practical use and lethality.

Many bowmen were now freshly equipped with more of the deadly rapid-firing arbalests. These were crossbows whose range and velocity were dramatically improved by steel bows.

Gómara proudly describes the Spanish force:

> As soon as the brigantines were launched Cortés held a review. He counted 900 Spaniards: 86 of them mounted, 118 armed with crossbows and harquebuses, and the rest with pikes, shields, and halberds [a long pole with an ax-like blade], besides the swords and daggers that they all carried. They also had several corslets [chest and back upper-body armor], and many cuirasses [torso armor] and leather jackets. He counted, besides, three heavy guns of cast iron and 15 small bronze pieces, ten hundred-weight of powder and plenty of shot. Such were the army, the weapons, and the munitions of Spain with which Cortés undertook the siege of Mexico, the greatest and strongest city of the Indies and the New World.[31]

Second, in the late fall of 1519 and the winter of 1520, a smallpox epidemic had proved devastating to the congested city, especially to a virgin population without some of the acquired immunity of the Spanish that so often mitigated what otherwise usually proved a fatal disease. While estimates that half to three-quarters of the Aztec population were wiped out by the smallpox are possibly exaggerated, nonetheless, the epidemic became a force multiplier of war and starvation.[32]

Even in the waning months of the epidemic, the population of the city continued to diminish, while thousands of survivors were often ill or debilitated, and hardly able to offer resistance. The plague had also spread to the hinterlands, reducing the empire's outlying labor force and additionally contributing to food shortages in the city. That the disease was rightly equated by the Aztecs with the arrival of the Spanish only added to the Spaniards' deadly mystique of invincibility—as if smallpox was almost a divine bioweapon that had wiped out entire swaths of the Aztec population. Years later Bernardino de Sahagún provided a detailed description of the pandemic:

> [The disease] brought great desolation; a great many died of it. They could no longer walk about, but lay in their dwellings and sleeping places, no longer able to move or stir. They were unable to change position, to stretch out on their sides or face down, or raise their heads. And when they made a motion, they called out loudly. The pustules that covered people caused great desolation; very many people died of them, and many just starved to death; starvation reigned, and no one took care of others any longer . . . After sixty days it abated and ended . . . The Mexica warriors were greatly weakened by it. And when things were in this state, the Spaniards came.[33]

Of course, smallpox devastated the indigenous allies of Cortés as much as it did the Aztecs. But the key difference was that the Spanish leadership mostly survived the outbreak, while many of Tenochtitlán's ruling hierarchy did not. The political and religious complexity of the Aztecs' hierarchically ranked top-down system of governance made the loss of its elite far more disastrous, given the tens of thousands of lives regimented from the palace.[34]

Third, the dynamics of the war had at last transformed from battles in the plains to the siege of Tenochtitlán itself, as the once great Aztec Empire was collapsing due to defections and new Spanish alliances. Aside from the psychological value of showing his indigenous allies that the Spanish were on the offensive, Cortés drew on a long

Spanish and indeed European tradition of siegecraft recently honed during the final sieges of the *Reconquista*, or Christian "reconquest," of Spain from Muslim overlords, and wars against the Ottomans.

In contrast, the Aztecs had never yet faced a host in strength intent on storming their city, much less one with technologically superior weapons and with an intent to destroy rather than merely weaken their civilization or take captives. A fragment from an Aztec chant reflects the institutionalized arrogance that Tenochtitlán was invulnerable: "Here no one fears to die in war. / This is our glory . . . / Who could conquer Tenochtitlán? / Who could shake the foundation of heaven?"[35]

Regardless of the modest size of his own forces, Cortés had gambled that a skilled besieger, with a small well-equipped and well-supplied army, navy, artillery, and missile troops, and bolstered by native allies, might turn the supposedly formidable island into a prison rather than a fortress. That is precisely what the conquistadors accomplished, as they systematically began to cut off the city by land and sea from its inland empire, and interrupted all avenues of support to Tenochtitlán, even as the Spanish occasionally paused to regroup and let the trapped population stew amid famine and lingering disease.

Cortés had clearly intended a conventional European sea-based siege, rather like Alexander's brutally successful capture of the island fortress of Tyre (332 BC), a supposedly impregnable city that was finally taken by both a naval blockade and the Macedonians' construction of a quay out to the island. Cortés addressed his troops on the new advantages accruing to his conquistadors, once the brigantines were finally launched into the lake to stop thousands of Aztec canoes from attacking his infantry:

> My brothers and comrades, you now see these brigantines finished and ready for action, and you know how much work they have cost us, and how much sweat they have cost our friends. A very great part of the hope I have to take Mexico lies in them, because we shall either quickly burn all the canoes of the city, or seal them up in the canals. In this we shall do the enemy as much harm as the land

forces can do, because the enemy can no more live without canoes than without eating.[36]

Cortés could have high confidence, based on European experience, that such a combined-arms siege would work. Yet he still had no inkling of just how long the siege would last given the superhuman frenzy of the Aztecs, or indeed how the reassembled brigantines would navigate on the unfamiliar lake and winds.

In fact the final battles, around and against the city, took almost four months, from late April through mid-August 1521. During these months the Spaniards continued to lose men to Aztec bands that roamed the battlefield seeking to knock down, overwhelm, bind, and carry off Spanish stragglers and the wounded. During breaks in the fighting, the conquistadors could gaze at the killing shrine atop the distant pyramid at Templo Mayor and take in the gruesome sacrifices of their captured comrades followed by Aztec cannibal feasts.

As long as the Aztecs, even in the penultimate phases of the final siege, were able to swarm and bind exhausted conquistadors to be sacrificed as food for their pantheon, then the Mexica assumed their gods were still on their side. Consequently, they entertained no thought of surrender. But the fewer of the Spanish and their allies who fell into the hands of Aztec warriors, and thus the more famished their bloody deities became, so all the more the gods seemed to have abandoned Tenochtitlán to the conquistadors.

And what a city it was! The conquistadors' first impression in November 1519 of the city's monuments had stunned Cortés's seasoned veterans. Some compared it to the canalled republic of Venice, then also at its zenith in power and wealth. In fact only Venice, along with Paris and Naples, may have rivaled the size of Montezuma II's imperial city. For a few of the awestruck and well-traveled Spaniards, Tenochtitlán was even more impressive than the richest of the Italian and Spanish cities, especially due to its unique use of and adaptation to the lake.

The city center was a model of sophisticated construction, most notably the so-called Templo Mayor sanctuary dedicated to the religious and ceremonial duties of the empire. Two side-by-side shrines capped a monumental flat-topped pyramid with expansive stairways that towered ninety feet above the city and the other, lesser pyramidal temples of the sanctuary. In the main two shrines were, respectively, the images of Tlaloc, the rain deity, and the frightening Huitzilopochtli, the Aztec god of war. Both were carnivorous, and to be appeased by frequent gifts of human flesh and blood.

The Spanish had seen firsthand human sacrifice prior to their arrival at Tenochtitlán. They had been first baffled and then sickened by the spectacle, as Cortés himself later reported to Charles V in his first letter of 1519:

> They have another custom, horrible, and abominable, and deserving punishment, and which we have never before seen in any other place, and it is this, that, as often as they have anything to ask of their idols, in order that their petition may be more acceptable, they take many boys or girls, and even grown men and women, and in the presence of those idols they open their breasts, while they are alive, and take out the hearts and entrails, and burn the said entrails and hearts before the idols, offering that smoke in sacrifice to them. Some of us who have seen this say that it is the most terrible and frightful thing to behold that has ever been seen.[37]

Yet the Spanish were now awed that what had been seen haphazardly in the satellite villages between the coast and Tenochtitlán had been transmogrified here at the capital into a virtual industry of mass death by the Aztecs. And they were to be further sickened when human sacrifice became the fate of hundreds of their own compatriots captured after the Noche Triste, while on patrols in the Mexican hinterlands, and during the subsequent four-month siege of 1521.

There were other contrasts beyond human sacrifice between the Spanish invaders and their Aztec hosts that can help us understand why the Spanish ultimately destroyed the very foundations of Tenochtitlán. Unlike Montezuma, or for that matter Alexander the

Great who was head of the government, army, and state religion of his country, the thirty-five-year-old Cortés was a minor Spanish colonial functionary with almost no prior military experience. He was thus subject to an array of audits and limitations the moment he reentered any Spanish jurisdiction in the New World. He may have been considered all powerful in the wild interior of Mexico, but otherwise he was a veritable nobody among the legions of officers and soldiers in Spain's huge imperial bureaucracy, fleet, and army.

Cortés had spent the last fifteen years as an aspiring but not particularly successful Cuban landowner, intriguer, and minor magistrate. There were in theory thousands of aspiring Cortéses in Spain, all eager in the first half century of New World discovery to become rich across the Atlantic. In other words, contemporaries had found nothing especially exceptional in Cortés in the years before he landed on the east coast of Mexico.

As an amateur adventurer, Cortés claimed legitimacy only through a dubious and apparently temporary charter from the Spanish colonial government in Cuba to explore the Mexican interior. His grant was uncertain because Governor Velásquez, at the moment of the departure of Cortés, had developed second thoughts about assigning a potentially lucrative expanse to such an ambitious but otherwise socially unimpressive freelancer.

When Cortés's small army first entered the Aztec capital on November 8, 1519, followed by roughly a thousand of the Aztecs' despised tributary subjects, the Tlaxcalans, the motley band seemed to pose no ostensible threat to Montezuma II, much less to his considerable empire. Cortés was unlike an Alexander, Scipio, or Mehmet II, who all knew precisely what they intended to do when they neared their targeted cities. He likely had little initial inkling that within two years the ultimate result of this fatal first encounter would be the leveling of the city and the collapse of its huge empire.

Yet, despite the uncertainty of the Spanish mission to Mexico and the unimpressive prior history of its leader, the unlikely Hernán Cortés would soon prove among the most capable military minds in history, and surely among the most indomitable. Even if the Aztecs initially had no idea whether he was a deity, in comparison to other

Spanish adventurers of his generation he was certainly godlike in his abilities. Or to put it more graphically, in extremis, Cortés, like Alexander the Great, proved a natural-born, highly skilled killer.[38]

There are at least half a dozen explanations for why the Spanish seemingly so quickly conquered the Aztecs. All such exegeses are contested. Many are embedded within contemporary ideological and political controversies. Spanish technological superiority over the Aztecs was not in itself determinative in the conflict. But the superior weaponry of the conquistadors served as a force multiplier of an array of other advantages that included animals, attitudes, culture, tactics, strategy, and generalship completely foreign to the Aztecs.[39]

As mentioned, until recently it has been popular to cite cultural bewilderments on the part of the Aztecs. First, at some point many of the Aztec elite supposedly conflated the Spanish arrival with a prophesy of an imminent visit of the god Quetzalcoatl to his worshippers' capital; therefore they did not instantly utilize the full potential of their overwhelming numbers and home advantages. According to this narrative, the Aztecs could not initially address this existential threat to their very survival because they were never sure whether killing off the Spanish would mark some elemental sacrilege inviting divine retribution. Perhaps the Spanish arrival was part of some divine plan. Yet even if the accounts of Aztec religious bafflement were true, surely within days of the Spanish arrival such shock vanished once the Aztecs familiarized themselves with the greedy and lustful Spanish.

Earlier we discussed the implausibility of the related idea that the Aztecs for long thought the Spaniards were gods themselves, that they were returning deities. This notion could of course at least partly explain why the Aztec hierarchy foolishly allowed Cortés and his men into their city in the first place, and granted them access to the emperor. The reported debate between Montezuma and his brother Cuitláhuac about this very issue, though, suggests otherwise. Again, it is not clear that the Aztec leadership ever believed the Spaniards were gods. Earlier we cited Montezuma's comments to Cortés confessing his own mortality. Certainly, the idea of Spanish divinity does not account for the furious resistance the Aztecs soon mounted.[40]

Second, there remained a constant cultural disconnect between the tactics of the two military forces. True, the Aztecs' so-called "flower," or ritual wars—staged with the main purpose of capturing victims for sacrifice—along with their more traditional conflicts of conquest without protocols or rules against neighboring cities, were brutal. About two decades before the arrival of Cortés, the Aztec Empire fought a huge flower war against the combined armies of the states of Huejotzingo, Tlaxcala, Cholula, and Tliliuhquitepec on the plains of nearby Atlixco, beneath the landmark Popocatépetl volcano. Despite its ritualized formalities and protocols, contemporary reports suggested that perhaps forty thousand on both sides died or were enslaved and sacrificed.[41]

Battle in Mesoamerica in the century before the arrival of Cortés was largely intended to capture prisoners for later sacrifice, not immediately to kill them, although in extremis the protocols sometimes broke down and the logic of killing overtook the efforts to seize sacrificial victims. In any case, the mere existence of this objective proved to be an Aztec disadvantage when confronting the Spanish. Like Cortés himself, the Spanish soldiers were first highly skilled killers who saw that victory usually went to the side that killed or wounded, or drove off more of the enemy in efforts to render an opposing force combat ineffective. They certainly were not interested in taking captives unless there was some immediate advantage in either enslaving them or using them as informants.

Granted, many earlier Aztec wars were waged to absorb neighboring peoples, to exploit the vanquished populations, and to magnify the power and wealth of the empire, formally known as the Aztec-dominated "Triple Alliance." It was really a sort of coerced league of smaller and weaker states run by the three Nahuatl-speaking lakeshore city-states of Texcoco, Tlacopan, and Tenochtitlán. Nevertheless, by the time of the Spanish arrival, wars to capture victims for sacrifice were more common than conflicts of conquest. In the flower wars, general rules privileged the prowess of individual, captive-taking warriors, given the overriding common and insatiable need for human sacrificial victims. In other words, what the Aztecs considered war, the Spanish might have termed deadly but still formalized jousts.

Yet while scholars sometimes have suggested that in reality hostage-taking was subordinated to killing the enemy, in many Triple Alliance conflicts the Spanish discovered otherwise: the Aztecs, at least initially, really did put a higher premium on trying to bind and carry away rather than kill conquistadors in battle. Cortés's men found the Aztec practice of combing the battlefield for sacrificial captives horrifying. The Aztecs seemed to "want to impale themselves on the points of the Castilians' swords so as to lay their hands on their owners," wrote Bernal Díaz.[42]

Yet the Spaniards soon discovered that despite the horror of human sacrifice, the tactic of capturing sacrificial victims rather than killing enemies also worked to their great advantage, especially given that they were always vastly outnumbered. It was far easier for well-armored Spanish to kill their enemies outright than for lightly clad Aztecs to stun, capture, bind, and pass armored men to the rear as future food for their gods. Surely this must have been one of the hardest tasks for an Aztec soldier in hand-to-hand battle with a Spaniard swordsman intent on killing him.

Nonetheless, during the Spanish conquest numerous accounts offer graphic descriptions of outnumbered, heavily armed conquistadors swarmed, pulled down, and bound by hordes of attackers, only to then be shuttled out of battle to await their turn atop the Templo Mayor. The entire effort to accumulate captives required scores of Aztec warriors to shepherd them out of the melee and thus take themselves out of battle. In contrast, again, a Spanish soldier had no interest in anything other than killing or disabling the Aztec fighter in front of him; this was part of his group's larger tactical methods of achieving Cortés's strategic objective of a foot-by-foot advance into the center of the city. In sum, hundreds of killers enjoyed advantages over tens of thousands of body snatchers.

At the decisive battle of Otumba, for example, which followed the Spanish retreat during the Noche Triste, about eight hundred conquistadors held off a much larger Aztec force that may have numbered some twenty thousand warriors, suffering very few casualties, again, because the Aztecs too often insisted on trying to knock down and capture individual Spanish soldiers instead of killing them.

Cortés himself was in the thick of the fighting, but only suffered a slight wound to his hand as the enemy sought to capture rather than kill him. He and his small guard, however, were able to spot the Aztec leader Matlatzincatl in the melee and charged directly at him through the throng. With Cortés leading the assault, his henchman Juan de Salamanca may have actually killed Matlatzincatl and captured the Aztec standards. The result was a growing panic among the enemy, who now lost any sense of overall command as well as the rallying point to which they might bring back their captives. The conquistador and veteran of the fighting Francisco de Aguilar later described the close-run battle:

> As Cortés battled his way among the Indians, performing marvels in singling out and killing their captains who were distinguishable by their gold shields, and disregarding the common warriors, he was able to reach their captain general and kill him with a thrust of a lance. . . . While this was going on, we foot soldiers under Diego de Ordaz were completely surrounded by Indians, who almost had their hands on us, but when Captain Hernándo Cortés killed their captain general they began to retreat and give way to us, so that few of them pursued us.[43]

There were other tactical differences between the Spanish and the Aztecs. Almost all Aztec fighters were individual warriors, rather like Achilles and other premier heroes as portrayed in the *Iliad*, whereas the Spaniards in contrast were soldiers, used to fighting together and cooperatively—both cavalry and pikemen. Of course, Aztec warriors could be adept killers. They were certainly brave. But in some sense, they were not professional soldiers, who coordinated their offensives in concert.

Aztec leaders did not see their strategic aims as always achieved by killing as many of the enemy as possible to collapse resistance or capture enemy-occupied ground. Instead, as individual fighters, Aztec warriors' greatest rewards for bravery came from piling up scores of captives for later adulation and individual rewards. At the end of a battle, the Aztecs knew which warriors were to be given credits for individual captures destined for human sacrifice. Later, back in Tenochtitlán during the ritual murdering of the prisoners, their individual captors might wear the skins of the sacrificed. In contrast, it is likely that no conquistador had any accurate idea of how many Aztecs he had personally killed, much less had a desire to wear Aztec regalia, but he certainly could calculate the advance or retreat of his comrades.[44]

So the Aztec warrior, who wanted sole credit for the killing or capture of a Spaniard, more often worked in solitary Homeric fashion rather than in concert with his fellow fighters. If falling back or pressing forward was to the small Spanish army's tactical advantage, then Cortés's men followed orders to retreat or advance in unison, oblivious to the wishes of individual soldiers. That idea of maintaining group solidarity and cohesion was likely foreign to the warrior ethos of the Aztec fighter, who would have considered even a collective tactical retreat as proof of his individual cowardice.[45]

Third, a much more plausible example of "cultural bewilderment" was the Aztecs' complete unfamiliarity with Spanish weapons: cavalry horses, war dogs, gunpowder, steel swords, steel armor, pikes, crossbows, and large ships with mounted cannons. Most importantly, these weapons not only were unfamiliar to the Aztecs, but also were far superior to their own. Bernardino de Sahagún later related how the sound of gunpower and the nature of Spanish steel terrified the Aztec elite:

> It especially made [Montezuma] faint when he heard how the guns went off at [the Spaniards'] command, sounding like thunder . . . fire went showering and spitting out . . . it had a very foul stench . . . it turned a tree to dust; it seemed to make it vanish, as though someone had conjured it away. Their war gear was all iron. They

clothed their bodies in iron, they put iron on their heads, their swords were iron, their bows were iron, and their shields and lances were iron. And their deer [horses] that carried them were as tall as the roof . . . And their dogs were huge creatures . . . When Montezuma heard it, he was greatly afraid.[46]

Anecdotes abound that the Aztecs were at first bewildered by the horses of the Spanish. They had never experienced anything like the sound of gunpowder. They were terrified by steel blades that shredded their cloth armor with ease. They discovered that harquebuses and crossbows made their own arrows seem like playthings in comparison, and initially might be explained only by superhuman construction. When the Aztecs encountered the conquistadors on the field of battle, they never quite could make sense of their deadly array of weapons and animals.

In a society completely lacking in large domesticated animals, both horses and the armored men who rode them were completely incomprehensible and terrifying. Military historians note how European cavalry could nullify the vast numerical superiority of the Aztecs:

> It is extraordinary what havoc a baker's dozen of horsemen could inflict on a vast horde of Indians and indeed it seems as if the horsemen did not do the damage directly, but that the sudden appearance of these "centaurs" (to use Díaz del Castillo's word) caused so much demoralization that the Indians faltered and enabled the Spanish infantrymen to dash at them with renewed force . . . The Indians had no idea how to deal with this supernatural beast, half animal and half man, and simply stood paralyzed while the pounding hoofs and flashing swords cut them down.[47]

One might compare the Aztec bewilderment by horses to the initial Roman reaction to elephants, likely first encountered at the battle of Heraclea against the Epirot general Pyrrhus (289 BC). However, the Romans recovered fairly quickly from their terror of such strange beasts (known initially as Lucanian "oxen"), but the Aztecs never really did. Unlike the Romans, they had no experience of warriors riding on the backs of large animals, or with helmets, breastplates, arm and leg greaves, metal skirts, neck-protecting gorgets, shoulder and elbow guards, and gauntlets that protected their lower arms, wrists, and hands.[48]

The Spaniards' animals and weapons were not just terrifyingly new, but they were also extremely effective against Aztec warriors. Nearly protected from head to foot in steel shells, Cortés's men were all but invulnerable when facing the obsidian-tipped blades of native opponents—if the conquistadors could even stay on their feet for hours on end of slashing and stabbing. When a Spaniard occasionally went down, it was usually under the collective hammering, tripping, grabbing, and sheer weight of his swarming attackers. Exhaustion also doomed some, especially in the spring and summer equatorial heat and humidity that intensified the weight of steel armor, the constant blows of obsidian-tipped blades, and the nonstop effort of wielding a three-foot sword. Once again Bernardino de Sahagún notes how amid the carnage the Spaniards alone could survive given their armor and weapons:

They surrounded them [the Spanish] on all sides, the Spanish started to strike at them, killing them like flies. No sooner were some slain than they were replaced with fresh ones. The Spaniards were like an islet in the sea, beaten by waves on all sides. This terrible conflict lasted over four hours. During this many Mexicans died, and nearly all the Spaniards' allies and some of the Spaniards themselves. When it came noon, with the intolerable exertion of battle, the Spaniards began to lag.[49]

Archers and javelin throwers were the most effective of Aztec soldiers, given their numbers and the fact that the edges of their obsidian, single-use arrow- and javelin-heads kept their sharp edge when striking their targets. Nonetheless, rarely could such missile weapons penetrate Spanish helmets, breastplates, or wood and leather shields. Small Spanish antipersonnel cannon, harquebuses, and crossbows were not dramatically effective. They were all slow firing, having been designed to penetrate the steel armor of rival massed European foot soldiers, not to reap the swarms and pockets of lightly protected Aztec warriors. Rapidity rather than velocity of fire would have been more advantageous for the Spanish against the Aztecs. Nonetheless, when protected by swordsmen, such artillery troops could send focused volleys into the occasional mass of Aztec attackers with devastating results, not least among them the psychological terror that such unfamiliarly loud and penetrating weapons spread.[50]

But most importantly, our contemporary sources constantly emphasize the advantages of Cortés's mounted Spanish lancers, some of the most lethal warriors of sixteenth-century Europe. Riding stout Arabian-bred horses with ample armor, cavalrymen were nearly invincible as they plowed back and forth through the Aztec masses, stabbing with nine-foot wooden lances tipped with steel, slashing with their Toledo blades, and often trampling solitary Aztec soldiers. It became almost impossible for Aztec warriors to pull Spanish lancers from their mounts, as these cavalrymen were accustomed to fighting an assortment of far better armed European and Islamic enemies.[51]

Amid the horsemen and foot soldiers, Spanish war dogs, usually huge mastiffs or breeds similar to contemporary wolfhounds and deerhounds, joined the fray. Mastiffs might reach two hundred pounds in weight and were often protected by light steel and leather plates. The hounds could easily rip apart unprotected Aztec limbs. Both trampling horses and biting dogs were terror weapons of a sort, given that native peoples had never encountered either. Just as the Aztecs initially were not certain whether men and their mounts were not centaur-like hybrid beasts, so too they envisioned mastiffs and wolfhounds as more akin to jaguars than to their own small and usually hairless canines. And Bernal Díaz felt that such huge dogs had played an important role in fighting the Aztecs:

> While staying at Zautla, a mastiff belonging to Francisco de Lugo barked most of the night. The people of Zautla asked some of the Cempoallans [an ally of the Spaniards] accompanying the

Castilians whether it was a [jaguar] or just an animal to kill Indians. The Cempoallans explained that the Castilians took dogs with them in order to kill anyone who annoyed them.[52]

As was true since antiquity, heavily armored European knights and foot soldiers were as invulnerable en masse as they were near-defenseless in isolation and on open ground. Accordingly, the Spaniards sought to multiply their enormous technological superiority by fighting in disciplined, phalanx-like ranks, with cavalry and missile troops protecting their vulnerable flanks.

In response to the deadly offensive power of Cortés's small but highly organized formations, the Aztecs preferred to attack conquistadors in transit or on the open plains where the Spaniards' tiny numbers and single-column marches often invited ambushes and entrapment. Yet by the time of the final siege of the city, both sides understood that horsemen on land and brigantines on water had finally ensured that Spanish ranks would not easily be outflanked, and thus could not be stopped. The best chance for Aztec warriors was simply to mass around Spanish soldiers, in hopes that the effort to cut dozens down would eventually exhaust the conquistadors and allow Aztec reinforcements to beat and pull down the wearied targets.[53]

Perhaps it was the unfortunate fate of the Aztecs not to have met a century later English interlopers of the sort who landed at Plymouth Rock 2,800 miles to the north. Pilgrim civilians fled Britain to North America as religious refugees and would-be agrarian settlers and merchants with wives and children. In contrast, Cortés's warriors, many of whom were colonists from the Caribbean, arrived in the New World with few women and fewer children. Even the stories of the few females who accompanied the conquistadors in Mexico were not of a maternal but of a martial nature—such as that of the legendary *conquistadora* María de Estrada, who supposedly eagerly charged Aztec ranks shouting her war cry of "Santiago!"[54]

Cortés and his adventurers had come not as our familial home-steaders or refugees from perceived religious persecution. They were not pilgrims but rather warrior emissaries in service to the Spanish imperial crown. As New World crusaders of a sort, the conquista-dors' victories were seen as adding converts to the global struggle to save embattled Catholicism from both ascendant Protestant apos-tates and Islamic jihadists, as well as ensuring the sixteenth-century golden age of Spanish political dominance in Europe under Charles V. All the while, the New World conquistadors also sought to become rich in gold and farmland, and eventually in sizeable haciendas with hundreds of indigenous slave workers.

Cortés himself combined these motives—spreading Catholicism and advancing the crown interests while getting rich—in his inspi-rational speech to the troops before marching back to Tenochtitlán with his newly resupplied army and recently completed brigantines:

> The principal reason for our coming to these parts is to glorify and preach the faith of Jesus Christ, even though at the same time it brings us honor and profit, which infrequently come in the same package . . . Let us go then and serve God, honor our nation, mag-nify our king, and enrich ourselves, for the conquest of Mexico is all these things![55]

More importantly, the conquistador fought as a beneficiary of the experience gained during nearly eight hundred years of violent struggles in the Reconquista against Islam. When María de Estrada shouted her war cry of "Santiago!" she was simply voicing the trade-mark rallying cry of Reconquista warriors in battle against Islam—an appeal for divine help from Saint James, the patron saint of Spain.

In addition, concurrent with the long and brutal effort to liberate Spain from Muslim imperialists were constant expeditionary Span-ish raids and wars along the coast of North Africa. The Aztecs, of course, had little conception of the radical improvements in Spanish tactics that had developed in just the three decades before Cortés landed in Mexico. In the last battles of the Reconquista, the Spanish had honed their tactical and strategic doctrines by fielding mass formations of specialist pike-wielding phalangites in emulation of the Swiss. They were accompanied by lighter-equipped swordsmen with shields, plus harquebusiers and crossbowmen. All were the immediate precursors of the feared *tercios* ("thirds"). These were the dreaded Spanish tactical formations of ten companies of three hundred troops each—resulting in highly skilled and cohesive units of three thousand soldiers divided into twenty-four hundred pikemen and six hundred harquebusiers—that would soon wreak havoc on the European battlefield. Tercios would prove to be among the best examples of the so-called military revolution unfolding in Europe as armies transitioned from muscle-powered weaponry to the increasing use of personal firearms and field artillery.[56]

Finally, the often neglected factor of logistics paradoxically favored the Spanish. By the sixteenth century, the Spanish had mastered the naval arts of transoceanic navigation, bravely and most often successfully sailing the treacherous six thousand miles across the tempestuous Atlantic from Spain to the Caribbean and the Mexican coast. That mostly reliable supply chain meant that Cortés ultimately had more access to Spanish imperial resources than a besieged Tenochtitlán had to its surrounding Aztec empire.

The reality that the conquistadors had come from far away as invaders, while the Aztecs played the role of the stationary and defensive party, also proved of enormous psychological advantage to the Spanish. The opposite scenario of Montezuma II leading an Aztec fleet from Vera Cruz to Malaga was absurd. The Aztecs knew basically nothing about the origin or homeland of the invaders. They gathered that the Spaniards came from a place called Castille, but had only the haziest idea of where it was. To them, the most significant characteristic of the newcomers was the collection of strange animals they brought with them, such as horses, war dogs, and livestock and poultry for consumption: chickens, cows, goats, sheep, and pigs. To Nahua ears, the ending of the word "Castilian" sounded like the "-tlan" suffix of many Nahua locations (e.g., Tenochtitlán). And the new borrowed from Nahuatl word for "chicken" (*caxtil*) was "Castile." So they may have decided that the Spaniards had come from a distant place known as "the land of the chickens."[57]

In sum, the conquistador of fifteenth-century Spain was perhaps the most audacious and dynamic contemporary manifestation of a long European tradition of martial lethality. His embattled world of European religious and political rivalries was envisioned as a nonstop *bellum omnium contra omnes* ("war of all against all"). Whereas the pre-Columbian Aztecs fought enemies mostly familiar to themselves and on battlefields close to home, the sixteenth-century Spanish were global warriors who battled all comers—the British navy on the high seas, Ottoman Janissaries and Moorish foot soldiers across the Mediterranean, and the mounted condottieri on Italy's home ground.[58]

Indeed, when Cortés arrived at Tenochtitlán, the end of the centuries-long Reconquista was not yet thirty years in the past. The Inquisition was still at full bore. The Grand Inquisitor Tomás de Torquemada had died only two decades prior. The European wars of religion between Protestants and Catholics were newly inaugurated while Cortés bivouacked in Tenochtitlán. And the landmark victory of Don Juan—illegitimate son of Charles V and half-brother of King Philip II of Spain—over the Ottoman navy at Lepanto was just a half century distant on the horizon.

Entire generations of young Spaniards were nursed on and expected endless war. Recently they had gained access to cheap printed books, given the invention a half century earlier of Gutenberg's movable type. Accordingly, information about the wonders, riches, and opportunities in the New World captivated readers throughout early-sixteenth-century Spain. And novels of chivalrous knights crisscrossing the new and old worlds—*The Adventures of Esplandián* by Rodríguez de Montalvo is a good example—were especially popular among the lower ranks of the aristocracy, who saw military expeditions abroad as a shortcut to social advancement and riches.[59]

Cortés's men were either veterans of these endless conflicts, or were schooled from youth in the arts that had given an otherwise naturally poor Spain its empire in the face of such an array of formidable enemies. Their creed was to do well for themselves in the New World by acquiring land, gold, and slaves that extended the reach and power of imperial Spain at the expense of its European rivals.

The successes of both conquistadors and Spain ensured for their god the conversion of all native peoples to an embattled orthodox Catholicism, whose future the Spanish felt was uncertain due to a rising army of Protestants throughout Europe. So the Aztec priests with their knives atop the pyramids were not the only religious zealots. Religious passion just as powerfully incited the Spanish, who saw the Aztecs not only as enemies of their crown, but also as devilish idolaters antithetical to their Christian god.

When Cortés met Montezuma II and the exotica of Tenochtitlán, he no more suffered from cultural confusion than did his compatriots when fighting northern and southern Europeans, Turks, or Arabs, with their impressive diversity of arms, tactics, and strategies. Today in the Anglosphere it is sometimes a canard that the legions of the empire of Charles V were medieval relics, captives to Don Quixote–like fantasy and romance novellas, hunting down the Fountain of Youth or cities of solid gold, bound by superstition, and on the wrong side of an emerging transatlantic future.

In fact, the Spanish tercio, galleon, and imperial viceroyalty were among the most effective and spirited military and diplomatic institutions of the preindustrial era. They help to explain why a resource-poor Iberian Peninsula ruled the European world of the sixteenth century. It was against just a few hundred Spanish conquistadors and their lethal traditions that the warlike but hapless Aztecs fought for their lives and their civilization.

The Spanish, like many sixteenth-century Europeans, also had mastered the complexity of continental rivalries, dynasties, alliances, and nonstop wars of succession. Key was a common Roman imperial inheritance of *divide et impera*—the canon of "divide and conquer" immortalized in the popular *Commentarii de Bello Gallico* of Julius Caesar. That ancient tradition of expanding national power trained the Spanish almost immediately to seek out and enlist as client states both long-standing enemies of Tenochtitlán and its dissatisfied allies. Cortés was schooled enough in the great game of constant warring not to be bothered by the mercurial fealty of the Texcocans and occasionally the Tlaxcalans. He instead considered all allies of Tenochtitlán always liable to defection given the right incentives, usually defined by the specter of Aztec defeat and Spanish victory. The enemies of the Aztecs on a particular day were his welcomed allies—at least for that day.[60]

Cortés likely entertained some intention of keeping his promises that after the conquest alliances would eventually earn indigenous peoples full autonomy and the perpetual friendship of the Spanish. Although the Tlaxcalans did not quite achieve the promised independence, they later did enjoy special treatment from the Spanish. For decades, they were given aristocratic titles, allowed semiautonomy for their villages, and, most importantly, were permitted to own Spanish firearms. In the end, their nonagenarian king Xicotencatl the Elder conceded that if the Tlaxcalans' likely futures were problematic under Cortés and a powerful and wealthy Spanish viceroyalty, they were without hope under continued imperial Aztec domination and its cult of mass death. Or as Cortés, in self-serving fashion, later put it in a letter to Charles V:

> When they heard through me of Your Highness and of Your very great royal power, they said they wished to become vassals of Your Majesty and my allies and asked me to protect them from that great [Aztec] lord who held them by tyranny and by force and took their children to sacrifice to his idols.[61]

Could the Spanish have conquered the Aztecs without the genius of Hernán Cortés? After all, the thirty-four-year-old minor functionary had almost no combat experience when he landed in Mexico in March 1519, and little support—and soon open hostility—from Spanish authorities in Cuba. He was also surrounded by an array of brilliant Spanish conquistadors, some with more experience in both New and Old World fighting and with better aristocratic connections and influence. Pedro de Alvarado, for example, was of the same age as Cortés, but with better support among the New World Spanish elite and more martial experience prior to landing at Vera Cruz. The younger Gonzalo de Sandoval on endless occasions helped salvage the often seemingly hopeless Spanish predicament. Cristóbal de Olid and Alonso de Avila proved invaluable lieutenants.

Still, it is hard to imagine any of Cortés's gifted subordinates regrouping after the Noche Triste. Who would have been able to lead wounded and exhausted men to fight and defeat the Aztecs at Otumba, or to organize the creation of a navy, or to form so successfully coalitions of native cities to join the Spanish? Who else combined the calm restraint to craft alliances with the unchecked fury to lead his outnumbered men into the throngs of Aztecs?

Consider the following juxtaposition: Had Cortés been left behind at Tenochtitlán in May 1520, while the hothead Pedro de Alvarado marched to deal with Narváez at Vera Cruz, it is likely there would have been neither an ensuing Noche Triste, nor the much-needed absorption of Narváez's troops and supplies. Cortés would likely not have butchered the Aztec aristocracy, and Alvarado would not have had the diplomatic savvy to win over Narváez's men. No leader of the Spanish conquest exhibited such relentlessness, such uncanny abilities of recovery after setback and defeat, and such talents to cajole, inspire, and coerce men to do what they assumed was hopeless.[62]

Add up singularly lethal Spanish militarism, the technological advantages and military traditions of the West, the deadly genius of Cortés, the opportune alliance with the Tlaxcalans, and the often rigid military and political rituals of the Aztecs—and the once improbable idea of fifteen hundred Spaniards destroying an empire of millions in roughly two years no longer seems so improbable.

The destruction of Tenochtitlán and the entire Aztec "Empire"—in truth a loose, coerced fealty of hundreds of smaller towns to Tenochtitlán—poses a paradox of sorts. As stated, on the Spanish side, Cortés from his first visit onward expressed wonderment at the impressive size and complexity of the city. He professed a desire to expropriate the marvelous metropolis of the lake for his newly envisioned Spanish viceroyalty. Or as Cortés put it in his second letter to his king, Charles V, after only six days inside Tenochtitlán he had decided to imprison Montezuma as a tool by which to control the city for the Spanish crown:

It appeared to me, even from what I had seen of it and the country, that it would be conducive to Your Royal Highness's service, and to our security, that Montezuma should be in my power, and not at his entire liberty, so that he might not relax his intention and disposition to serve Your Highness.[63]

Cortés later reiterated an ostensible intention ideally to dominate and pacify the Aztecs, assume sovereignty over their empire, and then preserve their capital and its domains as a tribute-paying province of the crown. In other words, he originally wished to replace the leadership at Tenochtitlán, not level the magnificent city. That idea would have followed a pattern analogous to the recent Ottoman absorption of Constantinople, rather than the earlier Roman leveling of Carthage.

Cortés also at first assumed that, given the radical demographic asymmetry between the Aztec population and the tiny Spanish presence in the early-sixteenth-century New World, Montezuma II or his successors and replacements could serve as client-king enforcers of the New World Spanish order. His subjects additionally would supply much-needed labor for Spanish plans for farming, ranching, and municipal construction.

Yet within weeks of what would prove to be an eight-month initial Spanish stay in Tenochtitlán, Cortés fathomed that any sort of accommodation with the Aztec hierarchy was impossible. The incompatibility of the Mexica with the tenets of Catholicism and Spanish imperial customs and mores was far too great for any compromise or conciliation. Even a subordinate but still intact Aztec empire had no place in New Spain.

Cortés entertained no objection per se to the widespread Aztec enslavement of its defeated enemies. As Spanish imperialists, the invaders admired, in a way, the ability of the imperial city to conquer central Mexico and craft an exploitative empire. As a warlike people, the conquistadors also found it logical that the elite of Aztec society were the military aristocracy and the religious clergy. Cortés's soldiers quickly came to admire—and fear—the ferocity of the Aztecs in battle, and to dread what might follow after it. When the last emperor of the Aztecs, Cuauhtémoc, finally was forced to surrender among the ruins of his city, he would offer his neck to Cortés to put a quick end to his misery. But Cortés instead praised his fiery leadership and the courage of his men, thus sparing his life, at least for a few months. Cortés the conquistador noted that the Spanish warrior ethos was to admire the fierceness of the defeated.

But all that said, to the Spanish mind the entire culture of the Aztecs quickly became symbolic of almost everything their church and king defined as precivilizational and anti-Christian: gruesome human sacrifice, cannibalism, the polytheistic worship of stone idols, polygamy, and overt homosexuality, to name a few of the many elements they saw as odious in Aztec culture and a permanent impediment to Spanish rule in the New World. In his *Second Letter* of October 1520, in the dark days following the Noche Triste, Cortés described the eerie construction of Aztec idols:

> They are made of a mass of all the seeds and vegetables which they eat, ground up and mixed with one another, and kneaded with the hearts blood of human beings, whose breasts are opened when alive, the hearts being removed, and, with the blood which comes out, is kneaded the flour, making the quantity necessary to construct a great statue. When these are finished the priests offer them more hearts, which have likewise been sacrificed, and besmear the faces with the blood.[64]

Such sins in the Spanish mind were not haphazard, but institutionalized on a grand scale and imprinted upon the very Aztec way of life. Indeed, religion so permeated every aspect of Aztec society that it was impossible to envision its continuance without its bloodthirsty deities, or so the Spanish concluded.

As a result, Cortés separated in his mind Tenochtitlán, the material city and nexus of Mexican wealth, from the odious Aztec culture that had built it. Perhaps within days of his arrival Cortés dreamed of a third alternative—again, something like Sultan Mehmet II's plans for a conquered Constantinople—as preferable to either destroying the city or allowing an Aztec Tenochtitlán to remain a tribute-paying client. Instead, he would seek to preserve intact the Aztec capital—but without the Aztec ruling elite, whose army and culture would have to be destroyed along with much of the population. Cortés in his third letter of 1522 after the conquest, claimed even after the Noche Triste on his way back to Tenochtitlán that the Spaniards still had believed they could incorporate a conquered but intact city into a new Spanish colony:

> I have always sought, Most Powerful Lord, to win the people of Temixtitan [Tenochtitlán] to our friendship by every way and means I could; on the one hand because I did not wish them to provoke their own destruction, and on the other in order to rest from the hardships of all the past wars; but principally because I knew it would conduce to Your Majesty's service.[65]

But eventually, in the bitter last days of the final siege, Cortés saw that the destruction of the physical city of Tenochtitlán was inseparable from the end of its culture, given that the defenders had turned their homes and shrines into a veritable sixteenth-century Stalingrad:

> Seeing that they were so rebellious and showed such determination to defend themselves to the death, I inferred two things: first that we should recover little or none of the treasures they had taken from us, and the other, that they gave occasion and forced us to totally destroy them. This last reason caused me the greater grief, for it weighed on my soul and made me reflect on what means I might employ to frighten them, so that they should realize their error and the injury they would sustain from us; and I kept on burning and destroying the towers of their idols and their houses.[66]

In addition, that the Aztecs were regarded as the most warlike of the Nahuatl-speaking tribes meant their annihilation would discourage lesser people's resistance to the Spanish. The idea of instilling realist deterrence no doubt also factored into Cortés's decision.

We cannot be sure precisely when Cortés in his two-year effort realized that his indigenous alliance increasingly possessed the ability to destroy the city, and that he would be pressured to do so by aggrieved allies. Nor is it clear at what point Cortés's sense of the rational advantages of saving and reinventing Tenochtitlán was overwhelmed by the furies of revenge unleashed by the ferocity of the Aztec resistance and dedication to human sacrifice. Yet while we do not know the moment of the decision to raze the Aztec capital or the exact balance of reasons, we do understand the advantages the Spanish saw in its obliteration—rationales both similar to and different from those of the conquerors discussed in prior chapters.

Alexander the Great quite spontaneously leveled Thebes out of wrath at the city's defiance, and the danger its revolt might pose for his agenda of unifying the Greek city-states into a huge coalition that would support and supply his looming invasion of the Persian Empire. Once he arrived in Boeotia, there was little doubt on either side that a successful Macedonian siege and retaliation were foreordained. But once Alexander grasped the full extent of Theban hatred, he then concluded that only crushing the resistance and destroying the city—rather than merely capturing it—would end Greek notions of opposition to Macedon. And it did just that in his lifetime. What doomed Thebes was the city's own fierce and unyielding devotion to political independence. Such defiance posed an unacceptable danger to Alexander's home front while he was marching eastward in Asia.

The Romans leveled Carthage because they were enraged by, exhausted from, and fed up with 118 years of conflict. Carthage was seen as a recrudescent enemy that after each of its prior two defeats seemingly arose again phoenix-like as a rival to their growing imperial plans for a Roman Mediterranean. The specter finally contributed to near paranoia among the Romans. The mere existence of even the much diminished second-century-BC city seemed to pose as much of an existential threat to ascendant Rome as its once majestic empire had to its beleaguered grandfathers.

Of course, there were innate differences between Punic and Roman culture, especially their religions. But the centuries-long rivalry grew largely from economic and commercial disputes. Hellenic culture for half a millennium had been absorbed by the Phoenician-founded Carthage. By the time of the First Punic war, Rome and Carthage both drew on a rich common Hellenic inheritance, from sophisticated agronomy to military practice to literature.

So the siege of Carthage was seen by both sides not as a third Punic war in an endless series of conflicts. Instead, the siege was silently agreed upon from the outset to be the *last* Roman-Carthaginian war. Carthage assumed the role of Germany in 1939–1945, when the Allies finally determined that, after 1870–1871 and 1914–1918, a third German "problem" would be solved for good by postwar partition, occupation, and the destruction of both Prussian militarism and National Socialism.

As for Mehmet II, he took Constantinople because by 1453 its hollowed-out defenses suggested he could. The city's infrastructure, wealth, location, and defenses made it the ideal capital of an ascendant Ottoman Empire poised for further westward expansion. Expropriating the infidels' Hagia Sophia as a mosque was natural for the Ottoman Muslims; they saw Christianity as an old rival as well as an inevitably spent religion whose cities and monuments were to be properly transmogrified and put into service to Islam. In contrast, it would have been impossible for Cortés to save the blood-soaked shrines of the Templo Mayor and turn its pyramids into Catholic monuments.

Cortés had only two years' experience with the Mexica. Unlike our previous cases, the final siege was not part of decades, much less centuries, of bitter Spanish-Aztec contests for power. Another final and particularly important factor in his decision was the hatred of the Aztecs by his all-important allies. Many of Tenochtitlán's neighbors despised the Aztec empire more than they did the Spanish newcomers. Even less was there any indigenous desire to lead a crusade for pan-Mexican freedom and lasting autonomy from a well-known Spanish imperial overlord.

As recorded in the Florentine Codex, most Aztec subjects felt the same as the Nahuatl people of Teocalhueyacan, who supposedly "told Cortés that the Mexica were inhuman and oppressive . . . They also complained to the captain of the bad treatment that Montezuma and the Mexica had given them, loading them down with much tribute and great afflictions, and they told them that if they left them, they were going to give them more bad treatment, because the Mexica were cruel and inhuman." Cortés's indigenous allies soon realized that while no subject state in the past had a prayer of storming Tenochtitlán, Hernán Cortés certainly did. Thus, his strange appearance offered a one-time opportunity that might not return.[67]

Cortés was given no brief from the governor of Cuba or the Spanish crown about the fate of Tenochtitlán. He operated by instinct. He set policy in response to the appetites and demands of his own men and his native allies. Indeed, his ad hoc directives later provided fodder for his enemies and rivals, who charged him with megalomaniacal insubordination and treason against the Spanish crown. Even when he handed over much of Mexico to the Spanish king, his critics hounded him for his gratuitous cruelty to indigenous people, his personal aggrandizement, and his supposedly unnecessary destruction of Tenochtitlán, a potential Spanish asset.

Cortés did not seek to destroy the city just to signal to Aztec subject states that the fate of Tenochtitlán would be their own payment for resistance, though of course such a spectacle was not without its advantages in consolidating Spanish control of Mexico. Instead, perhaps after the Noche Triste, Cortés surmised that he could find no peaceable means to exact what he initially thought was great wealth from the Aztec Empire. The fleeing Spaniards' hordes of gold had been lost in the lake during the Noche Triste. Nothing comparable would ever again be given up to the Spanish by their hosts.

Strategically, as long as a rival and powerful imperial system based at Tenochtitlán existed, the Spanish could never fully colonize and exploit Mexico. That fact was immediately known to insightful Cuauhtémoc, the second successor to Montezuma II, who galvanized Aztec resistance in a way Montezuma II had not. Once the beleaguered Aztecs changed their defensive strategy to street-by-street brawling and ambushes among their homes and monuments, Cortés's suspicions, as he later wrote to his king, were confirmed that there was no way to root out the imperial system without knocking the Aztecs' infrastructure down upon them.

Such revised decisions are common throughout military history. Near the end of World War II, US Army Air Corps general Curtis LeMay and the American B-29 bomber command decided the only way to destroy Japan's dispersed manufacturing, which was deeply embedded within the small neighborhoods of Tokyo, was to ignite the city—and tens of thousands of those working within it. LeMay's original mandate to use precision, high-level bombing to attack strictly industrial targets with high explosives was quickly deemed too costly and ineffectual.

When Cortés rebuilt Mexico City as the capital of Spanish Mexico, it was designed to rise atop the Aztec ruins as their complete antithesis, with the foundations of churches on top of crushed pyramids, and priests in them instead of human sacrificers. In some sense, Cortés did in Tenochtitlán what a series of Islamic caliphs had done in Jerusalem when they built, expanded, and rebuilt the Al-Aqsa Mosque atop the Temple Mount complex, the site of Herod the Great's Jewish Second Temple.

———————

Were the Aztecs delusional about their likely fate? Could they have avoided their annihilation, becoming analogous to Tlaxcala as a vassal of New Spain—just as Thebes could have been as quiescent under Alexander as were Athens or Corinth; or as Carthage might have become if relegated to a Romanized client city like Ephesus, which had been inherited and absorbed intact from its Hellenistic Attalid rulers?

The Aztecs did not think they were doomed, any more than had the Thebans, Carthaginians, or those on the walls of Constantinople. True, embedded within their religious orthodoxy were visions of the apocalypse—for some, fueled on the eve of the Spanish arrival by some two decades of occasional strange reports of white, bearded warriors along the coast of Mexico. This idea of the end of Tenochtitlán was not purely abstract, given that the Aztecs constantly viewed in their larger environs the all too real ruins of prior civilizations such as the monumental relics of the Toltecs dotting the plains of central Mexico.

Each of the two adversarial powers was in its golden age and had reached a zenith of wealth and influence that seemed to preclude serious rivals, much less any inkling of imminent decline. The Aztecs chose to fight Cortés to the death because, with the loss of Montezuma II, they quickly and rightly conjectured that otherwise, under any proposed settlement, peaceful coexistence was impossible. In defeat they would surely lose their religion, wealth, and power, as well as their customs and traditions.

But we should not therefore conclude that a willingness to fight to the death was synonymous with a death wish. The Aztecs had understandable expectations of defeating the invaders, especially after the rout and slaughter of the Spanish during the Noche Triste. In their minds, they still had considerable advantages in numbers, familiarity with their homeland's territory, tried weapons, fierce warriors, plenty of allies, and a religious mandate given their slavish attention to the appetites of their hungry gods. More specifically, while the Aztecs may have assumed there were tens of thousands more conquistadors in the far-off murky places from which Cortés came, all with the ability to reach their empire, they concluded that their best chance of survival was to exterminate Cortés's tiny advance army before his successors came in far greater numbers and force. This would also provide a warning for future conquistadors to stay away.

Granted, there were likely some Aztec officials—as there had been in Thebes, Carthage, and Constantinople—who foresaw that their city's resistance would ensure their collective obliteration; thus they sought to persuade their leaders to agree to terms, however humiliating and servile they might be. Spanish records occasionally note informal peace feelers from uncertain Aztec sources. But we have no record of any such Aztec leader seriously offering to surrender to save Tenochtitlán, at least not until the city was already mostly surrounded and half destroyed—despite chronic defections of groups of sick, starving, or homeless Aztecs who sought to flee the city before its final destruction.

Miscalculation and naïveté were not entirely culpable for the Aztecs' annihilation. Their end also arose from a reasoned and empirical decision to resist, with real hopes of victory. The Aztec strategy of defense in depth relied upon concentric rings of allied resistance. Tributary cities would blunt Cortés's advance toward the capital, ensuring his forces would be continually diminished by the time they reached Tenochtitlán. That plan eventually became futile once the Spanish took their fleet to Lake Texcoco, once Cortés began to flip most Aztec allies to his side, once he cut off water and food from the city, once he let smallpox do its work, and once he systematically began destroying Tenochtitlán block by block. Yet until the last weeks of their existence, the Aztecs had never imagined the erasure of their city was on the horizon; thus they never entertained any serious diplomatic means of avoiding it, given that it was synonymous with collective slavery.

Because Cortés's army was overwhelmingly indigenous, and given that the Aztec Empire grew out of the subjugation of the surrounding Nahua, the Aztecs had good reason to believe that the small number of Spanish, despite their horses and technological advantages, would not achieve a result different from the past defeats of Tenochtitlán's enemies.

However, the Aztecs' assumptions were disastrously wrong, for several reasons. If part of Aztec power had been grounded in its Nahua rivals' fear of its systematic institutionalization of mass sacrifice, the Aztecs sorely miscalculated the effects of their gory practices upon the Spanish. While Spanish contemporaries recorded the horrific sights of their fellow conquistadors being sacrificed, the eerie effect was just as likely to incite anger as terror, or rather a desperate furor fueled by vengeance. Each time a cadre of Spanish was publicly sacrificed, Cortés was reminded by his men that such a death machine had to be annihilated rather than compromised with.

Nor did the Aztecs have the opportunity ever to obtain technological parity. Although after the Noche Triste they occasionally found success by using lances tipped with captured Toledo blades, there were never enough of such appropriated swords, crossbows, or lances to make a difference in the fighting. And they certainly did not capture Spanish weapons, or master the few that came into their hands, to any degree similar to the later experience of the Incas. The latter, over the course of a much longer forty-year resistance, sometimes learned to ride Spanish horses and were on occasion equipped with captured Toledo steel. The siege of Tenochtitlán, if we can term it properly a siege, is one of the best examples in history where the technological disparity between attacker and attacked characterized the entire battle.[68]

Finally, as long as the death houses on the Templo Mayor stood, dead-ender Aztec warriors in the final frays were still trying to club and stun rather than just kill conquistadors. Indeed, at one of the final battles near the lake at Xochimilco, the Mexica unhorsed and swarmed Cortés himself. Had they ceased such efforts to capture and bind him and just killed him outright, Cortés would have perished, and the Spanish besiegers would have become leaderless. Instead, the Mexica continued to believe that if their gods drank Spanish blood, then their deities could do what their own obsidian blades could not.

The scale of death and destruction at the siege of Tenochtitlán invites many comparisons. One is the Battle of Verdun (February 21, 1916–December 18, 1916), where over some ten months some three hundred thousand died—a number comparable to the Aztec, Tlaxcalan, Spanish, and other native fatalities in the last thirteen months of near-continuous warring. But unlike the dead of World War I, who for the most part perished by artillery, machine guns, and illness, most of the native and Spanish dead, aside from the toll of smallpox and other epidemics, were killed by hand-held or hand-thrown weapons, suggesting a muscular fury unmatched in modern times.

There are no accurate numbers for native fatalities from the Spanish destruction of Tenochtitlán, at least for the period from the late-March 1519 Spanish landing on the Mexican coast to the final end of Tenochtitlán, when the defiant last Aztec emperor Cuauhtémoc and his remnant forces surrendered what was mostly only rubble on August 13, 1521. Somewhere between 200,000 and 400,000 city dwellers were now homeless or dead. A good guess is that at least 200,000 Aztec warriors, civilians, and allies had perished outright during the two-year war.

Many, of course, were sacrificed and eaten by the Tlaxcalans and Spain's other indigenous allies. Francisco Gómara later noted that "Cortés begged his Indian lords not to kill these poor wretches, for they were giving themselves up; but the temptation was too great, and some 15,000 were killed and sacrificed."[69]

The idea of being an Aztec vanished with the city, as the remnant survivors lost their culture, religion, and eventually even most of their language. The majority of the survivors melted away into the indigenous and eventually mestizo population. Eighty years after the fall of Tenochtitlán, many of the surviving old Aztec royal and aristocratic families had long since been given Spanish names and honorific and bureaucratic appointments to oversee the indigenous population. Yet most were largely without knowledge of the world of their long-dead grandparents, even if they retained a vague sense that their ancestry had once been majestic and imperial.[70]

Because of the material splendor and complexity of Aztec civilization, it is often common for today's Mexican population and its diaspora to claim direct descent from Aztec forebears. But it is much more likely that the indigenous, Nahuatl-speaking population that did survive what might reasonably be called an Aztec genocide were the besiegers of, not the doomed residents in, Tenochtitlán. Likewise, today's Mexican populations are more likely related to the victorious, surviving allies of the Spanish—and, as mestizos, to the conquering Spaniards—who destroyed the Aztecs than to any survivors of what they wrought.[71]

If the Aztecs, per se, were wiped out, the larger Nahua people survived. Indeed, Nahua continue to the present day in central Mexico, although almost all their descendants now speak Spanish and are partially descended from Spaniards. James Lockhart, principal historian of the post-conquest Nahua, summarized the subsequent post-Aztec five hundred years as a three-stage phenomenon of continual assimilation between the smaller Spanish overclass and much more numerous Nahua:

> (1) a generation (1519 to ca. 1545–50) during which, despite great revolutions, reorientations, and catastrophes, little changed in Nahua concepts, techniques, or modes of organization; (2) about a hundred years (ca. 1545–50 to ca. 1640–50) during which Spanish elements came to pervade every aspect of Nahua life, but with limitations, often as discrete additions within a relatively unchanged indigenous framework; and (3) the time thereafter, extending forward to Mexican independence and in many respects until our time, in which the Nahuas adopted a new wave of Spanish elements, now often more strongly affecting the framework of organization and technique, leading in some cases to a true amalgamation of the two traditions.[72]

Over the ensuing five hundred years, tiny islands of exclusively Nahuatl-speaking peoples persisted—approximately 1.5 million in 2005 among the 130 million population of contemporary Mexico. Many, although nominally Catholic, still worship a few pre-Spanish gods, retain pre-conquest customs and traditions, and have little if any Spanish ancestry. They remain a reminder that everything, and yet nothing, eventually comes to a complete end.[73]

Somewhere over two thousand Spanish conquistadors died during the war. The great majority perished from disease, fell in combat, drowned in the lake during the Noche Triste, or were captured in battle and later sacrificed by the Aztecs. Sources suggest that well over twenty thousand Tlaxcalans died, almost all males, in combat. Perhaps a like number of other indigenous allies died as well. The toll from smallpox—probably first brought into Mexico by the Narváez contingent—or enteric disease and other introduced pathogens is not known but its effects during the actual years of the conquest may have often been exaggerated. No one knows the number of indigenous people who eventually died from *all* imported diseases in the decades following the fall of Tenochtitlán, but the number could have been in the many millions.[74]

While Cortés and his successors eventually fudged on many of his pre-conquest agreements of autonomy with his native allies, the Spanish nonetheless did not exterminate them in the way they had done the majority of the Aztecs. Instead, the Spanish saw the indigenous population as crucial for a new Spanish-Mexican nation of plentiful and often forced labor, Catholic subjects, and wealth for the crown.

Cortés himself did not leave the lake upon the destruction of the city. He became as zealous in replacing Tenochtitlán with what would soon become the capital of New Spain (now Mexico City), and a site of a Spanish viceroyalty, as he had been just months earlier in destroying it. He had several reasons to build atop the ruins. Cortés reasoned that the Aztecs had wisely used the lake as a nexus for trade and the protection it offered, as well as because of the rich farmlands that ranged beyond it. At one time the site had also been surrounded by over a million residents of satellite villages, offering a plentiful supply of labor. More importantly, even more millions in Mexico, for better or worse, were acculturated to the idea that the greatest city in the New World was at the site of Tenochtitlán. Here is how Cortés summarized the reasons for his decision in his post-conquest third letter:

> I debated where to establish another town within the circuit of the lakes; for it was needed for the greater security and peace of all these parts. Considering also that the city of [Tenochtitlán] was a thing so renowned and had made itself so important and memorable, it seemed to us that it was well to rebuild it, for it was all destroyed. . . . In the four or five months since the rebuilding of the said city of [Tenochtitlán] was begun, it is already very beautiful, and Your Majesty may believe that each day it will become nobler, so that it was before the head and mistress of all these provinces, so it will be henceforward.[75]

By design, Cortés sought to remind natives of Spanish superiority—having destroyed Tenochtitlán, he erected a new urban center in its exact location, reusing many of the stones of the old city's monuments. In some sense, Cortés understood how the pyramidal societies of the Aztecs and their New World neighbors operated. He sought to supplant the vanquished hierarchies with his own, on the premise that such conquered peoples would be susceptible to new but also similar top-down orders from the very site of their former masters.

The new city that followed soon exceeded even the expectations of the victorious Spanish. A grid was superimposed on the former irregular blocks of Tenochtitlán, even as the old Aztec center of the city became the main square of the rising Mexico City. On top of the ruins of the Templo Mayor rose the cathedral of St. Francis, its foundations supplied by the wrecked stone statues of the old Aztec gods. The Spanish built homes mostly of reused stones in their own quarter, and welcomed some thirty thousand native peoples to live in their new city. It was not exactly clear which tribes composed the new indigenous population of Mexico City. But most were not Aztecs per se, given the carnage of the conquest.

The rapid building of the new capital later drew the ire of Spanish Counter-Reformation clerics, who criticized Cortés for the prior slaughter of the innocent, further noting the exploitation of thousands of native laborers used to clear and reuse the site. It was a peculiarity of the legalistic imperial Spanish bureaucracy that what seemed a brutal, often ad hoc conquest had to be authorized by government writs and post facto be audited by an army of clerks and inspectors.

In sum, to explain why such a huge, complex, and ascendant city fell so quickly to so few, we have seen both recurring and singular causes at work in the end of the Aztecs. Yet the Spanish conquest was also a wholly asymmetrical war, unlike any previously discussed. The collision was not only that of entirely different technologies, religions, governments, military protocols, numbers, cultures, and civilizations that worked to the advantage of the vastly outnumbered Spanish, but also one of innately antithetical mentalities. The Spanish and the Aztecs did not just hold different assumptions about the human condition, but were of mindsets unfathomable to one another, and in the end wholly incompatible.

But we also see in this chapter a recurring, universally human theme across time and space. The doomed, at the brink of civilizational destruction, have an attitude partly born of hubris and partly of naïveté, perhaps best summed up as "It cannot happen to us."

HOW THE UNIMAGINABLE BECOMES THE INEVITABLE

Now there is a field of grain where Troy once was, and the earth—cut by the scythe and rich with Phrygian blood—has grown rich. The half-buried bones of heroes are struck by the curved plow, and weeds hide the ruined houses.

(*Iam seges est, ubi Troia fuit resecandaque falce, luxuriat Phrygio sanguine pinguis humus; semisepulta virum curvis feriuntur aratris ossa, ruinosas occulit herba domos.*)
    —**Ovid,** *Heroides*

ANNIHILATION OF CULTURES and civilizations is certainly an apt characterization of the fate of our four cities and their environs. Before Alexander, ancient Thebes had been a unitary city-state with its own unique identity going back a thousand years. Yet it was nonetheless a mere tenth the size of late-stage Carthage or Tenochtitlán. If classical Thebes was nearly as large in population as a diminished Constantinople in the last years of its existence, nonetheless the area of Thebes was a fraction of the thirty-five hundred acres inside the walls of the great Byzantine city. Its small size explains much of its easy destruction.

The Thebans before 335 BC had been living in the city for ten centuries, certainly since Mycenaean times. They were never again to do so following Alexander's destruction. The Macedonians either killed off or enslaved the population. Most of the city was leveled. The Thebes that had provided the mythological fodder for the

Aeschylean, Sophoclean, and Euripidean tragedies of Oedipus, Antigone, and Pentheus was gone for good.

Those who reoccupied the site may have been mostly Greek Boeotians, somewhat similar in dialect and ethnicity. But they were not known, by themselves or others, as the original Thebans who had defined themselves for a millennium as a distinct Greek people from a particular place. The refounded city that followed brought in a new Greek people without connection to the past. No more would there be a Boeotian federation anchored by its capital in classical Thebes.

More than that, the destruction of Thebes also marked the wider end of the independent classical poleis and the finale to the golden age of Greece. So more than just one city-state was destroyed. In a very real sense, an entire way of life based on autonomous self-government ended when Alexander entered the gates of Thebes, wiped it out, and offered it as a Panhellenic model of what would happen to any Greek city-state dreaming of its old independence.[1]

Similarly, traces of the Punic language continued for over six hundred years in many regions of North Africa after the destruction of Carthage, especially in rural areas. Yet the notion of a Punic Mediterranean civilization beyond North Africa, or even of Carthaginian urban areas within it—with a cohesive religion, national character, and shared national past—was over, even as a century later Roman Carthage grew to be the second-greatest city of the Roman Empire in the West.

Some Greeks who survived the slaughter and enslavement of Constantinople continued to live as inferior Christian subjects or Islamic converts, or as slaves in the new Kostantiniyye. That new city repurposed the majestic Constantinople's religious and governmental monuments, along with its language, laws, and customs in service to Islam, Turkish culture, and the Ottoman imperium. There remained scattered populations of Greek-speaking Orthodox peoples in Asia Minor, at least until the 1922 destruction of Smyrna, the slaughter or expulsion of almost the entire remnant Greek population, and the final 1923 population exchanges of Greek and Turkish peoples. But the idea of a cohesive Byzantine civilization that had established a Hellenic and Romanized culture outside of Greece and its islands had ceased to exist in Asia Minor by 1453 and in mainland Greece by 1460.

There are some Mexican citizens today, in central and southern Mexico and parts of Central America, who speak derivatives of the Nahuatl language better than they do Spanish. There are millions of indigenous people who as Christians and citizens of Mexico keep alive vestigial customs of their ancestors who lived in or around Tenochtitlán. Nonetheless, there was no Aztec civilization to speak of, at least as it had existed in the past, after 1521. Its independent emperors, formal religion, temples, and customs of cannibalism, human sacrifice, and polygamy were all but extinguished. Aztec dress, weaponry, and even diet were absorbed into a new mestizo culture. There was never again to be an Aztec national identity, although, as noted in chapter 4, the idea of an Aztec *past* is still very much a romantic part of modern Mexican identity.

In sum, if a Greek in 200 BC said, "I live in Thebes of old," or a resident announced in 100 BC, "I am a citizen of Punic Carthage," or a Greek-speaker in 1500 claimed, "I am a resident of Greek Constantinople," or someone in 1600 pronounced, "I dwell in Mexico City of the Aztecs," he or she either would be considered completely unhinged or contextualized as really meaning they were a Boeotian subject of a Hellenistic king, or a Roman citizen in North Africa, or a second-class resident foreigner, or a slave in an Islamic city of Turks, or an indigenous or mixed-race resident of Spanish Mexico City.

Even centuries after the obliteration of these civilizations, their fates remained immortalized in popular culture. End-of-days allusions in music and poetry lamented the doom of these once powerful and majestic fallen states. Sometimes common themes warned that even the mighty could not escape fickle fate. Sometimes the message was one of divine revenge for hubris. But more often songs and poems simply bemoaned the loss of vanquished civilizations that did not deserve what their moral inferiors had meted out.

The theme of a "Carthaginian peace"—the needless annihilation of an already defeated Punic foe, with intimations of the later fate of the victor—was common in Western poetry and prose from Virgil to T. S. Eliot and W. H. Auden. In the case of the end of Byzantium, ritual Greek dirges lamented the ensuing cost to Hellenic and Christian civilization. Constantine Cavafy's 1921 poem "Captured" ends with "Let it be read, let it be mourned, let your heart be broken. / Woe to us, alas for us Romania has been captured." W. B. Yeats's equally famous poem "Sailing to Byzantium" describes spiritual immortality within an aging body, by comparing that paradoxical human condition to the immortal mystical majesty of Byzantium that persisted, regardless of the contemporary condition of Constantinople,

> An aged man is but a paltry thing,
> A tattered coat upon a stick, unless
> Soul clap its hands and sing, and louder sing
> For every tatter in its mortal dress,
> . . .
> And therefore I have sailed the seas and come
> To the holy city of Byzantium.

And there at Byzantium remains the immortal memory of the once great haunt:

> Or set upon a golden bough to sing
> To lords and ladies of Byzantium
> Of what is past, or passing, or to come.

Contemporary Aztec ritual lamentations inaugurated a long genre of commiserating over the end of Tenochtitlán. One Mexica poem ends: "Tears are pouring, teardrops are raining there in Tlatelolco. The Mexican women have gone into the lagoon. It's truly thus. So all are going. And where to, comrades? True it is. They forsake the city of Mexico. The smoke is rising, the haze is spreading."

In modern times, the fate of the Aztecs remains a popular topic of poetry, and none more so than in the work of William Carlos Williams. In his collection *In the American Grain*, Williams grieved the end of Mesoamerica: "The land! don't you feel it? Doesn't it make you want to go out and lift dead Indians tenderly from their graves to steal from them—as if it must be clinging even to their corpses—some authenticity." And in a long prose poem, "The Destruction of Tenochtitlan," Williams romanticized the end of Montezuma: "He had done all that he could and he was beaten. Placing his hand upon the hilt of Cortez's dagger he asked the Spaniard to draw it and plunge it into his heart. Cortez refused. Later the Conqueror tried to rebuild the city. Viva quien vence!" ("Long live he who conquers!")[2]

Even though our choice of these four destructions was driven in part by their historical significance, it is otherwise rather difficult to find a more recent example of a significant political and cultural annihilation following the end of the Aztecs and Incas. There is no longer a Soviet Russia, for example, but certainly the Russian people, language, and culture continue under the autocratic Russian Federation.

Even indigenous peoples like the Apaches or Zulus, who were soundly defeated and greatly and deliberately diminished, survived, although their language, culture, and population were subject to the control of a conquering power. Nevertheless, today there are both a politically recognized Zulu community and Native American tribal political entities, the former in South Africa, the latter in the United States.

Even a more recent parallel of the obliteration of "Prussia" and "Prussianism" during the first half of the twentieth century does not quite equate with the fates of the doomed in these chapters. Prussia, both before and after the creation of the German nation, was the dominant force in Europe from roughly 1850 to 1918. Once a small, peripheral, fifteenth-century state, created and ruled by the Teutonic Knights, Prussia struggled for independence against more powerful Poland, Sweden, and Lithuania. A series of competent rulers soon led Prussia to control almost all the territory from Belgium to Vilnius.

A Prussian statesman of Machiavellian genius, Otto von Bismarck (1815–1898), then crafted the foundations of the German

Empire. In some sense, his creation was Greater Prussia by a different name, and dominated by aristocrats from the former and now extinct territory of Old Prussia, along with its characteristic extreme militaristic ethos. Defeat in World War I cost Germany West Prussia, and the destruction of Germany in World War II saw the end of East Prussia (the original state), along with its historic capital at Königsberg.

Most of the territory of Old Prussia was then purged of Germans. The city of Königsberg was nearly destroyed, the remains of its historic castle dynamited in 1968 on the orders of Leonid Brezhnev, general secretary of the Communist Party of the Soviet Union. The Russians, and equally the Western Allies, saw the events of the 1871 Prussian defeat of France, the 1914 German invasion of France and Russia, and the 1939 Nazi attack on Poland as a persistent "Prussian problem." The Western allies intended that Prussian culture, nomenclature, and infrastructure should pay atonement by vanishing into a new Germany that would be modern, democratic, liberal—in a word, un- or anti-Prussian. But Prussians, quite unlike those in Thebes, Carthage, Constantinople, and Tenochtitlán, were absorbed into a kindred ethnic and political entity.

Nazi Germany sought to use twentieth-century technology and industrial practice to wipe out the Jewish people, religion, culture, and identity—and succeeded through the Holocaust in exterminating two-thirds of all the Jews in Europe. Yet because Jews were not confined to one nation but dispersed from the Atlantic to Russia—and throughout North America, Britain, its empire, and the Middle East—and because Germany could not win a war against the combined power of the British Empire, Soviet Russia, and the United States, Hitler's Final Solution ultimately failed to complete its hideous mission.

A crumbling Ottoman Empire between 1915 and 1917 sought to eliminate the Armenian population of over two million in Anatolia. It may have succeeded in destroying half of the Armenians under Ottoman control; only the collapse of the Central Powers aborted the final solution plans of the crumbling sultanate. One of the cruel paradoxes of these holocausts was that they ended not because of global outrage over such government-planned genocides, but because Nazi Germany and the Ottomans found themselves on the losing side of a world war, and would soon cease to exist as governments before their macabre plans could be completely realized.

Another reason why the compete destruction of a civilization is rare in war is that there are plenty of warnings that an impending war can presage defeat, and defeat in turn annihilation. As a result, most cities or states choose to capitulate under even humiliating terms rather than be wiped out to the last person. In contrast, the annihilations of our four cities offer eerily similar lessons across time and space about what we might call the "Melian Dilemma," the awful choice between calculated survival and brave extinction. Or to put it another way, there is an eternal dilemma in the free choice of the doomed either to fight on, despite likely annihilation, or to survive in an assured humiliating subservience.

In addition, the end of civilization can be both gradual and finally abrupt. Or to paraphrase the novelist Ernest Hemingway's famous observation in *The Sun Also Rises* about bankruptcy that progresses "gradually, then suddenly," the finale of these civilizations was the explosive manifestation of what had been an ongoing enervating process. Decline did not ensure extinction, but it certainly limited the options for surviving an invasion. It can be best defined as the gradual deflation of a state's viability, until scarcely more than the capital itself and the immediately surrounding territory survive.

There is also a certain formula that recurs: Alexander's Macedon was on the upswing; occupied Thebes was in descent. Carthage was stripped of most of its empire by 149; Rome was on the cusp of becoming a Mediterranean superpower. Constantinople had fields of weeds growing within the walls; the Ottomans were eager to head toward Vienna. Spain was heading into its golden age of Charles V and Philip II; the relatively young Aztec Empire was already beginning to calcify and splinter into factions.

Theban control of the surrounding Boeotian city-states had waned long before Alexander's final Macedonian siege, especially after the catastrophic defeat three years earlier of Theban and Athenian forces at the 338 BC battle of Chaeronea. That debacle emboldened disaffected anti-Theban Boeotians to triangulate with their Macedonian overlords against the capital at Thebes. When Alexander arrived, Thebes was no longer the arbiter of the large Boeotian Confederation but a single city on its own.

As the crisis mounted, Thebans and Macedonians alike assumed that there would be no Theban preemptive invasion of Macedon—at least in the earlier fashion of Epaminondas's great invasion of Laconia in 370 BC that had ended the serial Spartan projections of power into Boeotia. Accordingly, Theban allies and neutrals wisely calculated that Alexander was more likely to be at the gates of Thebes than Theban hoplites were to surround the Macedonian palace at Pella.

By the time of the Roman invasion of North Africa in 149 BC, a once vast Carthaginian empire had been reduced by a century of Roman-Carthaginian hostilities to little more than Carthage itself. Destroy Carthage and there were no major satellite cities in Spain to continue Punic civilization, and only a few in North Africa (Utica, for example). During some 115 years of conflict and tensions with Rome, Carthage had been stripped of its considerable buffer states along the North African coast and in Spain, along with a frequent presence in Sicily. If its European colonies in Spain had once threatened Italy while offering defense in depth to Carthage, the bulwark of the empire by the outbreak of the Third Punic War was solely the walls of Carthage.

By 1453 the thousand-year-old Byzantine Empire at Constantinople no longer ruled over a near-continental empire, one that at its greatest extent had once stretched from near Gibraltar to Persia, and from the Nile Valley to the Alps. "Byzantium" before the final storming of the city had been reduced to enclaves around Constantinople and the Black Sea, plus some swaths of mainland Greece, as Venetians, Genoese, Turks, Franks, and Arabs squabbled and devoured a once formidable Byzantine domain.

Most of the provinces that survived for a few years after the decapitation of Constantinople, such as the Byzantine Despotate of Morea, with its capital in the Peloponnese at Mystras, had long been semiautonomous anyway. These holdouts would be wiped out within a decade of the loss of Constantinople. Certainly, there were no more generals like the sixth-century Belisarius and Narses who had brought war home to Byzantium's enemies a thousand miles distant from Constantinople.

The ruthless genius of Hernán Cortés was not just in his systematic destruction of the huge capital at Tenochtitlán. Rather, following the Noche Triste, he had systematically pruned away key allies of the Aztecs. Such defections made it almost impossible for Tenochtitlán to rely on reinforcements of men and materiel, much less to send out preemptive expeditionary armies to enforce imperial obedience and resistance to the Spanish arrival. By April 1521 conquering Tenochtitlán was synonymous with destroying the Aztec Empire.

Were all these cities then doomed, their fates preordained given the asymmetrical power of the invader and invaded?

Not necessarily. The defeats of Carthage in the first two Punic Wars had not ended in the complete destruction of the empire, much less of Carthage itself. As the elderly and often paranoid Cato remarked after a visit to Carthage on the eve of the third war, the city seemed never to have been more prosperous. Moreover, some of history's most famous brutal and asymmetrical sieges—ancient Syracuse (415–13), Malta (1565), Vienna (1683), Gibraltar (1779–83), Leningrad (1941–44)—failed.

Constantinople and its empire had been looted, occupied, and expropriated by the Frankish buccaneers of the aborted Fourth Crusade (led by Dandolo, the ninety-five-year-old, blind doge of Venice) more than two centuries earlier than its fall. Yet if Constantinople's thirteenth-century imperial domains under the so-called Frankokratia had in large part been parceled out to an array of Frankish and Venetian lords, nonetheless by the end of that same century the Byzantines had reacquired power over their capital and key parts of Greece as well. And they would hold on to this empire for another century and a half.

In other words, there were enough resources to command a stouter defense, well aside from any anticipated succor from the millions of Western Christendom. An alternate history is plausible in which the brilliant Genoese Giovanni Giustiniani Longo was not injured on the walls or did not order that he be carried away wounded to his ships, and Constantinople then lasted the necessary few days needed to discourage the sultan's besiegers. The latter by May 29, 1453, were despairing of ever breaching the city's massive walls and eager to withdraw.

Tenochtitlán was larger than most major European cities of the age. Despite the genius of Cortés, his large Mexican alliance, and his overwhelming technological advantages, it remains indisputable that at any given time Cortés never marshaled an attack on the huge city with more than fifteen hundred conquistadors.

For an example of survival against great odds, the aggregate successful forces in 1565 under the command of the Knights Hospitallers of Malta never numbered much more than six thousand. The huge Ottoman besieging force of forty thousand should have easily wiped out the fortress, and with it the entire order of the Knights of Malta, if not for their brilliant leadership and fanatical resistance, and Ottoman incompetence.

To return to Thucydides's "Melian Dialogue" about a savage Athenian invasion of a neutral island state in 416 BC, there is even tragic irony here when the envoys of the maritime attackers lecture about the hopelessness of the Melian defenders' cause and hence the futility of their resistance. Such advice of the Athenian realists is contrary to their own prior heroic and *successful* resistance against overwhelming odds at Salamis during the Persian Wars, some sixty-four years earlier.

In sum, there are similar scenarios in which each of the four cities under discussion might have survived through abject surrender and humiliation, or adroit diplomacy. For Thebes, a reversion to the subservient status of other Greek city-states meant giving up to the Macedonians a few Greek patriots and insurrectionists—to be likely executed by Alexander the Great. And they had done just that 144 years earlier and thereby saved their city from fellow Greek attackers, after they and their Persian allies were humiliated at the battle of Plataea (479 BC).

For the Carthaginians, after agreeing to hand over all their weapons and burn their fleet, the ante of submission was upped to the abandonment of their magnificent city and relocation away from the coast. That is, continued life for five hundred thousand residents, but without full autonomy, their prior prosperity, or any prospect of future security.

For Constantinople, capitulation to the sultan at the outset of the siege spelled either an impoverished exodus from the city or continued life in a Muslim city as third-class residents.

For the Aztecs, surrender entailed a physically intact city (minus the pyramids and temples) and population, but as a Spanish-controlled metropolis, stripped of its old gods and ancient customs of human sacrifice, cannibalism, and polygamy. Whether the victors would have honored their final terms is debatable; whether the targeted could have ensured their continued independence, power, and influence against such forces outside their wall was unlikely.

So why did these targeted states resist? What were the general strategic errors or political miscalculations they shared? And what can we learn from their catastrophes, given that obliteration of a capital and extinction of a civilization is *not* how most wars end?

First, targeted states that prefer to die on their feet than to live on their knees, or doubt that aggressive would-be conquerors will abide by their terms upon surrender, naturally look for outside help. And it rarely arrives, as we can attest from the twentieth-century Jewish and Armenian genocides.

Like the doomed Melians, who clung to a vain hope ("danger's comforter") of Spartan succor, the trapped convince themselves that allies or friends are right over the horizon. Or at least surely they will lend assistance at the eleventh hour. But help to the likely doomed—pouring good money after bad, as it were in the cruel logic of advantage—is a fickle proposition, even in the case of aid from imperial subjects, client states, or sworn allies.

Thebes may have known that its historic nearby Boeotian rivals, the Thespians, Plataeans, and Orchomenians, would inevitably join Alexander. But the Thebans may also have been emboldened to revolt in expectation that their loud-talking fellow insurgents, the Athenians, would follow up their gift of arms with an army. They did not. Many in Thebes also apparently thought that sympathetic city-states in the Peloponnese would arrive in time. In fact, these saviors either did not muster, or their armies turned back once their generals got wind of the size and nature of the Macedonian army.

The Melian choices left for Carthage admittedly were similarly limited: obliteration or a humiliating, deracinated existence, and permanent demeaning subservience to Rome. But part of its hope of successful resistance was predicated on at least some allies, especially the nearby large seaside city of Utica, standing with their historical partner and denying entry ports to Rome's expeditionary forces.

The Carthaginians conceded that their Numidian enemies under their aged king Masinissa would seek to initiate war and bring the Romans to Africa on their side. Yet they were somehow shocked that few of their once subordinate states and allies in North Africa were willing to join them—at least once they calculated the size and intent of the Roman expeditionary army.

For a time, a desperate Carthage even believed the pretender to the Macedonian throne, Andriskos, might draw off Roman assets by starting and winning a fourth Macedonian war against Rome—especially after his army had all but annihilated an entire legion and killed its general Publius Juventius Thalna. But Macedon was far to the east of Rome. Even in victory it could render no immediate direct aid. Andriskos's success was a brief detour from a series of four Macedonian defeats in what would become four failed Macedonian Wars and end in the complete Roman absorption of Macedon.

Perhaps most tragic were the fruitless Byzantine calls throughout Christendom to save its historic window on the East. Until cut off by the Ottoman besiegers, the emperor Constantine XI Palaiologos clung to hope that the Latin West would for a moment unite with the Greek East in real rather than professed Christian unity and send a fleet to the Bosporus.

Yet frantic pleas from Constantinople to both France and England, exhausted from the Hundred Years' War, as well as to the opportunistic Venetians, were all but ignored. In the end, all of Western Christendom sent less than twenty ships and fewer than fifteen hundred soldiers. Indeed, there were likely far more Christians pressed into Ottoman service outside the walls than there were defenders inside. While the Byzantine Empire was vastly reduced, there were still sizable Hellenic outposts in mainland Greece and along the Black Sea. Yet all pleaded that their own vulnerabilities made it impossible to help the iconic city and heart of their culture.

Similarly, by early summer 1521, Tenochtitlán was beginning to fathom that there were hundreds of thousands of people wishing more for its demise than ready to defend it from the Spanish—given its yearly harvests of thousands of captives from towns of the surrounding valleys of Mexico. We talk of a Spanish victory, but in truth the overwhelming majority of Cortés's victorious army was native Nahua. The anti-Aztec Nahua saw Cortés as a tool, albeit a quite strange and dangerous implement, to realize their prior and long-existing agendas. That Tenochtitlán seemed to believe at first that its resistance to the Spanish would galvanize its imperial subjects—allies and even enemies in solidarity against a religiously, ethnically, and culturally antithetical foreigner—revealed the Aztecs' own ignorance of how hated they had become.

As a general rule, the besieged vainly counted on help that rarely appeared—especially if they were seen as likely to lose.

Second, the besieged were not just naïve in their expectation of outside help. The targeted states were also too confident in their fortifications and limited wherewithal. While acknowledging the power of their enemies, they still clung to the belief that their city walls or defenses in general were indomitable. Seven-Gated Thebes was a legendary fortress. Its walls had been reinforced in classical times after the city had surrendered to Panhellenic besiegers following the battle of Plataea (479 BC).

The ramparts of Carthage were also celebrated, well over thirty feet thick and forty feet high—and far taller at key junctures—and purportedly between eighteen and twenty-three miles in circumference. The series of walls constructed, enlarged, and repaired over a near millennium around Constantinople were more impressive still—in aggregate they were even wider, thicker, and longer than the massive fortifications at Carthage. And the island city Tenochtitlán on Lake Texcoco, due to its complex series of causeways and drawbridges, was considered nearly impenetrable.

No one in any of these cities in living memory had ever witnessed their defenses breached. So it was a perfectly natural reaction for the defenders to discount the enormous and deadly forces outside the walls, and instead to seek comfort in their ramparts, even if prior failed enemy sieges had all seen more defenders and fewer attackers than during the current danger.

Those surrounded looked to their own bastions and their past impregnability, rather than assessing realistically the unique and existential danger below the walls.

Third, all these vanquished civilizations struggled with factionalism and disunity, before and during the final battles. Thebes chose to revolt from Macedon only after exiled activists reentered the city and convinced its assembly to reject prior subservience. That was a radical step that may not have enjoyed the full support of the citizenry.

Hasdrubal the Boetharch, the leader of Carthage, had been jailed for his incendiary opposition to Rome. When he was released and canonized as the defender the city needed, he proved why he had been so unpopular to begin with. During the actual siege he sometimes cared as little for his own citizens as he did for the Romans. In the end, he was capable of executing both.

Constantinople fell in part because there was nearly as much strife inside as outside the walls. Some distant Western Christians were content to see the city fall. The Venetians and Genoese on the ramparts did not fight with the help of their governments, distrusted each other, and only united in their shared Western suspicion of their Greek hosts.

The Aztecs may have killed, or allowed the killing of, their own emperor even as the war began. By the time it was over, three different emperors—Montezuma II, Cuitláhuac, and Cuauhtémoc—had led the defense. The degree of ferocity of the native besiegers who joined the Spanish could be explained by the considerable number of their own citizens who had previously been bound and had their hearts ripped out by the Aztecs.

Prior discord often explained the vulnerability of the besieged, and its contribution to their defeat.

Fourth, the defenders had no accurate information about the excellence in siegecraft or generalship of their enemies, and no realistic appraisal of their own lack of ability. The twenty-one-year-old Alexander the Great had not yet demonstrated to the Greek world his full genius at storming cities that just three years after the destruction of Thebes was manifested at Tyre. There, his successful taking of the ancient and supposedly impregnable fortress displayed the most sophisticated arts of siegecraft then known in the ancient world. In contrast, Phoenix and Prothytes, the leaders of the Theban insurrection, have been mostly lost to history, but nothing suggests they had crafted any inspired strategy for success. Apparently, they and other returning exiles had naïvely counted on a Panhellenic uprising that withered away on news that Alexander was outside Thebes.

The Carthaginians, after stymieing three Roman generals—Manius Manilius, Lucius Marcius Censorinus, and Lucius Calpurnius Piso—assumed that Scipio Aemilianus would be similarly inept. They had no real notion that the young consul was a seasoned veteran of protracted Roman wars in Spain and Macedonia, and one of the finest military minds Rome had produced. Again, little is known about the Carthaginian commander Hasdrubal the Boetharch. He seems to have been at times tactically competent, since he conducted a three-year successful defense of the city against an array of consular armies. But the fact that his eleventh-hour capitulation earned him a safe retirement into old age on an Italian farm suggests that his overall strategic direction of Carthage's war effort was tainted by his own personal agenda and limitations.

Mehmet II was only twenty-one in 1453, but he had been given military and diplomatic commands by his father for nearly a decade. Moreover, the sultan had marshaled some seventy siege cannons and enlisted an army of logisticians in a fashion never seen before at Constantinople. Constantine XI was considered a successful and experienced emperor. He was certainly brave, and the best of the Byzantine aristocracy on the walls. He may have been prescient that Turkish offers to allow him and his people a safe exit to the Peloponnese were meaningless, given the Ottoman destruction of Byzantine civilization in Greece just a few years after the fall of Constantinople. Yet his inability to marshal on the walls any more than a twentieth of the forces outside them is a testament to his failure as a strategist and diplomat.

Unfortunately for the Aztecs, Hernán Cortés was not just an accomplished conquistador with the usual ambition of becoming rich and famous. He also was one of the most brilliant military commanders in Spanish history. Without him, the conquistadors might not have taken the city for decades. In contrast, the Aztecs' emperor Montezuma II was indecisive, weak, and at times delusional. He became and remained bewildered by the Spanish and missed dozens of occasions to destroy Cortés's small forces during their initial visit of 1519–1920. That the city offered a furious resistance in 1521 was largely due to Montezuma's demise and replacement by first Cuitláhuac and subsequently Cuauhtémoc. Had either been in command in 1519, they might have liquidated Cortés and his tiny band when they had the easiest opportunity.

The defenders rarely equate their present existential peril with the enemy military genius who reduced them to such straits. Nor can they accurately assess in comparison the mediocrity of their own leadership.

Fifth, prior to their annihilation, the defenders had often worked out some sort of understanding with their eventual destroyers that they thought would continue. In the modern case of the Jews of Europe, it seemed incomprehensible that a people who had heroically fought in World War I for a number of European armies and had become a professional elite in most of Europe's great capitals could be targeted for extinction. The same surrealism was true of the Armenians. True, like the Jews, they had been targets of past pogroms. But, also like the Jews, they had become a successful minority with considerable resources and influence, particularly in the capital at Kostantiniyye (Constantinople).

Thebes did not lose its freedom in 335 BC, but rather at the battle of Chaeronea three years earlier. Yet, along with perhaps more than a thousand other Greek poleis, Thebes had come to accept the inevitability of Macedonian power and rule over Greece. A prior enervating acquiescence made sudden insurrection far more difficult.

As noted, Carthage was put into a lose-lose dilemma by escalating attacks from Numidia, combined with Roman refusal to allow any counterattacks. Yet hitherto for over a century the Romans had accepted Carthage as a subordinate client state, and the Carthaginians thought that status could continue.

Byzantine emperors underappreciated the threat of Mehmet, in part because for the prior century they had grown accustomed to maintaining their existence by serially ceding territory and paying tribute to the Ottomans. They apparently believed that such bribery and concessions were permanently viable.

Montezuma and many of the deluded Aztec grandees around him had at least initially believed that Cortés might be some sort of super-plenipotentiary who would exact tribute but leave a subservient Aztec nation's infrastructure and customs intact.

Often defenders did not fully grasp, or were in denial, that their defeat would become synonymous with their disappearance, although it was certainly a logical deduction to make at the outset of hostilities. The Thebans knew well of Macedonian barbarity in the north and the razing of the city-state of Olynthus. But apparently they assumed their status as an iconic Greek polis, analogous to Athens, Corinth, and Sparta, meant that Alexander would once again defeat rather than erase them.

Carthage may have assumed that another brutal Scipio might conquer but not really (as he had warned) demolish the city, given that such exemptions had been accorded earlier after its defeats in two prior Punic wars. Constantinople had made all sorts of pragmatic agreements with the sultanate in the past. From trade concessions to subsidized custodianship of Turkish claimants to the Ottoman throne, its modus vivendi with prior sultans may have deluded the Byzantines into not taking seriously young Mehmet II's existential threats. And in the flower-war world of the Aztecs, defeat was commonly defined as humiliation, the mass human sacrifice of beaten warriors, tribute, enslavement, and loss of autonomy—but not vaporization.

The targeted never fully grasped that the antebellum negotiations and diplomacy that had allowed a final and brief respite no longer applied, either because politics had changed in the powerful party, or the technological and organizational capabilities of the enemy had evolved.

Sixth, the fierceness of the doomed grew with the bleaker odds. Yet such fanatical resistance only guaranteed the mercilessness of the victors' occupation. One reason of many why Alexander chose to obliterate Thebes was its frenzied defense on the eve of his expedition to Persia, which cost him five hundred of his crack troops.

Hasdrubal not only mounted a furious defense of Carthage for three years that may have cost Rome thousands of legionaries. Both to intimidate the attackers and to remind his defenders that defeat would be synonymous with extinction, the Carthaginian general also executed and mutilated Roman prisoners on the walls of the city in the full view of the besiegers. That barbarity confirmed that Rome would show no mercy in victory.

Despite the overwhelming forces of the Ottomans and their array of destructive artillery, during the fifty-three-day siege of Constantinople the Byzantine defenders may have killed more than twenty thousand of the attackers, or perhaps a quarter of their forces. And at one point, Constantine XI retaliated for prior Ottoman executions by beheading captive Turkish prisoners on the walls of the city. In the sultan's mind, his losses were unnecessary had the Byzantines simply accepted the inevitable, and so were to be paid back in kind when the city fell.

All contemporary Spanish accounts of the siege of Tenochtitlán attest to the fear of and anger over the ritual parading of captured conquistadors up the steps of the Great Pyramid at the center of the Templo Mayor sanctuary. Of the eighteen hundred Spaniards who died in battle—of disease and wounds, and while captives of the Aztecs—perhaps five hundred or more were sacrificed, a fact that ultimately galvanized the Spanish to eradicate Tenochtitlán.

There is also something quite different about a siege and urban warfare compared to a pitched battle in the field, something that especially whets the murderous appetites. Stealth and ambush recede as the enemy is confined, visible, and thus easily targeted. Population density is far greater, thus ensuring that violence becomes far more focused, lethal, and effective.

The longer the siege lasts, the more violence escalates, and the more savage the combatants become to end it. Civilians become indistinguishable from combatants. Wealth and booty are more concentrated in a confined space and become an added stimulus to storm the city. The targeted are also seen as the last obstacle of a larger war, in which the final investment of greater violence at the focused point ensures not just the end of risk and hazard, but the long-awaited moment of reward and profits—including the enslavement, torture, rape, and murder of civilians.

In other words, if the attacked fight with greater fervor when they realize that looming defeat is the equivalent of extinction, so too the attacker is enthused by the reality that his enemy is not going anywhere, but now is static, visible—and erasable.

The effort to destroy rather than merely defeat a trapped enemy ensures unprecedented savagery. And the zeal necessary to resist overwhelming odds eventually ensures a level of counter-violence that seals the fate of the defeated.

Seventh, what explains the conquerors' tallies of enemy dead was not primarily their leaders' individual intent, but the size and resources of their targets. In other words, the relative populations of Thebes, Carthage, Constantinople, and Tenochtitlán were the most important variables that account for the eventual toll of death and enslavement, not the comparative abilities, resources, or violence of the attackers. Had killers such as Alexander been at Tenochtitlán, or Scipio at Constantinople, the resulting body count would likely have been little different.

In this context, a certain remorse is predictable. After unleashing mass death, those in charge almost always post facto expressed shock at, or more likely tried to excuse, their own brutality, especially when they either immediately or in the future intended to reoccupy or reemploy the site of their destruction. In other words, whatever the original intention of the besieging general, at the moment of victory he either predictably lost control of his troops, who crossed the line from war to murder, or claimed he had. Such professed regret gained resonance because so often the destroyers of civilization were self-proclaimed men of letters.

Alexander, tutored by Aristotle, saw himself as Homer's Achilles redux and an emissary of Hellenism, packing his retinue with philosophers, poets, and historians. Scipio Aemilianus later created a philhellenic "Scipionic Circle" that included the comic playwright Terence and the philosopher Panaetius. Mehmet II fancied himself a man of letters, amassed a library of Greek, Latin, and Persian texts, and brought philosophers, historians, and men of science into his court. Cortés drew on classical thought and was accompanied by many writers, among them the great memoirist and chronicler of the conquest Bernal Díaz del Castillo. Beware of killers with pretensions of an enlightened intellect.

How inevitable that Alexander let loose his avengers to destroy Thebes, only later to regret the carnage he had unleashed. How typical that Scipio Aemilianus allowed his legionaries to murder the defeated, only later to recall that Rome's future might someday follow Homer's warning that a defeated Troy's fate would be that of the victorious Greeks as well. Did a suddenly philosophical Scipio feign remorse at what he had wrought? How predictable that after promising his Ottomans an orgy of rape, booty, and slaughter, a supposedly teary-eyed Mehmet II would soon claim regret that they had done what he had ensured: "What a city we have given over to plunder and destruction."

How banal that Hernán Cortés systematically destroyed Tenochtitlán block by block, yet claimed impotence when his Tlaxcalan allies murdered thousands of their unarmed civilian enemies, and then insisted he had only wished to preserve and improve upon the "Venice" of New Spain for posterity.

Once the victors are unleashed—and they always are—their commanders post facto express regret over their nihilistic cruelty, without any sense that they would do anything differently in the future. Education and pretenses of high culture empowered rather than limited the retribution of the conquerors.[3]

In our unstable contemporary globalized world, we should keep in mind all these considerations of what on rare occasions allows the unthinkable to become reality. In the war for Ukraine that broke out with the Russian invasion of February 2022, the use of apocalyptic weapons has been casually referenced since its outbreak, in a way not heard since the Cuban Missile Crisis of October 1962. In summer 2022 Vladimir Putin constantly suggested that the aggressor Russia reserved the right to use nuclear weapons if threatened with destruction. As Russia initially became stalemated in the months following its invasion, a few prominent Russians openly envisioned thermonuclear war to preclude defeat abroad rather than at home. On multiple occasions a nuclear Russia sought to confront the drones and planes from nuclear-protected NATO nations, while a nuclear China watched nuclear America's reaction as it assessed the pros and cons of invading Taiwan.

Strangely, throughout these tensions and threats, Western nations, which have provided Ukraine with billions of dollars in sophisticated weapons, often casually dismissed such nuclear saber rattling as the empty bluster of a sick leader, a frustrated and losing military, or a Russian nation in decline—albeit one armed with sixty thousand nuclear warheads. Perhaps the West disdained the seriousness of such nuclear threats because the attacker, Russia, was blanketing the skies of Kyiv with indiscriminate missiles and bombs, and thus surely could not seriously believe that the invaded had no right to reciprocate in kind. Or perhaps Americans just assumed that the doctrine of "mutually assured destruction" would deter even a madman from contemplating the use of a tactical nuclear weapon.

But as these chapters show, what is moral or logical bears no relation to the obliteration that may follow. Between a stronger attacker and a weaker attacked, the ancient Melian laws of "the strong do what they can, and the weak suffer what they must" prevail. And thus there is no such thing as reciprocity, proportionality, symmetry, or the "laws of war."[4]

Like a desperate Thebes, Carthage, Constantinople, or Tenochtitlán, Ukraine has been relying almost entirely on its allies to save it from Russia. Perhaps Kyiv should ponder its fate, especially since, through summer 2023, a well-armed and brave Ukraine had still lost about one soldier for every two Russians its forces killed. Russia's apparent plan was to use its hundred-million-person advantage, its ten-times-larger economy, and its thirty-times-larger territory to turn Ukraine into a Verdun-like deathscape.

North Korea is another flash point. Since its 2006 acquisition of nuclear weapons, and even as its ossified economy periodically descends into famine, Pyongyang has threatened South Korea, Japan, and the West Coast of the United States with nuclear attack. On New Year's Day 2018, North Korean dictator Kim Jong Un warned that he could hit any American city he wished with nuclear weapons—and that he had the launch button sitting on his desk. In response to such threats, in a tweet then-president Donald Trump almost immediately reminded Kim: "Will someone from his depleted and food starved regime please inform him that I too have a Nuclear Button, but it is a much bigger & more powerful one than his, and my Button works!"[5]

Of course, such North Korean nuclear threats soon resumed after the Trump administration. In November 2022, facing further criticism from the Biden administration for its reckless testing of long-range missiles, Kim warned both South Korea and the United States that they "would pay the most horrendous price in history." Any North Korean invasion of the South, on the premise that Seoul has no nuclear deterrent, would likely prompt the United States to remind both Pyongyang and its benefactor Beijing that South Korea is indeed protected by the American nuclear umbrella. Moreover, in the face of such serial threats, South Korea and other regional targets of North Korean and Chinese bullying, such as Australia, Japan, and Taiwan, might eventually consider that they have the means to become nuclear quite quickly and effectively.

Turning to China itself, which the United States has often designated its principal opponent, Chinese major general Zhu Chenghu warned the US in 2005 that "if the Americans draw their missiles and position-guided ammunition on to the target zone on China's territory, I think we will have to respond with nuclear weapons." Chenghu's nuclear threats over Taiwan have been occasionally echoed since.

For example, in July 2021 a Chinese government propaganda video briefly appeared, bragging of Chinese intentions to nuke Japan should Tokyo reaffirm its vows to help defend Taiwan from a Chinese invasion.[6]

Pakistan, another nuclear-armed potential flashpoint, in August 2021 again threatened India, in all too common Pakistani fashion, with possible nuclear war. Pakistani federal minister Sheikh Rashid went into some detail about the scenario of such an attack:

> If Pakistan gets attacked by India, there is no scope for conventional war. This will be a bloody and nuclear war. It will be a nuclear war for sure. We have very calculated weapons which are small and perfect. Our weapons will save Muslim lives and will only target certain regions. Pakistan's range now even includes Assam. Pakistan has no option in conventional war; therefore, India knows if something happens, it will be the end.

Rashid was only echoing a common nightmare of nuclear analysts, in which the stronger nuclear power uses its deterrence for advantage in a conventional conflict, thereby convincing the weaker power its only recourse is a first-strike preemptive use of the bomb.[7]

The acceptable bar since the Cuban Missile Crisis of not even referencing the use of nuclear weapons has certainly been lowered to the point of banality. In part, the culprit is the expansion of the club of nuclear powers during the last sixty years to include China, India, Israel, North Korea, and Pakistan—with many of these new nuclear states, unlike the small nuclear family of the past, sharing common borders while having diverse religions and ideologies. The more that current nuclear powers vow to consider using their arsenals, the more they fuel proliferation by their threatened non-nuclear neighbors. Had several embattled states—such as Libya, South Africa, and Ukraine—not given up their nuclear weapons or their intention to produce them, we might have already witnessed a wartime nuclear exchange.

Yet there are plenty of other nations and regions that equally risk sharing the fate of Thebes or Carthage, given their rather confined territories, their rough neighborhoods, their powerful enemies, their undependable allies, their small populations, and their assumptions that "it cannot happen here."

In 2002, the former Iranian president and then–Expediency Council chairman Ali Akbar Hashemi Rafsanjani, on the occasion of Al-Quds Day, outlined a scenario in which the acquisition of nuclear weapons might solve Iran's "Zionist-entity" problem. As reported by the Middle East Media Research Institute, in a lengthy speech Rafsanjani claimed "that Muslims must surround colonialism and force them [the colonialists] to see whether Israel is beneficial to them or not. If one day the world of Islam comes to possess the weapons currently in Israel's possession [meaning nuclear weapons]—on that day this method of global arrogance would come to a dead end. This, he said, is because the use of a nuclear bomb in Israel will leave nothing on the ground, whereas it will only damage the world of Islam."[8]

Former president Rafsanjani, once considered a "moderate" Iranian leader, also reportedly at one point remarked that Israel was conveniently "a one-bomb country." Apparently, Rafsanjani meant that half the world's Jewish population was concentrated in a relatively small region and thus could be liquidated with a single nuclear weapon.[9]

The specter of a soon to be nuclear theocratic Iran that professes it can survive a nuclear exchange, or at least find the ensuing postmortem paradise preferrable to the status quo ante bellum, ensures a dangerous state of affairs, especially amid recent proxy wars between Iran and nuclear Israel in Gaza, Lebanon, and Syria.

In December 2022, Tehran continued its two decades of existential threats with vows that any preemptive conventional strike on its nuclear enrichment facilities would earn a rain of Iranian missiles on Israel's Dimona nuclear reactor, followed by a flurry that would "raze Tel Aviv." Iran even released a video showing simulated missile attacks destroying Israel.[10]

Unfortunately, in addition to Israel, there are other nations and peoples that have a long and sad past of vulnerability and persecution, for whom a major war of escalation could threaten their very existences. These peoples reside in dangerous neighborhoods and have relatively small populations with limited resources, but long histories.

A good example is Western, Orthodox Greece of little more than ten million people, occupying some fifty-one thousand square miles of strategic real estate, with a population density of only two hundred persons per square mile, and without much natural wealth. It faces a hostile fellow NATO member, its historical conqueror and occupier—Turkey. The latter has increasingly shed the pro-Western, secular traditions of its founder, Mustafa Kemal Atatürk, and under its Islamist leader Recep Tayyip Erdoğan instead redefined itself as the rightful heir of the Islamic and expansionary Ottoman Empire that absorbed the Greek Byzantine Empire. The Turkish government has openly praised its Ottoman imperial heritage while downplaying its founder's secular vision. As part of its appeal to the Ottoman legacy of conquest, Turkey's First Lady has even praised the Ottoman harem as a supposed place of enlightened female companionship and learning.[11]

Turkey insists that its former occupation of Greek-speaking northern Cyprus, and the current puppet state of the Turkish Republic of Northern Cyprus (recognized only by Turkey), are permanent realities. Turkish President Erdoğan has repeatedly vowed to invalidate by force if necessary legitimate natural gas and oil claims of both Greece and Cyprus in the Eastern Mediterranean. Increasingly, Turkey does not recognize the Greek sovereignty of the major Greek islands off the coast of Asia Minor, and considers their status fluid and eventually Turkish.

As a result, in the Aegean, Turkey each month conducts dozens of provocative overflights of Greek territory, while insisting the islands remain demilitarized to avoid a Turkish invasion. Meanwhile, NATO member Turkey has grown closer to China, Iran, and Russia, while stepping up its anti-US and anti-European rhetoric.

In December 2022, Erdoğan explicitly warned Greece yet again that newly acquired Turkish missiles could strike Athens itself—"If you don't stay calm." Or as Erdoğan more unabashedly defined his threats:

Now we have started to make our own missiles. Of course, this production scares the Greeks. When you say "Tayfun" ["typhoon"],
the Greek gets scared and says, "It will hit Athens." Well, of course
it will . . . If you don't stay calm, if you try to buy something [to arm
yourself] from here and there, from America to the islands, a country like Turkey will not be a bystander. It has to do something.

Erdoğan has ominously further warned: "We can come down suddenly one night when the time comes."[12]

While Turkey remains officially both a NATO member and a
non-nuclear power, in the past Erdoğan has raised the possibility of
going nuclear. He has provoked a number of confrontations with the
United States, even to the extent of arguing over the exact status
of the American arsenal of B-61 nuclear bombs stored at the
American-leased Incirlik Air Base in Adana, Turkey. For example,
during the 2016 coup attempt against the Erdoğan government, it
was not certain that American personnel always had direct access to
or even complete ownership of the weapons. Erdoğan himself has
ominously warned the Americans not to remove their own nuclear
bombs from Incirlik. That paradox raises the specter that Turkey
believes it enjoys partial ownership rights to their use, or would itself
become a nuclear power should the weapons in Turkey be moved to
the United States.[13]

A resurgent Turkey and its surrogates have also revisited a number of their ancient one-sided rivalries with other vulnerable populations, particularly the Kurds and the Armenians. The Kurdish
people remain nationless, with considerable populations dispersed
among the borderlands of Iran, Iraq, Syria, and Turkey. The shifting
alliances of these host countries have traditionally ensured that
Kurds were periodically expelled from those borders, on occasion
had towns wiped out with poison gas, and were required to give up
their collective Kurdish identity. In December 2022, Turkish president Erdoğan threatened once again to enter northern Syria to clear
out its Kurdish population.[14]

Armenia in the modern era reemerged as an autonomous nation
only with the breakup of the former Soviet Union. It has suffered

two organized genocides that cost a million and a half lives at the hands of both the Ottoman sultanate and the emerging Turkish nation—prior to, during, and after World War I. The Armenian people's sad history serves as a reminder that they may still have little margin of error in any large-scale war of the great regional powers.

Armenia's current tiny population of three million, along with its Orthodox Christianity amid Islamic neighbors, renders it especially vulnerable. Moreover, Armenia's former inclusion within the Soviet Union, coupled with its strong ties to the United States due to the Armenian diaspora to America following the genocides, also add to its peril, especially during the frequent periods of Russian-American estrangement, like now.

The Turkish government continues to deny any truth to, much less culpability for, the past mass extermination of the Armenians. In September 2020, a dormant war reignited over the ongoing rival claims to the Nagorno-Karabakh borderlands. An armistice agreement temporarily ended the Nagorno-Karabakh conflict, but only due to Armenian concessions to the much larger, richer, and stronger Azerbaijan. The latter is a nation that enjoys three times the area and population of Armenia, along with notable oil and natural gas wealth. Concerning the ongoing Armenian-Azerbaijan territorial dispute, Erdoğan issued a thinly veiled threat that invoked the prior Armenian genocide: "We will continue to fulfill this mission which our grandfathers have carried out for centuries in the Caucasus region." By September 2023, Armenia had admitted defeat and apparently given up ancient claims to all Nagorno-Karabakh territory, as thousands of Armenian residents there were forced to flee their ancestral homes by the newly enlarged Azerbaijani state.[15]

Scenarios of annihilation arising out of these potential conflicts are not confined to nuclear escalation, or the vulnerability of smaller nations with conventionally armed historic enemies. As the world witnessed with the still-mysterious Covid-19 pandemic, biological agents may be more dangerous than nuclear bombs. By December 2022, the World Health Organization had estimated that fifteen million people had supposedly died from Covid in the two years from 2020 to 2021 alone.[16]

Further ahead, accelerating advances in artificial intelligence (AI) will inevitably be applied to war, with completely unknown consequences. Already, there have been simulated war-gaming exercises in which an AI missile system overrode presumed safety measures and "blew up" its operators. Or as a *Newsweek* account quoted the startled overseers of the hypothetical exercise:

> We were training it in simulation to identify and target a SAM [surface-to-air missile] threat. And then the operator would say yes, kill that threat. The system started realizing that while they did identify the threat at times the human operator would tell it not to kill that threat, but it got its points by killing that threat. So what did it do? It killed the operator. It killed the operator because that person was keeping it from accomplishing its objective.[17]

War is probably the oldest human endeavor, and its face of battle is constantly changing, with new challenges prompting counter-responses. Its novel and unforeseen dangers can never be underestimated. If the twenty-first-century nations do not tolerate the enslavement of the defeated, they certainly promiscuously warn about incinerating them with nuclear weapons.

Indeed, modern civilization faces a toxic paradox. The more that technologically advanced mankind develops the ability to wipe out wartime enemies, the more it develops a postmodern conceit that total war is an obsolete exercise, given that disagreements among civilized peoples will always be arbitrated by the cooler, more sophisticated, and more diplomatically minded. The same hubris that posits that complex tools of mass destruction can be created but never used, also fuels the fatal vanity that war itself is an anachronism and no longer an existential concern—at least in comparison to the supposedly greater threats of naturally occurring pandemics, meteoric impacts, man-made climate change, or overpopulation.[18]

If our brave new world has become more dangerous because of modern technology, age-old constants explain why and when wars of finality can still break out. Most conflicts will continue to end with either stalemate or concession, but not with the end of everything. I emphasize "most." The fate of the Thebans, Carthaginians, Byzantines, and Aztecs reminds us that what "cannot possibly happen" can indeed on occasion occur—when war unleashes timeless human passions, and escalation rather than reduction in violence becomes the rule of the conflict. In this regard, we should remind ourselves that we really do not know the boundaries of or the limitations to what may follow from a dispute in Ukraine, or a standoff over Taiwan, or strikes on nuclear facilities in Iran.

Like their predecessors, modern attackers will on occasion insist on impossible terms. They will sometimes become further enraged by prolonged and toxic resistance. They typically will go through commanders and strategies until they find those who guarantee victory even at the price of the extermination of the enemy. In extremis, they will either deliberately or inadvertently lose control over their own victorious troops, who in turn de facto redefine victory as annihilation. And they will certainly shed postmortem tears at what they wrought, as they claim annihilation was never their real intent.

In these rare cases, the targeted will also continue to quarrel and deny reality. They will believe that doomed resistance may not be so impossible, that the attackers will not consider extermination a necessary part of their victory, that allies and succor must be right over the horizon, that their defenses are underestimated while their enemies' powers are exaggerated, and that reason rules war.

And so they will hope that even their own defeat cannot possibly entail the end of everything.

NOTES

Introduction. How Civilizations Disappear

1. See the three-volume series by Jared Diamond on the end of states, peoples, and civilizations, which usually finds the culprit in either disease, climate changes, environmental damage, or mismatches between population and resources: *Guns, Germs, and Steel: The Fates of Human Societies; Collapse: How Societies Choose to Fail or Succeed;* and *Upheaval: Turning Points for Nations in Crisis.* Cf. G. Parker, *Global Crisis: War, Climate Change and Catastrophe in the Seventeenth Century;* W. Scheidel, *The Great Leveler: Violence and the History of Inequality from the Stone Age to the Twenty-First Century;* and my review of Scheidel's book, "Equal by Catastrophe," *Inference,* at https://inference-review.com/article/equal-by -catastrophe.

2. For a fascinating look at some of the obscure states that have been destroyed and mostly forgotten, consult N. Davies, *Vanished Kingdoms: The Rise and Fall of States and Nations,* including Tolosa, Alt Clut, and Rusyn.

3. R. Beaton, *Greece: Biography of a Modern Nation,* 415–444.

Chapter One. Hope, Danger's Comforter

1. Diodorus, 17.10.1. Diodorus's account of the siege is often questioned as the most rhetorical and least reliable. In fact, it is the longest and most detailed, and its main outlines are supported by Arrian and Plutarch: A. Bosworth, *Historical Commentary on Arrian's History of Alexander,* 81.

2. Despite the historic loss of Greek freedom at the battle at Chaeronea, there are few detailed ancient accounts of the battle. See Diodorus, 16.85.5–86.6; Plutarch, *Alexander,* 9.2; Polyaenus, 4.2.2. For the reaction and route of invasion of Alexander to Thebes, see N. Hammond and F. Walbank, *History of Macedonia,* 56; and 59–60 for the second thoughts of Theban allies. On the controversies over the battle and the lion monument, see

most recently, J. Ma, "Chaironeia 338: Topographies of Commemoration," 72–91.

3. Ancient treatments of the siege of and battle for Thebes are found in Diodorus, 17.16.8–15; Plutarch, *Alexander*, 11–12; Arrian, *Anabasis*, 1.7–8, Justin, *Epitome*, 11.3.6–7; and Aeschines, 3.133. See a summary in I. Worthington, "Alexander's Destruction of Thebes," 65; and 85 on Alexander's moderate terms; and in B. Antela-Bernardez, "A Furious Wrath: Alexander the Great's Destruction of Thebes and Perdiccas' False Retreat" in G. Lee et al., eds. *Ancient Warfare*, 94–105. Cf. also, A. Bosworth, *Conquest and Empire*, 32–35, 195–96. We are not sure whether the thirty thousand in Alexander's army refers to Macedonians only or included his Boeotian allies: Bosworth, *Historical Commentary on Arrian's History of Alexander*, 79; see 78 for the weakness in the Cadmea's defenses.

4. For the battles of Delium and Leuctra, see respectively V. Hanson, *Ripples of Battle*, 171–243; "Epameinondas, the Battle of Leuctra (371 B.C.), and the 'Revolution' in Greek Battle Tactics," 190–207. On the "lost cause" mentality, see *Ripples of Battle,* 94–118.

5. Plutarch, *Comparison of Pelopidas and Marcellus*, 1.1.

6. On the characteristics of the Theban army, see N. Hammond, "What May Philip Have Learnt as a Hostage in Thebes?," 362–371.

7. For Diodorus's graphic descriptions of the fighting, see 17.11.3–5. The bodily strength of Theban hoplites was generally recognized in antiquity. See a list of ancient references in V. Hanson, *Soul of Battle*, 421, nn. 17–19.

8. See Diodorus, 17.12.2–3.

9. On the Theban fortifications, see T. Manolova, "The Mytho-Historical Topography of Thebes," 84–85. On the classical reputation of Theban excellence in military architecture, cf. Diodorus, 14.84.3; Xenophon, *Hellenica*, 5.438.

10. On Theban wall builders, the role of Thebans in founding the great walled cities of the Peloponnese, and the "dancing floor of war," see variously V. Hanson, *Soul of Battle*, 424, 427; Plutarch, *Moralia*, 193E18.

11. Diodorus, 17.12.3.

12. For Thebes's walls and the city's relationship to surrounding towns and hamlets, cf. *Hellenica Oxyrhynchia*, 12.3; S. Symeonoglou, *Topography*, 35–36.

13. Arrian, 1.8.8. The "other" Boeotians, we know from different sources, also included the Orchomenians and Thespians. Cf. Diodorus 13.5; Plutarch, *Alexander*, 11.11.

14. Diodorus, 17.13.1–3.

15. On the vote of the Theban people, see A. Bosworth, *Historical Commentary on Arrian's History of Alexander,* 74.

16. Plutarch, *Alexander,* 11.10–12. On the Greek sources of our extant later accounts, especially the lost histories of Ephorus, Diyllus, and Cleitarchus, see, for example, R. Drews, "Diodorus and His Sources," *American Journal of Philology,* 83.4 (October 1962), 383–392; J. Yardley, *Justin: Epitome,* 84.

17. We have no accurate numbers on the population of Thebes in 335 BC, though more evidence about numbers for the entire surrounding region of Boeotia. Symeonoglou noted that the population was likely smaller than thirty thousand, although in theory the Cadmea alone had room for up to twelve thousand residents inside its ramparts, and the city itself could have accommodated up to a hundred thousand people. See S. Symeonoglou, *Topography,* 118, 146, 153–154. See also G. Vottéro, *Le dialecte béotien,* I.

18. On the poet Pindar's house, and the various categories of the exempted, see J. Hamilton, *Plutarch: Alexander, A Commentary,* 30–31. Cf. Plutarch, *Alexander,* 12.1–2 for the story of Timocleia. And cf. *Moralia (Mulierum virtutes),* 259e; and Aristobulus, *FGrHist,* 139 F2.

19. For Plutarch's additional observations, see *Alexander,* 11–12.5, and C. Mossé, "Plutarque, Alexandre et Thèbes," 968. See Thucydides, 7.29–30 for Mycalessos.

20. For a general discussion of the sources of Arrian and Alexander concerning the razing of Thebes, see N. Hammond, *Sources for Alexander the Great,* chapter 2.

21. For slave prices in connection with wartime defeat, see J. Yardley, *Justin: Epitome,* 99–101, and especially W. Pritchett, *War,* Vol. V, 243–245. In most classical hoplite battles, the losers lost somewhere between 10 and 20 percent of their troops, the victors about 5 percent. See P. Krentz, "Casualties in Hoplite Battles," *Greek, Roman and Byzantine Studies,* 26.1 (Spring 1985), 13–20.

22. Arrian 1.9.0.

23. See Justin, *Epitome,* 11.4.8. On the average daily wages in classical Greece, see A. Bergh and C. Hampus Lyttkens, "Measuring Institutional Quality in Ancient Athens," 279–310. Xenophon, *On Revenues,* 4, cites 180 drachmas as the price of a slave miner at the Laurion silver mines; presumably the largely female slaves at Thebes would be sold for less.

24. For the role and fate of the Theban exiles, see S. Gartland, "A New Boeotia? Exiles, Landscapes, and Kings," 149–151.

25. On the difficulties of destroying farmland, see in general V. Hanson, *Warfare and Agriculture in Classical Greece*. For the size of Boeotia, and the city proper of Thebes, cf. V. Hanson, *The Other Greeks*, 207–210; P. Cartledge, *Thebes*, 72–73.

26. For house destruction, roof tiles, and the burning of mud brick dwellings, see V. Hanson, *Warfare and Agriculture in Classical Greece*, 71–76, 107–109. For pro-Macedonian Boeotians likely using the spoils for later endowments and dedicatory buildings, see A. Schlachter, *Boeotia in Antiquity*, 113.

27. Arrian, 1.9.9.

28. On philosophical energy at Thebes and the Greek foundational myths involving Thebes, cf. P. Cartledge, *Thebes*, 111–131, 247–249. And for ancient references for Theban Pythagoreans and other philosophical schools, V. Hanson, *Soul of Battle*, 422, nn. 25, 27.

29. On the Macedonian propaganda of a Panhellenic strike against Persia, see Alexander's offer before the battle at Thebes, Diodorus, 17.9.5–6.

30. On the controversial number of twenty thousand mercenaries at Granicus, see W. McCoy, "Memnon of Rhodes at the Granicus," 413–433; N. Hammond, "The Battle of the Granicus River," 73–88.

31. For Philip's siege of Olynthus and political aftermath, see I. Worthington, "Alexander's Destruction of Thebes," 66–67, especially 83–85.

32. Justin, *Epitome*, 11.3.

33. On Boeotian city-states that joined the Macedonians to attack Thebes despite the otherwise mostly positive feeling of many Boeotians toward Thebes, see A. Schlachter, *Boeotia in Antiquity*, 113–114.

34. For key linguistic differences between Greeks and Macedonians, see the classic work of A. Jarde, *The Formation of the Greek People*, 324–325. For mass atrocities committed by Alexander, see V. Hanson, "Alexander the Killer," *Military History Quarterly*, 10.3 (Spring 1998), 8–19.

35. Justin, *Epitome*, 11.3.10–11.

36. On the speeches for and against leniency, cf. Justin, *Epitome*, 11.4.

37. Arrian 1.9.6–7.

38. On the killing of pro-Macedonian Thebans before the rebellion, see A. Schlachter, *Boeotia in Antiquity*, 126. For the idea that Alexander destroyed Thebes in retaliation for its support of Alexander's rival for

the throne, see I. Worthington, "Alexander's Destruction of Thebes," 85–86.

39. Few of the ancient sources were fooled by Alexander's pawning off responsibility for Thebes's fate to its Greek rivals. Cf. C. Mossé, "Plutarque, Alexandre et Thebes," 968–969. Soldiers usually received the same one-drachma daily wage as day laborers: W. Pritchett, *War*, Vol. I, 3–52; D. Engels, *Alexander*, 11–25.

40. For the legal pretexts cited by the victor to justify the city's destruction, see N. Hammond and F. Walbank, *History of Macedonia*, 64–66.

41. On the Macedonian military revolution and its relationship to Philip's years at Thebes, see N. Hammond, "What May Philip Have Learnt as a Hostage in Thebes?," 357–370.

42. Arrian (1.9.1–3) seems to have been the only ancient source who cited the role of exiles for stirring up the Theban dêmos to revolt. For their prominent role, see N. Hammond and F. Walbank, *History of Macedonia*, 56–57; A. Bosworth, *Historical Commentary on Arrian's History of Alexander*, 75.

43. For the lethality of the Macedonian phalanx for decades before the destruction of Thebes, see N. Hammond, "What May Philip Have Learnt as a Hostage in Thebes?," 362–363.

44. For the Athenian role in extending aid and more support but not needed soldiers, see Diodorus, 17.8.6; J. Trevett, "Demosthenes and Thebes," 184–202, especially 199. On the false rumors surrounding Alexander's death, see Arrian 1.7.4–11; Diodorus, 17.9.1; Plutarch, *Alexander*, 11.

45. On Athenian efforts to placate a victorious Alexander, see cf. Justin, *Epitome*, 11.3–5; Plutarch, *Demosthenes*, 23.2; *Alexander*, 13, Arrian, 1.1.1–3.

46. Diodorus, 17.9.3–5.

47. Archeological "evidence" for the destruction of 335 BC often consists simply of a hiatus in material remains between fifth century BC and the later refounded city of Cassander. Cf. T. Manolova, "The Mytho-Historical Topography of Thebes," 82; S. Symeonoglou, *Topography*, 148–150. For Hyperides and his freedwoman Theban mistress, see Plutarch, *Moralia*, 849D.

48. On later references to surviving named Boeotians or Thebans, and the multiplicity of scenarios that might explain the very few references to Thebans after the destruction of the city, see A. Schlachter, *Boeotia in Antiquity*, 160–164.

49. Arrian, 9.1–8. Cf. I. Worthington, "Alexander's Destruction of Thebes," 65–68.

50. The various agendas and motives of Cassander, and the associated reactions from both pro- and anti-Theban Boeotians, are discussed in Y. Kalliontzis and N. Papazarkadas, "The Contributions to the Refoundation of Thebes," 293–294. For the sources and discussion of the rebuilding, cf. N. Rockwell, *Thebes, A History*, 139–141.

51. See Diodorus, 19.53–4. For the details of Cassander's "new" Thebes and inscriptional evidence, see in general, K. Buraselis, "Contributions to Rebuilding Thebes," 159–170; S. Gartland, "A New Boeotia? Exiles, Landscapes, and Kings," 162; Y. Kalliontzis and N. Papazarkadas, "The Contributions to the Refoundation of Thebes," 293–294.

52. On the various fates of Hellenistic and Roman Thebes, see P. Cartledge, *Thebes*, 244–252.

53. The normal Greek word for "people" was *ethnos*, as in, say, the Medes or the Arcadians, but it only occasionally was used to denote a larger tribal organization or loose federation.

54. For the consequences of a small state losing a battle, and with it deterrence against attack and subsequent destruction, see V. Hanson, "Hoplite Obliteration: The Case of the Town of Thespiae," 210–211.

55. Thucydides, "Melian Dialogue," 5.84–116. On Io, see Aeschylus, *Prometheus Bound*, 750–751.

56. Arrian, 1.9.

Chapter Two. The Wages of Vengeance

1. Appian, *Punic Wars*, 19.129.

2. Appian, *Punic Wars*, 19.129.

3. Ancient and modern guesses of the population of Carthage range widely. Strabo (17.15.13) believed in normal times the city held 700,000 Carthaginians. D. Hoyos (*Hannibal's Dynasty*, 28) argued there were 200,000 males, which might suggest a total population including women and children of 800,000. Most scholars accept 200,000–500,000, which surely swelled from rural refugees at the onset of the siege. For a lower number, see B. Warmington, *Carthage*, 124–127.

4. Appian, *Punic Wars*, 19.131.

5. On Carthage and genocide, see B. Kiernan, "Sur la notion de génocide," 179–192.

6. On the numbers at Ecnomus, G. Tipps, "The Battle of Ecnomus," 436. Cf. A. Goldsworthy, *Punic Wars*, 109–115, and especially J. Lazenby, *First Punic War*, 81–96.

7. Cf. "Carthage, with her new resources and territorial dominions, was once again at least as powerful as Rome. The Romans with their Italian allies could call on about three-quarters of a million men of military age, in a total population of three to four million. Carthage with her chora, allies and subjects from Lepcis Magna to Gades will have had a population roughly similar." D. Hoyos, *The Carthaginians*, 199.

8. For an outline of the growth of Roman power and its confrontation with the Hellenistic kingdoms and the preliminary tensions with Carthage, see F. Walbank, A. Astin, M. Frederiksen, and R. Ogilvie, eds., *The Cambridge Ancient History, Volume 7, Part 1: The Hellenistic World*, 101–255, 412–472. And cf. F. Walbank, A. Astin, M. Frederiksen, and R. Ogilvie, eds., *The Cambridge Ancient History Vol. 7, Part 2: The Rise of Rome to 220 B.C.*, 466–559.

9. See the praise of Aristotle, *Politics*, 1272b; and cf. Polybius, 6.2–18, 51.

10. Pseudo-Scylax, *Periplus*, 111; S. Lancel, *Carthage*, 137–138; D. Hoyos, *The Carthaginians*, 41; J. Quinn, *In Search of the Phoenicians*, 88; R. Miles, "Vandal North Africa and the Fourth Punic War," 384–410.

11. Polybius, 6.52.

12. J. Quinn, "Tophets in the 'Punic World,'" 23–48.

13. Cleitarchus, *FGrHist*, 137 F9.

14. Appian, *Punic Wars*, 11.75. Modern scholars argue that ancient numbers are exaggerated, and the expeditionary force was more likely forty thousand to fifty thousand in number. Cf. A. Goldsworthy, *Punic Wars*, 340. Yet eighty thousand is not an unlikely number, given a much larger, earlier Roman force in 255, at a time in the First Punic War when Rome was far weaker, sought to sail back from North Africa, and was wrecked by a storm in the Mediterranean. It suffered *one hundred thousand dead* alone.

15. Appian, *Punic Wars*, 11.79. For the echoes of the Dialogue at Melos in the speech of the Carthaginians, see, J. Leavesly, "Melos and Carthage: Genocide in the Ancient World." On the weapons turned over to Rome, see Appian, *Punic Wars*, 11.75.

16. Appian, *Punic Wars*, 12.81. On the changing Roman demands, see Diodorus, 32.1–3. On the wages of Carthaginian appeasement and

disarmament, see D. Armstrong, "Unilateral Disarmament: A Case History," 22–27.

17. S. Lancel, *Carthage,* 432–433.

18. Appian, *Punic Wars,* 13.91–3. See Cassius Dio, 21.9.26.

19. Cf. D. Hoyos, *The Carthaginians,* 146, 217.

20. Appian, *Punic Wars,* 13.93–4; Diodorus, 32.9. On Carthage's ability to tap the resources of the hinterlands, see H. Delile, E. Pleuger, J. Blichert-Toft, and A. Wilson, "Economic Resilience of Carthage During the Punic Wars: Insights from Sediments of the Medjerda Delta Around Utica (Tunisia)," 9764–9769.

21. On the structural problems of the Carthaginian military vis-à-vis the Roman army, see Polybius, 6.52.

22. For the walls of Carthage, see Appian, *Punic Wars,* 14.95; cf. S. Lancel, *Carthage.*

23. For the events of the first year of the siege, see Appian, *Punic Wars,* 14.97–100. For the Roman first-year disaster, see the synopsis in A. Goldsworthy, *Punic Wars,* 344–346.

24. Thucydides, 7.87.5–6.

25. Appian, *Punic Wars,* 14.97–9.

26. For Scipio's exceptionalism, see Livy, 49; Cassius Dio, 21.70.4. For the elder Cato on Scipio, see Diodorus, 32.9a; cf. A. Astin, "Scipio Aemilianus and Cato Censorius," 159–180, especially 164–166. Aemilianus Paulus and Epirus: Livy, 45.33–4; Plutarch *Aemilius Paulus* 29.1–30.1.

27. Appian, *Punic Wars,* 16.109–11.

28. Appian, *Punic Wars,* 16.111.

29. Appian, *Punic Wars,* 16.111.

30. Appian, *Punic Wars,* 17.116.

31. Appian, *Punic Wars,* 18.118.

32. Appian, *Punic Wars,* 18.119–20.

33. Appian, *Punic Wars,* 18.121.

34. For the sea-fighting between the Carthaginians and Romans, see again Appian, *Punic Wars,* 18.122–3.

35. Appian, *Punic Wars,* 18.124.

36. Appian, *Punic Wars,* 20.133. For the convoluted early history of the myth of "salting the earth" of Carthage, see R. T. Ridley, "To Be Taken with a Pinch of Salt: The Destruction of Carthage," 140–46, in *Classical Philology* 81.2 (April 1986), 140–146. And for debate over the various "salting the earth" narratives, see S. Stevens, "A Legend of the Destruction of

Carthage," 39–41; B. Warmington, "The Destruction of Carthage: A Retractatio," 308–310.

37. Cassius Dio, 21.9.30. Dio's account is fragmentary and the chronology incoherent, given Cato could not have participated in the final debate over Carthage in 146, having died in late 149.

38. Polybius, 36.2–4.

39. Throughout the war, Rome was far more duplicitous than its Carthaginian enemies, who were often slurred with the charge of "Punic treachery": A. Goldsworthy, *Punic Wars*, 331–332. For the general criticism of Rome's instigation of the war, see N. Rosenstein, *Rome and the Mediterranean*, 233.

40. Masinissa's decades-long aggrandizement at the expense of Carthage, D. Hoyos, *Mastering the West*, 244–248.

41. Polybius, 10.15.4–5.

42. On Polybius and the tradition of Rome's various pretexts for launching an unnecessary war, see D. Baronowski, "Polybius on the Causes of the Third Punic War," 16–31.

43. On the phrase *"Carthago delenda est,"* see U. Vogel Weidemann, "Carthago Delenda Est: 'Aitia' and 'Prophasis,'" 79–95; C. Little, "The Authenticity and Form of Cato's Saying 'Carthago Delenda Est,'" 429–435. Cato either did not actually say at the conclusion of his speeches *Carthago delenda est,* or no one thought much of it, if and when he did. Only later, and apparently in imperial times, did Roman historians magnify and elaborate on the tradition of Cato's insistence on Carthage's destruction and thus recalibrated, or even invented, the famous phrase.

44. Plutarch, *Punic Wars*, 27.1; Pliny, *Natural History*, 15.74. On the fig story, see F. Meijer, "Cato's African Figs," 117–118.

45. The extent of Hannibal's damage to the Italian countryside is controversial. See V. Hanson, *Warfare and Agriculture*, 250–251, contra A. Toynbee, *Hannibal's Legacy*, and H. Sidebottom, "Philosophers' Attitudes to Warfare under the Principate," 248–250.

46. Appian, *Punic Wars*, 10.69.

47. N. Rosenstein, *Rome and the Mediterranean*, 237–238.

48. For the text of the Morgenthau Plan, see Works Cited, Primary Sources, US and Mexico Federal Documents. For Rome's rhetoric and appeasement after the First Punic War, and the settlement after the Second, see D. Kagan, *Origins*, 232–279.

49. Cf. F. Adcock, "'Delenda Est Carthago,'" 117–128.

50. On fear of a North African superstate, see, for example, C. Kunze, "Carthage and Numia, 201–149 B.C.," in D. Hoyos, ed. *Blackwell Companion to the Punic Wars*, 395–411. For Roman paranoias see Y. Le Bohec, "The 'Third Punic War,'" 434–435.

51. On the idea of Roman fear of Carthaginian radical democratization, see Y. Le Bohec, "The 'Third Punic War,'" 431–432, who noted Rome's fears of "flooding Rome itself like a wave."

52. Plutarch quote: *Moralia*, 200D–E; Plautus reference: *Epidicus*, 158–60. For discussion of the Plautus quote and in general on the greed motive for imperialism, see especially W. Harris, "On War and Greed in the Second Century B.C.," 1371–1385, especially 1385.

53. On incentives for war, see D. Hoyos, *Mastering the West*, 254–255.

54. For the Catullus and Juvenal quotations, see Catullus, *Poems*, 51.15–6; Juvenal, *Satires*, 6.292–3.

55. Sallust, *Jugurtha*, 41.

56. See Diodorus, 32.4. On the evolving nature of Roman imperialism and its manifestations abroad, see in general W. Harris, *War and Imperialism in Republican Rome*, especially 131–254; A. Eckstein, *Mediterranean Anarchy, Interstate War, and the Rise of Rome*, 117–118; N. Rosenstein, *Rome and the Mediterranean*, 2, 25–26, 211–212. Cf. A. Goldsworthy, *Punic Wars*, 149–150.

57. On Calgacus, see Tacitus, *Agricola*, 30.4. Eventually, Rome usually found ways to annex and absorb peoples and nations without annihilation, mostly through material enticement and military vigilance. See N. Morley, *The Roman Empire: Roots of Imperialism*, 38–69.

58. See Ennius (239–169 BC), Frag. 237: *Poeni suos soliti dis sacrificare puellos* ("Phoenicians accustomed to sacrifice to the gods their own little sons").

59. Appian, *Punic Wars*, 20.132. For the Homeric passage, cf. *Iliad*, 5.448–9 (Lattimore translation).

60. Cicero, *Tusculum Disputations*, 3.54.

61. Appian, *Punic Wars*, 20.135.

62. Amusingly, the senators claimed that "all the boundary lines of the city had been torn down and obliterated by wolves" (Appian, 20.136).

63. J. Prag, "Poenus Plane Est—But Who Were the 'Punickes'?," 1–37; cf. especially 11–21.

64. J. Quinn, *In Search of the Phoenicians*, 167–168.

65. For Christian Carthage in the age of Augustine, see P. Brown, *Augustine of Hippo*, 54; cf. 7–15, 423–430.

66. For the Vandal capture of Carthage and its subsequent destruction, see V. Hanson, *Savior Generals*, 52–93.

67. J. Quinn, *In Search of the Phoenicians*, 11–13.

Chapter Three. Deadly Delusions

1. E. Gibbon, *The Decline and Fall of the Roman Empire*, Volume XII, chapter 68.

2. For Constantine and the founding of the city, cf. W. Treadgold, *A History of the Byzantine State and Society*, 38–41.

3. For most of their history, the Byzantines referred to themselves, and were known, as *Rhōmaîoi*, the Greek transliteration of "Romans" (Latin *Romani*), to emphasize they were the direct and only surviving successors to the ancient Roman Empire, both east and west. The use of the Latinate *Romani* and Greek *Rhomaioi* eventually came to distinguish Western Roman Catholicism from Eastern Christian Orthodoxy. Of course, occasionally the Byzantines were referred to informally as "Greeks" (*Graikoí*/Γραικοί), and on occasion called themselves "Hellenes." "Byzantine" and "Byzantines" may have first been authoritatively used by Hieronymus Wolf, the German historian. In 1557 he published a compendium of imperial sources entitled *Corpus Historiæ Byzantinæ*—apparently in reference to the fact that Constantinople had been founded atop the classical Greek city of Byzantium; and because Western Europeans, especially "Roman" Catholics, perhaps resented the idea that Greek-speaking Orthodox Christians had appropriated the inheritance and nomenclature of Western Europeans and "Roman" Catholicism—as if Constantinople was the proper and exclusive successor to Romanitas. By the nineteenth century, the haphazard "Byzantine/Byzantines" became normalized for the Later Eastern Roman Empire, often by resentful Westerners who sometimes used the adjective and noun as pejoratives, purportedly to emphasize the corruption, querulousness, convoluted rituals, and bureaucratic complexity of Eastern Greek-speaking Orthodoxy in comparison to their own Latinate Western Catholicism.

4. For the contours of disagreements before the Great Schism, see P. O'Connell, "Nine Centuries of Schism: The Origins of the Schism," 168–175.

5. B. Ward-Perkins, *The Fall of Rome and the End of Civilization*, 59.

6. On East-West trade and the geography of Constantinople, see L. Dominian, "The Site of Constantinople: A Factor of Historical Value," 57–71.

7. See W. Kaegi, *Byzantium and the Decline of Rome*, 226–230. On the differences in state religion from later Western Europe and Byzantium, see J. Skedros, "'You Cannot Have a Church Without an Empire': Political Orthodoxy in Byzantium," 219–231; cf. 219–220.

8. For the tradition of Greek scientific achievement and its continuance in the Byzantine Empire, see A. Tihon, "Science in the Byzantine Empire," 190–206.

9. For Islamic and Byzantine scientific cross-fertilization, see H. Cohen, "Greek Nature-Knowledge Transplanted: The Islamic World," 53–76. Cf. M. S. Khan, "A Chapter on Roman (Byzantine) Sciences in an Eleventh Century Hispano-Arabic Work," 41–70.

10. On the spiritual effects of the monuments, architecture, and public places of imperial Constantinople, see J. Bogdanović, "The Relational Spiritual Geopolitics of Constantinople, the Capital of the Byzantine Empire," 97–154. For the fluid population size of Constantinople and its iconic buildings, see D. Jacoby, "La Population de Constantinople à l'époque Byzantine: un problème de démographie urbaine," 81–109.

11. For the land and seawalls, see D. Nicolle, J. Haldon, and S. Turnbull, *The Fall of Constantinople*, 104–138.

12. The 1204 successful siege by the Venetians of the Fourth Crusade breached the seawalls, as they controlled the sea.

13. On the singular nature of the walls in the ancient and medieval world, see M. Philippides and W. Hanak, *The Siege and the Fall of Constantinople in 1453*, 299.

14. An unmatched description and detailed analysis of the city's fortifications are found in M. Philippides and W. Hanak, *The Siege and the Fall of Constantinople in 1453*, 297–358, especially 306–310.

15. On the inner versus outer wall strategies, see the accounts of Laonicus Chalcocondylas and Leonardo of Chios in J. Melville-Jones, *The Siege of Constantinople 1453*, 42, 30–33.

16. On Gibbon and the Byzantines, see S. Runciman, "Gibbon and Byzantium," 53–60. On Hegel, see G. Arabatzis, "Hegel and Byzantium," 31–39.

17. Venice ruled Corfu until 1797. The Russian Orthodox theory of why Constantinople fell, as Moscow became the "Third Rome," faults the

eleventh-hour agreement of the Greek Orthodox patriarch of Constantinople to the Catholic terms of the union that supposedly had betrayed the true faith. See D. Strémooukhoff, "Moscow the Third Rome: Sources of the Doctrine," 84–101.

18. On the arrival of Turkish tribes into Asia Minor and the challenges they posed for Byzantium, see A. Beihammer, "Patterns of Turkish Migration and Expansion in Byzantine Asia Minor in the 11th and 12th Centuries," 166–192.

19. E. Luttwak, *The Grand Strategy of the Byzantine Empire*, 13–14. For the other consequences of the Justinian plague, see W. Rosen, *Justinian's Flea. The First Great Plague and the End of the Roman World*, 198–268.

20. On the fourteen-century outbreak, cf. M. Congourdeau, "La Peste Noire a Constantinople de 1343 a 1466," 377–389. W. Rosen, *Justinian's Flea. The First Great Plague and the End of the Roman World*, 198–268.

21. Y. Ayalon, *Natural Disasters in the Ottoman Empire. Plague, Famine, and Other Misfortunes*, 21–60.

22. D. Nicolle, J. Haldon, and S. Turnbull, *The Fall of Constantinople*, 98–99.

23. E. Luttwak, *The Grand Strategy of the Byzantine Empire*, 415–418.

24. D. Nicolle, J. Haldon, and S. Turnbull, *The Fall of Constantinople*, 81–84.

25. P. Rance, "Maurice's Strategicon and the Ancients," 217–255.

26. On Byzantine tactics, strategy, and armament, see W. Treadgold, *Byzantium and Its Army*, 87–117; D. Nicolle, J. Haldon, and S. Turnbull, *The Fall of Constantinople*, 56–58.

27. On the rise of the Seljuk Turks and Ottomans, see R. Crowley, *1453*, 29–35.

28. For the disunity, serial defeats of the Crusaders, and the collective fear of the Ottomans, K. DeVries, "The Lack of a Western European Military Response," 539–559.

29. D. Nicolle, J. Haldon, and S. Turnbull, *The Fall of Constantinople*, 198–200. Cf. M. Philippides and W. Hanak, *The Siege and the Fall of Constantinople in 1453*, 74–75.

30. For devshirme, see V. Ménage, "Some Notes on the 'Devshirme,'" 64–78. On resentment of exalted ex-Christians, see M. Greene, *The Edinburgh History of the Greeks, 1453 to 1774: The Ottoman Empire*, 22–56.

31. On the Janissaries and Varangians, see D. Nicolle, J. Haldon, and S. Turnbull, *The Fall of Constantinople*, 142–143, 198–199.

32. See the contemporary descriptions of Barbaro in J. Jones, *Nicolò Bararo. Diary of the Siege of Constantinople, 1453*, 63–64, 32–33.

33. On the European politics of the harem, see M. Iyigun, "Lessons from the Ottoman Harem on Culture, Religion, and Wars," 693–730.

34. On Constantine's earlier career, cf. R. Crowley, *1453*, 47–53.

35. See the account of Michael Ducas in J. Melville-Jones, *The Siege of Constantinople 1453*, 69.

36. On the exchanges between Mehmet and Constantine, see the account of Michael Ducas in J. Melville-Jones, *The Siege of Constantinople 1453*, 64–65.

37. See the version of Halil's remarks in the later account of Michael Ducas in J. Melville-Jones, *The Siege of Constantinople 1453*, 63.

38. For contemporary appraisals of Halil, cf. M. Philippides and W. Hanak, *The Siege and the Fall of Constantinople in 1453*.

39. Quoted in D. Nicolle, J. Haldon, and S. Turnbull, *The Fall of Constantinople*, 180.

40. D. Nicolle, J. Haldon, and S. Turnbull, *The Fall of Constantinople*, 159–169. Cf. George Sphrantzes in M. Carroll, *A Contemporary Greek Source for the Siege of Constantinople: The Sphrantzes Chronicle*, 54–56.

41. For the inability of the Turkish fleet to successfully engage Christian ships, see the contemporary narratives of Nicolò Barbaro, in J. Jones, *Nicolò Barbaro. Diary of the Siege of Constantinople, 1453*, 31–32, 35–36, 44–45.

42. J. Haldon, "Some Aspects of Byzantine Military Technology," 11–47; T. Salmon, *The Byzantine Science of Warfare: From Treatises to Battlefield*, 429–463.

43. See R. Cowley, *1453*, 52–64; M. Philippides and W. Hanak, *The Siege and the Fall of Constantinople in 1453*, 394–396, 411–413.

44. See the translation in M. Philippides and W. Hanak, *The Siege and the Fall of Constantinople in 1453*, 369–370. On the impossibility of aid from the outlands, see W. Treadgold, *A History of the Byzantine State and Society*, 798–799.

45. For ineptness of the Turkish fleet, see the account of George Sphrantzes in M. Carroll, *A Contemporary Greek Source for the Siege of Constantinople: The Sphrantzes Chronicle*, 49.

46. There are conflicting accounts of the number and composition of the defenders, as well as how many of some fifty thousand residents of the city were active or sometime combatants. Contemporary reports suggest

that the Greeks could deploy nearly five thousand professional soldiers (sometimes referenced as "4,773"), and there were over two thousand foreign volunteers or mercenaries, as well as hundreds of other uncounted and unnamed who arrived in smaller numbers or snuck in from surrounding Italian trading enclaves. Cf. M. Philippides and W. Hanak, *The Siege and the Fall of Constantinople in 1453*, 142–145.

47. For the nature of the gun and contemporary descriptions, see M. Philippides and W. Hanak, *The Siege and the Fall of Constantinople in 1453*, 413–425, 479–481. On the exaggeration of the importance of Ottoman cannon in general during the siege, cf. K. DeVries, "Gunpowder Weapons at Constantinople," cf. 353–357.

48. The most complete assessment of the arrival, role, and value of Giustiniani on the walls is found in M. Philippides and W. Hanak, *The Siege and the Fall of Constantinople in 1453*, 384–387; cf. Leonardo of Chios in J. Melville-Jones, *The Siege of Constantinople 1453*, 28–29.

49. Leonardo of Chios in J. Melville-Jones, *The Siege of Constantinople 1453*, 29.

50. K. DeVries, "The Lack of a Western European Military Response," 83–84.

51. For the number and armament of the defenders, see contemporary accounts of Giacomo Tedaldi and Leonardo of Chios in M. Philippides and W. Hanak, *The Siege and the Fall of Constantinople in 1453*, 53–57, 107–111; cf. D. Nicolle, *Constantinople, 1453*, 33. And cf. J. Melville-Jones, *The Siege of Constantinople 1453*, 1–41; D. Nicolle, J. Haldon, and S. Turnbull, *The Fall of Constantinople*, 204–205.

52. On the shortage of soldiers, see Leonardo of Chios in J. Melville-Jones, *The Siege of Constantinople 1453*, 24–26.

53. S. Runciman, *The Fall of Constantinople*, 188. But cf. his other assessment (189): "Nevertheless the date of 29 May 1453 marks a turning-point in the history. It marks the end of an old story, the story of Byzantine civilization."

54. On the weaknesses of the Ottoman naval forces, see H. Inalcik, "Mehmet the Conqueror," 408–427, especially 412–413.

55. See M. Philippides and W. Hanak, *The Siege and the Fall of Constantinople in 1453*, 554–558, for a comprehensive analysis of Ottoman strategy and tactics during the siege.

56. On the first few days of the siege, cf. D. Nicolle, J. Haldon, and S. Turnbull, *The Fall of Constantinople*, 104–138, 217–219. For the relative

positions of the Turkish army and fleet, see D. Nicolle, *Constantinople, 1453*, 38–43.

57. The deployment of various contingents is discussed by George Sphrantzes in M. Carroll, *A Contemporary Greek Source for the Siege of Constantinople: The Sphrantzes Chronicle*, 58–59.

58. For a contemporary account of the Byzantines' successful efforts to countermine the Ottomans' tunneling under the inner and outer walls, see the account of Nicolò Barbaro in J. R. Jones, *Nicolò Barbaro. Diary of the Siege of Constantinople, 1453*, 50–51, 55.

59. Leonardo of Chios offered a contemporary account of the various weapons and siege devices of the attackers and attacked: cf. J. Melville-Jones, *The Siege of Constantinople 1453*, 16–18, 22–23.

60. See the terms offered by the sultan in the near-contemporaneous account of Michael Ducas. Cf. J. Melville-Jones, *The Siege of Constantinople 1453*, 89. On the various contingents on the walls, see Nicolò Barbaro in J. R. Jones, *Nicolò Barbaro. Diary of the Siege of Constantinople, 1453*, 27–30.

61. Michael Ducas in J. Melville-Jones, *The Siege of Constantinople 1453*, 89–90.

62. Michael Ducas in J. Melville-Jones, *The Siege of Constantinople 1453*, 29, 92–93.

63. J. Melville-Jones, *The Siege of Constantinople 1453*, 6.

64. See Nicolò Barbaro, in J. Jones, *Nicolò Barbaro. Diary of the Siege of Constantinople, 1453*, 63–64, 32–33; D. Nicolle, J. Haldon, and S. Turnbull, *The Fall of Constantinople*, 231–232; and George Sphrantzes in M. Carroll, *A Contemporary Greek Source for the Siege of Constantinople: The Sphrantzes Chronicle*, 50–51. On burning oil and other efforts of the defenders, see M. Philippides and W. Hanak, *The Siege and the Fall of Constantinople in 1453*, 522–523.

65. J. Melville-Jones, *The Siege of Constantinople 1453*, 16–18, 36–37. On Giustiniani's wound, the subsequent Genoese panic, and controversy over the flight to the ships, see also the primary source accounts assembled in M. Philippides and W. Hanak, *The Siege and the Fall of Constantinople in 1453*, 521–546.

66. M. Carroll, *A Contemporary Greek Source for the Siege of Constantinople: The Sphrantzes Chronicle*, 77–78. On the controversies of Giustiniani's death, see M. Philippides and W. Hanak, *The Siege and the Fall of Constantinople in 1453*, 542–546.

67. Constantine quote: J. Melville-Jones, *The Siege of Constantinople 1453*, 36.

68. On the looting of Hagia Sophia and other atrocities inside the cathedral, cf. R. Guerdan, *Byzantium*, 217–222.

69. J. Melville-Jones, *The Siege of Constantinople 1453*, 104–105.

70. J. R. Jones, *Nicolò Barbaro. Diary of the Siege of Constantinople, 1453*, 69.

71. Michael Ducas in J. Melville-Jones, *The Siege of Constantinople 1453*, 16–18, 106–107. Cf. M Philippides and W. Hanak, *The Siege and the Fall of Constantinople in 1453*, 131–134.

72. H. Inalcik, "The Policy of Mehmet," 229–249.

73. For examples of the psychological shock in the West at the city's fall, cf. R. Crowley, *1453*, 238–239; and M. Kamariôtès, "Récit pitoyable de la prise de Constantinople," 771–778.

74. For various revisions to the idea of Ottoman military and technological backwardness, see J. Grant, "Rethinking the Ottoman 'Decline,'" 179–201.

75. On Mehmet's efforts to reboot Islamic Constantinople as a sort of international trading concession, see C. Dauverd, "Cultivating Differences," 94–124.

76. On the aspirations of post-1453 Islamic Constantinople, cf. R. Crowley, *1453*, 246–253.

77. For the absorption of Byzantium remnant enclaves after the fall, see S. Runciman, *The Fall of Constantinople*, 170–177.

78. S. Runciman, *The Fall of Constantinople*, 176.

79. M. Philippides and W. Hanak, *The Siege and the Fall of Constantinople in 1453*, 197; Runciman, *The Fall of Constantinople*, 183–184.

80. Byzantium and the Western Renaissance: K. Setton, "The Byzantine Background to the Italian Renaissance," 1–76. For the remarks of Pope Pius, see M. Philippides and W. Hanak, *The Siege and the Fall of Constantinople in 1453*, 195–196.

81. D. Nicol, *The Immortal Emperor*, 98–108; For the various myths and tales of Constantine's last minutes, see M. Philippides and W. Hanak, *The Siege and the Fall of Constantinople in 1453*, 234–235. On the beleaguered Balkans in the ensuring decades after the fall, see S. Runciman, *The Fall of Constantinople*, 176–177, and P. Kinross, *The Ottoman Centuries*, 123–137.

82. For contemporary Turkey's strategic importance and ambiguity, see the short essay of F. Zabun, "Strategic Ambiguity."

83. On Erdoğan's turn toward Islamism, see H. Fradkin and L. Libby, "Erdogan's Grand Vision: Rise and Decline," 41–50. On Greeks today in Turkey, see I. Magra, "Greeks in Istanbul," https://www.ekathimerini.com/society/diaspora/258839/greeks-in-istanbul-keeping-close-eye-on-developments/.

84. On the surviving Greeks of Asia Minor in the centuries after 1453, cf. P. Kitromilides and A. Alexandris, "Ethnic Survival, Nationalism and Forced Migration," especially 9–14. See too J. Harris, "Despots, Emperors, and Balkan Identity in Exile," 643–661.

85. For the quote, see K. Fleming, "Constantinople: From Christianity to Islam," 69–78. On the controversial career and death of Notaras, see primary sources concerning his career in M. Philippides and W. Hanak, *The Siege and the Fall of Constantinople in 1453*, 41–62, 58–264.

86. H. Inalcik, "The Policy of Mehmet II," 229–249, especially 238–241. On the postbellum effort to woo the Greeks of the city to stay, see P. Kinross, *The Ottoman Centuries*, 112–115.

87. See M. Philippides and W. Hanak, *The Siege and the Fall of Constantinople in 1453*, 197–214.

88. P. Kitromilides and A. Alexandris, "Ethnic Survival," 6, 9–44.

89. On Mehmet's rapid Islamization of Constantinople and efforts to increase its population, see H. Inalcik, "Istanbul: Islamic," 1–23. For the Kemalist effort to replace Ottomanism with the idea of the modern Turkish nation, see G. Brockett, "When Ottomans Become Turks," 399–433. On controversial DNA surveys of Turkish demographics and the ensuing political uproar, see *Newsroom Protothema*, "Turks Enraged as Ancestry.com Reveals the Truth: Most of Them are Greeks"; P. Antonopoulos, "Turkish DNA Project Calls for Boycott after Ancestry.com Highlights Many Greeks Were Turkified."

90. For the quote about King Constantine and the end of the Great Idea, see G. Kaloudis, "Ethnic Cleansing in Asia Minor and the Treaty of Lausanne," 59–88 and A. Dagkas, "Constantinople-Istanbul. Rêve et réalité pour les Grecs," 71–81, especially 72–78.

91. On the nature and origins of the Megali Idea and the idea of reclaiming Constantinople, see M. Finefrock, "Ataturk, Lloyd George and the Megali Idea," 47–66; and on the Greek aftermath of 1453 until the present, see W. Treadgold, *A History of the Byzantine State and Society*, 848–852. On the Greek population of Constantinople, see A. Dagkas, "Constantinople-Istanbul. Rêve et réalité pour les Grecs," 79.

92. Portuguese navigators, many of them Genoese by birth, under the patronage of Prince Henry the Navigator, had reached Senegal in 1445, and in 1446 almost to Sierra Leone.

Chapter Four. Imperial Hubris

1. F. Cortés, "Third Letter," in D. Carballo, *Collision of Worlds*, 225. On the letters in general, see A. Padgen, *Hernán Cortés: Letters from Mexico*. "Aztecs," a term the Mexica never used, is here for clarity employed at times interchangeably with the "Mexica," the noun most likely employed by the people of Tenochtitlán. Cf. C. Townsend, *Fifth Sun*, xi–xii.

2. For the key role of allies in Cortés's victory, see T. Brinkerhoff, "Re-examining the Lore of the 'Archetypal Conquistador,'" 169–187.

3. J. Bierhorst, *Cantares Mexicanos*, 319.

4. F. Aguilar, in P. de Fuentes, *Conquistadors*, 138.

5. D. Carasco, *The History of the Conquest of New Spain by Bernal Díaz del Castillo*, 69–70.

6. A. Tapia, in P. de Fuentes, *The Conquistadors*, 31.

7. For the omens, see B. Sahagún, *The Florentine Codex*, Book 12, chapter 1. On the idea that "cultural confusion" accounts for the Spanish victory, see V. Hanson, *Carnage and Culture*, 216–218.

8. See S. Colston, "No Longer Will There Be a Mexico," 239–258, who distinguishes various Aztec prophecies and omens as those either widely believed before the invasion, or others constructed in the aftermath of the end of Tenochtitlán.

9. F. Cortés, "Second Letter," in F. MacNutt, *Letters of Cortes*, 86.

10. For the growing native belief that the Spanish were not really divine, see W. Prescott, *History of the Conquest of Mexico*, 241–243, 278–279.

11. B. Sahagún, *The Florentine Codex*, Book 12, chapter 9.

12. See H. Thomas, *The Conquest of Mexico*, 179–187, on the various Aztec interpretations of who the Spanish were and why they came.

13. From the *Codex Ramirez*, in M. Leon-Portilla, *Broken Spears*, 61. The Codex, from the mid sixteenth century, is a Spanish account based on an earlier Nahuatl source.

14. Cf. H. Thomas, *The Conquest of Mexico*, 384, who has an in-depth description of Alvarado's various fears and excuses.

15. On the various excuses for Alvarado's butchery, see again H. Thomas, *The Conquest of Mexico*, 385–390.

16. *Florentine Codex*, 12, in M. Leon-Portilla, *Broken Spears,* 76.

17. F. Gómara, *Cortés, the Life of the Conqueror,* 222.

18. *Florentine Codex*, 12, in M. Leon-Portilla, *Broken Spears,* 76, 85–86.

19. For a classic graphic narrative of the Noche Triste and the battle of Otumba, see W. Prescott, *History of the Conquest of Mexico*, 441–465.

20. F. Gomara, *Cortés, the Life of the Conqueror,* 228.

21. H. Thomas, *The Conquest of Mexico*, 5–6.

22. For example, purportedly, Vasili Blokhin, chief executioner of the NKVD (the internal security agency of the Soviet Union, under control of Lavrentiy Beria) and perhaps the most lethal executioner in history, personally killed almost seven thousand people, one at a time, during the Katyn massacre, receiving the Order of the Red Banner for his efforts. "The methods employed . . . would have taken no more than a minute or two per individual," according to G. Sanford, *Katyn and the Soviet Massacre of 1940*, 102. If true, the killings at, say, one every three minutes, might have taken Blokhin more than an aggregate 350 hours to execute the seven thousand. The murder spree reportedly lasted some twenty-eight days. That calculus of death would have in theory required Blokhin to have spent a full twelve hours for each night of murdering.

23. For these gruesome details, see the descriptions in M. León-Portilla, *Broken Spears*, 107. On Aztec human sacrifice, see J. Ingham, "Human Sacrifice at Tenochtitlán," 379–400; cf. M. Harner, "The Enigma of Aztec Sacrifice," 46–51.

24. On the ingenious design, construction, and transport of the brigantines, see F. Cortés, "Third Letter," 255–257.

25. *Florentine Codex*, 12, quoted in M. León-Portilla, *Broken Spears*, 94–96.

26. F. MacNutt, "First Letter," Appendix 4, 182. For the background of the first letter, cf. E. Wright, "New World News, Ancient Echoes: A Cortés Letter and a Vernacular Livy for a New King and His Wary Subjects (1520–23)," *Renaissance Quarterly* 61.3 (2008), 711–749.

27. B. Díaz, *The History of the Conquest of New Spain*, chapter 156 in the original text.

28. F. Cortés, "Third Letter," in D. Carballo, *Collision of Worlds*, paragraph 111.

29. F. Gómara, *Cortés, the Life of the Conqueror*, chapter 114 in the original text.

30. B. Díaz, *Discovery and Conquest of Mexico*, 337–338, chapter 95 in the original text.

31. F. Gómara, *Cortés, the Life of the Conqueror*, 262–263, chapter 130 in the original text.

32. Revising smallpox deaths downward: for a more modest estimation of Aztec deaths from smallpox, cf. F. Brooks, "Revising the Conquest of Mexico," 1–29.

33. B. Sahagún, *The Florentine Codex* 12:29 (Nahuatl version).

34. R. Hassig, *Mexico and Spanish Conquest*, 102.

35. "Contares Mexicanos," fos. 19v–20t, in M. Leon-Portilla, *Pre-Columbian Literatures of Mexico*, 87.

36. F. Gómara, *Cortés, the Life of the Conqueror*, 263, chapter 130 in the original text.

37. See F. Cortés, "First Letter," in F. MacNutt, *Letters of Cortes*, 164.

38. F. Alva Ixtkukxochitl, *Ally of Cortés*, xxvi. Cf. V. Hanson, "Alexander the Killer," 8–18.

39. Compare various reasons for the Spanish victory, among them superior supply and logistics: G. Raudzens, "So Why Were the Aztecs Conquered," 87–104.

40. F. Cortés, "Second Letter," in F. MacNutt, *Letters of Cortes*, 86.

41. See F. Tezozomoc, *Crónica Mexicana*, 612.

42. D. Carasco, *The History of the Conquest of New Spain by Bernal Díaz del Castillo*, 2, 100.

43. F. Aguilar, in P. de Fuentes, *The Conquistadors*, 138. The credit for the killing of Matlatzincatl was a likely group effort, although the coup de grâce was probably delivered by Juan de Salamanca.

44. Cf. "What is notable about Mexica warfare is how little co-operative it was. The great warriors were solitary hunters . . . The novice was in direct competition with his peers, as he searched through the dust and confusion of the battle for an enemy of the same, or ideally just higher, rank . . . Intervention to aid a companion who was being worsted was liable to be interpreted as an attempt to pirate his captive." I. Clendinnen, *Aztecs*, 111–128. On the wearing of human skins of the sacrificed, see D. Carrasco, "Give Me Some Skin," 1–26.

45. On the ritualized nature and limitations in the Western sense of Aztec warfare, see I. Clendinnen, "The Cost of Courage," 44–89. See too D. Carballo, *Collision of Worlds*, 181.

46. B. Sahagún, *The Florentine Codex*, Book 12, 71.

47. J. White, *Cortés and the Downfall of the Aztec Empire*, 169. Cf. V. Hanson, *Carnage and Culture*, 226.

48. On comparisons between Spanish and Aztec weapons, see R. Hassig, *Mexico and the Spanish Conquest*, 78. For the Romans' initial encounters with elephants, see Pliny, *Natural History* 8.16.

49. B. Sahagún, *The Florentine Codex*, Book 12.

50. "Clubs and swords had effect, but Spanish steel armor was proof against most Indian projectiles, except perhaps darts cast from very close range. Indeed, Spaniards' wounds were typically limited to the limbs, face, neck, and other vulnerable areas not protected by armor." R. Hassig, *Mexico and Spanish Conquest*, 37–38.

51. C. Townsend, "Burying the White Gods: New Perspectives on the Conquest of Mexico," *American Historical Review* 108.3 (2003), 659–687; cf. 677. R. Denhardt, "The Truth about Cortés's Horses," *Hispanic American Historical Review*, 17.4 (November 1937), 525–532.

52. B. Díaz, *The Discovery and Conquest of Mexico*, I, 224.

53. B. Sahagún, *The Florentine Codex*, Book 12, 96.

54. On Spanish women in the conquest, see J. Johnson, "Bernal Díaz and the Women of the Conquest," 67–77.

55. F. Gómara, *Cortés, the Life of the Conqueror*, 241.

56. On Spanish military innovations, see F. González de León, "Spanish Military Power and the Military Revolution," 25–42.

57. J. Lockhart, *The Nahuas After the Conquest*, 277–278.

58. See V. Hanson, *Carnage and Culture*, 222–230.

59. Strikingly, Spain in the fifteenth century had the largest percentage of university students in Europe, 3 percent of young Spanish males, a level not achieved in Britain until 1950. Most were studying the law, like Cortés, without much hope of government employment. These upper-class men, with a sophisticated understanding of the world, were drawn into the New World adventure. These were not thugs from the wharf, but unemployed grad students. See R. Kagan, "Universities in Castille, 1500–1800," in L. Stone, *The University in Society*.

60. See D. Carasco, *The History of the Conquest of New Spain by Bernal Díaz del Castillo*, 156, for the impressive ability of the Spanish to create coalitions of native cities in common cause against the Aztecs.

61. F. Cortés, "Second Letter," in F. MacNutt, *Letters of Cortes*, 189.

62. For portraits of the brilliant lieutenants of Cortés, see H. Thomas, *The Conquest of Mexico*, 106–107, 149–155.

63. F. Cortés, "Second Letter," in F. MacNutt, *Letters of Cortes*, 238.

64. F. Cortés, "Second Letter," in F. MacNutt, *Letters of Cortes*, 263. For the idea of homosexuality as part of the Aztecs' more "natural" idea of "a range of sexual possibilities," see C. Townsend, *Fifth Sun*, 63.

65. F. Cortés, "Third Letter," in D. Carballo, *Collision of Worlds*, 40.

66. F. Cortés, "Third Letter," in D. Carballo, *Collision of Worlds*, 80–81.

67. J. Lockhart, *We People Here: Nahuatl Accounts of the Conquest of Mexico*, 165–167, containing a translation of *Florentine Codex*, 12:26.

68. C. Townsend, *Fifth Sun*, 125.

69. F. Gómara, *Cortés, the Life of the Conqueror*, 143, 291.

70. C. Townsend, *Fifth Sun*, 192–194.

71. For the survival of pre-Spanish religion and culture throughout the centuries of Spanish colonization, see F. Karttunen, "After the Conquest," 239–256.

72. J. Lockhart, *The Nahuas After the Conquest*, 429–430.

73. *Socio-Demographic Profile of the Population Speaking Nahuatl*.

74. On the tendency to exaggerate Aztec deaths from smallpox during the conquest, see F. Brooks, "Revising the Conquest of Mexico," 1–29. But his valid arguments were not intended to extend to all the aggregate deaths of indigenous peoples due to the many imported diseases during the decades following the fall of Tenochtitlán. The eventual total over several years may have eventually numbered from five to ten million fatalities rather than the larger totals argued by a number of scholars. For a good discussion, see R. McCaa, "Spanish and Nahuatl Views on Smallpox and Demographic Catastrophe in Mexico," 397–431.

75. F. Cortés, "Third Letter," in D. Carballo, *Collision of Worlds*, section 136.

Epilogue. How the Unimaginable Becomes the Inevitable

1. Classicists usually loosely define "Classical Greece" or the "Golden Age" as the period from the Persian Wars (beginning with Marathon in 490 BC or alternatively after the victory at Salamis in 480 BC) to either Alexander's final conquest of the city-states Greece in 335 BC or his own death in 323 BC, which began the Hellenistic era.

2. On the lamentations for destroyed Mediterranean cities, see in general, M. R. Bachvarova, D. Dutsch, and A. Suter, eds., *The Fall of Cities in*

the Mediterranean: Commemoration in Literature, Folk-Song, and Liturgy, especially 226–255. On Carthage: E. Cook, "T. S. Eliot and the Carthaginian Peace," 341–355; B. Wardropper, "The Poetry of Ruins in the Golden Age," 295–305. On Constantinople: A. Norman Jeffares, "The Byzantine Poems of W. B. Yeats," 44–52. On Tenochtitlán: D. Damrosch, "The Aesthetics of Conquest: Aztec Poetry before and after Cortés," 101–120; B. Clarke, "The Fall of Montezuma: Poetry and History in William Carlos Williams and D. H. Lawrence," 1–12; S. Park, "Mesoamerican Modernism: William Carlos Williams and the Archaeological Imagination," 21–47.

3. On Alexander the Great, see P. Merlan, "Isocrates, Aristotle and Alexander the Great," 60–81. For doubts about the importance of the Scipionic Circle, see: F. Walbank, "The Scipionic Legend," 54–69. For the library and court of Mehmet II, cf. J. Raby, "Mehmed the Conqueror's Greek Scriptorium," 15–34. On Cortés, see J. Elliott, "The Mental World of Hernán Cortés," 41–58.

4. Thucydides, 5. 89.

5. P. Baker, "'I Too Have a Nuclear Button, but It Is a Much Bigger & More Powerful One': Trump Taunts Kim Jong-un," https://www.nytimes .com/2018/01/02/us/politics/trump-tweet-north-korea.html.

6. J. Watts, "Chinese general warns of nuclear risk to US," https://www .theguardian.com/world/2005/jul/16/china.jonathanwatts.

7. *Mumbai Mirror,* "Pakistan Minister Threatens India with Nuclear War Which Won't Harm Muslims," https://mumbaimirror.indiatimes .com/news/world/pakistan-minister-threatens-india-with-nuclear-war -which-wont-harm-muslims/articleshow/77675717.cms.

8. MEMRI, "Former Iranian President Rafsanjani on Using a Nuclear Bomb Against Israel," https://www.memri.org/reports/former-iranian -president-rafsanjani-using-nuclear-bomb-against-israel.

9. M. Oren, "Ex-envoy: Iran Deal Bad for Israel, U.S. and World," https://www.cnn.com/2015/07/01/opinions/oren-iran-nuclear-deal/index .html.

10. *Times of Israel,* "In Video, Iran Threatens to Raze Tel Aviv, Destroy Dimona, If Israel Hits Nuke Sites," https://www.timesofisrael.com/iran -threatens-to-raze-tel-aviv-destroy-dimona-if-israel-strikes-nuclear -sites/. As this book went to press, in early October 2023 terrorists from the Gaza Strip entered Israel and murdered well over twelve hundred civilians, taking hostages back to Gaza, beheading babies, executing women and children, and dismembering and desecrating the dead. The precivili-

zational savagery earned a prompt Israeli invasion into Gaza, given the reality that Hamas terrorists before and after the atrocities boasted that their aim was to destroy utterly Israel and the Jewish people in the Middle East.

11. P. Koelle, "Recep Tayyip Erdogan's Relationship with the Ottoman Empire," https://intpolicydigest.org/recep-tayyip-erdogan-s-relationship -with-the-ottoman-empire/. Cf. BBC World News, "Turkey's First Lady Praises Ottoman Harem," https://www.bbc.com/news/world-europe -35773208.

12. N. Stamouli, "Erdoğan Warns Greece That Turkish Missiles Can Reach Athens," https://www.politico.eu/article/erdogan-warns-greece -that-turkish-missiles-can-reach-athens%ef%bf%bc/.

13. M. Pomper, "Why the US Has Nuclear Bombs in Turkey, and Why It's So Tricky to Remove Them," https://www.businessinsider.com/us -nuclear-bombs-in-turkey-tricky-to-remove-2019-10. Cf., B. Fox, ed., "Turkey Warns It Could Kick Out US from Incirlik Nuclear Base," https:// www.euractiv.com/section/defence-and-security/news/turkey-warns -it-could-kick-out-us-from-incirlik-nuclear-base/.

14. S. Fraser and B. Mroue, "What's at Stake as Turkey Threatens to Escalate Conflict with Syrian Fighters?," https://www.timesofisrael.com /whats-at-stake-as-turkey-threatens-to-escalate-conflict-with-syrian -fighters/.

15. BBC World News, "Nagorno-Karabakh: Profile," https://www.bbc .com/news/world-europe-18270325. Cf. A. Youssefian, "Turkey's Escala- tions Pose an Existential Threat to Armenia," https://armenianweekly .com/2020/09/30/turkeys-escalations-pose-an-existential-threat-to -armenia/. Cf. Reuters, "Nagorno-Karabakh's Armenians Start to Leave En Masse for Armenia," September 25, 2023, https://www.reuters.com/ world/armenia-calls-un-mission-monitor-rights-nagorno-karabakh -2023-09-24/.

16. W. Msemburi et al., "The WHO Estimates of Excess Mortality Associated with the COVID-19 Pandemic," 130–137, https://www.nature .com/articles/s41586-022-05522-2.

17. A. Skinner, "Military Drone Attacks Human Operator in Hypo- thetical Scenario," *Newsweek*, June 1, 2023, https://www.newsweek.com /military-drone-attacks-human-operator-simulation-1803949.

18. This is not to dismiss the threat of existential dangers other than war, from climate change to supply chain interruptions and mass

starvation. Other threats of Armageddon exist that often have been dismissed as science fiction, including impacts from comets or large meteors (such as the Tunguska event or even the dinosaur-killing comet sixty-five million years ago). Perhaps even more worrisome is that our own technology might become our enemy, if the sensationalized "AI apocalypse" should come to pass and we face a superhuman "Skynet"-like entity. See, for example, M. Tegmark, *Life 3.0* or T. Ord, *The Precipice: Existential Risk and the Future of Humanity.*

WORKS CITED

Primary Sources

Classical Works

Aeschines, *Against Ctesiphon.*
Aeschylus, *Prometheus Bound.*
Appian, *Punic Wars.*
Aristobulus, *FGrHist*, 139 F2.
Aristotle, *Politics.*
Arrian, *Anabasis of Alexander.*
Cassius Dio, *Roman History.*
Catullus, *Poems.*
Cicero, *Tusculan Disputations.*
Cleitarchus, *FGrHist*, 137 F9.
Diodorus Siculus, *Biliotheca Historica.*
Ennius, Frag. 237.
Hellenica Oxyrhynchia.
Homer, *Iliad* (Lattimore translation).
Horace, *Epistles.*
Justin, *Epitome of Pomponius Trogus.*
Juvenal, *Satires.*
Livy, *Ab Urbe Condita.*
Plautus, *Epidicus.*
Pliny, *Natural History.*
Plutarch, *Cato the Elder.*
Plutarch, *Comparison of Pelopidas and Marcellus.*
Plutarch, *Life of Alexander.*
Plutarch, *Life of Demosthenes.*
Plutarch, *Moralia.*
Polyaenus, *Stratagems in War.*
Polybius, *Histories.*
Pseudo-Scylax, *Periplus.*
Sallust, *Jugurthine War.*

Strabo, *Geography*.

Tacitus, *Agricola*.

Thucydides, *Peloponnesian War*.

Xenophon, *Hellenica*.

Xenophon, *On Revenues*.

Primary Accounts of the Conquest of Mexico

Aguilar, F., in P. de Fuentes, trans. and ed. *The Conquistadors; First-person Accounts of the Conquest of Mexico* (Austin: University of Texas Press, 1963).

Alva Ixtlilxochitl, F. *Ally of Cortés: Account 13, of the Coming of the Spaniards and the Beginning of the Evangelical Law*, trans. D. Ballentine (El Paso: Texas Western Press, 1969).

Bierhorst, J., trans. and ed. *Cantares Mexicanos: Songs of the Aztecs* (Stanford: Stanford University Press, 1985).

Carasco, D., trans. and ed. *The History of the Conquest of New Spain by Bernal Díaz del Castillo* (Albuquerque: University of New Mexico Press, 2008).

Codex Ramirez, trans. L. Kemp, in M. León-Portilla, ed. *The Broken Spears: The Aztec Account of the Conquest of Mexico* (Boston: Beacon Press, 1992).

Cortés, F. "Third Letter," in D. Carballo, *Collision of Worlds: A Deep History of the Fall of Aztec Mexico and the Forging of New Spain* (Oxford: Oxford University Press, 2022).

Díaz, B. *The Discovery and Conquest of Mexico*, trans. A. P. Maudslay (New York: Harper & Brother, 1928).

Florentine Codex, trans. L. Kemp, in M. León-Portilla, ed. *The Broken Spears: The Aztec Account of the Conquest of Mexico* (Boston: Beacon Press, 1992).

Gómara, F. *Cortés, the Life of the Conqueror by His Secretary*, trans. L. Simpson (Berkeley: University of California Press, 1964).

Leon-Portilla, M., trans. "Cantares Mexicanos," fos. 19v–20t, in *Pre-Columbian Literatures of Mexico* (Norman: University of Oklahoma Press, 1969).

Lockhart, J., trans. and ed. *We People Here: Nahuatl Accounts of the Conquest of Mexico*, (Berkeley: University of California Press, 1994), 165–167, containing a translation of *Florentine Codex* 12:26.

MacNutt, F., trans. *Letters of Cortes: The Five Letters of Relation from Fernando Cortes to the Emperor Charles V* (New York: Putnam, 1908).

Sahagún, B. *The Florentine Codex, Book 12, The Conquest of Mexico*, trans. A. Anderson and C. Dibble (Salt Lake City: University of Utah Press, 2012).

Tapia, A., in P. de Fuentes, trans. and ed., *The Conquistadors* (Austin: University of Texas Press, 1963).

US and Mexico Federal Documents

Morgenthau Plan, http://docs.fdrlibrary.marist.edu/PSF/BOX31/t297a01 .html.

Socio-Demographic Profile of the Population Speaking Nahuatl (Gov. of Mexico, 2005).

Secondary Sources

"Former Iranian President Rafsanjani on Using a Nuclear Bomb Against Israel," MEMRI Special Dispatch No. 325, January 2, 2002.

"In Video, Iran Threatens to Raze Tel Aviv, Destroy Dimona, if Israel Hits Nuke Sites," *Times of Israel*, December 27, 2022.

"Nagorno-Karabakh: Profile," BBC World News, April 10, 2023. Cf. A. Youssefian, "Turkey's Escalations Pose an Existential Threat to Armenia," *Armenian Weekly*, September 30, 2020.

"Pakistan Minister Threatens India with Nuclear War Which Won't Harm Muslims," *Mumbai Mirror*, August 21, 2020.

"Turkey's First Lady Praises Ottoman Harem," BBC World News, March 10, 2016.

Adcock, F. "Delenda Est Carthago," *Cambridge Historical Journal* 8.3 (1946), 117–128.

Antela-Bernardez, B. "A Furious Wrath: Alexander the Great's Destruction of Thebes and Perdiccas' False Retreat," in G. Lee et al., eds., *Ancient Warfare: Introducing Current Research*, Volume 1 (Newcastle upon Tyne: Cambridge Scholars Publishing, 2015), 94–105.

Arabatzis, G. "Hegel and Byzantium (With a note on Alexandre Kojève and Scepticism)," *Philosophical Inquiry* 25 (2003), 31–39.

Armstrong, D. "Unilateral Disarmament: A Case History," *World Affairs* 126.1 (1963), 22–27.

Astin, A. "Scipio Aemilianus and Cato Censorius," *Latomus* 15.2 (1956), 159–180.

Ayalon, A. *Natural Disasters in the Ottoman Empire. Plague, Famine, and Other Misfortunes* (New York: Cambridge University Press, 2015).

Bachvarova, M. R., D. Dutsch, and A. Suter, eds., *The Fall of Cities in the Mediterranean: Commemoration in Literature, Folk-Song, and Liturgy* (Cambridge: Cambridge University Press, 2015).

Baker, P. "'I Too Have a Nuclear Button, but It Is a Much Bigger & More Powerful One': Trump Taunts Kim Jong-un," *New York Times*, January 2, 2018.

Baronowski, D. "Polybius on the Causes of the Third Punic War," *Classical Philology* 90.1 (January 1995), 16–31.

Beaton, R. *Greece: Biography of a Modern Nation* (London: Allen Lane, 2019).

Beihammer, A. "Patterns of Turkish Migration and Expansion in Byzantine Asia Minor in the 11th and 12th Centuries," in J. Preiser-Kapeller, L. Reinfandt, and Y. Stouraitis, eds., *Migration Histories of the Medieval Afroeurasian Transition Zone: Aspects of Mobility between Africa, Asia and Europe, 300–1500 C.E.* (Leiden: Brill, 2020), 166–192.

Bergh, A., and C. Hampus Lyttkens. "Measuring Institutional Quality in Ancient Athens," *Journal of Institutional Economics* 10.2 (June 2014), 279–310.

Bierhorst, J., trans. and ed. *Cantares Mexicanos: Songs of the Aztecs* (Stanford: Stanford University Press, 1985).

Bogdanović, J. "The Relational Spiritual Geopolitics of Constantinople, the Capital of the Byzantine Empire," in J. Bogdanović, J. Christie, and E. Guzmán, eds., *Political Landscapes of Capital Cities* (Denver: University Press of Colorado, 2016), 97–154.

Bosworth, A. *Conquest and Empire: The Reign of Alexander the Great* (Cambridge: Cambridge University Press, 1988).

Bosworth, A. *Historical Commentary on Arrian's History of Alexander. Volume 1: Books I–III* (Oxford: Clarendon Press, 1980).

Brinkerhoff, T. "Reexamining the Lore of the 'Archetypal Conquistador'": Hernán Cortés and the Spanish Conquest of the Aztec Empire, 1519–1521," *History Teacher* 49.2 (February 2016), 169–187.

Brockett, G. "When Ottomans Become Turks: Commemorating the Conquest of Constantinople and Its Contribution to World History," *American Historical Review* 119.2 (2014), 399–433.

Brooks, F. "Revising the Conquest of Mexico: Smallpox, Sources, and Populations," *Journal of Interdisciplinary History* 24.1 (Summer 1993), 1–29.

Brown, P. *Augustine of Hippo* (Berkeley: University of California Press, 2013).

Buraselis, K. "Contributions to Rebuilding Thebes: The Old and a New Fragment of IG VII 2419 ≈ Sylloge3 337," *Zeitschrift Für Papyrologie Und Epigraphik* 188 (2014), 159–170.

Carballo, D. *Collision of Worlds: A Deep History of the Fall of Aztec Mexico and the Forging of New Spain* (Oxford: Oxford University Press, 2022).

Carrasco, D. "Give Me Some Skin: The Charisma of the Aztec Warrior," *History of Religions* 35.1 (1995), 1–26.

Carroll, M. *A Contemporary Greek Source for the Siege of Constantinople: The Sphrantzes Chronicle* (Amsterdam: Hakkert, 1985).

Cartledge, P. *Thebes: The Forgotten City of Ancient Greece* (London: Picador, 2020).

Clarke, B. "The Fall of Montezuma: Poetry and History in William Carlos Williams and D. H. Lawrence," *William Carlos Williams Review* 12.1 (Spring 1986), 1–12.

Clendinnen, I. "The Cost of Courage in Aztec Society," *Past & Present* 107 (May 1985), 44–89.

Clendinnen, I. *Aztecs: An Interpretation* (New York: Cambridge University Press, 1991).

Cohen, H. "Greek Nature-Knowledge Transplanted: The Islamic World," 53–75, in H. Cohen, ed., *How Modern Science Came into the World: Four Civilizations, One 17th-Century Breakthrough* (Amsterdam: Amsterdam University Press, 2010).

Colston, S. "'No Longer Will There Be a Mexico': Omens, Prophecies, and the Conquest of the Aztec Empire," *American Indian Quarterly* 9.3, *American Indian Prophets: Religious Leaders and Revitalization Movements* (Summer 1985), 239–258.

Congourdeau, M. "La Peste Noire à Constantinople de 1343 à 1466," *Med Secoli* 11.2 (1999), 377–389.

Cook, E. "T. S. Eliot and the Carthaginian Peace," *ELH* 46.2 (1979), 341–355.

Crowley, R. *1453: The Holy War for Constantinople and the Clash of Islam and the West* (New York: Hachette, 2005).

Dagkas, A. "Constantinople-Istanbul. Rêve et réalité pour les Grecs," in M. Mansouri, *La prise de Constantinople. L'évenement, sa portée et ses échos (1453–2003)* (Tunis: Cahiers du CERES, 2008), 71–81.

Damrosch, D. "The Aesthetics of Conquest: Aztec Poetry before and after Cortés," *Representations* 33 (1991), 101–120.

Dana, C. *New American Cyclopaedia* (New York: Appleton, 1858–63).

Dauverd, C. "Cultivating Differences: Genoese Trade Identity in the Constantinople of Sultan Mehmet II, 1453–81," *Mediterranean Studies* 23.2 (2015), 94–124.

Davies, N. *Vanished Kingdoms: The Rise and Fall of States and Nations* (New York: Penguin Books, 2012).

Delile, H., E. Pleuger, J. Blichert-Toft, and A. Wilson. "Economic Resilience of Carthage During the Punic Wars: Insights from Sediments of the Medjerda Delta Around Utica (Tunisia)," *PNAS*, April 29, 2019, 116 (20), 9764–9769.

Denhardt, R. "The Truth about Cortés's Horses," *Hispanic American Historical Review* 17.4 (November 1937), 525–532.

DeVries, K. "Gunpowder Weapons at Constantinople," in Y. Lev., ed., *War and Society in the Eastern Mediterranean, 7th–15th Centuries* (Leiden: Brill, 1997), 353–357.

DeVries, K. "The Lack of a Western European Military Response to the Ottoman Invasions of Eastern Europe from Nicopolis (1396) to Mohacs (1526)," *Journal of Military History* 63.3 (1999), 539–559.

Diamond, J. *Collapse: How Societies Choose to Fail or Succeed* (New York: Viking, 2005).

Diamond, J. *Guns, Germs, and Steel: The Fates of Human Societies* (New York: Norton, 2005).

Diamond, J. *Upheaval: Turning Points for Nations in Crisis* (New York: Little, Brown and Company, 2019).

Dietrich, J. *The Morgenthau Plan: Soviet Influence on American Postwar Policy* (rev. ed.) (New York: Algora Publishing, 2013).

Dominian, L. "The Site of Constantinople: A Factor of Historical Value," *Journal of the American Oriental Society* 37 (1917), 57–71.

Drews, R. "Diodorus and His Sources," *American Journal of Philology* 83.4 (October 1962), 383–392.

Eckstein, A. *Mediterranean Anarchy, Interstate War, and the Rise of Rome* (Berkeley: University of California Press, 2009).

Elliott, J. "The Mental World of Hernán Cortés," *Transactions of the Royal Historical Society* 17 (1967), 41–58.

Engels, D. *Alexander the Great and the Logistics of the Macedonian Army* (Berkeley: University of California Press, 1980).

Farkas C., et al. "Analysis of the Virus SARS-CoV-2 as a Potential Bioweapon in Light of International Literature," *Military Medicine* 188.3–4 (March–April 2023), 531–540.

Finefrock, M. "Ataturk, Lloyd George and the Megali Idea: Cause and Consequence of the Greek Plan to Seize Constantinople from the Allies, June–August 1922," *Journal of Modern History* 52.1 (1980) D10, 47–66.

Fleming, K. "Constantinople: From Christianity to Islam," *Classical World* 97.1 (2003), 69–78.

Fox, B., ed. "Turkey Warns It Could Kick Out US from Incirlik Nuclear Base," *Euractiv*, December 11, 2019.

Fradkin, H., and L. Libby, "Erdogan's Grand Vision: Rise and Decline," *World Affairs* 175.6 (2013), 41–50.

Fraser, S., and B. Mroue. "What's at Stake as Turkey Threatens to Escalate Conflict with Syrian Fighters?" *Times of Israel*, December 10, 2022.

Gartland, S. "A New Boiotia? Exiles, Landscapes, and Kings," in S. Gartland, ed., *Boiotia in the Fourth Century B.C.* (Philadelphia: University of Pennsylvania Press, 2016), 147–164.

Gibbon, E. *The Decline and Fall of the Roman Empire* (London: Strahan & Cadell, 1776–1789).

Goldsworthy, A. *The Punic Wars* (London: Weidenfeld & Nicolson, 2000).

González de León, F. "Spanish Military Power and the Military Revolution," in G. Mortimer, ed., *Early Modern Military History, 1450–1815* (London: Palgrave, 2004), 25–42.

Grant, J. "Rethinking the Ottoman 'Decline': Military Technology Diffusion in the Ottoman Empire, Fifteenth to Eighteenth Centuries," *Journal of World History* 10.1 (1999), 179–201.

Greene, M. *The Edinburgh History of the Greeks, 1453 to 1774: The Ottoman Empire* (Edinburgh: Edinburgh University Press, 2015).

Guerdan, R. *Byzantium* (New York: Perigee, 2000).

Haldon, J. "Some Aspects of Byzantine Military Technology from the Sixth to the Tenth Centuries," *Byzantine and Modern Greek Studies* 1 (1975), 11–47.

Hamilton, J. *Plutarch, Alexander, A Commentary* (Oxford: Clarendon Press, 1969).

Hammond, N. *Sources for Alexander the Great: An Analysis of Plutarch's Life and Arrian's Anabasis Alexandrou* (Cambridge: Cambridge University Press, 1993).

Hammond, N. "The Battle of the Granicus River," *Journal of Hellenic Studies* 100 (1980), 73–88.

Hammond, N. "What May Philip Have Learnt as a Hostage in Thebes?," *Greek, Roman and Byzantine Studies* 38 (1997), 362–371.

Hammond, N., and F. Walbank, *History of Macedonia. Volume III: 336–167 B.C.* (Oxford: Clarendon Press, 1988).

Hanson, V. "Alexander the Killer," *Military History Quarterly* 10.3 (Spring 1998), 8–19.

Hanson, V. "Epameinondas, the Battle of Leuctra (371 B.C.), and the 'Revolution' in Greek Battle Tactics," *Classical Antiquity* 7.2 (1988), 190–207.

Hanson, V. "Equal by Catastrophe," *Inference* 3.2 (August 2017).

Hanson, V. "Hoplite Obliteration: The Case of the Town of Thespiae," in J. Carman and A. Harding, eds., *Ancient Warfare* (Cheltenham: History Press, 2009), 203–218.

Hanson, V. *Carnage and Culture* (New York: Doubleday, 2001).

Hanson, V. *The Other Greeks* (New York: Free Press, 1995).

Hanson, V. *Ripples of Battle* (New York: Doubleday, 2003).

Hanson, V. *The Savior Generals: How Five Great Commanders Saved Wars That Were Lost—From Ancient Greece to Iraq* (London: Bloomsbury, 2013).

Hanson, V. *The Soul of Battle* (New York: Free Press, 1999).

Hanson, V. *A War Like No Other: How the Athenians and Spartans Fought the Peloponnesian War* (New York: Random House, 2005).

Hanson, V. *Warfare and Agriculture in Classical Greece* (Berkeley: University of California Press, 1983).

Harner, M. "The Enigma of Aztec Sacrifice," *Natural History* 86.4 (April 1977), 46–51.

Harris, J. "Despots, Emperors, and Balkan Identity in Exile," *Sixteenth Century Journal* 44.3 (2013), 643–661.

Harris, M. "On War and Greed in the Second Century B.C.," *American Historical Review* 76.5 (1971), 1371–1385.

Harris, W. *War and Imperialism in Republican Rome 327–70 BC* (Oxford: Clarendon Press, 1979).

Hassig, R. *Mexico and the Spanish Conquest* (Norman: University of Oklahoma Press, 1994; rev. ed. 2006).

Hoyos, D. *The Carthaginians* (London: Routledge, 2010).

Hoyos, D. *Hannibal's Dynasty: Power and Politics in the Western Mediterranean* (London: Routledge, 2003).

Hoyos, D. *Mastering the West: Rome and Carthage at War* (Oxford: Oxford University Press, 2017).

Iacurci, G. "Long Covid Has an 'Underappreciated' Role in Labor Shortage, Study Finds," CNBC, January 30, 2023.

Inalcik, H. "Istanbul: Islamic," *Journal of Islamic Studies* 1 (1990), 1–23.

Inalcik, H. "Mehmet the Conqueror (1432–1481) and His Time," *Speculum* 35.3 (1960), 408–427.

Inalcik, H. "The Policy of Mehmet II toward the Greek Population of Istanbul and the Byzantine Buildings of the City," *Dumbarton Oaks Papers* 23/24 (1969), 229–249.

Ingham, J. "Human Sacrifice at Tenochtitlán," in *Comparative Studies in Society and History* 26.3 (July 1984), 379–400.

Iyigun, M. "Lessons from the Ottoman Harem on Culture, Religion, and Wars," *Economic Development and Cultural Change* 61.4 (2013), 693–730.

Jacoby, D. "La Population de Constantinople à l'époque Byzantine: un problème de démographie urbaine," *Byzantion* 31.1 (1961), 81–109.

Jarde, A. M. R. *The Formation of the Greek People,* Dobie, trans. (London: Routledge, 1996).

Jeffares, A. Norman. "The Byzantine Poems of W. B. Yeats," *Review of English Studies* 22.85 (1946), 44–52.

Johnson, J. "Bernal Díaz and the Women of the Conquest," *Hispaniola* 82 (September 1984), 67–77.

Jones, J. R., trans. *Nicolò Barbaro. Diary of the Siege of Constantinople, 1453* (Jericho, NY: Exposition Press, 1969).

Kaegi, W. *Byzantium and the Decline of Rome* (Princeton: Princeton University Press, 1968).

Kagan, D. *On the Origins of War and the Preservation of Peace* (New York: Doubleday, 1995).

Kagan, R. "Universities in Castille, 1500–1800," in L. Stone, ed., *The University in Society* (Princeton: Princeton University Press, 1974).

Kalliontzis, Y., and N. Papazarkadas. "The Contributions to the Refoundation of Thebes: A New Epigraphic and Historical Analysis," *Annual of the British School at Athens* 114 (2019), 293–315.

Kaloudis, G. "Ethnic Cleansing in Asia Minor and the Treaty of Lausanne," *International Journal on World Peace* 31.1 (2014), 59–88.

Kamariôtès, M. "Récit pitoyable de la prise de Constantinople," in V. Deroche and N. Vatin, eds., *Constantinople 1453: des Byzantins aux Ottomans: Textes et Documents* (Toulouse: Anacharsis, 2017), 771–778.

Karttunen, F. "After the Conquest: The Survival of Indigenous Patterns of Life and Belief," *Journal of World History* 3.2 (Fall 1992), 239–256.

Kennedy, P. *The Rise and Fall of the Great Powers: Economic Change and Military Conflict from 1500 to 2000* (New York: Random House, 1987).

Khan, M. S. "A Chapter on Roman (Byzantine) Sciences in an Eleventh Century Hispano-Arabic Work," *Islamic Studies* 22. 1 (1983): 41–70.

Kiernan, B. "Sur la notion de génocide," *Le Débat* (Paris) 104 (Mars–Avril 1999), 179–192.

Kinross, P. *The Ottoman Centuries: The Rise and Fall of the Turkish Empire* (New York: HarperCollins, 1979).

Kitromilides, P., and A. Alexandris. "Ethnic Survival, Nationalism and Forced Migration," *Bulletin of the Centre for Asia Minor Studies* (1986), 6–14.

Koelle, P. "Recep Tayyip Erdogan's Relationship with the Ottoman Empire," *International Policy Digest*, June 13, 2019.

Krentz, P. "Casualties in Hoplite Battles," *Greek, Roman and Byzantine Studies* 26.1 (Spring 1985), 13–20.

Kunze, C. "Carthage and Numia, 201–149 B.C.," in D. Hoyos, ed. *Blackwell Companion to the Punic Wars* (Oxford: Blackwell, 2011), 395–411.

Lancel, S. *Carthage: A History*, A. Nevill, trans. (Oxford: Blackwell, 1995).

Lazenby, J. *The First Punic War: A Military History* (Stanford: Stanford University Press, 1996).

Le Bohec, Y. "The 'Third Punic War': The Siege of Carthage (149–146 BC)," in D. Hoyos, ed., *A Companion to the Punic Wars* (Oxford: Blackwell, 2011), 430–445.

Leavesly, J. "Melos and Carthage: Genocide in the Ancient World," https://www.academia.edu/31572631/Melos_and_Carthage_Genocide_in_the_Ancient_World.

Little, C. "The Authenticity and Form of Cato's Saying 'Carthago Delenda Est,'" *Classical Journal* 29.6 (March 1934), 429–435.

Lockhart, J. *The Nahuas After the Conquest* (Stanford: Stanford University Press, 1992).

Luttwak, E. *The Grand Strategy of the Byzantine Empire* (Cambridge: Harvard University Press, 2009).

Ma, J. "Chaironeia 338: Topographies of Commemoration," *Journal of Hellenic Studies* 128 (2008), 72–91.

Magra, I. "Greeks in Istanbul Keeping Close Eye on Developments," *Ekathimerini.com* 22.3 (05.11.2020).

Manolova, T. "The Mytho-Historical Topography of Thebes," *Hirundo* 8 (2009/2010), 80–94.

McCaa, R. "Spanish and Nahuatl Views on Smallpox and Demographic Catastrophe in Mexico," *Journal of Interdisciplinary History* 25. 3 (1995), 397–431.

McCoy, W. "Memnon of Rhodes at the Granicus," *American Journal of Philology* 110.3 (1989), 413–433.

Meijer, F. "Cato's African Figs," *Mnemosyne* 37.1–2 (1984), 117–118.

Melville-Jones, J. *The Siege of Constantinople 1453: Seven Contemporary Accounts Translated* (Hakkert: Amsterdam, 1972).

Ménage, V. "Some Notes on the 'Devshirme,'" *Bulletin of the School of Oriental and African Studies, University of London* 29.1 (1966), 64–78.

Merlan, P. "Isocrates, Aristotle and Alexander the Great," *Historia: Zeitschrift Für Alte Geschichte* 3.1 (1954), 60–81.

Miles, R. "Vandal North Africa and the Fourth Punic War," *Classical Philology* 112.3 (2017), 384–410.

Morgenthau, H. *Germany Is Our Problem* (New York: Harper & Brothers, 1945).

Morley, N. *The Roman Empire: Roots of Imperialism* (London: Pluto Press, 2010).

Mossé, C. "Plutarque, Alexandre et Thebes," in S. Bianchetti, et al., eds., *Poikilma* (La Spezia: Agorà, 2001), 167–172.

Msemburi, W., et al. "The WHO Estimates of Excess Mortality Associated with the COVID-19 Pandemic," *Nature* 613 (2023), 130–137.

Nicol, D. *The Immortal Emperor: The Life and Legend of Constantine Palaiologos, Last Emperor of the Romans* (Cambridge: Cambridge University Press, 1992).

Nicolle, D. *Constantinople, 1453: The End of Byzantium* (Oxford: Osprey, 2000).

Nicolle, D., J. Haldon, and S. Turnbull. *The Fall of Constantinople* (Oxford: Osprey, 2007).

O'Connell, P. "Nine Centuries of Schism: The Origins of the Schism," *Studies: An Irish Quarterly Review* 48.190 (1959), 168–175.

Ord, T. *The Precipice: Existential Risk and the Future of Humanity* (New York: Hachette, 2020).

Oren, M. "Ex-envoy: Iran Deal Bad for Israel, U.S. and World," CNN, July 1, 2015.

Padgen, A. *Hernán Cortés: Letters from Mexico* (New Haven: Yale University Press, 2001).

Park, S. "Mesoamerican Modernism: William Carlos Williams and the Archaeological Imagination," *Journal of Modern Literature* 34. 4 (2011), 21–47.

Parker, G. *Global Crisis: War, Climate Change and Catastrophe in the Seventeenth Century* (New Haven: Yale University Press, 2014).

Philippides, M., and W. Hanak. *The Siege and the Fall of Constantinople in 1453* (Farnham: Ashgate, 2011).

Pomper, M. "Why the US Has Nuclear Bombs in Turkey, and Why It's So Tricky to Remove Them," *Business Insider*, October 24, 2019.

Prag, J. "Poenus Plane Est—But Who Were the 'Punickes'?," *Papers of the British School at Rome* 74 (2006), 1–37.

Pritchett, W. *The Greek State at War*, Vol. I (Berkeley: University of California Press, 1975).

Pritchett, W. *The Greek State at War*, Vol. V (Berkeley: University of California Press, 1991).

Prescott, W. *History of the Conquest of Mexico* (New York: Harper and Brothers, 1843).

Quay, S. "Led by Science: The COVID-19 Origin Story," *Select Subcommittee on the Coronavirus Crisis*, June 26, 2021.

Quay, S., and R. Muller. "The Science Suggests a Wuhan Lab Leak," *Wall Street Journal*, June 6, 2021.

Quinn, J. "Tophets in the 'Punic World,'" *SEL* 29–30 (2012–13), 23–48.

Quinn, J. *In Search of the Phoenicians* (Princeton: Princeton University Press, 2017).

Raby, J. "Mehmed the Conqueror's Greek Scriptorium," *Dumbarton Oaks Papers* 37 (1983), 15–34.

Rance, P. "Maurice's Strategicon and the Ancients: The Late Antique Reception of Aelian and Arrian," in P. Rance and N. V. Sekunda, eds., *Greek Taktika. Ancient Military Writing and Its Heritage* (Gdańsk: Akanthina, 2017), 217–255.

Raudzens, G. "So Why Were the Aztecs Conquered, and What Were the Wider Implications? Testing Military Superiority as a Cause of Europe's Pre-industrial Colonial Conquests," *War in History* 2.1 (March 1995), 87–104.

Ridley, R. T. "To Be Taken with a Pinch of Salt: The Destruction of Carthage," *Classical Philology* 81. 2 (April 1986), 140–46.

Rockwell, N. *Thebes, A History* (London: Routledge, 2017).

Rosen, W. *Justinian's Flea: The First Great Plague and the End of the Roman World* (London: Penguin, 2008).

Rosenstein, N. *Rome and the Mediterranean, 290 to 146 B.C.: The Imperial Republic* (Edinburgh: Edinburgh University Press, 2012).

Runciman, S. "Gibbon and Byzantium," in G. W. Bowerstock, J. Clive, and S. R. Graubard, eds. *Edward Gibbon and the Decline and Fall of the Roman Empire* (Cambridge: Harvard University Press, 1977), 53–60.

Runciman, S. *The Fall of Constantinople* (Cambridge: Cambridge University Press, 1957).

Salmon, T. "The Byzantine Science of Warfare: From Treatises to Battlefield," in S. Lazaris, ed. *A Companion to Byzantine Science* (Leiden: Brill, 2020), 429–463.

Sanford, G. *Katyn and the Soviet Massacre of 1940: Truth, Justice, and Memory* (London: Routledge, 2005).

Scheidel, W. *The Great Leveler: Violence and the History of Inequality from the Stone Age to the Twenty-First Century* (Princeton: Princeton University Press, 2017).

Schlachter, A. *Boeotia in Antiquity. Selected Papers* (Cambridge: Cambridge University Press, 2016).

Seaman, M. "The Athenian Expedition to Melos in 416 B.C.," *Historia* 46.4 (1997), 385–418.

Setton, K. "The Byzantine Background to the Italian Renaissance," *Proceedings of the American Philosophical Society* 100.1 (1956), 1–76.

Sidebottom, H. "Philosophers' Attitudes to Warfare under the Principate," in J. Rich and G. Shipley, eds., *War and Society in the Roman World* (London: Routledge, 1993), 241–264.

Skedros, J. "'You Cannot Have a Church Without an Empire': Political Orthodoxy in Byzantium," in G. Demacopoulos and A. Papanikolaou, eds., *Christianity, Democracy, and the Shadow of Constantine* (New York: Fordham University Press, 2017), 219–231.

Skinner, A. "Military Drone Attacks Human Operator in Hypothetical Scenario," *Newsweek*, June 1, 2023.

Stamouli, N. "Erdoğan Warns Greece That Turkish Missiles Can Reach Athens," *Politico Europe*, December 11, 2022.

Stanzel, V. "Germany and Japan: A Comeback Story," *Globalist* (March 7, 2015).

Stevens, S. "A Legend of the Destruction of Carthage," *Classical Philology* 83.1 (January 1988), 39–41.

Stimson, H., and Bundy, M. *On Active Service in Peace and War* (New York: Harper, 1948).

Strassler, R., ed. *The Landmark Thucydides* (Richard Crawley translation) (New York: Free Press, 1996).

Strémooukhoff, D. "Moscow the Third Rome: Sources of the Doctrine," *Speculum* 28.1 (1953) 84–101.

Symeonoglou, S. *The Topography of Thebes from the Bronze Age to Modern Times* (Princeton: Princeton University Press, 1985).

Tegmark, M. *Life 3.0: Being Human in the Age of Artificial Intelligence* (New York: Knopf, 2017).

Tezozomoc, H. *Crónica Mexicana* (Mexico City: Imprenta y Litografía de Ireneo Paz, 1878).

Thomas, H. *The Conquest of Mexico* (London: Random House UK, 1993).

Tihon, A. "Science in the Byzantine Empire," in D. Lindberg, and M. Shank, eds. *The Cambridge History of Science, Vol 2. Medieval Science* (Cambridge: Cambridge University Press, 2013), 190–206.

Tipps, G. "The Battle of Ecnomus," *Historia* 34.4 (1985), 432–465.

Townsend, C. "Burying the White Gods: New Perspectives on the Conquest of Mexico," *American Historical Review* 108.3 (2003), 659–687.

Townsend, C. *Fifth Sun* (Oxford: Oxford University Press, 2019).

Toynbee, A. *Hannibal's Legacy: The Hannibalic War's Effects on Roman Life* (London: Oxford University Press, 1965).

Treadgold, W. *Byzantium and Its Army* (Stanford: Stanford University Press, 1995).

Treadgold, W. *A History of the Byzantine State and Society* (Stanford: Stanford University Press, 1997).

Trevett, J. "Demosthenes and Thebes," *Historia: Zeitschrift Für Alte Geschichte* 48.2 (1999), 184–202.

Vogel Weidemann, U. "Carthago Delenda Est: 'Aitia' and 'Prophasis,'" *Acta Classica* 32 (1989), 79–95.

Vottéro, G. *Le dialecte béotien*, 83. (Paris: A.D.R.A., 1998).

Walbank, F. "The Scipionic Legend," *Proceedings of the Cambridge Philological Society* 13.193 (1967), 54–69.

Walbank, F., A. Astin, M. Frederiksen, and R. Ogilvie, eds. *The Cambridge Ancient History, Volume 7, Part 1: The Hellenistic World* (Cambridge: Cambridge University Press, 1984).

Walbank, F., A. Astin, M. Frederiksen, and R. Ogilvie, eds. *The Cambridge Ancient History Volume 7, Part 2: The Rise of Rome to 220 B.C.* (Cambridge: Cambridge University Press, 1990).

Ward-Perkins, B. *The Fall of Rome and the End of Civilization* (Oxford: Oxford University Press, 2005).

Wardropper, B. "The Poetry of Ruins in the Golden Age," *Revista Hispánica Moderna* 35.4 (1969), 295–305.

Warmington, B. "The Destruction of Carthage: A Retractatio," *Classical Philology*, 83.4 (October 1988), 308–310.

Warmington, B. H. *Carthage* (London: Robert Hale, 1960).

Watts, J. "Chinese General Warns of Nuclear Risk to US," *Guardian*, July 15, 2005.

White, J. *Cortés and the Downfall of the Aztec Empire* (New York: St. Martin's Press, 1971).

Worthington, I. "Alexander's Destruction of Thebes," in W. Heckel and L. Tritle, eds., *Crossroads of History: The Age of Alexander* (Claremont, CA: Regina Books, 2003), 65–86.

Yardley, J., trans. *Justin: Epitome of the Philippic, History of Pompeius Trogus,* Classical Resources Series. No. 3 (Atlanta: Scholars Press, 1994).

Zabun, F. "Strategic Ambiguity: Explaining Foreign Policy Under the Erdogan Presidency," *MENA Politics Newsletter,* 3.1 (Spring 2020).

INDEX

ABOUT THE AUTHOR

The Hoover Institution

Victor Davis Hanson is a senior fellow in military history and classics at the Hoover Institution at Stanford University and a professor emeritus of classics at California State University, Fresno. He is the author of over two dozen books, including *Carnage and Culture*, *A War Like No Other*, *The Second World Wars*, and *The Dying Citizen*. He lives in Selma, California.